# THE NINJA

## ANCIENT
## SHADOW WARRIORS
## OF JAPAN

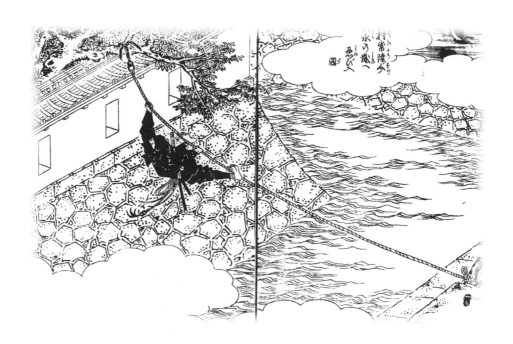

THE SECRET HISTORY
OF NINJUTSU

# THE
# NINJA

ANCIENT
SHADOW WARRIORS
OF JAPAN

Dr. KACEM ZOUGHARI

TUTTLE Publishing
Tokyo | Rutland, Vermont | Singapore

Published by Tuttle Publishing, an imprint of Periplus Editions (HK) Ltd.

Library of Congress Cataloging-in-Publication Data

Zoughari, Kacem.
  The ninja : ancient shadow warriors of Japan / Dr. Kacem Zoughari. -- 1st ed.
    191 p., [16] p. of plates : ill. (some col.) ; 27 cm.
  Includes bibliographical references.
  ISBN 978-0-8048-3927-3 (hardcover)
1.  Ninjutsu. 2.  Martial arts--Japan.  I. Title.
  GV1114.73.Z68 2009
  796.80952--dc22
                    2009032926

ISBN 978-4-8053-1404-3

Paperback Edition:
25 24 23 22 21    5 4 3 2    2105TP
Printed in Singapore

## "Books to Span the East and West"

Tuttle Publishing was founded in 1832 in the small New England town of Rutland, Vermont [USA]. Our core values remain as strong today as they were then—to publish best-in-class books which bring people together one page at a time. In 1948, we established a publishing office in Japan—and Tuttle is now a leader in publishing English-language books about the arts, languages and cultures of Asia. The world has become a much smaller place today and Asia's economic and cultural influence has grown. Yet the need for meaningful dialogue and information about this diverse region has never been greater. Over the past seven decades, Tuttle has published thousands of books on subjects ranging from martial arts and paper crafts to language learning and literature—and our talented authors, illustrators, designers and photographers have won many prestigious awards. We welcome you to explore the wealth of information available on Asia at www.tuttlepublishing.com.

Distributed by

**North America, Latin America & Europe**
Tuttle Publishing
364 Innovation Drive
North Clarendon, VT 05759-9436 U.S.A.
Tel: 1 (802) 773-8930
Fax: 1 (802) 773-6993
info@tuttlepublishing.com
www.tuttlepublishing.com

**Japan**
Tuttle Publishing
Yaekari Building, 3rd Floor
5-4-12 Osaki, Shinagawa-ku
Tokyo 141 0032
Tel: (81) 3 5437-0171
Fax: (81) 3 5437-0755
sales@tuttle.co.jp
www.tuttle.co.jp

**Asia Pacific**
Berkeley Books Pte. Ltd.
3 Kallang Sector #04-01
Singapore 349278
Tel: (65) 6741-2178
Fax: (65) 6741-2179
inquiries@periplus.com.sg
www.periplus.com

# Contents

# Foreword

It is with the greatest honor that I write a foreword for this book. Dr. Zoughari's visionary work connects old ways with the new, breathing life and new meaning into an often controversial subject in a way that benefits all who will read these pages.

In all honesty, I was unsure what to offer in prelude that affords justice to the significance of this work. This book will prove to be a beacon, allowing us to pass into a new territory of times long past. It will lead the reader into a deeper understanding and serve as a bridge to a new perspective on the ancient art of ninjutsu.

Perhaps it's simplest to say that ninjutsu is a timeless and elusive art that is infinitely valuable to all who come to know its form.

Christopher Davy
December 2009

**Shihan Christopher Davy** holds a tenth degree black belt under Dr. Masaaki Hatsumi Soke of Noda City, Japan. He has traveled to Japan many times to train and research the Bujinkan arts. He has been training in martial arts for over thirty-three years and is Shidoshi at the Bujinkan Yume Dojo in Lost River, West Virginia.

# Introduction

For as long as I can remember, the image of the ninja from movies and books fascinated me by the way they could disappear, use improvised weapons, and execute incredible techniques. I didn't understand that this image was rooted in a very profound and logical way of using the body for the art of survival. After many years of research and encounters with many masters, I realized that *ninjutsu* goes beyond the form and the fixed methods of sport or other classical martial arts. Ninjutsu is something that is alive and ever changing. This is why ninjutsu is different; it's always evolving and adapting to the environment. The knowledge and wisdom of using the body is complex and subtle at the same time. It is complex because each technique that makes up the art is born from the blood of many warriors. It's subtle and very deep because the defense of life is based on time, wisdom, and knowledge. The art of the using the body in ninjutsu must be unpredictable and is, thus, difficult to see and to grasp. The only thing I can say is that to master this way of using the body asks us not to be ambitious but to be patient. In other words, to understand the value of what it really means to be patient is to understand the value of the moment. To control ego and master the subtleties of body mechanics without extensive forethought or great physical strength demands time and a singular state of mind. The heart of this, again, is patience.

I didn't initially set out to write a book on ninjutsu, even though I had already written many articles on ninjutsu, *bujutsu*, and *koryū* in general. However, thanks to the "miracle of various meetings" with English-speaking partners requesting training, I decided to develop an English book on ninjutu.

Through my international travel to conferences and seminars, I became aware that the majority of ninjutsu practitioners, other marital arts practitioners, and members of academia were confused about the true nature of the art. They only knew bits and pieces of information—generally, what they'd gleaned from the Internet.

This book is a new level of research into the art of ninjutsu. This new approach is not lightly undertaken. It was not quickly translated or compiled from various current works on the subject. It is not about delving into a study of various esoteric works based entirely in the classical Japanese language, called *kanbun*. Rather, this book is the fruit of more than 10 years of study, practice and research on different *bujutsu*, *koryū* and, more particularly, ninjutsu.

This approach was developed during my studies at the National Institute of the Eastern Languages and Civilizations in Paris (INALCO). Thus, because of my academic experience and training, particularly in Japanese studies, I undertook a serious and precise research study, far from any "parochialism."

If my studies and choice of material drew me closer to Master Hatsumi Masaaki, it is because his knowledge of the subject matter is so highly regarded, and also because I initially avoided following the pack of so-called experts in the field. Master Hatsumi Masaaki remains one of the only masters to have had an authentic contact with the one of the last true ninja, Takamatsu Toshitsuga. This unique relationship was one-to-one, a master with a disciple, which continues still today through Sōke Hatsumi.

Thus, this isn't an attempt to extol the glory of Master Hatsumi, or of the Bujinkan, but rather it is a study of ninjutsu seen through the eyes of a practitioner, and the practitioner is Master Takamatsu Toshitsuga.

I don't seek to enter into a critical debate with the other organizations created by alumni of Master Hatsumi Masaaki nor with the keen defenders of *koryū* and other *budō*. Although I can prove the conclusions of my research to anyone who wants to see it, the goal remains to provide an alternative, honest, and serious reading of historical ninjutsu and its practice.

I have divided this book in several parts. Each chapter deals with a different aspect of ninjustsu, including relevant studies of the history, philosophy, and wisdom. In each of these aspects, I have presented different authors, historians, chronicles, and scrolls in order to impart a wider and deeper understanding. I didn't focus on translating the quoted passages word for word, but rather I tried to impart a clear sense of the writer's main concept, which (as you'll see) was always based upon how to survive, how to hide, how to move subtly, how to be more effective, and so forth. I worked to preserve the original essence of all the translations. In order to do this, I had to include the historical explanation of classical Kobujutsu schools for completeness. I've also included appendices that deal with other aspects of ninjutsu (ninja names, chronologies, and the like) in order to give adequate background information for those of you who wish to take your research of ninjutsu beyond this book. I took care to add the kanji for each term, title, scroll, and so forth, in order to be as precise as possible.

I hope this book will enlighten you and build your interest in the various aspects of ninjutsu and how it relates to the history of Japan. If this work can help you to practice and study more deeply (no matter the art) and allow you to view the world with a broader perspective and one without preconception, then I have achieved my goal in writing this book.

The love of training requires a particular gift: the gift of one's devotion. This dedication is based on single-minded focus. All the major martial art practices have in common requiring ongoing dedication. This gift allows one to transcend and to overcome the prejudices and other insignificant aspects of our ego, detriments that keep our eyes closed at a time when they should be open.

But the wise know that the eyes alone are not sufficient.

Kacem Zoughari
December 2009

# CHAPTER 1

# What Is Ninjutsu?

When one inquires about ninjutsu or the ninja to a Japanese martial arts instructor, student, or enthusiast, their response is often surprising. Many who claim to have knowledge of Japanese techniques of combat describe a ninja as a kind of scientist who blends most of the known *budō* (jūdō, karate-dō, aikidō, kendō, *jō-dō*, and so forth) with wilderness survival skills and other ascetic disciplines.

For the Japanese, ninja are warriors, or rather "ghosts" capable of superhuman prowess, devoting themselves to occult and esoteric practices.

It is tempting to believe that these fantastic tales are true, but that simply isn't the case. Actually, ninjutsu does not enter into any of the known sporting and martial art categories, because its evolution has always remained in the shadows of greatest secrecy, at the fringes of a constantly evolving society.

Because it is difficult to fully comprehend ninjutsu without having a firm knowledge of the historical foundations of combat techniques, I'll define the combat practices of Japan first. With a brief definition of these combat practices, one can better understand ninjas' operating mode, the reason for their existence, and their use, which arose from the continual upheaval throughout Japanese history. These practices later gave rise to the sports-based martial arts in the twentieth century.

One must avoid making a false connection between contemporary sport martial arts and ninjutsu. For one thing, ninjutsu has historically never been respected as a legitimate practice, and this left room for a great deal of confusion to grow within the minds of many martial artists and martial arts researchers.

In Japan, when one refers to the techniques of combat, commonly called martial arts, the terms *bujutsu*, *bugei,* and *budō* are generally used. These terms convey the history of the Japanese warrior class.

## *Bujutsu, Bugei,* and *Budō*

The *Tsuki no shō, densho* written in 1642 by Yagyū Jūbei. Famous handwritten scroll that concerns *shinkage-ryū's* strategies and fighting techniques. Private collection.

According to the book entitled *Suikoden* (水滸伝: *At the Edge of Water*), composed at the beginning of the Ming dynasty (the second half of the fifteenth century) in China, the term *bugei* (arts "*gei*" 芸 of war "*bu*" 武) meant the use of weapons, such as the bow, sword, spear, halberd, axe, and so forth; and *bujutsu* (techniques "*jutsu*" 術; of war "*bu*" 武) meant "all of the techniques necessary to fight." This includes physical skills such as swimming and horsemanship.

After the rise of the *samurai* class to power in Japan during the Kamakura period (1192–1333), martial arts and martial styles started to be classified. Indeed, the practice of martial arts as a true combat practice included a whole range of martial art subject areas called *bugei jūhappan* (武芸十八般: eighteen warrior disciplines).[1] This vast martial arts repertoire included the use of the sword, hand-to-hand combat, horsemanship, lance wielding, and so on.

Categorizing these skills is the foundation of *bujutsu*, which made it possible for the samurai families to be able to protect themselves from one another. Each samurai family developed these formal alternatives and technical innovations and, starting from these experiments on the battlefield, the schools of combat (*ryū-h*) were born.[2]

Practical *bujutsu* was a solitary art, and the transmission of the wisdom and knowledge that made up the *ryū-ha* was restricted to only the elite members of the warrior class. The schools were few in number and did not have formal classes, a *dōjō*, or any public venue.

The main reason that the particular techniques of any given style were not normally spread nor shared with the general public, but rather given only to the elite classes, was to preserve one's advantage during conflict with another warrior. The special knowledge behind any particular school,

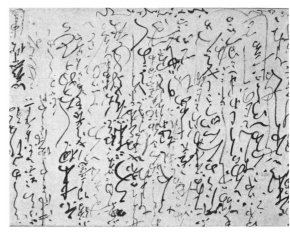

Inside the *Tsuki no shō* section concerning the art of using the body and mind, written by Yagyū Jūbei. Private collection.

or *ryū*, remained exclusively in the hands of the current master or founder of the style. We see that the spreading of particular styles of *bujutsu ryū-ha* throughout the country began when masters started traveling across Japan to test themselves against others. It was a form of evaluation and verification wherein the practitioner applied his knowledge against others to see the validity of the style and to prove his understanding through physical expression. *Bujutsu* has always required a deep and sincere devotion to one's practice. During this period, passing down the knowledge of survival was a very serious responsibility because it opened up the possibility that the master would be betrayed and killed by his student. Choosing the correct, sincere disciple in order to pass on the major principles of the school (*ogi* 奥義, *gokui* 極意) was the main intent of the practice of the art.

*Ogi* represents the core principles and top-level techniques as well as the secret and subtle way of using the body and weapons.

*Gokui* represents the philosophical essence of the school.

*Bujutsu* includes the use and mastery of various weapons and techniques. These techniques were developed in response to the volatile nature in the historical period in Japan, where there was constant war and personal combat. Indeed, *bujutsu* comprises various martial techniques that address confrontations with or without armor, known as *gekitō* (撃刀), *kumitachi* (組太刀), *tachi uchi* (太刀打ち), or *yoroi kumi-uchi* (鎧組討ち).

*Gekitō*, *kumitachi*, and *tachi uchi* are the arts of using various types of Japanese swords at both close and long ranges. In these three arts, one can have armor, light armor, or even no armor, but the practice is not exclusive to sword usage and can be used to mean the application of all weapons.

*Yoroi Kumi uchi* is combat with armor that includes combat with and without weapons.

*Bujutsu* training was inconsistent,

Picture taken in middle of Meiji era, showing warriors from various *bujutsu* schools. Private collection.

because there was no specific, unified method to pass on the school's knowledge and wisdom. It was necessary that the disciple develop a particular acuity in order to mimic the master's technique, watching the movement, action, and techniques until the learner could imitate what was observed to perfection.

It was a widespread practice in Japan, where *bujutsu* disciples attempted to reproduce the techniques of combat, which came from the experimentation of their particular master. These techniques were relatively simple yet powerful because most combat was done while wearing armor. The *bujutsu* masters of the time, all members of the warrior class, undertook personal research on the most effective techniques, based on experience gained through combat. The passing of the knowledge and wisdom of the *bujutsu* school culminated with the transfer of three documents to the disciple. They were *kiri-gami* (切紙: a letter attesting to the student's achievement of mastery over the first practical level of *bujutsu* instruction), *inka*[3] (印可: a certificate of complete license for the school), *mokuroku* (目録: an index containing the names and the description of the techniques of the school) or *e-mokuroku* (technical sketches 絵目録). The contents of these documents, written by the master, presented the philosophy of the school since its creation and the directives to be followed, as well as the technical lexicon.

*Bujutsu* was a logical evolution of the primitive practice to which the warriors prior to the Kamakura period devoted themselves. The techniques of combat used before, during, and after the Héian (782–1190) period were the direct expression of a destructive impulse—the art of war.

Picture taken in Yokohama at the beginning of the Meiji period, showing a warrior sitting in his garden. Private collection.

Famous picture taken in the Meiji era showing two partisans of the Bōshin's war or Bōshin sensō (1868). Private collection.

Picture taken during the Meiji era showing a warrior using the ninja's famous black zukin. Private collection.

The famous Yamaoka Tesshū (1836–1888), politician, philosopher and martial artist, founder of the Ittō Shōden Mutō-ryū. Picture taken in the Meiji era. Private collection.

In a great number of studied cases and schools, it is evident that the practice of *bujutsu* went hand in hand with spiritual research. This research provided the focus that allowed practitioners to find the ultimate technical level of their art. Most of the schools were created after a dream or vision wherein the founder received technical and spiritual initiation.

It can be concluded that *bujutsu* is a collection of the all-encompassing techniques of combat, which included a great number of gruesome skills focused primarily on the art of war, and where spirituality holds a unique place. The amount of spirituality varied according to the degree of skill and belief of the practitioner.

As one delved deeper into the study of martial arts, there was an increasing need to understand the intentions of potential adversaries, who could only be assumed to be studying with the same zeal. It is not surprising that living on this "razor's edge" with death opened one up to the importance of the spiritual realm. That this was prevalent in many *bujutsu* schools cannot be discounted.

*Budō* (the way "*do*: 道" of war "*bu*: 武")[4] remains difficult to explain, because the meaning of the term is ambiguous, even for Japanese people and martial artists.

Kondo isami nosuke, famous master of the Tenren rishin-ryū school and captain of the Shinsen-gumi. Picture taken in the Meiji era. Private collection.

The term is a relatively recent one, having been first used at the beginning of the Meiji period (1868–1912) in a climate dominated by the need to defend the threatened Japanese state. *Budō*, in the Meiji period, draws from concepts of the warrior practice of *bujutsu* from the Edo period (1603–1863). Indeed, during the Edo period, the *shōgun* of the Tokugawa family established and stabilized control over all of Japan. They imposed a strong central government on the country, ensuring a long period of peace lasting until the reopening of the country to foreign powers in the nineteenth century.

During this long period of peace, warriors gradually had to accustom themselves to the times and seek other avenues to hone and perfect their combat techniques. This radically changed the transmission of knowledge and wisdom and, thus, the manner of

The Kashima *shintō-ryū kumi-tachi e-mokuroku*, scroll written by Yoshikawa Tsunedate in 1691. Private collection.

Portrait of Ittō Ittōsai, the founder of *Ittō-ryū*. Private collection.

teaching. Indeed, the practice, which until that time was transmitted only to an elite class, gave way to the teaching of the masses.

This opening of martial arts instruction to all social classes was done through the establishment of formal schools, public demonstrations, and the formation of groups of followers and disciples. One parallel to note is that with the proliferation of new schools, the drafting of transmission documents (scrolls and *densho,* which were the official documents of the school itself), became increasingly sophisticated, and research shows that this helped move schools towards specialization.

It is through the practice of *dō,* the way, that the concept of "*dō*" came, little by little, to be associated with a deep sense of duty towards each warrior's lord. The warrior, who accepted this concept of "*dō*," then had to seek a way to advance in *bujutsu* without really killing the opponent, contrary with the ideology of *bujutsu,* which consists of methods of killing. The martial techniques became increasingly sophisticated and coexisted with spirituality.

These *budō* arts gradually became less and less deadly, eventually reaching a point where some were not deadly at all. Increasingly subtle, *budō* techniques were developed to take advantage of the freedom of movement that the dress of the period offered; as the style of clothing changed, so did the application of *budō* techniques. Thus, little by little, certain disciplines of *bujutsu* (*kenjutsu, bōjutsu, jōjutsu,* and the like) reached a high degree of refinement, but without the danger of mortal consequences.

The practice of these disciplines through the concept of *budō* aims to train the follower physically and psychologically, two inseparable aspects of the practice.

It was during this period, in the middle of the eighteenth century, that certain schools of *kenjutsu* began to use the *shinai* (swords made with plates of bamboo) as well as protective armor. The *shinai* was actually created a few centuries before and was called a *fukuro shinai*[5] by Kami Izumi Nobutsuna (1508–1577), the founder of *Shinkage-ryū* (新影流).[6]

The use of both the *shinai* and armor spread through the end of the eighteenth century. At present, modern kendō (剣道) owes almost all of its evolution to a genius named Chiba Shūsaku (1794–1855), master of the sword and founder of the current *Hokushin Ittō-ryū* (北辰一刀流), which descended from the famous school, *Ittō-ryū* (一刀流).[7]

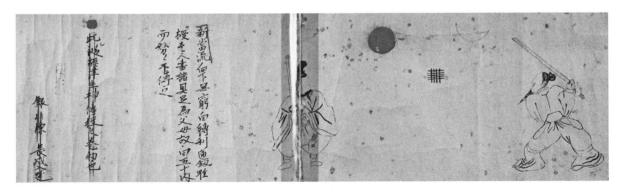

The Kashima *shinkage-ryū mokuroku,* scroll written in 1865. Private collection.

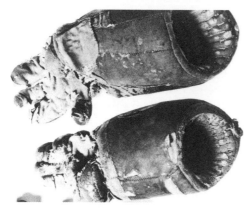

*Kote*, hand and forearm protection, used during the Edo period in the practice of *Ittō-ryū kenjutsu*. Private collection.

Scroll from the *Ittō-ryū* school written at the end of the Edo period. Private collection.

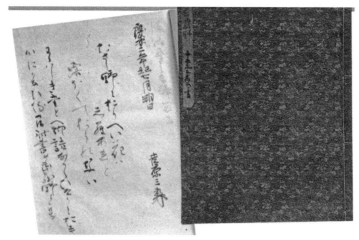

*Densho* (a document of transmission) concerning the history and strategies of *Ittō-ryū*. Private collection.

*Ittō-ryū* was created by Itō Ittōsa, a great master of the sword at the end of the sixteenth and beginning of the seventeenth century. After the Second World War, thanks to the assistance of modern-day masters like Nakayama Hakudōi (1872–1959) and Takano Saburō (1870–1960), a reform effort returned most of kendō to these roots.

The practice of modern kendō, even at the most senior levels, has lost much authenticity that one finds in the practice of traditional *kenjutsu*. Indeed, in the art of the *kenjutsu*, traditionally all the weapons

Scroll of Hokushin *Ittō-ryū* founded by Chiba Chūsaku. Private collection.

were studied, because it was necessary to be able to answer every type of weapon and attack. With the introduction of armor came a lack of flexibility, and so the principle inherent to the practice of the sword as relating to body movement was discarded. The positions (*kamae*) of the traditional sword were shortened, which implies that the mobility of the body as a whole was restricted. This severely reduced overall body movement and seriously impacted natural timing.

The lack of flexibility of kendō is indicated in their practice. One can add that, contrary to traditional *kenjutsu*, kendō remains very limited. And, it is in this limitation of movement that leads some *kendō-ka* to search for a form of freedom, a "formlessness of pure movement."

This principle continues to be found in the *budō* that emerged during the Meiji period (1868–1912). Jūdō and Karatedō are striking examples of the search for "formlessness of pure movement" through disciplines limited to the field of the war, espionage, guerrilla warfare, real combat, and the like.

Photograph taken at the beginning of Meiji showing the last member of the Hattori family. Private collection.

## Jūdō

From the middle of the nineteenth century, as described earlier, the closed and autocratic society of feudal Japan was shaken by the perceived Western threat. The arrival of the Americans with Admiral Perry upset many of the warrior practices, much as had happened a few centuries before with the introduction of firearms by the Portuguese in 1540.

The transitioning cultural environment became a place where all the knowledge and warrior traditions from Japanese history were abandoned in order to take advantage of new and innovative Western industrial techniques. It was in this period that Kanō Jigorō (1860–1930) worked out a new model of training, drawing from the concept of *dō* which was derived from the warrior traditions of ancient Japan. This new training approach judiciously combined the knowledge of Western thought and the model of action of the *bushi* (warrior). It was the birth of Jūdō (柔道: the way of flexibility).

After having studied the *jūjutsu* (柔術)[8] of two traditional schools, *Tenshin shinyō-ryū* (天神真楊流)[9] and *Kitō-ryū* (起倒流),[10] and comparing it with various Western methods of physical conditioning, Kanō concluded that *jūjutsu* was the most effective and balanced.

Concentrating mainly on the educational and gymnastic aspects within *jūjutsu*, Kanō skillfully eliminated the parts that he considered dangerous. He founded his private school, *Kōdōkan*[11] (講道館: residence where the way is taught) in 1882 and developed jūdō, a discipline based on the physical practice and morality of a modern world. Jūdō quickly became a great success.

However, Kanō always publicly tried to promote Kōdōkan Jūdō as a physical method formed by the "modernization" of *jūjutsu*, so that no one would mistake jūdō for a technique of combat or a form of warrior arts, as in *bujutsu*. After his death, and the rise of Japanese militarism, jūdō was incorporated, little by little, into formal military training and gradually came to be falsely identified as true *bujutsu*.

In addition to the adoption of jūdō by the military, the publication of the novel *Sugata Sanshirō* by Tomita Tsuneo in 1942, very popular at the time in Japan, surely contributed to the confusion which many today regard jūdō as a true combat art.[12]

Modern jūdō is very different from Kanō's original jūdō. Today it is based mainly on the use of physical

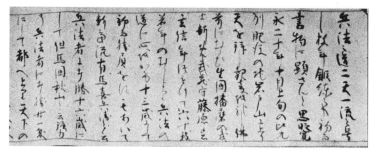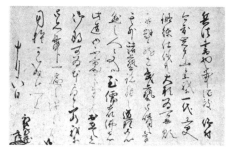

A version of the *Gorin no sho* written in 1655 by Terao Umanosuke, disciple and successor of Miyamoto Musashi. Private collection.

force driven only towards sport competition. The true essence and freedom of movement is completely forgotten. Indeed, one of the concepts dear to Kanō, "the soft one exceeds the hard"[13] seems lost to many modern jūdō-ka. The study of martial practices, including blows, strikes, the use of weapons, and dangerous techniques are not approached anymore or even studied in the practice of "modern jūdō," whereas they were practiced in the Kōdōkan jūdō of Kanō. One only needs to note that Kanō himself continued to research traditional *bujutsu*. Master Kyozō Mifune, who in addition to being a virtuoso of jūdō, was a noted and assiduous practitioner of *jūjutsu*. Of course, there are always some practitioners who are very attached to the concepts of Kanō and who claim to have and teach "true jūdō." But how could these claims be true in the absence of a master who received instruction directly from Kanō?

## Karate

In the 1920s, karate was imported from Okinawa to Japan by Funakoshi Gishin (1868–1957), under the name of Okinawa Tōte (沖縄唐手: Chinese technique of Okinawa).[14] This "new" technique of combat did not have any common point with the ancient practice of *bujutsu* and even less with the concept of *dō* of *budō*.

This martial art was later called karate-dō during the 1930s. The name was changed because of the rise of Japanese nationalism and a rejection of all that was not purely Japanese. Karate-dō only consisted in repeating *kata* (preestablished sequences of movement) without any clear application in situational combat. This was not the case in the techniques of *bujutsu*. With *budō* and kendō, for example, there is a re-creation of combat through attacking and defending that is still practiced.

All of the techniques of *bujutsu* aim at direct applications in real combat situations. Any tradition of combat application in karate from Okinawa was not transmitted to Japan via Funakoshi. This explains the efforts of certain notable Japanese marital artists, like Konishi, Otsuka and others, who tried to raise the quality of karate by integrating *budō's* concept of *dō*.

For these Japanese martial artists, deeply experienced in the tradition of *kenjutsu* and other disciplines of traditional *bujutsu*, the content and design of a martial art is inseparable from the practice of combat. Indeed, for a great number of masters of the time, karate-dō represented a "folk dance" coming from their "country cousins in the sea," and it was not of the same pedigree as the *bujutsu* of the "Japanese *bushi.*"

It must be remembered that in Okinawa, karate-dō was practiced in fields and hidden places, in the greatest secrecy. There is no proof that karate-dō grew from combat techniques born in the battlefields like *bujutsu*. However, one only need remember that the archipelago of Okinawa knew the same political upheaval and had many wars, just as in Japan.

Okinawa formed "a bridge" for the relations between Japan and the remainder of Asia, for example,

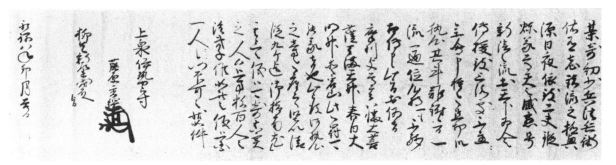

The *Ichinin ikkoku inka* written in 1565 by Kamiizumi Hidetsuna for Yagyū Muneyoshi.

Taiwan, China of the south, Malaysia, and so forth.[15] It was essential that Okinawa display a certain level of political neutrality and, thus, avoid war with their more powerful neighbors.

By the time karate-dō was imported to Japan, it had undergone its first transformation, passing from basic techniques of martial self-defense to an exercise routine intended for the education of schoolboys.[16] In Japan, karate-dō was developed primarily for the academic world.

Thereafter, eminent colleagues of Funakoshi came from Okinawa to Japan to make known and to develop their unique practice and style of karate-dō. These were Kenwa Mabuni (1889–1952), founder of *Shitō-ryū*; Chojun Miyagi (1888–1953), founder of *Gojū-ryū*; Kanbun Uechi (1888–1937), founder of *Uechi-ryū*; and Choki Motobu (1871–1944), founder of *Motobu-ryū*, who brought a level of realism to karate-dō through his personality and dedicated personal practice. Two pupils of Funakoshi established their own schools of karate-dō. Otsuka Hironori (1893–1982) was the founder of *Wadō-ryū*, and Oyama Masutatsu (1923–1994), who was the founder of *Kyokushin-kai karate*.

## Aikidō

The last pillar in the development of *budō* was Ueshiba Morihei (1883–1969), founder of aikidō. Aikidō started from his experimentation in several traditional *bujutsu* schools, and it influenced by his mystical and esoteric religious beliefs. Ueshiba remains truly remarkable, and, compared to Funakoshu and Kanō, was the only one who had direct contact with traditional *bujutsu*, combined with a sincere and deep religious conviction.

This deep tie to spirituality and close association with religious practices often went hand in hand with the practice of *bujutsu* with the majority of the warriors of feudal Japan. The foundation of certain schools, such as *Tenshin Shōden Katori Shintō-ryū* (天真正伝香取神道流)[17] and *Kashima Shin-ryū* (鹿島神流)[18] are examples where the practice of combat and spirituality coexisted for the warrior class since the Kamakura period.

Ueshiba studied the sword and spear techniques, and *jūjutsu* of many schools, including *Yagyū Shingan-ryū* (柳生心眼流),[19] before meeting Master Takeda Sokaku (1860–1969).[20] Master Takeda, founder of *Daitō-ryū* (大東流),[21] deeply affected Ueshiba in his martial practice and in the future development of aikidō (合気道).

Ueshiba also became the disciple of Onisaburō Deguchi (1871–1947)[22] principal pillar of *Omoto-kyō* (大本教). Aikidō, created in 1942, is a synthesis between *Ueshiba's* martial experiments and the precepts of Deguchi's Omoto-kyō.

To promote aikidō, then called *Ueshiba-ryū*, Ueshiba approached the political powers of the time and acquired many disciples who were highly ranked Japanese naval officers. Ueshiba's incredible control of combat techniques brought him many supporters from the military. He took on many challenges

The founder of the *Asayama ichiden-ryū taijutsu*, Asayama Ichiden-sai. Painting from the Bukei haykunin-shū. Private collection.

and attracted numerous pupils, among whom one finds an envoy of Kanō![23]

But do we really understand Ueshiba? To know him would be to know his style and practice, particularly since he "lived aikidō." Nowadays, aikidō is very different from what was created by Ueshiba. Indeed, his late son, Kisshomaru, instituted a technical reorganization of aikidō. This reorganization came about because, even though his father was a martial teacher beyond compare, Ueshiba belonged to the old generation of masters who demonstrated their techniques rather than explaining them.

As in traditional *bujutsu*, the aikidō disciples had to develop the mental discipline to grasp the essence of the techniques based on their impressions during the moment of technical exchange with the master. However, as aikidō attracted more and more followers and as Ueshiba began to dissociate from *Daitō-ryū*, it became apparent that a formal technical progression program, something suitable for aikidō, was needed in order to be able to form and develop the art.

At present, the Aiki-kai[24] of Tōkyō, set up by the late Kisshomaru, remains the only organization where a great number of high-level instructors had some direct contact with the founder. However, the nature of this contact varied according to the individual in question. Some remained with Ueshiba for only a short amount of time, others trained with him longer. Some of Ueshiba's students, such as Tomiki, Mochizuki, and Shioda, studied during a time when the founder was still under the technical influence of *Daitō-ryū*, and others, such as Saito Morihiro, witnessed the transformation and the technical foundation of aikidō.

Many charismatic figures teach and pass on the message of Ueshiba. But in regard to the essence of that art and style created by the founder himself, it seems that only a meticulous study of several *bujutsu*, combined with a deep, intrinsic introspection would produce an epiphany similar to Ueshiba's.

Presently, the practice of aikidō tends to alter the reality of combat, as there is a tacit agreement between the partners during the confrontation. The famous "*aiki*" (合気: union of energies, meetings of energies, merging into one energy),[25] is directed towards synchronization and mutual timing to the detriment of interference, which is the foundation of combat in general. In the meantime, a certain number of old schools of sword and combat technique continue to pass down their techniques in traditional form, but only with an extremely limited number of followers.

The founder of the Tagaki yōshin-ryū school of jūjutsu, Takagi Umanosuke. Painting from the Bukei haykunin-shū. Private collection.

Today, in Japan, the meaning of the word *budō* has become more and more vague, at the same time the disciplines that claim to have a part, for example, *iai-dō, battō-dō, jōdō, tai-dō*, and so forth, have multiplied. The followers of modern *budō* justify themselves with the assertion that the differences between "sport combat" and physical education were blurred because all martial arts practice was confined by General Douglas MacArthur and the Supreme Command of Allied Power (SCAP), during the occupation of Japan, to only those activities not deemed "militaristic" or "martial."

Yamada Nobuo, famous master of *kusarigama jutsu*, from the Bukei haykunin-shū. Private collection.

Interestingly, in Japan, as in the rest of the world, there are martial art philosophies that seem to have the form of *budō*. Many of these post-Meiji efforts claim the authenticity of a *budō* tradition, but they appear incomplete as they try to compensate for their lack of the *bujutsu* spirit that *budō* draws from. One can find schools that insist on an austere, violent, and even bloody attitude. The effort, even the physical suffering, are evident in their practice. In fact, they often take pride on the amount of pain and suffering practitioners have to bear.

Other schools claim a spiritual, or even mystical, approach to combat, with an attitude of going beyond aggressiveness, and they are critical of the more austere schools, which they see as primitive and unworthy of the tradition of *budō*. Among these modern expressions of *budō* are the vacillating philosophies that blend in "sport" speeches, colored with various "enlightenments," preaching well-being and health. Some of these schools taught an approach to competition that focused only on tournament presentation, style, and "flash", while in others, research of the effectiveness of their style is paramount, and they preach "the *budō* spirit" or "the spirit of the samurai" combined with a Spartan and dangerous physical regime as they struggle to understand the unspoken, undocumented intent of their founders.

In the final analysis, what benefit comes from these approaches? All that remains is a pain-ravaged student with a body broken by the effects of a practice regime too austere, who doesn't gain a form of spiritual enlightenment as his body is forever damaged. Then there is the compulsion to pursue medals and honors from a variety of tournaments and sport competitions. All of this comes from a martial practice and history where the very essence demands that one persevere in humble practice. Perhaps our Western mindset, so prevalent in martial arts today, has simply discarded the importance of pleasure and individual well-being.

A saint once said, ...there are as many ways [to salvation] as pilgrims.[26] With each school of thought in modern martial arts, one has to find what is most appropriate and fulfilling, without forgetting to keep "open the eyes of the heart" in order to avoid all missteps.

Izasa Choisai, founder of the Tenshin Shōden Katori *Shintō-ryū* school. Painting from the Bukei haykunin-shū. Private collection.

# Ninjutsu

After reviewing the development of "mainstream martial arts" in Japan, we can now turn to the very different development of ninjutsu. The representation of this discipline outside of Japan has seldom been edifying. This is not to say that some presentations of ninjutsu haven't been accurate, but the "myth" of the ninja seems to be the point of reference for the world. So, as we explore the "myth" and the art of ninjutsu, you will gain a better overall comprehension of a martial art that is as important as it is mysterious.

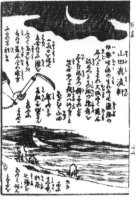

Yamada Yoshinaru, famous master of *bujutsu*. Painting from the Bukei haykunin-shū. Private collection.

Hikita Bunguro and Yagyū Muneyoshi, two masters of *Shinkage-ryū* and Kamiizumi's top disciples. Painting from the Bukei haykunin-shū. Private collection.

The origins of ninjutsu are surrounded by mysteries and legends, seemingly developed to scramble its tracks. One cannot speak about ninjutsu without evoking the image of the terrifying devotee, who devoted body and heart to it: the ninja, the "superspy", who left fear and death on his wake. The ninja was, and remains, in the fullest sense of the word, a specialist, a veritable combat expert, fluent in the handling of a variety of weapons, a remarkable scout, tracker, acrobat, and illusionist.

However, what most know of the ninja and ninjutsu is only a pale reflection of reality. For instance, the commonly held image of the ninja clad all in black is itself a recent invention. Indeed, it appeared at the same time as all the legends and myths, during the Genroku era (1688–1704), when the first paintings representing the ninja were created, starting with the military chronicles (軍記物: *gunki-mono*).[27]

From there, a whole class of fantasy literature developed, making the ninja out to be a superman, giving him awesome and terrifying magical capabilities. Cultural influences resulting from the "floating world" (浮世絵: *ukiyo-e*) in 1780, also seized on this image, which, at the same time created both fear and fascination.

The image of the warrior clad in black, a color which gave him a demonic and mysterious visage, developed at the same time as all the legends regarding ninjutsu and the supposed skills obtained through its practice.

Certain paintings showed the ninja as an honest warrior, being introduced furtively into a castle or using his psychic abilities to detect danger. Others, on the contrary, showed violence and the perceived threat that characterized it. Another collection of paintings, *shunga* (春画), shows the ninja in scenes of eroticism taken to the extreme. These representations show a black clad ninja, with disproportionately enhanced sexual anatomy, subjecting his partner to a whole series of erotic flexibility exercises that would make any yoga master blush! *Ehon Futami-gata* (1803),[28] a book of illustrations attributed to Hokusai (or possibly to Utamaro) shows a ninja raping a woman. All the details of the clothing of

Illustration of *Edo hokapiki*, or Edo's law enforcement's, man in action. From the *Zahei mongatari*, written in 1769. Private collection.

the ninja are represented perfectly there. This painting is one of the first to show the ninja as a man dressed in black.

Most of these paintings draw inspiration from certain parts of *kabuki*, where the ninja played a role. The part *Meiboku Sendai Hagi*[29] was originally written for *jōrori* (theater of the puppets) and offers us one of the best examples of the ninja portrayed as a magician. The character of Nikki Danjō, a follower of ninjutsu, is transformed into a rat, using incantations and a form of ritual magic. This character became the most famous theatrical ninja. In the play *Kikutsuki Irafune Banashi*,[30] there appears a ninja by the name of Tenjiku Tokubei, who is transformed into a giant frog, using a magic ritual that he executes with his fingers. There are many parts where warriors are presented like ninja and, under cover of the intimidating, dark clothing, they carry out their misdeeds.

Famous painting from Hokusai showing a ninja climbing.

The famous history of the 47 Rōnin, which became one of the most popular works of Japanese literature, also promotes the myth of the ninja. The night attack launched by the faithful avenging vassals against Kira Yoshimoto implied the complicity of the darkness and the secrecy that the night offers. Two books of illustrations clearly depict the scene of the night raid against the house of Kira during which the 47 Rōnin were clad in black like ninja.

In the *Chūshingura*[31] (a version of the history) of Sadahide (1807–1873), certain members of the 47 Rōnin are shown carrying the hood of the ninja. Another illustration, attributed to Kunisada, in a part of the *kabuki* entitled *Kanadehon Chūshingura*[32] gives perfect examples where ninja are shown controlling a woman and holding a lantern, which has all the characteristics of a lantern used by the ninja. And the list goes on. However, these popular caricatures give only vague information on ninjutsu. This image of the ninja appears in almost all the epic and fantasy novels of Japan.

Samurai disguised as a ninja in observation. From the Ehon Taira gunki by Kunisada Tadachūji, in 1852. Private collection.

It is this image that the Japanese have in mind when they think of ninja and ninjutsu. Westerners are no different. Most see ninjutsu as arcane, combining occult practices with extremely effective combat techniques. Is this really true?

Ninjutsu is not a *bujutsu*, nor is it a sporting practice resulting from *budō*. It cannot even be classified as being like *budō*. It did not follow the way traced by *budō* as it cut a path during the Meiji period. Rather ninjutsu practitioners observed the changes in martial arts from deep in the shadows and watched the evolution of *budō* from *bujutsu*. To observe, to spy, to predict, and to stop danger, this, in a few words, is how ninjutsu is summarized.

Ninjutsu, or *ninpō*, is a *kakutō-jutsu* (格闘術), that is a true science of survival and combat born of necessity to predict and protect one from danger. Although, technically, the difference is obvious when compared with *bujutsu*, the contrast lies mainly in one's frame of mind. Ninjutsu shows how to be a ghost to one's enemy and to "disappear" in front of him.

Defined in the English language often by the phrase "the art of remaining unseen" or "the invisible art," even these definitions of ninjutsu do not fully illustrate that invisibility, anonymity, and secrecy are

Ise Saburō, famous ninja warrior and friend of Minamoto no Yoshitsune. Painting from the Bukei haykunin-shū. Private collection.

keystones of the art, and that these aptitudes can be acquired only through an iron discipline, where deception plays a prevailing role.

Deception is the foundation of all warrior strategies, and ninjutsu is no exception. However, it should be noted that in the use of tricks or stratagems, ninjutsu exceeds all others disciplines by far. This is why the lords of feudal Japan surrounded themselves with practitioners of ninjutsu.

One can also define ninjutsu as "the use of tricks" and the manner of putting them into practice. All the weapons and techniques of the ninja were created with the aim of misleading, of deceiving the enemy and, thus, overcoming him. By using deception, the ninja could survive. It is the prerogative of spies, and ninja are no exception.

Each warrior culture had its own rules and precepts. For example, an old Arab work of the end of the thirteenth century was titled *The Book of Tricks*. The anecdotes and councils reported in this work show a remarkable similarity to the principles of ninjutsu.

> Put more trust in your tricks than in your bravery, and give more importance to your circumspection than to your courage in combat, because war is a continual effort to mislead the enemy. It is truly a struggle for those who rush blindly into an operation but only a momentary cloud for those who remain wary.[33]

Although Japan and Arabia are societies with different warrior cultures, the science of using deception in combat does not differ. The advice in this Arabic work shows a certain resemblance to the principles of ninjutsu that consists of using deception and tricks continuously against the enemy.

From a deeper perspective, it also shows the cautious, careful, and attentive character of the ninja, who did not dive blindly into the mouth of the wolf. It is very interesting to note a similarity with the attitudes and techniques of combat that one finds among the tribes of Native Americans.

As a practice intended to predict and defeat danger, ninjutsu demonstrated a control of time and information, which are essential for survival and success during a confrontation. Ninja did not engage in protracted battles but were deployed sparingly when it would impact the outcome successfully. Also, rather than face the enemy head on, ninja would use all the fraud, deceit, and trickery that were necessary to successfully carry out the battle or the mission. An example drawn from the same work illustrates this well:

Tsukahara Bokuden, famous warriors who founded the Kashima shintō-ryū. Painting from the Bukei haykunin-shū. Private collection.

> Have no fear of employing deception in war, because it enables you to arrive at the goal in a way more certain than the battle of body to bloody body.[34]

The ninja was a specialist in evasion, and in direct and rapid action. A ninja's role as a spy was to sow disorder and confusion in the enemy troops after having carried out his mission of information gathering.

# Ninja Attributes

To illustrate the methods of subterfuge used in ninjutsu, outside entities (particularly Chinese martial artists) would often draw comparison to the behavior of savage animals. Animal behavior gives some insight into how the ninja behaved in combat. The ninja, however, would not be dominated by animal instincts, as these did not take into account an intelligent sense of timing. All animals, especially the wildest and most dangerous, are captured or killed by more intelligent adversaries.

A key to understanding ninjutsu is knowing that the birthplace of this art was in the provinces of Iga and Kōga, which were mostly uninhabited wild areas. The observation of nature, of the practices and habits of people as well as the climatic phenomena, plays a considerable role in practice of ninjutsu. One can easily understand that the first ninja, practicing in the wild mountains of these areas, developed very keen skills in observation and adaptation. To know how to observe is an essential capacity for a ninja, because all his strategies started with careful observation.

To be crafty is not enough. It is also necessary to have physical and psychological conditioning, a potent combination that makes it possible to be most effective. Especially necessary for the follower of ninjutsu, one must develop clarified determination, which makes it possible to adapt to any situation and to effectively and judiciously use deception and stratagems. There was not, as many believe, a great number of ninja who had all skills

Ittō Ittōsai, the founder of *Ittō-ryū*, and his successor, Migami Tenzen Tadaaki. Painting from the Bukei haykuninshū. Private collection.

necessary to disappear at the first inkling of danger. Only from the purity of his deepest convictions could one in a thousand ever arrive at this level. It is for this reason that the skills and deepest essence of ninjutsu have always been passed only to the person who gathers the deepest of human qualities. With this in mind, consider the following:

> What one calls ninjutsu was, in the beginning, a discipline of the *kobujutsu* (traditional techniques of combat). Having changed its form, part of this art remains in Japan. Ninjutsu does not consist in attacking men or taking life without reason, as many would like to believe.
>
> The character *nin* (忍) of ninjutsu, is read *shinobu* or *shinobi*. To apply one's thoughts and ego to the edge of the sword; to be constantly vigilant of one's self and one's surroundings and to have courage with endurance . . . such is the intention of the word, *shinobu* (忍ぶ).
>
> If one exerts his will in an unreasonable way, the blade stops us at once, and cuts us; and, thus, to act under the constraint of a blade prevents us from being driven by the winds of change. To act by controlling one's ego, such is true essence of the character *nin* in *ninpō* (忍法).[35]

By understanding the various intepretations of the character *nin*, we begin to get a clearer picture of the follower of ninjutsu and can see that it is far from that reported by novels and films. Although there is no technical information given in this example, it shows the state of mind necessary for the practice of ninjutsu.

Ninjutsu is more than a simple set of techniques for guerrilla warfare. The heart of the techniques in ninjutsu lies in the practice of vigilance, by finding and exploiting an opening from all directions, by retaining flexibility *and* strength forged by endurance.

For practitioners of ninjutsu, it all came down to survival in order to help and to protect their families during a period of history where the slightest dissent could mean death. Just as the great religions appeared during very disturbed periods in history, so did ninjutsu. Ninja were trained to endure and to avoid danger by seeing it, accepting it, and adapting to it.

The following is another impression, different from the first but also indicative of the practice:

> The spirit of the ninja is based on the ability to endure shame without exerting resentment. It is not a question of dangerous actions, in wounding people by putting a sharp blade to the heart but rather like the flower, flexible, to be full of love and peace.
>
> In short, to naturally evade the sword of the enemy, to be invisible, and for the people and the nation to overcome the enemy by using the five phases of Nature, such are the principles of the ninja.[36]

In this passage, one realizes that the level of endurance goes well beyond any ordinary example. It is a question of enduring and of overcoming the seemingly insurmountable without "exerting resentment," which for an ordinary person would be rather difficult. Only one with a disciplined body and who lives in perfect spiritual harmony would be able to maintain this level of endurance.

## Disciplines of the Ninja

To be able to disappear, to "be erased" in the mind and eye of the enemy, and use nature judiciously, requires more than one simple technique; rather, it requires a very focused state of mind. It requires a vision of a very precise way of living that appears when one's life and lifestyle are threatened. It is honed by developing a pragmatic approach to combat. This brings us back to the issue of the ninja's many specializations and to the spirit and tactics used. In understanding the dispassionate yet focused manner in which a ninja can accomplish the mission at hand, one might be led to suspect that there would be a certain number of mentally or emotionally disturbed practitioners. But how can one claim to have a unity of body and spirit, and in a certain manner to truly be spiritual, if one is flawed in mind and body? The philosophy and teaching of *ninpō* is a useless jumble of great words and ideals if one does not have a certain physical, mental, emotional, and spiritual balance—to be, quite simply, human.

Therefore, it is necessary to maintain a level of psychological health through physical discipline, combining flexibility and adaptation. The first stage of ninjutsu practice has to do with the control of various disciplines, which are dependent

Warriors from the last Tokugawa's shogunate on a visit to Kyoto. Picture taken in the Meiji era. Private collection.

The *Kage-mokuroku* scroll written by Kamiizumi Hidetsuna, founder of the *Shinkage-ryū*. Private collection.

on a common thread, allowing one to start from a single movement, one breath, rate of movement, or rhythm, and to generate from that an infinite number of movements and applications. It is the control of the union between the body and the spirit that makes it possible to reach this level.

Ninjutsu is composed of eight fundamental disciplines, whose generic title is *ninja no hachimon* (忍者之八門: eight disciplines of the ninja) or *ninja no hakkei* (忍者之八景). They are:

✦ *Ninja no kiai* (忍者の気合): Practical synthesis of breathing and energy
✦ *Koppō tai-jūtsu* (骨法体術): Techniques for bare-handed combat based on the laws which govern the human skeleton and framework
✦ *Ninpō no ken* (忍法の剣): Swordfighting techniques
✦ *Yari-jutsu* (槍術): Spear techniques
✦ *Shuriken* (手裏剣): Techniques for the throwing and handling of sharp blades and objects
✦ *Ka-jutsu* (火術): Techniques for using fire in all its forms, from setting fires to using explosives
✦ *Yūgei* (遊芸): Cultural pusuits: music, painting, dance, and the like
✦ *Kyōmon* (教門): Religious practice

In the case of other schools of ninjutsu, like *Togakure-ryū ninpō* (戸隠流忍法), these eight disciplines carry the generic title of *happō biken* (八法秘剣): eight secret rules of the sword. In addition to their secret techniques, the ninja used the long sword (*daitō*) and short sword (*kodachi*). The *happō biken* includes the following disciplines:

✦ *Gun-ryaku* (軍略): Military strategy
✦ *Tenmon* (天門): Meteorology, astronomy
✦ *Chimon* (地問): Geography, geometry, distances, and angles
✦ *Shuriken-jutsu* (手裏剣術): Techniques for throwing edged weapons
✦ *Senban-nage-jutsu* (銛盤投術): The technique of throwing four-pointed metal discs
✦ *Tonpō* (遁法): Methods of escape—also including *goton* (五遁): five methods of escape, based on the five phases and *jūton* (十遁): ten methods of escape
✦ *Jō-jutsu* (杖術): A technique for using the 4-foot staff
✦ *Hanbō-jutsu* (半棒術): A technique for using the one meter stick
✦ *Bisentō-jutsu* (眉尖刀術): technique for using the battlefield halberd (which has a very broad blade like a scimitar)
✦ *Naginata-jutsu* (薙刀術): A technique for using the ordinary halberd
✦ *Rokushaku-bō-jutsu* (六尺棒術): A technique for using the 6-foot staff
✦ *Sō-jutsu* (槍術): A technique for using the spear

✦ *Kisha-jutsu* (騎射術): Horsemanship, including mounted combat, shooting with a bow while on horseback, and the like[38]

To be a ninja, in the spirit of the term, was to control all these disciplines to fulfill his function as a spy. This shows that the ninja's reputation for warriorship was not overrated. Nevertheless, it's hard to imagine how the ninja could master all these arts and so many various techniques of combat.

Obviously the ninja had to set aside a considerable amount of time for training. The essence of training in these various disciplines lies in *ninpō-tai-jutsu* (忍法体術): technique for using the body according to rules of endurance, perseverance and survival. This is a natural and unified approach to combat, where the harmony of the body and the spirit allows one's actions to flow with natural movement and enables one to hide and suppress one's injuries, adapting to all situations.

The study of ninjutsu included various fields, such as strategy, combat in all its forms, medicine, psychology, and so on. Ninjutsu showed how to use nature or the enviroment and the body to "disappear" and to attain this the practitioner needed to lose himself (lose his ego) and study deeply.

It is about a deep knowledge of the union of opposites that one acquires through a discipline dedicated to survival in the face of the threat of obliteration. Knowing the nature of danger makes it possible to circumvent it, just as knowing weapons and their use allows one to stop them or to use them with accuracy. Of course, this is not simple and it is not for everyone. As the old saying goes, "Many are called, but few are chosen." It is one of the reasons that ninjutsu was (and continues to be) taught to select individuals.

## Defining Ninjutsu

As mentioned, in the first character of the word ninjutsu, one can perceive the state of mind of one devoted to the art. The character *nin* (忍) covers several significant levels; therefore, the follower of ninjutsu, the ninja, cannot be restricted to only one definition. Indeed, when it is pronounced *shinobu*, it has the meaning "to endure," "to support," and "to be tenacious," and when it is pronounced *shinobaseru*, it has the meanings "to hold hidden," "to hide," "to be furtive," "to be secretive."

In looking at the meaning of the character *nin*, one begins to understand that the practitioner of ninjutsu is a person who acts in secrecy and that ninjutsu is the practice that makes it possible to act in secrecy through the use of deception. By breaking up the character *nin*, one finds two other characters: heart (心) and blade (刃).

The tengu-shō section of the *Shinkage-ryū heihō mokuroku no koto*. The scroll was written by Yagyū Muneyoshi, successor of Kamiizumi Hidetsuna. Private collection.

柳生三嚴

Portrait of Yagyū Jūei Mitsuyoshi, eldest son of Yagyū Munenori and grandson of Yagyū Muneyoshi. Edo-yagyū shinkage-ryū's second headmaster. Private collection.

One can interpret the meaning of the character *nin* in two ways. The first interpretation depicts the state of mind of one who suffers, supports misfortune, and must moreover hide—for instance, to conceal and suppress pain and weakness, as described earlier. The second interpretation refers to a way of practice in which one's willpower becomes as sharp as a spinning blade. The body, terribly effective, is the tool of expression for this will. This evokes, consequently, the control of the spirit upon the body.

The concept of the "way of practice" with ninjutsu is different from that identified with the concept of *budō*. Contrary to the latter, one did not commit oneself to find personal enlightenment or intrinsic realization but rather to survive in combat and protect oneself by forming alliances. Therefore, one can say that the follower of ninjutsu, a ninja, is a person (者) who endures and perseveres despite all adversity, and embodies the experience rising from survival. A ninja understands the forces that temper the heart of an enduring person. *Ninpō* (忍法), as a doctrine (法), means the rule that governs self-discipline, endurance, and perseverance in all situations, as well as the techniques of pragmatic combat, drawn from actual situations, for the purposes of survival.

The following is a more general definition of ninjutsu or *ninpō*:

Ninjutsu, or *ninpō*, is a collection of adaptable survival techniques that allows one to face the uncertainties of life and to respond to dangerous situations, through physical and psychological discipline, where one uses orthodox weapons in unorthodox ways.

# CHAPTER 2

# The Public Record of Ninjutsu

The purpose of this chapter is to describe, as precisely as possible, the details of historical events concerning ninja and the practice of ninjutsu, based on the most serious and accurate testimonies.

A historical account does not have to be exciting or astounding; all that we ask is that it be accurate. To understand the true history of ninjutsu, it is necessary for one to give up a great number of legends and myths. Then one is left with details of a technical nature, the combat techniques.

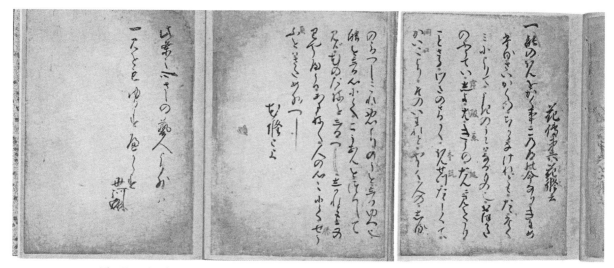

The *Koyō Gunkan*, a text about the Takeda family's tactics and strategies. Private collection.

One also needs to discard the image of the black-clad man, a popular image that first appeared in illustrated books between 1770 and 1780.[1] Added to this is a whole mixture of heroic legends, esoteric religious practices, of magic and invisibility, and so forth, which brings to mind the charismatic image of the "superspy ninja."

To discover the history of an art such as ninjutsu, and thus of the ninja, one must research the history of the military class, the *bushi* and their superior martial skills. In almost all the wars that Japan experienced, warring sides used the ninja for information gathering, guerilla tactics, assassinations, and the like. The history of the ninja simply represents a vital part of the history of the Japanese warriors—something often forgotten. Because ninjutsu is a practice of the shadows, the ninja did not belong to any social class. In short, they are the men who acted in the shadows to maintain law and order.

Although it is difficult, even impossible to define by whom, where, and when ninjutsu was created, leading Japanese historians Yamaguchi Masayuki,[2] Koyama Ryōtarō,[3] Tobe Shinjūrō,[4] and Sugiyama Hiroshi,[5] have fixed five dates where ninjutsu played a major part in the history of Japan.

These dates extend over the Muromachi, Sengoku, and Edo periods. These were major turning points in the history of Japan. During these periods, major developments formed the basis for unification of the country.

We begin our study of the role of the ninja with a look at all of the unconventional aspects of the historical Japanese battles ranging between the Muromachi, Sengoku, and Edo periods. In particular, we will examine accounts of activities ranging from espionage to assassination, of guerilla warfare to night raids, and missions of any unorthodox military operations from which the ninja could not be dissociated. That implies a study of the historical facts of certain chronicles of battles (*gunkimono* or *gunki-monogatari*).

These epic stories, similar to Homer's *Iliad*, tell the exploits and combat of great warriors during the continual wars of eleventh through sixteenth centuries. Although these battle chronicles are often unconfirmed or dubious, they bring many insights on the value and combat techniques of the warriors of the time.

The ubiquitous military treatise on strategy and espionage, written by Sun Zi, is a point that one should not neglect in the search for unorthodox operations at the time of these battles.

The final chapter of that treatise places great importance on the use of expert spies for misinformation, espionage, guerilla warfare, assassination, and the like. For Tobe Shinjūrō[6] and Koyama Ryōtarō,[7] the work of Sun Zi seems to have been a traditional necessity for the training of any Japanese military strategist.

To accurately determine the history of the ninja and of ninjutsu, we must give up looking for these specific terms, as both are recent names. These terms were used for the Edo period in a work entitled *Buyō Benryaku*[8] written in 1684.

The most widespread term in the historical chronicles of wars is that of *shinobi no mono* or simply *shinobi*. However, one also finds a whole list of names and expressions relating to the acts of the ninja. The *Hōjō Godai-ki* (北条五代記),[9] among other things, uses the terms *rappa* and *seppa*, and the *Kōyō Gunkan* (甲陽軍鑑: chronicle of the Takeda family) uses the term, *kagimono-kiki* (嗅物聴).[10]

In order understand the Muromachi period (1333–1467) to any degree, one must first gain an understanding of the preliminary historical background concerning the Heian and Kamakura periods, as well as have a familiarity with the "War between the Court of the North and the Court of the South" (*Nambokuchō sensō*). Indeed, if we start directly with the first date when the term ninja first appears, we omit a rich history of events that helped develop ninjutsu.

So that one can clearly see the lineages, we will start with the origins of ninjutsu, in particular, by looking at all their interactions, influences, and exchanges. These, according to the historians quoted above, are at the epicenter of ninjutsu.

## Theories Related to the Historical Origins of Ninjutsu

When a historian who specializes in the history of feudal Japan discovers the character of the ninja or *shinobi no mono* through readings and research, he or she becomes intrigued.

A mysterious figure, with seemingly incredible capabilities and accomplishments, a true chameleon of combat and spy without peer, the ninja is hidden in the shadows of all the wars, often acting to turn the tide and snatch victory from the jaws of defeat. Who are the ninja? What is the source of the practice of ninjutsu?

There are many theories advanced regarding the beginnings of ninjutsu, with a seemingly wide variety of proposed origins. These theories are reinforced by the obvious diversity of techniques employed in the martial art. It is difficult to see clearly through this clouded historical lens. One saying goes:

忍者の世界は迚も奥が深い所です [11]
The world of the ninja is deep and complex.
忍びの歴史は長く古い [12]
The history of the ninja is long and old.

These sentences, which one finds in the majority of the Japanese works "specializing" in ninjutsu and

View of the Hakuho castle of Iga's Ueno city. Private collection.

the ninja, show how difficult it is to seize upon the true origins of ninjutsu.

Although it is nearly impossible to determine the exact time, place, and origin of ninjutsu, there are some reasonable inferences that can be made. The military treatise on strategy, *Sonbu no heihō* (孫武之兵法) contains the teachings of the famous Chinese strategist Sun Zi, who lived in the sixth century BCE It also contains a body of oral doctrines supplemented by Se Ma during the same period, then further by Zi from the third century BCE This combined body of work was introduced in Japan as early as the sixth century CE.

A chapter concerning espionage at the end of the treatise, according to historians Yamaguchi and Tobe, contains the fundamental principles that are at the heart of the practice that will later be called ninjutsu.

Ninjutsu would be a practice of combat, or a martial art, that would make it possible to realize the theories of invisibility and deceit, preached by Sun Zi.

彼を知り己を知れば百戦致て危うからず

If you know the enemy and know yourself, you need not fear the results of a hundred battles.[13]

This famous maxim attributed to Sun Zi, on which generations of soldiers meditated, represents the essence of ninjutsu, that is, a deep and fundamental knowledge of the psychological and physical aspects of adapting to extreme situations and turning obstacles into advantages.

However, that doesn't exactly pinpoint the precise origin of ninjutsu, because, if it is undeniable that the ninja was a spy-warrior without equal, it is also necessary to include and understand the reasons for which this system of combat was invented.

What later became *shinobu ho* (忍ぶ法: the old reading of the term ninjutsu), a highly systematized and scientific method of combat, espionage, and defense, sprang from various sources in reaction against the forces of the current dominating political, economic, and social traditions of the Japanese classes.

As early as the seventh century, many immigrants arrived from the mainland, in particular from China and Korea, and among these immigrants were monks, wise Taoists, military officers, potters, merchants, and craftsmen, all having fled their country of origin for various reasons.

It is likely that *genjutsu* (玄術: techniques of illusion, conjuring), and *kenpō* (劍法, 拳法: Chinese combat techniques with bare hands and with weapons) arrived in Japan and developed jointly thereafter with the local combat techniques.[14]

Temple in the Yagyū village in Mie prefecture. Private collection.

At the same time, new religious branches of esoteric Buddhism, such as *mikkyō* (密教), were imported into Japan, In addition to ascetic and shamanistic practices developed in the mountains, there also arose the practice of *onmyōdō* (陰陽道: way of yin and yang) also known as *inyō gogyō setsu* (陰陽五行説: theory of the five phases yin and yang).[15]

Between the 8th and 11th century, a great number of immigrants, as well as defeated and displaced Japanese *bushi* started to form autonomous groups, withdrawn in the mountains in order to hide far from the major urban centers. These homeless and lord-less warriors often escaped into the wilderness after the armies to which they belonged were routed and defeated in battle.

The provinces of Iga (伊賀) and Kōga (甲賀), due to their remote locations and inhospitable venue, represented the ideal place for these cultural groups. The separation from mainstream Japanese society allowed these expatriates to freely research combat techniques that would be the origin of ninjutsu and also many other Japanese martial schools. Despite the many legends attributing the development of ninjutsu to ancient mythical gods, the art probably developed between 10th and the 14th century.

Indeed, it is the fruit of the interaction of religious sources and soldiers who produced a uniquely Japanese approach regarding the use of nature, cosmic laws (meteorology, astronomy, divination, etc.), of psychology and physiology of man in order to permanently affect history in order to obtain the means of physical and spiritual survival. This complete knowledge, after all, was regarded as a means of facing the various challenges in life, and achieving the necessary goals in all these situations. However, it is erroneous to believe that all of this developed in a vacuum, without other influences. There is a theory that Japanese pirates could also have contributed to the origin of ninjutsu.

It is a historical fact, since antiquity up until the Edo period (1603–1867), that the Japanese seas were infested with pirates known under the name of *kaizoku* (海賊).[16]

Kumano, an area located south of Iga, is an ancient stronghold of the shintō religion. Pirates, depending on sanctuary from the shintō priests of Kumano, practiced combat techniques that contained a great deal of religious influence.

It was under similar circumstances that the creation of the famous schools of *kenjutsu, Tenshin Shōden Katori Shintō-ryū* and *Kashima Shin-ryū*, were both founded under the inspiration of warriors who lived in the sanctuaries Katori and Kashima.

Priests, who offered and managed the sanctuaries of Katoria and Kashima in the area of Kantō, influenced a great number of combat technique schools. One finds the name of the temple at Kurama (鞍馬寺)[17] in Kyōto prominent in the genealogies of many of traditional bujutsu schools, particularly *Nen-ryū* (念流). One of the principal instructors of *Kurama-ryū, Tozawa Hakuunsai*, is reputed to have been a ninji, and his name appears in various genealogies of old schools of ninjutsu.

All the warriors of the time sought out the celebrated warrior Minamoto Yoshitsune, initiated into the martial arts by Kiichi Hōgan, head of the *Kurama-ryū kenjutsu* school that possessed a military study of strategy and combat called the Rikutō Sanryaku (六韜三略). Yoshitsune later founded his own school, *Yoshitsune-ryū ninjutsu*.[18]

One can easily conclude that a great number of temples had secret circles where there were taught a whole series of special combat styles, which can be called a form of ninjutsu; all obviously practiced in private, away from prying eyes.

The Kuki (九鬼氏) family, who were reputed pirates, was distinguished in two ways. They were recognized socially and accepted in the warrior caste. They enjoyed great influence in the sea of Kumano and the Ise area. They were also well known for their school of combat, which still exists today under the name of *Kukishinden-ryū* (九鬼神伝流).

One of the scrolls (*makimono*) of this school shows the techniques and tools used that found their way into other arts. When boarding enemy ships, the pirates of this school used a hook, like many others. However, this hook, called a *kagi-nawa*, formed an integral part of the arsenal used by the ninja during their various missions. The use of this hook with a fine cord, generally made from braided woman's hair, gave rise to many combat techniques included in the practice of ancient ninjutsu.

These disciplines are:

- ✦ *kaginawa-jutsu* (the technique of using the hook and cord)
- ✦ *kusarigama-jutsu* (the technique of using the chain and sickle)
- ✦ *torinawa-jutsu* (the technique of using the cord to bind the adversary in combat)
- ✦ *kusari-jutsu* (the technique of using the chain)

It is a solid assumption that the techniques used by Japanese pirates influenced ninjutsu, as well as many other combat styles. This influence was part of the range that affected ninjutsu, helping it to become an evolutionary combat style used for evasion and self-defense.

## Birth of Primitive Ninjutsu Practice during the Heian Period (782–1190)

In 782, the capital in Nara was transferred to the town of Heian-kyō, present-day Kyōto. It was a period of great change that enriched nobility and established many great houses. It is during this period that the Tendai doctrines of China are brought back by Saichō monks and Shingon doctrines, another Chinese esoteric Buddhist system, is brought back by Kūkai.[19]

*Shugendō* (修験道), Buddhist ascetics founded by In no Gyōja between the seventh and the eighth century, developed and had considerable influence into the twelfth century in the Kumano area, south of the peninsula of Kii. Many temples and sanctuaries related to this practice were found here.

*Onmyōdō* (陰陽道: the way of yin and yang), a science of predicting the future based, among other things, on the astronomy of ancient China combined with the theory of the five male and female phases (五行説: *gogyō setsu*), was introduced in Japan at the same period.

The practices of *shugendō* and *onmyōdō*, which some at the time found amusing, influenced the practice of ninjutsu, which was, according to Koyama,[20] still in its infancy. These two doctrines were largely

Illustration showing the Prince Yamato acting as a ninja. From the One Hundred Aspects of the Moon by Yoshitoshi Kakusai in 1886. Private collection.

widespread among the ascetics, *yamabushi* (hermits of the mountains), shaman, and warriors of the time.

One must note that these beliefs, while scoffed at by some, were not restricted to the hermits, monks, and warriors. In the case of *onmyōdō*, many well-read men of the time were believers and practitioners. Indeed, these scholars were the source of the introduction and the development of these doctrines in Japan. Their interests in these beliefs were different from those of the warriors and hermits, because knowledge of the sciences from China gave one great prestige and status. This knowledge was of capital importance in order to pass the examinations needed for promotion among the senior government officials of the period.[21] Powerful, warrior families, such as the Minamoto and the Taira clans, maintained close relations with various *yamabushi*, hermits, and shamans.

The reputation of these ascetics, who lived in the farthest reaches and deepest recesses of the mountains, instilled a certain level of fear in the population. This was a considerable asset when the yamabushi moved from one area to another, collecting vital information. Many researchers and historians saw in the *yamabushi*, ascetics, hermits, and warrior monks, the characteristics and personalities that formed the precursors of the ninja.

Ninjutsu evolved as a martial art without a preestablished code. Since it developed in locations where hermits, ascetics, dissidents, and deposed warriors came to seek refuge and live peace, it is understandable that this "melting pot" of various religious practices influenced the development of the art over time.

Relationships with the great warrior families of the time started to emerge. This later made it possible for ninjutsu to be incorporated into the disciplines of combat that these families used while following imperial orders, which consisted of removing Ainu and other rebels representing a possible threat.

At the principle temples of the time, it was common to find a number of monks who were able to handle the staff, the bow, and sword. They put these skills to use defending the goods and interests of the temples.

The great establishments, Enryakuji and Onjoji, which formed the two branches of Tendai, Kōfukuji and Todaiji of Nara, had the most troops and often entered in conflict against each other and sometimes in support of the local provincial governor.[22]

These warrior monks, often called *akusō* (悪僧: bad monks) or *sōhei* (僧兵: monk soldiers), became a major element of the Japanese warrior structure starting in the eleventh century and remained a dominant element until the end of the sixteenth century.

In the light of these facts, one can conclude that a great majority of the temples provided training in combat techniques via the warrior-monks, and as a result of sharing the same geographical locations, primarily in the mountains, it is not unthinkable that relationships developed with dissidents, hermits, ascetics, and future ninja.

Many of these so-called "outcasts" belonged to a class that was part of the hierarchy set up during the Heian period. However, as mentioned previously, they returned to live in the mountains, living like nomads, obeying no lord.

Mainstream government classified them as "outcasts" at the time, because they were not included in the local government's tax rolls. This "separateness" allowed them a great freedom of movement.

It is easy to presume that the large temples and ambitious warrior families maintained close relations with these "outcasts," which enabled the mainstream participants in society to act in the shadows without dirtying their hands directly.

This illustration shows the famous warrior Benkei, friend of Minamoto Yoshintsune. Private collection.

Qualified personnel were required to manage these great tracts of property and fields owned by the temples and the warrior families. These worker castes, the *saka-hinin* (坂非人: people of the banks, outcasts practicing all the trades in connection with butchery and tanning, and the like), included a small group of specialists who were entrusted to collect information and conduct espionage. This group was bound by religious conviction and profit, as well as any alliances that allowed for the survival of their particular clan.

One can suggest that the precursors of the ninja, as well as the ninja themselves, find their origin among outcasts called the *shōmonji* (声聞師: reciting), a kind of traveling acrobat or magician. One can attribute the lack of consistent, clear historical evidence of the relationships of ninja to outcasts in this period of history to the simple fact that the ninja could change appearance and thus their level of social condition in order to carry out the entrusted mission.

It is difficult to be categorical about the existence of the ninja during this period. However, there were many factors that make it possible to assert that various minority groups in the fringes of society were devoted to practices that would quickly evolve into ninjutsu.

It wasn't until the twelfth century, with the emergence of great warrior families of Momochi, Hattori, and Fujibayashi in the Iga and Kōga provinces, that ninjutsu became an independent and recognized technique of combat.

A turning point for Japan and the development of ninjutsu came at the end of the Heian period. A combination of the weakening of the central government, the intrigues and plots in the imperial palace and the competitions between the warrior families, like those of the Minamoto and Taira clans, supported the development of ninjutsu as a method of combat and espionage. Little by little, ninjutsu became an essential pursuit for the warrior families of this period.

The precursors of ninjutsu, alive in the provinces of Iga and Kōga that were located near the towns of Kyōto and Nara, the great metropolitan centers of the time, all offered their various services and made alliances with the future government leaders, the temples, and new warrior classes starting to emerge.

## The Emergence of the Warrior Class

The Kamakura period (1192–1333) marked a great turning point in the history of Japan. Indeed, following a period of great conflict and at the end of ten years of social and political crisis, Minamoto no Yoritomo, leader of victorious the Minamoto clan came to power. Minamoto no Yoritomo defeated the Taira clan (in the battle known as Gempei), set up his new regime in Kamakura, away from the provinces of Kinai (the area located around the imperial capital, Kyōto). This new regime constituted a governmental framework, making it possible for the warrior classes to ensure their political domination of the country for more than seven centuries.

With the Yoritomo ascension to power, the emperor and court no longer controlled Japan, but rather the country was led by a succession of shōgun dynasties or powerful families, exerting their influence on the emperor. This period was punctuated by bloody conflicts with the head of the regime, where assassination played a dominant part in order to destabilize and divide opponents.

Even the family of Yoritomo did not escape assassination. The second and the third shōgun of the minamoto family fell to "unexplained deaths." Sanetomo, the third and the last Minamoto shōgun, fell to an assassin in 1219, on the steps leading to the Hachiman temple in Kamakura.[23]

A warrior monk in action. Private collection.

For Sugiyama Hiroshi,[24] the use of spies and killers during this period was common. Because of (or thanks to) all these scheming and political disturbances, there was no shortage of work for the skilled spy and assassin.

Wanting to remain anonymous, the powerful families, such as the Hōjō clan, selected skilled adepts who were accustomed to hiding the relationships that allowed the clan to achieve their surreptitious goals without rousing the suspicions of the government.

A *sōhei*, monk warrior using a *tetsubō*, iron staff as a shield. Private collection.

Each new war gave the *bushi* an opportunity to test and refine their combat skills, and to acquire fame. However, for the groups of spies, it was a time when they worked behind the scenes, doing all the basic work (espionage, assassinations, and guerilla warfare) vital to the victory.

Koyama explains why the operatives, thereafter called ninja, were like the immersed part of an iceberg in any battle. They were the bedrock of every battle in which they participated, and they used unorthodox methods in which the Kamakura era warrior class had not been trained.

Unlike the samurai of the time, the ninja did not directly face their adversaries. Operating in the shadows as advisors, they were not in a position to open hostilities. In contrast to the bushi with their ideal of loyalty towards their lord, the ninja represented, in Japanese warrior history, an example of a mercenary paid for a specific job, and did not attach any particular honor to being the first thrown into battle.

Towards the end of the Kamakura period, in 1336 (the first year of the Engen era or the third year of the Kenmu era) Japan was divided between two warring states, each of which asserted its legitimacy to control the whole country.

Picture taken during Meiji period showing a *Sōhei*, a warrior monk. Private collection.

This political crisis is known in Japan under the name of the period of the Court of the North and the Court of the South (南北朝時代: *Nanbokuchō jidai*). The origin of this crisis was the attempt at restoring the imperial rule by Emperor Godaigo (1319–1338), who tried to throw off the shōgunate set up by Yoritomo.

Small bands of mountain warriors assisted Godaigo, as well as a great number of dissatisfied *akutō* (悪党: gangsters, bad people), who were not in the service of the *bakufu* (shōgun). All of these disaffected people joined under the banner of Godaigo and were led by a famous military genius named Kusunoki Masashige (1294–1336). He led the resistance with great effectiveness. According to Tobe Shinjūrō,[25] the fact that the Kusunoki family originated in the province of Iga, proves that Kusunoki Masashige was a ninja.

In fact, Sugiyama[26] insisted that Kunosoki Masashige was a specialist in unconventional warfare, which was a method of the ninja and that, among the warriors who were at his side, there were certainly experts in guerilla warfare and unorthodox techniques of combat.

Completely ordinary mountain warriors carried out the majority of the extraordinary techniques and raids, such as the night raid on the Mount Kasagi. These simple warriors were motivated by a strong desire to survive, and demonstrated remarkable ingenuity in the field.

Masashige later committed *seppuku*, a ritual specific to the *bushi*, which would not have been done by a ninja. Indeed, ninja, being warriors who could turn against their current employer, held no particular loyalty towards any lord. Kusunoki Masashige symbolized the *bushidō* code, established later, during the Edo period, namely, honesty to all, regardless of rank.[27]

The accounts of the military campaigns, like all the stratagems used by Kusunoki Masashige, are contained in one of the most famous *gunkimono*, a blend of historical fact and romantic fiction, called *Taiheiki* (太平記), compiled between 1360 and 1380.

Like the *Heike Monogatari* (平家物語), as a historical source, certain facts in the *Taiheiki* are of doubtful validity, but from another point of view, it admirably depicts the values that the *bushi* held in this period, as well as the battles and unorthodox techniques at the beginning of the fourteenth century.

One finds there many references to traditional Chinese military and philosophical thought, including, of course, the treatise of Sun Zi. In contrast to the *Heike Monogatari*, the *Taiheiki* abounds with anecdotes that we can infer are practices of ninjutsu, because of the many examples of strategies and topography.

However, there is no proof of the use of a group of ninja as a special or unique unit in any of the anecdotes described by the *Taiheiki*.

## First Mention of the Ninja During the Muromachi Period (1333–1467)

The Muromachi period (1333–1467) starts with the beginnings of the reign of the shōgun Ashikaga Yoshimitsu (1368–1394), and concludes at the end of the war of Ōnin (1467–1477) with the coup d'etat perpetrated in Kyōto in 1493 by Hosokawa Masamoto, a major lord and minister. It was a transitional period marked by instability and insurrection in all the sectors of society.[28] In these troubled times, a new type of warrior appears who left his mark on Japanese military history.

The entrance of Mochizuki's ninja museum in Iga's Ueno city, Mie prefecture, private collection.

The events of the war of Nambokuchō, (1336–1392), took place in a geographical location not far from the provinces of Iga and Kōga, two areas which are forever bound as the cradle of ninja and ninjutsu.

The province of Iga, today part of the prefecture of Mie, is located east of Yamato (less than one hundred kilometers from Kyōto). It is a kind of basin surrounded by a nearly perfect chain of mountains whose peaks culminate at an altitude of 1,640 to 1,970 feet (five to six hundred meters) in the north and the west, and around 3,280 feet (one thousand meters) in the south. To the north of Iga and contiguous to the latter, the district of Kōga (340 miles or 548 kilometers from Kyōto, today part of the prefecture of Shiga), is characterized by a landscape of hills that sharply run into cliffs towards the lake Biwa. Towards the south, the mountaintops rise to an altitude of 2,625 feet (eight hundred meters).

The two provinces share a similar geography. They represented the ideal hiding-place for all the escaping warriors, fugitives, gangsters, and those dissatisfied with the battles between the two courts. They were a place of refuge for those who wished for seclusion and peace, far from the large cities of the time.

The annals of the Muromachi Bakufu, *Nochi Kagami* (後鑑), provide the first written reference that mentions and associates the ninja with the provinces of Iga and Kōga. In a particular article quoted by Sugiyama Hiroshi, one finds the following:

> With regard to the ninja, it is known that they were native to the provinces of Iga and Kōga, and could easily slip secretly into enemy castles.
>
> They observed the hidden things, and were able to pass as allies to the eyes of their enemies. In the countries of the West (in China), one called them saisaku (細作). The strategists called them kagimono-kiki (嗅物聴).[29]

This description concerning their activities, including secret intrusion into enemy castles, coincides with what will be discussed later in the numerous reports of

Ashikaga Yoshihisa's grave situated in Magari district in Ōmi prefecture. Private collection.

attacks on castles. The article also mentions the specific actions to which people of Iga (伊賀之者: *Iga no Mono*) took part. In this same article, the word *shinobi* is used rather than ninja:

> In the camp of the shōgun Ashikaga Yoshihisa in Magari, there were shinobi whose names were known by all in the area.
>
> When Yoshihisa attacked Rokkaku Takayori, the family of Kawai Aki no Kami of the area of Iga, in the service of Yoshihisa in Magari, obtained considerable recognition as shinobi in the forefront of the large army of the shōgun.
>
> Since then, successive generations of warriors from Iga were admired. This is the origin of the warriors of Iga.[30]

The names of Rokkaku Takayori and the shōgun Ashikaga Yoshihisa, who reigned from 1473 to 1489, enable us to identify in which area and on which date this event (鈎の陣: *Magari no Jin*) occurred. This was in 1487 in the village of Magari in the province of Kōga. This episode took place at the end of an event of great importance in the history of the Japanese warriors, the Ōnin War (1467–1477).

The ninth shogun, Ashikaga Yoshihisa (1465–1489). Yoshihisa fought against Rokkaku Takeyori at the battle of Magari, where ninja from Kōga helped Takeyori. Private collection.

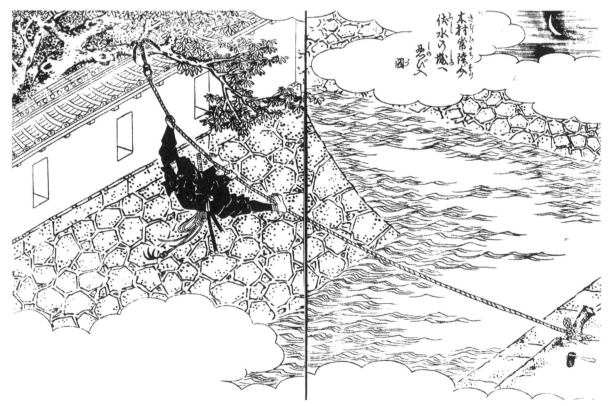

Ninja sneaking into a castle. The caption on the right side reads: "Kimura Hitachi no suke sneaking in the Fushimi castle." From the *Ehon Taikō-ki*, a romance based on the life of Toyotomi Hideyoshi. The *Ehon Taikō-ki* was written by Takenouchi Kakusai, and illustrated by Okada Gyokuzan, and was published in 1802. Private collection.

Warriors climbing a castle's walls. From the *Ehon Taikō-ki*.

This illustration shows how an intruder was stabbed by a fatal and unexpected blow though the interior wall of the house. From the *Ehon Taira gunki* by Kunisada Tadachūji, in 1852. Private collection.

This war began from conflict over succession to the shogunate between members of the Ashikaga family. Yoshihisa, mentioned above, was still a child when put among these applicants to the shōgunate.

Rather than one major battle or a clash of armies in the field, the Ōnin War was primarily made up of street battles during which the capital and the prestige of the bakufu were devestated.[31]

This war lasted ten years, and Yoshihisa, who gained the right to the title of shōgun at nine years of age by his father, Yoshimasa, sought to restore the military prestige of his family as soon as he was of age.

His chance came in September 1487 (or 1488). In this year, 46 landowners of the province of Ōmi, among those who appeared to be owners of the province of Kōga, sought the assistance of the shōgun against the excesses made by a *shugo* of Ōmi, named Rokkaku Takeyori. Rokkaku planned to seize the lands of each. This type of action was not unusual for the time. Indeed, the shugo, who were provincial governors selected by Ashikaga, had benefited from the chaos caused by the Ōnin War, rebelling against the shōgun. They were supposed to manage the territories that belonged to the shōgun. These *shugo*, called *daimyō*, instead had built autonomous principalities and were the cause of the many wars that took place between 1490 and 1600.

The young and proud, Yoshihisa would not tolerate the rebelling *shugo* and personally undertook the business of reestablishing the dominance of his shōgunate. With his army, Yoshihisa besieged Rokkaku Takeyori in his castle with Kannonji-in, in the province of Ōmi. The siege camp was based close to the village of Magari, where several sympathizers of the cause of the shōgunate joined them.

In spite of the good progress made by his army, Yoshihisa's health was not equal to his ambitions, and he succumbed to disease, dying without driving out Rokkaku. His army broke camp and moved to Kyōto. Yoshitane, Yoshihisa's cousin and successor, returned to Ōmi in 1491 and defeated Rokkaku.

According to Sugiyama, there is no proof to conclude that there were ninja used at Magari.[32] Indeed, when Yoshihisa, and then Yoshitane attacked Rokkaku Takeyori; he twice escaped in the direction of Kōga and Iga. Only when the shōgun's army again launched a siege against the castle at Ōmi did help appear from a small group of mercenaries using unorthodox methods.

It is only a question of whether it was the Iga or Kōga ninja. One did not enter Iga or Kōga without the knowledge and permission of the warriors who lived there. During his escape towards these two areas, the same warriors surely helped Rokkaku, but they were used against him shortly thereafter. This lack of filial loyalty, changing colors without hesitation in support of his own goals, is a mercenary behavior attributed early on to the warriors of Iga and Kōga; and affirmed throughout the history.

A warrior monk holding his *naginata*. Private collection.

# Organization

If we put aside these facts and anything else regarding the ninja during the Muromachi period, the question arises whether ninjutsu was created at this time or if a purely local practice that focused on united self-protection already existed.

According to Souyri,[33] the provinces of Iga and Kōga were organized by groupings of local warriors, *jizamurai* (地侍), who formed mutually beneficial confederations or leagues. In Iga, this league was structured on two levels: the villages of the province formed the first level, and then all were federated at a central level.

The military force of the league consisted of the agricultural work force that supported the local warriors during times of need. This league was entitled on confer to the mobilized peasants (足軽: the *ashigaru*) the status of samurai and to offer, thus, the possibility of social elevation. The leaders of the league also had the right to execute members who would refuse to obey.

In *jizamurai*, this league corresponded to an organization of solidarity, an agreement between small local lords at the regional level. In this province, the leadership of the nobility over the local warriors seemed well organized.

In the old field of Kashiwagi, which occupies a good share of the administrative district of Kōga, one finds small groups of warriors, the *Ban*, the *Kōga*, and the *Mochizuki*, who each dominated one of several villages that made up the communes. These communal regroupings were in turn federated in an alliance gathering the communes under the domination of these three warrior families.

This collective organization, dominated by the small group of warriors, *jizamurai*, was an alliance also in military matters: preventing the intrusion of more powerful external forces.

These local warriors often called themselves *kokujin*, (国人) "the men of the country," which indicates that they viewed the imperial authorities in Kyōto and in the other close provinces as outsiders.[34]

However, Iga did not regard the federation in nearby Kōga as foreign. On the contrary, a spontaneous alliance had been

Outside view of the Momochi family's house. Private collection.

initiated because these regional federations ran up against common enemies.

So, where did these warriors come from? What were their aptitudes in combat, and where did they gain these skills? How did they manage to organize the various groups and keep them in agreement?

As Souyri explains it, the traditional ninja who was born in these areas was the product of a defeat.[35] Indeed, as explained previously, the majority of the warriors who had taken refuge in these provinces were survivors of the war of Nambokuchō or immigrants looking for reclusive places such as these.

The knowledge of combat and the military disciplines of these deposed warriors, combined with knowledge of the immigrants from overseas, former Chinese and Korean warriors, for example, added to a strong appreciation of defeat in all its forms, and it surely gave rise to pragmatic and evolutionary combat. This approach made it possible for these warriors to protect their homes and to sell their extraordinary skills to a great number of warriors of the time. As Koyama recalls, the ninja were *jizamurai* who, to escape the pressures and the threat of the shōgunate and to oppose the *shugo*, developed a perfect technique of combat.[36]

It is safe to assume that even if the first appearance of the ninja occurred during the siege of the castle of Rokkaku Takeyori in Magari by Ashikaga Yoshihisa in 1487, the birth of the techniques of ninjutsu as well as the formation of leagues and federations of local warriors, surely were not done overnight.

This takes us to the Sengoku period, which was a period of much disorder and confusion because of the constant warfare between opposing warlords. This conflict naturally gave rise to an increased reliance on mercenaries like the ninja.

## Use of Ninja During the Feudal Wars of the Sengoku Period (1477–1600)

Following the terrible Ōnin War (Ōnin no Ran 1467–1478), the central government could no longer exert its power beyond the capital; efforts to control the surrounding areas met with much difficulty. Indeed, Japan entered a new period called the Sengoku Period (戦国時代: Sengoku Jidai) or "warring-states" or "age of the country at war." This was a period of long civil war in the history of Japan, from the middle fifteenth to the early seventeenth centuries. It started in the late Muramachi period in 1467 lasting through the entire Azuchi-Momoyama period, until finally peace and order was achieved in 1615 during the Edo period.

Starting with, and continuing after, the Ōnin War, the central ruling authority of the Ashikaga or Muromachi shogunate in the capital of Kyoto was ruined, leading to a complete breakdown in social order and civil war throughout Japan. Outside of the capital, the provincial *daimyō* and magistrates that relied on the shogunate for their own authority and power, found themselves isolated and vulnerable to not only external but also internal forces.

During these wars for control, the warlords bypassed the conquest of Kyōto and control of surrounding areas, because the policy of religious autonomy and other characteristics in the region prevented the construction of a strong state. The wars overall seemed to be the means, however, of resolving these contradictions.[37]

This period in the history of Japan is very rich with documentation of the activities of the ninja. It is during this period of history that they were most active, because of the confusion and the chaos of the time.

An account that depicts the ninja in a way that we are accustomed to seeing is located in one of the most reliable references in connection with the ninja of Iga, namely, a story about a man who is able to furtively steal into a place considered impenetrable.

This particular account appeared in a chronicle known by the title of *Tamon-In Nikki* (多聞院日記). The Eishun Abbot of Tamon-In, a monk of the famous monastery of Nara, the Kōfuku-ji, possessed this newspaper.

Road to Yagyū's village, Mie prefecture. Private collection.

Many monasteries, such as the Kōfuku-ji, chronicled events that occurred in the provinces, and sources such as *Tamon-In Nikki* are, according to all historians, sources of the highest reliability.

Here is how the *Tamon-In Nikki* related the story about an infiltration of a group of ninja from Iga:

> At the beginning of the twenty-sixth day of the eleventh month of the tenth year of the Tembun era (1541), Iga-shū had entered into the castle of Kasagi in secrecy and had set fire to the monks' quarters.
>
> They also set fire to the out buildings and various places inside San no Maru, and they captured Ichi no Maru and Ni no Maru.[38]

The castle in question was the same one that was defended during the wars of Nambokuchō, at the time of the raid of the troops of Kusonuki Masashige. However, we can note that it fell in the usual manner.

The term *maru* refers to an internal part of the castle where the defenses are located and is equivalent to the palisades of defense in the European castles. *Shū* is defined as a directed group, band, or unit.

This chronicle contains only the quotation presented above. but it makes it possible to understand what had occurred at the time of this attack. The defender of the castle of Kasagi was a certain Kizawa Nagamasa, one of the minor *daimyō*, who had benefited from the extreme weakness of the central government because of the wars of Ōnin, and who enjoyed some influences in the provinces of Yamato and Kawachi.

In 1540, at the time when the feudal wars were at their height, an ambitious seventeen-year-old warrior, named Miyoshi Chōkei, invaded the territory of Kizawa. His uncle, Masanaga, and a great number of allies assisted him.

Tsutsui Junshō led the army of Kizawa, an ally of Miyoshi attacked Kasagi. Tsutsui Junshō was the leader who used the Iga-shū against the army of Kizawa. The group of ninja fulfilled its contract. Kizawa Nagasama was seriously wounded, and the castle fell at the hands of the army from Miyoshi.

During this period (Sengoku), the services of people of Iga and Kōga were in high demand. All the warlords wanted to pay for the very special services of those that possessed this elite talent and ability to infiltrate fortified towns considered impenetrable, to commit selected assassinations, and to conduct guerilla warfare.

A minor *daimyō*, but one who would become a great shōgun thereafter, was bound closely with the ninja of Iga and Kōga. This was none other than Tokugawa Ieyasu (1542–1616). The close links between Tokugawa and the ninja of Iga were in place right after bloody revolt of Iga in 1579–1581. However, reliable sources attest that his use of the ninja of Kōga precedes the revolt.

Ieyasu was born into a former family of warriors, the Matsudaira clan, in the minor province of Mikawa on the Tōkaidō route. Caught between two powerful war chiefs, Oda Nobunaga and Imagawa Yoshimoto, Ieyasu spent his childhood as a hostage between these two chiefs of war. He suffered much from this practice of keeping political hostages like many of his contemporaries. These hostages made it possible to have control of allies, and when those allies were recalcitrant, the hostages' throats were cut.

With the passing of years, the fortunes of Ieyasu changed, and, little by little, he ascended the warrior hierarchy of the Imagawa family. This family wanted to march on Kyōto and control the shōgunate, but ran up against the army of Oda Nobunaga. The battle was inevitable.

The battle took place in Okehazama, and it ended with the decapitation of Imagawa Yoshimoto. By chance, Ieyasu was not in the headquarters where Yoshimoto was killed. With the death of Yoshimoto, Ieyasu was free to continue to serve the Imagawa family, which he did almost his entire life. Ieyasu was still too weak to become a *daimyo*. His only choice was to join forces with the conqueror of the moment, Oda Nobunaga.

However, Yoshimoto had a son named Ujizane who, not having the military talent of his father, was a considerable source of pressure on Ieyasu. His family, including his wife, were retained as hostages in Sumpu, the castle of Ujizane, and they would undoubtedly die if Ieyasu changed allegiances.

Ieyasu acted prudently and intelligently by contracting a secret alliance with Oda Nobunaga, while seemingly remaining faithful to the Imagawa family. It did not take long for the situation to fall apart, and Ieyasu was faced with a dilemma.

On one hand, Oda Nobunaga wanted Ieyasu to provide him a more concrete allegiance, and on the other hand, Ujizane required the same faithful service that Ieyasu had given his father. These two problems were solved during a dramatic attack in 1562, with help from a group of ninja.

The Imagawa family had a castle named Kaminojō, which was their main stronghold, under the command of a certain Udono Nagamochi. The capture of this castle represented the means for Oda to test the loyalty of Ieyasu.

Ieyasu thought that all the hostages taken at the time of the attack of Kaminojō could be exchanged for his remaining family with Sumpu. Ieyasu had to act as soon as possible before information could be leaked, in which case Ujizane would be likely to kill his family.

He gave the mission of leading a fast attack to one of his men, Matsui Sakon Tadatsu. The document relating to this event is *Mikawa Go Fudo-Ki* (三河後風土記):

Monogashira Mitsuhara Sanzaemon says:

> As this castle is built on an incredible cliff, we will suffer many losses at the time of the attack. But by chance, there is here, among the go-hatamoto, men having relations with Kōga-shū of the province of Ōmi. Let us convene Kōga-shū via their compatriots, and they will be able to infiltrate the castle.[39]

This text makes it clear that the aptitude at infiltrating castles was well known to be a specialty of the Kōga-shū. The leader of the Kōga-shū was a certain Tomo Tarōzaemon Sukeie (according to Yamaguchi his name was Tomo Yoshichirō Sukesada), who commanded 80 soldiers, each skilled in the use of *shinobi-jutsu*:

> One ordered this group to hide in the shadows and to hide in various places. And, on the night of the fifteenth day of the third month, they were to infiltrate the castle and, without waiting, to put fire at the turns within the fortress.[40]

In other words, they carried out a traditional raid as taught by their practice in *shinobi no jutsu*, under the cover of darkness. However, Mikawa Go Fudo-Ki reveals some very interesting points.

First, they infiltrated, attacked, and killed without giving signal, so that the insurrectionists believed that traitors coming from their own garrison had attacked them. Yamaguchi adds that the ninja wore the same clothing of the defenders.[41] This indicates that for this night attack, they were not equipped with the famous black battle dress! This surely sowed a great deal of confusion in the minds of their enemies. They communicated only with each other, by using a password selected in advance.

Their chief apparently used a spear, sometimes thought to be a disadvantage when climbing along the walls, but for a ninja, the frequent use of a spear, like the *kama-yari* (spear with hook), made it possible to fight and climb along walls without issue. Here is the continuation of the account:

> . . . The garrison was completely dispersed and destroyed. The guard of the castle, Nagamochi Enfuya ran towards Gomadō (the "hall of prayer") located in the northern part of the castle. When Tomo Yoshichirō Sukesada discovered where he was, he ran towards Nagamochi, impaled him with his lance and took his head. The children, Fujitarō Nagateru and Katsusaburō Nagatada were captured alive by Tomo Hoki no Kami Suketsuna.[42]

Two hundred people from the garrison of Udono perished in the flames. By taking the castle, Ieyasu showed his loyalty to Nobunaga, but more importantly, he could exchange survivors of Udono for his family held by Imagawa Ujizane.

Once he was rejoined with his family, Ieyasu was free to choose his path for the future. From this moment he started his rise to power. Yamaguchi brought back a *kansha-jō* (a letter of thanks) written by Ieyasu for Tomo Sukesada, thanking him for his action with Kaminojō.

This letter was preserved in the documents of the Iwane family, a prominent ninja family of Kōga:

> As for the battle where Udono Fujitarō Nagateru was defeated, it was an act of unequaled bravery. Following this battle I was preoccupied with business and I neglected to write to you for years. I wish you good health and hope to have the honor to congratulate you in person. It was enchanting to hear the account of such a hero of this battle by my two men, Matsui Sakon Tadatsugu and Sakai Masachika.[43]

Regarding this document, the source is unknown and the date of its origin remains elusive. However, according to Yamaguchi, it is authentic.[44] In addition, this is the sole letter addressed to a ninja leader throughout all of Japanese history and represents, according to Yamaguchi, the only documentation showing the regard Ieyasu had for the abilities of this ninja leader. However, nothing is certain with the documents of the ninja, which were frequently falsified.

The services of the ninja of Iga and Kōga were essential, and as noted for Tokugawa Ieyasu, there are many battles where they were present. Of course, we cannot quote them all.

## A Mercenary's Mindset

Before moving on from the topic of the ninja of Iga and Kōga, we present the following, because it illustrates the awe-inspiring aspects of the ninja mercenary.

The Asai family employed various groups of Iga ninja against Rokkaku Yoshitaka, grandson of Takeyori who took part in the battle of Magari no Jin in 1487, where he opposed the shōgun Yoshihisa, and his successor, Yoshitane. His grandfather, Rokkaku Yoshitaka (or Sasaki according to other sources), often employed the ninja of Iga, and these same ninja later turned against him.

Asai Nagasama (1545–1573) was one of these traditional Sengoku *daimyō* during the time of the feudal wars. He was very familiar with the families of ninja of the province of Iga and Kōga, as his stronghold was in the north in the province of Ōmi, where his family was at war with the Rokkaku family for three generations.

In 1561, Asai Nagamasa made the decision to retake the castle of Futō (in the current prefecture of Maibara) in the east of the lake Biwa, which had fallen recently into the hands of the Rokkaku clan.[45] The castle was under the command of two generals, who apparently were not very qualified. Nagamasa ordered an attack and gave the command to two able men: Imai Kenroku and Isono Tamba no Kami.

Isono Tamba no Kami employed three men of Iga Shima Wakasaka no Kami, Iwakō Chikuzen no Kami, and Kanda Shurito. These men were to handle the seemingly impossible task of conducting a night attack, which would supplement the conventional attack prepared by the ordinary *bushi*. It is interesting to note the high rank that the suffix "*no Kami*" implies; it has as a meaning similar to "lord of."

Two chronicles report on this battle. They both recount the beginning of the action of Iga no Mono. In *Shima-Kiroku* (島記録) one finds the following:

Iga-shū entered in secrecy and burned the castle. At this signal, the guard and the second palisade were destroyed.[46]

*Asai Sandai-ki* (浅井三代記) provides another brief summary of this action:

We employed shinobi no mono of the province of Iga. . . . they were contracted for the burning of the castle.[47]

These quotes are only bits of information that suggest the direct action of the ninja of Iga. There was confusion at the time of the battle. Here is how, using the information reported by the two chronicles quoted above, the events of the night of the first day of the seventh month proceeded:

The shinobi of Iga were at their station, whereas the conventional troops, impatient, had begun their attack. It was clear to the leader, Imai Kenroku, who was on a close-by hill, that the shinobi had not followed the order to advance.

When he reproached them regarding their hesitation, they answered and made him understand that a samurai from the northern area of lake Biwa could not understand the tactics of the shinobi-jutsu, and that they would wait for a more favorable moment.

However, the troops were already moving. The night attack where the shinobi were to set fire to the castle was behind schedule and, like the mercenaries they were, they refused to attack and threatened to return to their homes if they were prevented from carrying out the operation as they saw fit.

The head ninja, Shima Wakasa no Kami, suggested to Imai Kenroku that he gather his men, and if he withdrew his troops for approximately an hour, the shinobi would carry out the raid on the castle. The signal to attack would be the burning of the castle.

Imai Kenroku agreed to act according to the advice of the ninja chief, but the result was disastrous. His army made the error of crossing the road in front of that of his comrade in arms, Isono Tamba no Kami, who had not been informed of the new operation, and the warriors of the second army concluded that an "enemy" attack was launched against them.

A rider of first line, named Kishizawa Yoichi, ran towards this "enemy" force to achieve the ideal of all samurai: to be the first in battle. He galloped towards the "enemy" army of Imai Kenroku, who hopelessly sought to regain control of his army. He impaled Imai Kenroku in the back with his lance.

Working to prepare his attack and thinking that only allies were behind him, he was too surprised to offer any resistance. Imai Kenroku fell from his horse and died.

The two allied armies began the combat between them, and approximately twenty warriors were killed before restoring order.

Finally, the shinobi set fire to the castle and those remaining of the two armies took the castle by storm. The castle of Futō was conquered but at the price of the life of one of the best born leaders of the Asai family.[48]

It can be concluded, then, that the mercenary aspect of the ninja of Iga and Kōga rests indeed on a firm historical basis.

Although there is no doubt that ninja were skilled in changing camps, ninja native to other areas, completed the same types of tasks without acting as mercenaries.

There are many excellent reports of the use of ninja during the feudal wars, who did not have any relation or connections with those of Iga and Kōga.

However, the precursors to their appearance were similar: the fall of the central authority held by the shōgun after the terrible Ōnin Wars and the rise of the *daimyō* and their principalities.

This time, the difference lies in the fact that contrary to the nature of ninja of Iga and Kōga, these ninja were clansmen to whom the *daimyō* entrusted a mission.

In the chronicles of battle that follow, the ninja form an integral part of the army of the *daimyō*, and are used for espionage or as an elite force, like a small commando unit, to sow disorder and confusion in the enemy lines, carrying out the operations in support of the action on the battlefield.

The famous war chief Takeda Shingen used spies against his major rival Uesugi Kenshin, and none seemed to be employed mercenaries. They all were loyal men of the Takeda generals. What is particularly interesting is that Takeda had taken the precaution to retain the women and children of his spies as hostages. Takeda Shingen had surely studied Sun Zi and feared double agents!

He had three groups of "secret agents," composed of ten men who were under the orders of three generals, Amari, Itagaki and Iidomo. These agents collected information and then forwarded it to these three generals, who sent it to Takeda in his headquarters with Kofu, using fast and skilful riders. Tobe Shinjūrō reports that these secret agents were *watari-ninja* (渡り忍者: the ninja who crosses, who circulates).

In connection with the ninja employed by the Takeda family, one finds the following in the chronicle *Kōyō Gunkan* (甲陽軍鑑):

> For example, concerning the changing fortunes of the Takeda family, the involvement of the watari-ninja natives of the province of Iga was considerable.
>
> During their spare time, by using the various techniques of ninpō, they aided in the industrial exploitation of the area, the best example being the exploitation of the mines.
>
> The ninja had what one would call today an aptitude for mathematics. In parallel with an uncanny sense of direction, they had the techniques of calculation, which made it possible to measure angles and distances.
>
> The gold coins of the Takeda family, called Koshūban, were extracted from the mines by the ninja. Once gold was extracted, from the same rock they extracted quartz and crystal, which became the basic elements of the particular products of the province of Kai.[49]

This is a surprising example; the ninja was far from being a simple mercenary, as many seem to believe. Ninjutsu, as a practice, was far from being restricted to combat only; in fact, it was also used to provide for daily needs and even mining techniques. Another edifying example shows how the ninja used his daily work to understand the martial qualities of even the most menial task:

> Even for the control of the course of a river, it seems that it was the case. The dam called Shingen-tei, built to control water of the Kamanashi River, was also a "technology" of the ninja. To overpower the enemy, the ninja caused the dam to break, which flooded the river. But, they also knew methods to avoid the rupture of the dams. The shingen-tei built by the ninja, was cut at intervals on the sides so that at when a flood occurs, water can run out. The flow of the water that escaped was dispersed by another dam on the outside and created a cascade effect. This process is an application of the techniques of the ninpō to control water. The ninja were scientists.[50]

This example shows the general-purpose character of ninjutsu and one of its most fundamental principles, namely adaptation. All the inventions must be easily repaired and maintained by fine soldiers or with daily labor. All ninja were not experienced "scientists" or skillful artisans, but each within a certain group had a well-defined function.

Another description of battle comes from *Hōjō Godai-Ki* (北条五代記), a chronicle telling of the exploits of five generations of the Hōjō family, compiled in 1600 by a vassal of Hōjō named Miura Jōshin.

The Hōjō family had been a potent force using unorthodox means, and the family subsequently controlled the whole of Kantō plain. The report reveals the use of ninja of the Satake clan against the Hōjō clan in 1575.

The terms used for ninja in this report were *shinobi* and *kusa* (草: the grasses). The use of the term *kusa* indicates the ninja were highly skilled in blending in with nature, a very advanced form of *Goton no Jutsu*. Aside from espionage, the Satake family used *kusa* as sentinels in the enemy lines to intercept spies. One can think of them as the anti-ninja ninja!

> . . .After having established the camp, men came as scouts to familiarize themselves with the area. They were very good riders, and all had great qualities.
>
> These warrior scouts, could go by horse to the borders of the stronghold to observe possible signs or go to any place, from which they could observe the enemy troops and return quickly to their lines.
>
> However, when a general opened hostilities and sent his army against the enemy, the first warriors to confront enemy lines were the ashigaru (足軽: foot soldiers).
>
> The latter remained carpeted in grass, spying on the enemies, and returned at dawn. They were called kusa or shinobi. Some of these "night kusa" could remain hidden until middle of the following day.
>
> The front lines of the enemy were not aware that they were being observed, and when they advanced, the kusa rose at once, cut off their retreat, and killed them. The Kusa were also very good riders, they could effectively retreat without regard to difficult terrain.[51]

This description of the *kusa* reported by Jōshin in *Hōjō Godai-ki* is characteristic of the methods of espionage and combat used by the ninja of Iga and Kōga. In addition, horsemanship was an essential skill for a warrior, and ninjutsu offered a range of techniques applicable to equestrian combat.

**Woods close to the Mochizuki's house in Iga's Ueno city. Private collection.**

# The Takeda Family's Encounter with the *Rappa*

Another report from the same chronicle refers to an action that occurred five years after the one mentioned previously. This time, it was the Hōjō who used the ninja against their enemies, the Takeda.

The name used was *rappa* (乱破) rather than *kusa*, but according to the context, it appears clear that their role was similar to the traditional role of the ninja, namely to sow confusion in the enemy lines.

The leader of the *rappa*, was Kazama Kotarō (or Fuma Kotarō), which seems here the most famous ninja leader of Kantō.

> A long time ago, as we saw, when the chaos reigned in Kantō, our bows and our arrows were always ready. In those days, there were villains called rappa.
>
> They were like thieves, without really being thieves. These bad people were intelligent and brave and had a special place in the army of a daimyō.
>
> Whatever the reasons for which they were called rappa, they could skillfully track their quarry, force them to flee their own territory, and defeat them.
>
> They infiltrated the neighboring provinces. Night piracy, robbery, attacks, and abductions were among their techniques. They were intelligent and conceived plans and plots that ordinary people would never have considered.
>
> In studying the old books, they learned how to mix truth with forgery, and they combined the aspects of wisdom judiciously with those of deception.[52]

As the report continues, it reveals an interesting anecdote regarding the *rappa*:

> Hōjō Ujinao controlled the eight provinces of Kantō, of which all the neighboring provinces were enemies, which caused ceaseless wars.
>
> During the autumn of 1580, Takeda Katsuyori and his son Takeda Nobukatsu commanded the armies of Shinano, Kai, and Suruga. They initially made movement towards Sanmaibashi with Suruga, to cover their flank with the wide and dangerous Kisegawa river. All the army established the camp in the full one with Ukishimagahara.
>
> Ujinao, consequently, led his army of the eight provinces of Kantō and established the camp with Hatsune ga hara and Mishima, in Izu.
>
> Ujino had two hundred rappa under his command that were all in his pay. One of them was a gangster by the name of Kazama.
>
> He was terrible for many reasons. Under the command of Kazama, there were four chiefs. Two had been bandits from the mountains and the other two had been thieves.
>
> The two bandits had a great knowledge of the mountains and rivers, and the two thieves could infiltrate enemy lines.
>
> These two thieves were called hosoru nusubito (細る盗人) and had skill in shinobi-jutsu. These four chiefs primarily carried out night raids.
>
> Their units of two hundred men were divided into four sections and would attack during the night whatever the weather.
>
> Each night they crossed the enormous Kisegawa and infiltrated secretly in the camp of Katsuyori. They kidnapped individuals, and freed horses of their reins and saddles.
>
> Moreover, during their night attacks, they set fire to all things and joined their cries to those of the soldiers, in order pass for their allies.

All the camp was in a state of shock and sank into chaos. Amplifying this confusion, the infiltrators bore the armor of their enemies. Not knowing friend from foe, the hapless solders turned against their companions.

The rappa ended up setting fire to all of the camp and sowed confusion and panic.

With a paddle, they examined the heads of the victims and discovered that during the combat, the low-ranking soldiers had taken the heads of their superiors and that children had taken the heads of their fathers.[53]

The losses of the Takeda family were considerable, but a small group of survivors attempted to take revenge against Kazama and his *rappa*. Here is how the account continues:

Kazama Kotarō is the general of the rappa. We will give our lives to kill him. This evening he will return for a new attack. We will await them on the road by which they should come.

They will be spread out, and we will secretly infiltrate their ranks until the moment that they congregate.

Kazama is a man of great stature, who cannot pass undetected among his two hundred men. He measures 7 shaku 2 sun (approx. 2.5 m or 8 ft), and is built like a wild beast.

His intelligence exceeds his herd of men by far. He gives the impression that he has eyes in the back of his head. He has a black moustache and his mouth is particularly broad.

His head resembles Fukuroku-ju, his nose is edifying, and if he raises the voice, he can be heard 50 chō round about. On the other hand, if he speaks gently, his whisper is like the sound of the wind. Based on this description, you can recognize him easily.

If you seize Kazama, do so resolutely, with your only intent being to take your revenge on account of our deposed lords, our late parents. This mindset will greatly bolster the fury of your attack. Then, along the road by which they would pass, the ten men waited in grasses. Kazama came to carry out his night attack, and the ten men mixed into the group unnoticed.

When the men of Kazama joined together in preparation to attack, they lit torches, and in response to a secret signal, they rose suddenly.

Not being aware of the secret signal, the infiltrating would-be avengers were caught off-guard, and were discovered and killed.[54]

This anecdote illustrates the intelligence of the *rappa*, who used signals and passwords to thwart any plans for revenge.

Even if the description of Kazama is an exaggerated example, it still renders something we can understand: that he was an uncommon warrior, whose image brought terror to all his enemies.

This rendition also includes many anecdotes where Fuma Kazama Kotarō is depicted with wonder and awe. However, my goal is to present the ninja of the Sengoku period.

There are still many examples of the same type of warriors described in other chronicles, such as *Or Eikyo Gunki* (奥武永亨軍記)[55] or *Chūgoku Chiran-ki* (中國知覽記),[56] where the ninja are *ashigaru* (lower class warriors) or as in the description of the *rappa* of Hōjō, of the infiltration of specialists into enemy lines.

The difference from the traditional ninja of Iga and Kōga still lies in the fact that these other ninja remained faithful to their lord and acted on the order of their lord like a special operations unit. The ninja of Iga and Kōga were independent in their acts, as in their choices, and this clearly explains their frequently shifting loyalties. This freedom enabled them to be at peace with their ideals and, thus, they could not accept the control of some warlord whose interests differed from theirs.

## The Death of Uesugi Kenshin

We cannot discuss the terrible battle of Iga (1579–80) without evoking the mysterious death of a famous Sengoku *daimyō*, Uesugi Kenshin (1530–78). His death is suspected to be an assassination, an act over which ninja claimed unequaled mastery, and which gave birth to a great number of stories.

Once the Takeda family was crushed in Nagashino, Oda Nobunaga attacked his rival Uesugi Kenshin. Without revealing any source, here is how the death of Uesugi is reported, according to one of the most famous ninja anecdotes:

Uesugi Kenshin was wary of the ninja of Oda and had taken utmost precaution; thus, he also secured the services of a group of ninja directed by a certain Kasumi Danjō.

However, one night, the ninja of Oda succeeded in penetrating the fortress of Uesugi, but Kasumi had discovered the breach and hunted them with three of his men.

Finding a suspicious shadow at the end of a corridor, the bodyguards of Uesugi sprang, only to discover too late that the shadow was a lure set up by the infiltrating ninja. . . .

The invaders, hanging from the ceiling like spiders, rained a hail of shuriken on Kasumi and his men, leaving them for dead. Without losing a moment (fearing an alarm would be raised), Ukifune Genpachi, the leader of the ninja of Nobunaga, leapt into the room where Uesugi rested.

Ukifune did not have time to carry out Oda's assassination order. Suddenly looming out of the shadows before him was Kasumi Danjō himself, who had not been wounded by the shuriken trap but had merely feigned death under the corpses of his three men. Kasumi restrained Ukifune Genpachi by breaking his arms before breaking his neck.

. . . . Uesugi had little time to congratulate Kasumi for his quick thinking. Indeed, the next attempt on his life would be more successful.

Shortly thereafter, Oda Nobunaga sent an exceptional ninja after him, Ukifune Jinnai, who bided his time in order to strike when Uesugi had dropped his guard.

Jinnai was only one meter [3.28 feet] high, and had trained himself to live, concealed, in a terra cotta earthenware jar.

He developed a plan that would take advantage of his diminutive stature; thus, the ninja gained entry into the latrines of the castle of Uesugi, and he clung beneath the boards that covered them in a most uncomfortable position. He remained there a long time.

Finally, when Uesugi sat above him, Ukifune Junnai impaled Uesugi with his sword. When Kasumi and the Uesugi's samurai ran to his howls of pain, Uesugi had collapsed dead already and could only be carried out.

Nobody found his assassin, who had at once dropped himself into the sewage, breathing through the sheath of his sword. Ukifune Jinnai arose from the pit and escaped when the way was free. . . .[57]

The circumstances of Uesugi's death were very well reported and do not significantly contradict the ninja anecdote.

It appears that he suffered from a crisis while he was in the toilet and died three days afterwards, during which he did not pronounce a word. The Kenshin-Gunki (兼信軍記) reveals:

. . . At the ninth day of the third month, he had a stomachache in the bathroom. Unfortunately, this evil persisted until the thirteenth, when he died.[58]

This report is to be taken into consideration with that of a chronicle, *Tōdaiki* (東大記), by a man in the service of Tokugawa, called Matsudaira Tadaaki, who noted the following in a footnote that in the fourth month:

> This spring, Kagetora died at 49 years of age. The cause of his death would be an enormous worm.[59]

It is clear that something happened to Uesugi while in the toilet. However, even if the ninja anecdote seems plausible, Uesugi Kenshin-den reports that he was seriously sick and that his death, although unexplainable at the time, arose as a complication of an incurable disease he had contracted a few years before.

"He moved using a stick and drank heavily," noted Naoe Kanetsugu, one of his more faithful companions. During the ninth month of the year 1577, during a night when he had remained with him, Naoe maintained that the condition of the *daimyō* went from bad to worse.

The ninja theory remains plausible, considering there was no autopsy at the time. However, given the fact that Uesugi was seriously sick, it is more probable that he died of a cerebral hemorrhage. One thing is certain: the right-hand men of Uesugi assumed that he had died from a disease. If we grant that a ninja did assassinate Uesugi, he committed the perfect crime.

## Riot in Iga and the End of Ninja Freedom

Since the beginning of the feudal wars, the province of Iga had remained a place unaffected by the upheaval that all Japan knew, thanks to the mountainous terrain and the safety it provided, it was a "dream come true" for any mercenary. All of this changed in 1579, when the Iga no Mono were forced to fight for their lands and for their very survival.

The Hattori pass in Mie prefecture, the place where Hattori Hanzō helped Tokugawa Ieyasu
get home to Mikawa during the trouble of Honnō temple. Private collection.

The chronicle of this obscure and bloody war, translated ages ago into French, provides insight into another dimension of the skill of the inhabitants of Iga regarding *shinobi no jutsu*. They now used their talents for guerilla action enhanced by an effective network of information.

The principal sources for information on these military campaigns are *Seishū Heiran-ki* (正集平乱記), a history relating the events of the province of Ise with some references to Iga, and *Shinchōkō-ki* (信長公記), a history reporting the detailed life of Nobunaga.

The most interesting chronicle remains *Iran-ki* (伊乱記),[60] written by Kikuoka Nyogen, probably a monk of Iga, where he describes the events of the battle against Iga. This chronicle has many rich details and offers a tantalizing description of the events and places.

The area of Iga, like that of Kōga, was not of great strategic interest. However, it could not remain eternally without control, and it was necessary to put an end to any desire for independence and autonomy held by the families who lived there.

The origins of the revolt of Iga (伊賀の乱: *Iga no Ran* 1579–1581) start with the events that occurred in the neighboring province of Ise, which, because of its close proximity, had relations with Iga.

The terrible Ōnin War marked the fall of the shōgunate's authority and heralded the expansion of the *shugo* who were proclaiming themselves *daimyō*. However, unlike most of Japan, it had not affected the province of Ise significantly.

This province had gone through a transition from the rule of a *shugo* to that of a *sengoku-daimyō* of the Kitabatake clan, a family of great warriors. Living during these very turbulent times was none other than Kitabatake Tomonori (1528–1576). He was a famous *kenjutsu* master and a pupil of the great *kenjutsu* master, Tsukahara Bokuden.[61]

The Nikki family controlled the province of Iga. Like the Kitabatake family, they respected the qualities and skills of the warriors of Iga and left these autonomous families free to offer their skills in *shinobi-no-jutsu* to other lords.

The expansion of Oda Nobunaga's power in 1560 marked the beginning of the confrontation with Kitabatake.

After the battle of Okehazama in 1560, Nobunaga swiftly rose to power. In 1568 he conquered Kyōtō and defeated the last shōgun, Ashikaga Yoshiaki. Nobunaga now reigned as regent but was surrounded by enemies like the Mōri, Takeda and Uesugi.

In 1568–69, his army invaded the province of Ise in order to control an important transportation route, the Tōkaidō, shared by the strongholds of Owari and Mino.

Kitabatake Tomonori fought valiantly, but he lost the castles of Kambe and Kuwana, the latter being on the strategic road of Tōkaidō.

Nobunaga besieged Okawachi for 50 days, after which a peace was struck. The *Seishū Heiran-ki* (正集平乱記), records the facts as follows:

> The lord Nobunaga sent Chasen-maru, who was twelve years old, accompanied by Kiboku Shuji-no-suke, to become the adoptive son of Tomonori and, with that, peace was restored.[62]

Chasen-maru was the name of child of the second son of Nobunaga Nobuo. Nobunaga established a headquarters in Okawachi and offered the land of the province of Ise as a reward to his generals.

As for Kitabatake Tomonori, he continued to control Ise, but was more of a puppet *daimyō*. His "consolation prize" was that once he died, his principal heir would be the son of Nobunaga Nobuo.

Tomonori died, and his stronghold became the property of Oda "Kitabatake" Nobuo. However, the survivors of the Kitabatake family did not accept this succession submissively.

The younger brother of Tomonori, Tomoyori, was a monk in a temple of Nara, and, learning the news, left his religious life to avenge his brother. Many Kitabatake faithful joined him, and among them, according to Tobe Shinjūrō, there was the son of the great sword master, Tsukahara Bokuden. Many men of Iga joined the forces of Kitabatake, which directly plunged, for the first time, the province of Iga into conflict with Nobunaga.

The ninja Manabe Rokurō, from the Hatano family, tries to kill Oda Nobunaga in his Azuchi castle. From the *Shinsen Taikō-ki* by Toyonobu Muramasa in 1883. Private collection.

The Nobunaga's first commander, Takigawa Saburōhei Kazumasu, broke this rebellion, supporting Nobuo and restoring balance to the situation in the province.

Many deposed samurai who were faithful to Kitabatake, fled towards the safety of the mountainous area of Iga, where they made the error of asking for the assistance of a mortal enemy of Nobunaga, Mōri Motonori.

The land of Mōri was the last in Japan that had not been disturbed by the expansion of Nobunaga. The threat that Mōri represented would precipitate calamitous events, and the son of Nobunaga, Nobuo, would be charged with restoring the peace.[63]

The events of the Ia no Ran are divided into three phases. The first is the battle of Maruyama. The second is the invasion of Iga by Nobuo, with an army of 12,000 men who received a crushing defeat at the hands of Iga no Mono. The third was when six armies attacked Iga on several fronts, simultaneously burning the stronghold and slaughtering the inhabitants.

It's beyond the scope of this book to discuss all the battles in detail. However, by focusing on the last phase of the offensive, namely the destruction of Iga, one can appreciate the tragedy.

The history of the Revolt of Iga, according to Koyama and Tobe,[64] started correctly in 1579, when a dissatisfied *jizamurai* of Iga named Shimoyama Kai no Kami visited Oda Nobuo in Ise to protest against the "excesses" of the men of Iga. This complaint provided the pretext and the opportunity sought by Nobuo, as he well knew about the great military reputation of Iga, as well as its geographical position.

A few years before, his late adoptive father, Kitabatake Tomonori, had built a castle on a hill, named Maruyama, which was almost in the center of Iga, with the aim of conquering the warriors of Iga.

These dreams of conquest regarding areas such as Iga, were common to all the lords of the Sengoku period. Becoming fearful of the reputation held by Iga and its men, Tomonori abandoned the project and made no further attempts. Such a place represented an essential location for the operations of Nobuo and he delegated to Takigawa Saburōhei, who was also a *fushin-bugyō*, with the mission of rebuilding the castle of Maruyama for him.

The castle of Maruyama was built in a fortified town, 180 meters (590.5 feet) high, dominating the Hijiki River. Takigawa did spectacular work and, according to the *Iran-ki*, he sent his own *shinobi* for reconnaissance missions during the rebuilding.

It was a beautiful building, constructed so that its true nature as a fortress might pass unperceived to the eyes of the inhabitants of Iga. However, the families of the local warriors were shrewd and took precautions using their traditional talents:

> The true significance of the building was propagated by word of mouth. The kanchō (間諜 spies) that remained behind with Matsugashima had become plowmen working for the castle, in order to gain knowledge of the castle. Consequently, they were able to evaluate all the weak points of this splendid castle.[65]

The chiefs of the families of Iga decided that the castle had to be attacked before it was finished, and that with any luck they could also kill Takigawa Saburōhei, whom they hated.

The families of Iga (the *Iran-ki* reports all these surnames)[66] joined together and attacked by surprise. Takigawa tried to resist with his army, but he had to flee towards the village neighborhoods for safety. Yet there, too, other warriors of Iga, operating in small groups, attacked him.

Those who remained in the castle sought to come to assistance of those who had fled, but by then it was too late, and they learned first-hand why the *Iga no Mono* were famous for infiltrating castles.

The fighting continued until night, and the darkness favored *Iga no Mono* since they had familiarized themselves with the area. With this advantage, they continued to attack the troops of Takigawa in the fields and forests. The victory was complete. When Nobuo learned the news, he wanted to invade Iga immediately, but the majority of his men prevented him from doing so, because they knew about the reputation of the *Iga no Mono*.

However, for revenge, Nobuo planned an attack on the three principal mountain roads that made it possible to go into Iga. Yet, despite this, the *Iga no Mono* exercised their penchant for spying and prepared their defense. As one might expect, it was a disaster for the 12,000 men of Nobuo who were not familiar with the geography of Iga and not accustomed to fighting with "shadows."

This defeat was even more of a humiliation because Nobuo received a letter from Nobunaga. This rebuke coming from Nobunaga multiplied the hatred that Nobuo felt towards the warriors of Iga.[67]

Because he was preoccupied with other more urgent tasks, Oda Nobunaga had not personally seen to the task of ridding the countryside of the autonomous warriors of Iga. But, when Fukuchi Iyō, a native of the village of Tsuge in Iga, offered assistance to Nobunaga as guide in Iga for a new invasion plan, the occasion to achieve revenge for the disaster of 1579 presented itself.

The *Iran-ki* reveals that Oda Nobunaga himself led the attack against Iga. He understood the error made by his son at the time of the first attack and developed a plan of invasion based on an attack synchronized on six different roads leading to Iga.

At the beginning of the ninth month of the year 1580, a council of war was held in Azuchi, during which the order to attack on the six key roads was given.

According to the *Iran-ki*, for Nobunaga, the attitude the warriors of Iga held defied all the rules of the samurai. Here is what he said on this subject:

> The number of rebels in Iga increases daily, more presumptuous and more costly than ever, they've exhausted our patience.

Those that ply this outrageous trade do not make any distinction between the high and low, rich or poor classes.

This attitude is a mystery to me; they disparage the hierarchy and do not have any respect for the warriors of high rank.

They practice disobedience and dishonesty; they heap dishonor on my name, the old court, and military practices alike.

Because they are traitors, they are guilty and we will punish these rebelious families. Let us go forward into Iga and punish them![68]

The place that used to be the home of Kikuoka Nyogen, the author of the *Iga no ran* chronicle and other diary entries and notes about ninjutsu and ninja from Iga. Mie prefecture, Iga Ueno City. Private collection.

The *Iran-ki* diligently reports the strategy used to invade the area of Iga, and Shinchōkō-ki and Seishū Heiran-ki corroborate these facts.

Nobunaga surrounded the area of Iga with his armies concentrating on the six principal roads leading to the Iseji villages, Tsuge, Tatamaki, Yamato Hase, Kasama and Tarao. Each was attacked at the same time. No village was spared.

The warriors of Iga knew that they did not have the resources necessary to fight six armies on six fronts. This time the number of enemy soldiers was greater than the two preceding battles of 1579.

Therefore, they gathered their principal forces in two fortified towns: at the Heiraku-Ji, a temple on a hill in the middle of the village of Ueno near the current site of the castle of Ueno, and in the fortress of Tendōyama, near the castle of Maruyama.

Ambushes were out of the question, except for some occasional raids, as the following passage of the *Iran-ki* describes. Once again, the action of the ninja of Iga is reminiscent of the actions of the *rappa* of Hōjō:

The enemy became increasingly negligent, including the guards outside the castle. Thus, skillful *Iga no Mono*, thirty men who had mastered the shinobi no jutsu, set fire to various places outside the castle.

Night after night, they made frequent secret incursions and raids on all the generals' camps, setting fires by various tactics.

Because of this mayhem, the enemy became more vigilant and reinforced the guard. Each one remained alert, because everyone knew what would befall. The enemy carefully prepared its defenses.

The camp of Niwa Nagahide was attacked during the night again and again, and many of the guards were killed.

More than one hundred men were killed, and news of this made the enemy tremble, and sleep deprivation reduced their vigilance.[69]

Another interesting passage recalls an incident at a time when the army advanced towards the road of Tatamaki that winds through the area of Kōga, and shows clearly that the warriors and the ninja of the villages in the neighborhoods of Kōga had joined forces with the men of Iga.

The surname mentioned is that of the Mochizuki clan, a ninja family of Kōga ancestry:

An inhabitant of Kōga, Mochizuki Chotarō, was a mighty warrior with a nervous disposition. He had broad and long tachi (long sword) of 4 shaku and 5 sun (1.5 m or about 4.9 ft), that he held up transversely (during the combat).

Furiously advancing, he mowed down his adversaries with his tachi. A fleeing inhabitant, Yamauchi Zaemon-dono of Shimo-tomoda, approached with his sword to cross iron with Chotarō. Chotarō accepted the challenge and moved in for the kill.

Chotarō parried the attack of Yamauchi and then suddenly attacked again and broke Yamauchi's legs. He killed him without hesitation. He was a remarkable sword master, a model for all of the samurai in the province.[70]

However, even the best techniques and tactics of *shinobi no jutsu* were not enough to allow them to hold their ground indefinitely. Even though there were some remarkable clashes, the end result of the battle was clear.

Food became scarce. Seeing the cruelty of the troops of Nobunaga, certain warriors of Iga did not hesitate to kill their own wives and children in order to prevent them from being taken by their enemies.

The final attack unfolded in Hijiyama, where a fortified Buddhist temple, named Kannonji, was the last redoubt of the warriors of Iga. The outcome of the final attack on Hijiyama was not decided by the sword or the spear, but rather by fire.

The dry and windy weather offered ideal conditions for the use of the most deadly weapon of the *bushi* arsenal: fire. Fire did the work for the troops of Nobunaga, as it had a decade earlier in the notorious battle against the monk-soldiers (*sōhei*) of the Hiei Mountain.

Ujisato, Hidesama, Junkei, and the rest of the men had suffered greatly. . . . but now they felt that the victory was close.

They set fire to all the temples in a broad perimeter. This time, there was no rain to intervene.

The flames blazed and were seen in the sky, like an omen. The inferno eventually died out, but many months passed before the black ashes disappeared.[71]

Kannondō of Hijiyama was entirely burned, and its destruction signaled the end of any resistance on the part of Iga. The invaders either killed the fugitives outright or threw them into the still burning flames.

The invasion of Iga continued and all the other villages fell one by one. The *Iran-ki* reported all names of the principal ninja family of Iga, included the Hattori, who died during the battle.[72]

Once he subdued the rebellion and pacified the area, Oda Nobunaga inspected this crucible of resistance that had caused him so many problems. According to Shinchōkō-ki, the visit of Nobunaga at the time of his arrival in Iga, was limited to an inspection of the principal bastions of the resistance of *Iga no Mono*.

Later, when he was in Ichinomiya, warriors of Iga tried to assassinate him. Iga had been devastated, but the spirit that gave purpose to the people of this area was not yet destroyed. Three *jizamurai* of Iga named Kido, Harada and Jindai, who had fought for Kashiwabara, waited for the much-despised Nobunaga.

One of the three *jizamurai*, Kido of the village of *Neba*, was skillful in *shinobi no jutsu*. When Nobunaga and his men appeared the three opened fire using *ōzūtsu*, a kind of gun made from a tree trunk. They tried to kill Nobunaga in crossfire from three different directions. The blasts did not kill him, but they were powerful enough to kill seven or eight men who surrounded him.

That these men were able to come by the military intelligence to prepare such an attack behind enemy lines was proof of the skill of the ninja of Iga.

Crossfire triangulation is still taught today in many military organizations throughout the world.

The author of the *Iran-ki* ends his account as follows:

With regard to these men, the one called Kido of Neba had mastered arcane espionage techniques as well as methods of arson (using gunpowder). There are some who continue to follow this tradition. They are the shinobi of Iga, the descendants of these men.[73]

*Shinchōkō-ki*, written by one of Nobunaga's men, probably glosses over these details for political reasons. Whereas in the *Iran-ki*, there is a more exhaustive report, complete with the role attributed to the ninja of Iga.

The province of Iga was completely destroyed and any thought of autonomy was subdued. However, the destruction of Iga did not mean the end of the independent spirit that lived there. The indigenous art of *shinobi no jutsu* survived. This shadowy warrior tradition would reemerge in years to come.

There is evidence that the destruction of Iga in 1581 by Nobunaga resulted in the migration of those who knew regional *shinobi* practices to other areas of Japan. Some survivors escaped from the carnage and found asylum in other areas, where they dedicated themselves to the service of local lords.

One of these *daimyō*, who had already used the ninja of Kōga, was none other than Tokugawa Ieyasu himself. The links between Tokugawa Ieyasu's army and the ninja of Iga were very close. One of Ieyasu's sixteen generals was a warrior from a famous family of ninja of Iga. He was named Hattori Hanzō.

Among the survivors of the invasion of 1581, some fled towards the province of Kii and others towards Mikawa, where they had already a point of escape thanks to Iga no Mono present in the army of Tokugawa Ieyasu.

One can reasonably conclude that a great number of warriors in service to Ieyasu had lost family and friends during the invasion of Iga. However, the adoption of the ninja of Iga appears to have occurred following the incident that occurred at the Honnō temple in 1582 (本能寺の変).

This incident culminated with the suicide of the ambitious conqueror Oda Nobunaga, facilitated by Akechi Mitsuhide, one of his generals. Nobunaga intended to personally support Toyotomi Hideyoshi, who fought Mōri.

He sent a significant number of men, which he hoped to follow the next day, after spending the night in Honnō-ji temple. Akechi took the advantage of the small number of guards and mounted a surprise attack. Nobunaga was obliged to commit *seppuku*. Determined to continue, Akechi wanted to exterminate Nobunaga's entire family, as well as his allies.

When the incident occurred, Tokugawa Ieyasu, allied with Nobunaga, was visiting the town of Sakai. Only a few men accompanied Ieyasu in a bid to regain his stronghold of Mikawa. He was not prepared to face an attack from Akechi's troops controlling the roads. The choice of another route was crucial to Ieyasu's survival. The only choice was a road that crossed Yamashiro and Iga. The mountains were infested with gangsters and dissidents, as well as Akechi's men.

The existence of gangsters and dissidents reveals the presence of a group still on the fringes of society, living autonomously in the mountains despite the crushing blow delivered to the independent families of Iga. It is not surprising that the area of Iga is still sought out by individualists. With the assistance of sympathizers, Ieyasu and his men were guided on their way. They crossed the Kizu River, which runs along Mount Kasagi, in a wooden boat that they destroyed upon reaching the other bank.

Here is the continuation of the account relating these events as revealed by the *Mikawa Go Fudo-ki*:

Hattori Hanzō Masanari, the famous ninja from Iga who served Tokugawa Ieysu. Private collection.

The Hattori river pass Monument that explains the circumstances of the rescue and escort of Tokugawa Ieyasu. Private collection.

A different view of the Hattori river pass.

From here until Shigaraki, they were only chasms and mountainous roads infested by gangsters. Yamaoka and Hattori accompanied them, defying any gangster of the mountains as those who resembled yamabushi. . . .

Hattori Sadanobu was thanked mainly for his honesty and offered a wakizashi forged by Kunitsugu. The fifth day, Yoshikawa Shūma no Kuke was thanked and accepted one ko-dachi.

Yamaoka, the father and the son, took their way beyond the pass of Tomi at the border of Iga. Wada Hachirō Sadanori accompanied them the entire way . . . and for his efforts and his faithfulness, he accepted a letter of introduction (kansha-jō).[75]

The quoted names, like that of the famous Hattori family, all belonged to ninja families that once lived in perfect harmony and autonomy in these rural back areas where the techniques of the *shinobi no jutsu* were necessary for survival.

One can see that all these families were interlinked, as the guides were able to lead Tokugawa Ieyasu from village to village, all the way to the border of Iga. Iga had a great number of allies waiting:

Hattori Hanzō Masashige was Iga no Mono. Sent by Sadakatsu, he took the guided us on the roads of Iga.

The previous year, when the Oda lord invaded Iga, he had ordered: "The Jizamurai of Iga must all be killed." Because of this they had fled towards the territory of Tokugawa, Mikawa and Totomi, where it was decreed that they be treated with consideration and kindness.

Consequently, for this act of hospitality, their families were indebted. That started with Tsuge Sannojō Kiyohiro, his son, two or three hundred men of the village of Tsuge, and one hundred other jizamurai of Kōga under Shima Okashi no Suke and others . . . that he (Ieyasu) found useful. . . .

They passed in the middle of the mountains where the den of the gangsters was located. The two or three hundred men of the village of Tsuge escorted them to a place of safety, and then they left. Tsuge Sannojō was thanked in particular because he had served them magnificently.[76]

Thanks to knowledge of Hattori and the bonds of friendship dependant between the ninja families of the mountainous areas, Tokugawa Ieyasu could recover and regain his stronghold at *Mikawa*. According to Koyama, he had a debt towards the men of Iga, which he discharged by taking three hundred men of *Iga* and *Kōga* into his service permanently.

These free warriors who were without lords, became the loyal servants of Ieyasu. He was the only *daimyō* who would bring the famous *Iga no Mono* into his service, and the only master they served beyond their own convictions.

The two hundred men from Iga, named *Iga-gumi Dōshin* (伊賀組同心) were under the command of one of the most famous ninja, Hattori Hanzō Masashige, who was the guide during Ieyasu's trek through Iga. Hattori had been born in 1543, the son of Hattori Yasunaga, a loyal servant of the Matsudaira family, the descendant of an important family of ninja of Iga.[77]

His baptism by fire was the night attack of the castle of Udo in 1557 when he was 16 years old. Thereafter, he was present during the battles of Anegawa (1570) and Mikata ga Hara (1572). His nickname was Oni Hanzō, "Hanzō the demon" which distinguished him from another famous samurai of Mikawa, Watanabe Hanzō. In Mikawa Monogatari, Yamaguchi recorded the following sentence:

> The best warriors of the Tokugawa lord were Hattori Hanzō, Watanabe Hanzō, and Atsumi Gengo.[76]

He died in 1596 at the age of 55, and his son, Hattori Iwami no Kami Masanari, succeeded him as the head of the Iga shinobi of Tokugawa.

After 1580, the number of minor *daimyō* fell considerably. All the small strongholds, which had abounded in 1540, fell to the law of the survival of the fittest, being absorbed by the strongholds belonging to a small number of lords who held greater power.

After 1590, thanks to glorious military campaigns led by Toyotomi Hideyoshi, a warrior of Oda Nobunaga, Japan was united. Not satisfied to control Japan, his great dream was to invade Korea and from there, to enter to China. When the first attempt to invade Korea was made in 1592, a number of *shinobi* from Iga were among those sent.

The campaign started in May 1592, and the force was made up of two divisions, the first controlled by the General Konishi Yukinaga and the second by his rival, General Katō Kiyomasa.

After the capture of Pusan and the invasion of Seoul, they were halted at the fortress called Chigūju. The chronicle reporting the events of this action is the *Taikō-ki* (太閤記), in which there is a reference relating to the use of ninja by Konishi.[78]

Incursions into Korea were not very successful and Toyotomi Hideyoshi died in 1598, leaving a child as his only heir. Toyotomi Hideyori was only five years old when dissension began to appear, and two rival groups with different interests formed.

One was faithful to the son of Hideyoshi, and the other with Tokugawa. Those siding with Ieyasu cited a lack of leadership because of the youth of Hideyori.

War was the only way to resolve the differences, and in autumn of the year 1600, the greatest battle ever held on Japanese soil unfolded in Sekigahara.

The preliminary movements of the battle of Sekigahara consisted of a series of attacks on and seiges of castle, which each of the two factions tried to retain or gain. Indeed, these castles were generally strategic locations along the two principal roads of Tōkaidō and Nakasendō.

The most important castle was that of Fushimi to the southeast of Kyotō. The Torii family, who were faithful to Tokugawa, held this castle. During the siege of Fushimijo, several hundred warriors of Kōga helped the Torii family; some defended of the interior, while others harassed those besieging them outside.

Ieyasu had already recognized the skill of *Kōga no Mono* from their attack on the Kaminojō castle in 1562, but in Fushimi, they were overcome and more than one hundred died in combat.

After the conclusive victory of the battle of Sekigahara, Tokugawa rewarded the late families, among whom names like Mochizuki and Arakawa were quoted.

Once the castle of Fushimi fell, nothing could prevent the two factions from meeting for the decisive battle of Sekigahara. Each of the two factions sent *shinobi* spies into the opposing camps.

However, the action of the *shinobi* of Shimazu of Satsuma was significant. He had developed a particular style incorporating the use of firearms. Shimazu was among the first to realize the importance of firearms, as well as the first to use them.

Used during the sieges and on the battlefields, like that of Nagashino in 1575, firearms changed warrior's doctrine since their introduction to Japan by the Portuguese in 1542.

According to Yamaguchi, the *shinobi* of Shimazu had developed many tactics and techniques known by the generic title of *Satsuma Ninpō*. They caused many losses in the ranks of Tokugawa, but that did not change the inevitable outcome of the battle.

## Instruments of Authority in the Edo Period (1603–1867)

Tokugawa Ieyasu secured a great victory at the time of the decisive battle of Sekigahara, His army defeated a coalition of lords faithful to Toyotomi Hideyoshi, gathered around Mōri Terutomo.

In 1603, in honor of this victory, Ieyasu accepted from the Goyozei emperor the title of shōgun, an honor that his two predecessors had never managed to attain. Ieyasu set up new a *bakufu* in the town of Edo.[80]

This new era was characterized by a long period of peace, during which the nature of the *shinobi* changed. Indeed, guerilla warfare and other secret operations in which ninja excelled no longer existed. However, they resumed their service as spies for the shōgun at the time of two great battles, the siege of the castle of Osaka in 1614 and the battle of Shimabara in Kyūshū in 1637.

The son of Hideyoshi, Toyotomi Hideyori, became an adult and secluded himself in the fortress of his late father in Osaka, surrounded by many samurai who were dissatisfied with the seizure of power by Ieyasu. Among these samurai, there were many rōnin, as well as other victims of Sekigahara. The threat was too great for Ieyasu to ignore, and in the winter of 1614 he besieged the castle of Osaka, whose perimeter measured 20 kilometers. The siege of the castle was accomplished in two phases.

The first phase was the assault in winter 1614, when, according to Yamaguchi, Tokugawa Ieyasu used ninja of

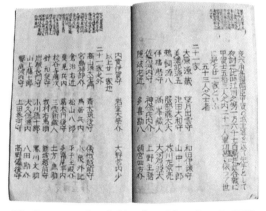

The *Iga mono taiyu shoki*, a chronicle written in 1798 by Kōgi Kudemon. This chronicle has to do with the ninja families of Iga. Private collection.

Iga and Kōga under the command of Hattori Masanari for the first attack and Yamaoka Kagetsuge for the second. Of note is the participation of Negoro-shū, survivor of the destruction of the Negoro temple by Nobunaga.

The second phase was the assault of summer 1615, when after a short truce, Ieyasu began again to besiege the castle of Osaka, which culminate in a violent battle in Tennōji, to the south of the castle. The ninja fought openly beside the regular troops.

When the besieged Hideyori sounded the retreat, Ii Naotaka, one Ieyasu's principal commanders at the time, cut off the enemy's retreat using heavy artillery brought for the occasion. The castle fell and Hideyori committed suicide through *seppukku*.

The second battle where the ninja were again in service was the battle of Shimabara in 1637. Right before the battle of Osaka of 1614, the Tokugawa government published a decree prohibiting Christianity in all of Japan.

In the south of Kyūshū, where dissatisfaction against the Tokugawa government grew, Christianity was widespread. The Mastukura lord of the Shimabara castle then initiated severe policies with regard to the peasants, who ended up revolting and overcame his army.

The peasants of the island of Amakusa and the old vassals of the Christian lords joined them. Thirty-eight thousand people, the majority of them Christian peasants, occupied the castle of Hara under the command of a 16-year-old boy, Amakusa Shirō Tokisane, called "the child from heaven."

The rebels raised a cross at the top of the castle and fought under flags decorated with crosses and icons of the Blessed Virgin Mary. To overcome the rebel peasants, government forces spent five months gathering 120,000 warriors. The government even accepted military aid from the Dutch, who laid down cannon fire onto the castle from their ships.

In this situation, it is not surprising to see the use of the ninja of Kōga. The government turned to them to infiltrate the fortified towns and spy. The records relating to their investigations in the castle of Hara are very detailed and provide a very good illustration of the work of the ninja.

Katsuyama, a descendant of Kōga Ukai Kanemon, a ninja who participated in this action, provided a good summary of the actions of the Kōga ninja:

> The sixth day of the first month . . . one ordered them to go into the castle of Hara and determine the plans of construction of the castle of Hara and to provide a report on the distance from the ditches to the second palisades, the depth of the ditches, the state of the roads, the height of the walls, and the form of the faults.
>
> All this information was put into a report by the soldier Kanematsu Tadanao, envoy with Edo and presented to the shōgun Iemitsu on the nineteenth day of the first month.[81]

Another anecdote of the battle and the actions of the ninja is reported by the *Amakusa-gunki* (天草軍記), where a synonym of ninja is used:

> Each night, the ongyō no mono (隠形之者) could slip furtively into the castle and leave again as they pleased.[82]

The record of the Ukai family reveals a particular raid to seize the provisions of the garrisons carried out by the men of Kōga:

Painting showing Commodore Perry's black ship in Edo bay in 1852. Private collection.

Entrance to the Mochizuki home in Iga, Mie prefecture. The Mochizuki were a prominent Iga ninja family during the fifteenth century. Private collection.

The twenty-first day of the first month . . . the raid on the castle of Hara was, according to the orders of the commander-in-chief Matsudaira Nobutsuna, only one simple raid on the provisions of the garrisons.

From the camp of Kuroda in the east of the beach, they made a descent and aided in the seizure of about thirty bags of food, on which the enemy depended.

This night also, they infiltrated the enemy castle and quickly returned with the secret passwords.[83]

However, a more animated raid occurred six days afterwards:

The twenty-seventh day of the first month . . . we had dispatched spies prepared to die inside the castle of Hara.

Then, at midnight, from the camp of Hosokawa, we went to the castle. Those who had returned had taken an enemy standard by force.

Arakawa Shichirōbei and Mochizuki Yoemon met both a strong resistance and suffered serious wounds during the forty days.[84]

The vase where the Sawamura family's explosive powder was concealed. Private collection.

The *Kōga no Mono* were under the command of Mochizuki Yoemon, and a raid was launched using firearms on the camp of Hosokawa to create a diversion.

Covered by the noise of the firearms, the *Kōga no Mono* were introduced into the castle, where alarm had been given. Arakawa and Mochizuki were the first to enter and mixed, undetected, with the men of the garrison.

They were not hidden by the dark as in "traditional" combat operations but were very conspicuous in the light of the full moon, specifies Yamaguchi. It seemed that they were clad in the same manner as the men guarding the garrison.

To prove that they had indeed infiltrated the castle, they stole one of the many banners bearing a cross. When they escaped, while going down along the walls, they were subject to the attacks of the insurrectionists, receiving their many wounds.

Food started to become increasingly rare, and the fateful moment of the final attack was near. The men of the garrison, weakened by the lack of sleep and food, prepared to repel the final attack.

The twenty-fourth day of the second month . . . the Generals launched their raids with increasing frequency.

The group of Kōga ninja under the direct command of Matsudaira Nobutsuna, seized the first and second palisades. After that, until the fall of the castle, they were under the command of Suzuki Sankurō Shigenari and his group of ten men, including Nakafusa Mino no Kami, the chief of the ninja sent by the bakufu.

Their purpose was to signal the onset of the final attack in order to coordinate the various groups.[85]

Various types of spears in the Sawamura family home in Mie prefecture. Private collection.

The *Kayaku-jutsu no heihō mokuroku* scroll written in 1675 by Sawamura Yotaemon. The text deals with pharmaceuticals, gunpowder and poison recipes. Iga Ueno city, Mie prefecture. Private collection.

Amakusa Shirō Tokisane made a courageous attempt at a frontal attack, but to little effect. When the final attack began, as the preceding excerpt mentions, Kōga ninja took part in combat and coordinated the various groups, which took the castle by storm. The fall of the castle of Hara and the extermination of the Christians who gathered there, marked the last appearance of the ninja in a battle.

## The Ninja's New Peacetime Role

The majority of the ninja of Iga and Kōga became auxiliaries of Tokugawa, distributed according to their aptitudes. Some became the bodyguards of the family of the shōgun in the castle at Edo under the name of *Oniwaban* (御庭番), with responsibility for protecting the part of the private castle where the family and concubines lived.

Others became the spies charged to surveil the actions of the *daimyō*. They answered the name of *Onmitsu* (隠密).[86] As spies employed by the government, *Onmitsu* provided information on the lords most distant from Edo, the capital.

During the reign of Iemitsu, younger son of Ieyasu Tokugawa, (1633–1639) Japan adopted measures to impose greater control of the country. This was solidified in the field of internal politics by a reinforcement of control on all the fields.

These measures obliged the *bakufu* to strengthen their information gathering and, thus, employ more and more ninja. The highly technical skills developed by the ninja, such as their vast information-gathering network, were skillfully used by each of the various shōgun from the Tokugawa family.

The other type of ninja was, as alluded to earlier, known as *Oniwaban*. They had the responsibility of protecting the interior of the castle of Tokugawa, the part reserved mainly for the family of the shōgun, the concubines, and the like.

This was not the first time that ninja acted as guards of the Tokugawa castle because, as shown previously, many bonds existed between the ninja of Iga and the Tokugawa family.

Indeed, Ieyasu was protected by ninja of Iga. Since the time of the incident at Honnō temple, Ieyasu kept them in his service and, by 1590, the ninja kept the east door of the castle of Edo. It was called later *hanzō no mon* (判蔵門: the gate of Hanzō) where the residence of the famous ninja, Hattori Hanzō, was estblished.[87]

The role of *Oniwaban* was not restricted to simple guard duty. They carried out their rounds at nightfall, and one easily understands why, considering their skill and capability to act quickly and silently. But what remains most interesting is that they constituted a kind of internal police force that provided surveillance and protected the residents of the castle.

During the Edo period, duels and other combat between warriors was punished by death, normally through ritual suicide if the condemned was allowed to do so. In addition, in the enclosure of the castle of Edo, it was formally decreed that one had to remove one's sword or any other weapons that could be used in a duel.

Let me stress that it is during the Edo period that the peace founded by Tokugawa forced a great number of warriors to reexamine their practices of combat. It is during this period that the creation of schools and the drafting of manuscripts (*densho, makimono, shuki,* and the like), as well as technical specialization gained prominence.

Most of the schools of *bujutsu* that were born during this period carry in them the characteristics specific to this time of history. Ninjutsu did not escape this phenomenon, and a great number of techniques were adapted to the new requirements of peace.

Outside view from the Momochi family's house. Private collection.

However if you think about it, the purpose of the techniques used by ninjutsu was to ensure the survival of those who used them, and thus it is understandable that they were considered too radical at the time these new laws were brought into force.

During this period of peace, it was necessary to avoid killing as much as possible. It is within this framework that techniques of combat like *mutōdori* (無刀捕 – to disarm with bare hands), *shinken shirahadōme* (真剣白刃止 – to disarm or stop with bare hands), *nawa-jutsu* (縄術 – techniques of the rope to disarm and bind), and so forth, were developed to avoid killing.

Note that these techniques were not exclusive to the *Oniwaban*, but were also used by the police force that emerged in the new and ever-growing capital, Edo. Weapons like the *jutte*, the *mojiri*, the *sodega-rami*, and the like were used by the ninja during the period of feudal war, and they were rehabilitated for their new function, to apply the law.

This shift could not have been accomplished if not for one of the basic tenets of ninjutsu: adaptabilty. In other words, a person can be a ninja, insofar as one has the capacity to produce something of consequence from a little bit and this production, whether a technical or physical creation, is adaptable and evolutionary.

Let us not forget that the *metsuke* (目附), a kind of spy, paid for unconventional operations, was also related to the ninja. The survivors of the temple Negoro (根来寺), whose control of gunpowder and firearms interested the *bakufu* early on, were at the forefront of the armed forces that emerged in the town of Edo.

According to Koyama, a great number of them were ninja. That is possible, because the ninja did not come from only one class. On this subject, the *Nihon ninja Retsuden* (日本忍者列伝) reveals this:

> However, the survivors of the Negoro temple had returned to the service of Tokugawa Ieyasu. They were at the origin of the armed bodies that emerged in the town of Edo.
>
> Later, they were called Okubo hyakunin-shū (大久保百人衆: the hundred men of the band ōkubo) and they took shelter with Okubo hyakunin-chō (大久保百人町).

Although they were called the haykunin-shū (the group of the hundred men), their band consisted of approximately a hundred and twenty people.

Living very close to the Koshū road, when the shōgun left, they protected it and another band called Hachiōji sennin-shū possibly (八王子千人衆) joined them.

At the beginning of the Edo period, the people who formerly were named ninja, hid in the company under the name of teppōtai (鉄砲隊: armed bodies), being used for the close protection of the shōgun.[88]

As these lines reveal, the ninja, particularly those of the Negoro, made a success of their conversion. However, authenitc ninja, in the true sense of the term, were very few. Certainly, many acted the part but seldom did they possess the science of ninjutsu in all its forms. Only the specialized ninja who had a rare technique or a particular knowledge that interested the *bakufu* were allowed to practice their art.

The less fortunate ninja, unable to make the conversion, turned to farming as peasants or to tradecraft as merchants and, thus, their skills lapsed from memory.

It is during the Edo period that the most extravagant stories on the exploits of the ninja and their arts developed. The ninja were transformed into "supermen" without faith or law, clad in black, defying human logic and resembling demons. All this mythology developed in parallel to the image of samurai, the great valorous, loyal warrior without fear.

Although the ninja were free warriors capable of a diabolical ingenuity to survive, stories of their exploits were extremely exaggerated. Until Meiji, ninjutsu was taught in the military academies, less like an evolutionary technique of combat and more like an espionage technique.

The tradition of deadly combat was forgotten, leaving only theoretical teaching based on experimentation. All the documents, weapons, and armor found are displayed for the public in museums like the Iga Ueno in the Mie prefecture or the Togakushi in Nagano.

Today, for a great number of Japanese and neophytes, the battle dress, weapons, and documents that sustain the myth of the terrifying ninja warrior are only echoes of an all-but-forgotten history.

# CHAPTER 3

# The Private History of Ninjutsu

As was mentioned in the introduction, the history of ninjutsu and the ninja has two distinct aspects. The public aspect of history, previously presented from historical sources that have been found to be most reliable, and a private aspect of history, which is to say, the history conveyed by the instructional documents and scrolls of the school in which, for generations, the master has transmitted to his disciple.

In contrast to the public history, and particularly with regard to certain historical points (such as the battle of Iga), the private history covers certain historical events from a different point of view and hints at other possible origins. It remains, however, on many points, a corroborating record of the overall development of ninjutsu.

It is interesting that the private history presents another view of the genesis of ninjutsu and the ninja, and this offers a more plausible possibility in certain cases than all those others mentioning immigrant Chinese, Koreans, *shugenja*, Buddhist monks, ascetics, Taoists, farmers, robbers, magicians, and other conjurers.

Indeed, the private history of ninjutsu provides just as valid an interpretation as what can be concluded from the multitude of public records, where various threads of information intermingle and where it remains difficult to distinguish truth from forgery.

Facts remain obscure, and it is not easy to identify precisely all the historical details, especially when they are very old. This is a problem found in historical research in general.

The private history that I present here comes primarily from parts of scrolls of an authentic school of ninjutsu, *Togakure-ryū ninpō* (戸隠流忍法), which was founded, according to those same scrolls, in the Kamakura period (1192–1333). This school has continued the initiatory chain of transmission from master to disciple uninterrupted to present day.

The text is written in traditional language, *kanbun*, in a cursive style similar to calligraphy. The writing is based on the personality of the author and reflects their individual level of literacy. This is found to be the case in almost every historical archive kept by traditional schools of combat.

The *Shinkage-ryū heihō mokuroku no koto*, describing technique called *Kinhira-bō*.
The scroll was written by Yagyū Muneyoshi, successor to Kamiizumi Hidetsuna. Private collection.

In keeping with ninjutsu's precepts of remaining hidden, of being invisible, and covering one's tracks, much of the documentation is in the form of quasi-illegible writing, using Sino-Japanese characters. In these cases, the *kanji* is indecipherable.

One can conclude that the other scrolls (巻物: *makimono*, 絵巻: *e-maki*) as well as the three instructional documents (伝書: *densho*) that accompany it were written during the Edo period (1603–1867).

The section generously entrusted to me was not marked with any date. Also, it is difficult to be categorical in regard to what time period it was written in.

The part of the scrolls (*makimono*) that I present here reports certain historical facts very briefly. When necessary, I've added some explanations in order to be clear and create an understandable parallel with the recognized historical facts.

The home of Hattori Hanzō in the Edo's castle's gate known as *Hanzō no Mon* (Hanzō's gate). Picture taken during the Meiji era. Private collection.

During the transmission of the school's wisdom and knowledge, all of the writings and objects are given to the heir. In the case of *Togakure-ryū*, there are several *makimono* (scrolls), including the part presented here, which are three books of "secret" lessons (*hi-densho*) and the principal weapons of the school.

One should not restrict the study of *Togakure-ryū* to only a limited a number of documents, because there are other writings (such as *oboe-gaki* 覚書, *Shuki* 手記, *Nikki* 日記, and *kuden-sho*, 口伝書) that allow one to better understand the master documents.

Among the scrolls, one contains the basis of ninjutsu from the creation of the school, as well as the course of instruction to be followed. The other scrolls explain the genealogy. As for the three technical instructional books (*densho*), they contain explanations on all the combat techniques, battle strategies, tricks, the descriptions and instructions on use of weapons.

However, the study of this kind of writings remains very difficult. Indeed, the *makimono* and *densho* are written in such an obscure manner that only the heir to the school could understand, with the major points hidden "between the lines."

What this implies is that in addition to prerequisite qualities and aptitudes, the training of the heir must be based on a profound level of personal experience. Without this, it is almost impossible to decipher the writings of the school.

It is for this reason that I restricted this study to a translation of documents that the clearly present historical facts, for instance, a genealogy. To convey the private history of ninjutsu, I will start with a presentation of the principal works written during the Edo period (1603–1867) by authentic ninja.

## Principal Transmission Documents Written by the Ninja

Although there have been a great number of schools of ninjutsu, particularly during the Sengoku period (1477–1600), when, according to estimates, there were between 70 and 80 different schools, the transmission documents of the technical and practical knowledge were very restricted.

During Japanese history, and particularly during certain periods, such as the Sengoku period, a great number of schools were created. The proliferation of schools was due, largely, to the frequent economic and political upheaval. The schools evolved, beginning with their adaptation to the various requests of the government, the imperial court, and the various warrior families.

The entrance to the Yagyū castle, Yagyū village. Private collection.

The ninjutsu schools multiplied to meet to the ever-increasing need for their services precipitated by a period of disorder and intrigue. The majority of the ninjutsu transmission documents come from families living in the same area, the provinces of Iga and of Kōga, the historical and technical cradle of ninjutsu.

The transmission documents were passed on from generation to generation, within schools founded around an extensive and evolving body of military experience and knowledge.

Some schools sprang up when founding families were isolated because of military issues or economic development, when only creative thought and action could guarantee survival.

Others were established for a specific action, which is to say, in order to support the cause of one local lord, to bring protection and information to an ambitious warrior family, or to protect the interests of a religious group. Once the work was completed, they dispersed.

Many potential heirs would not survive to attain the necessary level of skill to succeed their master. Japan knew periods of successive wars where truces were a rarity.

This explains why, in spite of the many schools, little knowledge actually endured. For many schools, the surviving documents contain only technical instruction and practical knowledge. However, regardless of the school of combat, instruction written in the peaceful Edo period was much more likely to survive to the present.

During periods of war, it was very difficult to produce and preserve historical records—but not impossible. This may be the case for a great number of schools, and in particular, those founded during the Edo period, so one should keep an open mind about what documents may exist. Historical works, collections of poems, sutras, religious texts, and so forth have crossed the ages and survived the wars, so the same is possible regarding the transmission documents of the schools of combat. This is a point that should not be forgotten when one studies the technical documents of instruction. For example, there are documents of certain schools of *kenjutsu* and *jūjutsu* that were written between 1450 and 1550. Documents from the *Shinkage-ryū* (新影流) and *Takenouchi-ryū* (竹内流) schools prove this.

Among *hi-densho* (秘伝書), secret transmission documents written by the ninja, the most well known are *Bansen Shūkai* (万川集会), *Shōnin-ki* (正忍記), *Ninpiden* (忍秘伝), and *Ninpō-hikan* (忍法秘巻). For historical study, "theoretical" approaches to certain technical usage; these works remain the most useful to historians.

They represent the sum of knowledge, like *Bansen Shūkai*, of all the schools of ninjutsu of the provinces of Iga and Kōga. The some of the originals, such as *Shōnin-ki*, are preserved at the national library of Tōkyō. Others one either finds in private collections or displayed in museums.

What these documents have in common is that they were written during the same period, the Edo period (1603–1867). As mentioned, this period in the history of Japan is characterized by a lasting peace, where it was easier to write a work or summarizing of what has been learned.

The style of language used is also common to all these documents; it is *kanbun*, the traditional language. The writing remains cursive and is, at times, illegible. One should note that sometimes, as in *Bansen-shūkai* or *Shōnin-ki*, the presence of drawings to illustrate the text.

However, in total, these documents contain only written indications and a few technical drawings. With only that, it is necessary for us to classify them as "sterile," stripped of any philosophical concepts, religious, or even Buddhist terminology, Taoist philosophy, or the like that would ideally be used by the various authors in order to clarify their ideas.

The major principles governing the combat techniques do not appear in them either. Indeed, the science and art of ninjutsu naturally was transmitted orally and through direct experience, very discretely, from generation to generation, and then only to a single heir. It is easy to advance the idea that the manuscript doesn't matter, that they only provide a superficial explanation ninjutsu.

*Kuden* (口伝: oral lesson), *shinden* (心伝: spiritual transmission, namely what is shown by the master; the memory of the movement and the words of the master), and *taiden* (体伝: physical transmission, namely the experience of the body, the memory of the body's movements during practice with the master and the internalization of those movements) are the true sources of the transmission of ninjutsu.

One must recognize that the ninja never documented the secret principles of their practice unless it was written in such a way that only one who had received *kuden*, *shinden* and *taiden*, would be able to decipher the *densho* and *makimono* of the school.

In these reference manuscripts, the historical contents, as well as the exact origin of the combat techniques, are often referred to in mythological terms or through some initiatory event that is impossible to prove. The specifics are generally hidden in the shadows. The practice that allows the ninja to cast his ego aside and unify his body and spirit to achieve fantastic feats simply cannot be transmitted in writing.

## General Description of These Reference Works[1]
### *Bansen-shūkai* (万川集会: Ocean of Ten Thousand Rivers)[2]

This manuscript is a kind of encyclopedia of ninjutsu. Writing in fourth year of the Enpō era (1676) by a ninja of the province of Iga named Fujibayashi Yasutake (or Masayoshi). The entire document is composed of twelve volumes in which the "secret" lesson of the forty-nine schools of ninjutsu is inscribed, and which formed the base of *Iga-ryū* (the school of the province of Iga) before the battle of Iga in 1580.

Among the twelve known volumes are treatises on strategy, espionage, astronomy, philosophy, and geography, in addition to one description of the construction and use of weapons and tools of the ninja. A part entitled "Gunyō-hiki" (軍要秘記: secret notes on the major military sciences) is included there.

# *Shōnin-ki* (正忍記: Writings Concerning the Uses and Techniques of the Ninja)[3]

This is a manuscript in three volumes written in the ninth year of the Enpō era (1681) by a master in military science named Natori Sanjūrō Masazumi.

These three volumes contain the theoretical lessons, as well as the combat techniques of the *Kishū* School (紀州流: school of the province of Kishū).

# *Ninpiden* (忍秘伝: Secret Transmissions of the Ninja)[4]

This is a manuscript in four volumes written in the second year of the Joō era (1654) by a descendant of the family ninja of Iga, Hattori, named Hattori Yasukiyo.

Three of the four volumes contain the teachings of the famous ninja of Iga and head of the secret police of the shōgun Tokugawa Ieyasu (1542–1642), named Hattori Hanzō.

# *Ninpō-hikan* (忍法秘巻: Secret Scrolls of *Ninpō*)[5]

Inue Masayasu, a descendant of a ninja family of the province of Iga, wrote this manuscript in a single volume during the Shōho period (1644–1648). The manuscript contains the "secret" lesson of the *Iga-ryū* Ninjutsu school.

## Principal Dates of the History of Ninjutsu

These dates are listed according to the transmission document of the *Togakure-ryū* school.

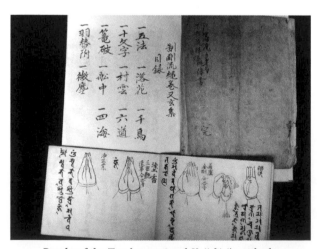

*Densho* of the *Togakure-ryū* and *Kuji-kiri's* methods.
Private collection.

Here is a translation of part of the *densho* from *Togakure-ryū ninpō*, transmitted to Hatsumi Masaaki, thirty-fourth successor of the school, by the thirty-third successor, Takamatsu Toshitsugu (1887–1972).

1. With the assistance of their techniques of war, the practice of ninjutsu was distinguished in the battles from the Jinmu emperor in order to control Yamato, and gave their support to the repression of the rebels known by the name of Ainu.[6]
2. During the Genko era (1331–1334), the ninja fought at the sides of the families of Nawa, Kusunoki, and Kitabatake.[7]
3. During the Kenmu era (1334–1336), [the ninja] raised an army of honest soldiers faithful to the court of the South based in the province of Yoshino, and had a great influence.[8]
4. During the Chōkyō era (1487–1489), the ninja harassed the troops with the Ashikaga family.[9]
5. During the Eishō era (1504–1521), they joined the army of the Sekia family and pursued the large army of Hosokawa Takakuni.[10]
6. During the Eishō era (1504–1521), at the time when Ashikaga Yoshitane sent his troops to the province of Ōmi to attack Ashikaga Yoshizumi, the ninja of the province of Kōga took the part of Ashikaga Yoshitane, whereas the ninja of the province of Iga were opposed to him. This was the basis of the discord between the ninja of Iga and Kōga.[11]
7. . . .
8. Between 1854 and 1859, the ninja were bound to the partisans of the emperor and rose against Shinsen-gumi, which was the last group of protection of Tokuguwa during the last days of the shōgunate.[12]
9. In 1863, certain ninja joined Tenchū-gumi, a group of extremists controlled by Yoshimura Toratarō and Fujimoto Tesseki, who attempted to overthrow the military government of Tokugawa. Although they raised an army of many dissatisfied soldiers, they all were captured and carried out.[13]
10. The ninja were distinguished on the battlefields against the government Tokugawa's forces. It was at the time of the battle of Toba Fushimi, right after the Meiji restoration was decreed in 1867, and they took the side of the Emperor.[14]

This part of the scrolls ends in the following sentence:

Ninjutsu is the use of all means in the pursuit of Justice.[15]

It is important to emphasize certain interesting facts. Indeed, as in many transmission documents passed on in the traditional martial arts schools, one notices that the origin of the school goes back to a mythical period of the Japanese history, called "the Age of the Gods," which tells of the foundation of the country by the gods.

In fact, it is commonly allowed that majority of martial arts schools, and the schools of ninjutsu are no exception, seek to cloak their genesis in legends in order to boast a certain legitimacy. Therefore, it is reasonable to conclude that these schools started to form in the Kamakura and Muromachi periods, as is with the case with *Togakure-ryū ninpō*.

Other facts will be presented that corroborate the points that I made above. One begins to realize that the formation of the ninja schools corresponds to periods of disorders and wars during the Kamakura period, at the time of the wars between the Two Courts, that of the North and the South.

The surname Kusunoki should be noted. The famous Kusunoki Masashige, a warrior of great prowess, was a genius of a military leader who had a great number of mountain warriors in his ranks, and in other circumstances, one finds ninja associated with him.

One finds the surname Kusonoki in the family trees of the Momochi and Kuroda families. Momochi was a notorious family of ninja from the province of Iga, and Kuroda was a notorious family of Akutō who lived in the southern part of Iga.

Various *densho* from *Tatsumi-ryū*, *Kage-ryū*, *Yōshin-ryū*, *Yasuda-ryū*, *Kotō-ryū* and *Kuji-kiri's* methods. Private collection.

Even if the facts concerning the implications and direct actions of the ninja were not accurately reported, because as spies they were compelled to act furtively and in the greatest of secrecy, the majority of the reports correspond well with those presented in the preceding chapter, regarding the public record of the ninja.

Note that the actions taken by Oda Nobunaga (1534–1582) against the ninja of the province of Iga, the terrible battles named Tenshō Iga no Ran (the revolt of the province of Iga of the Tenshō era) related in the previous chapter do not appear in the historical presentation in the scrolls of the school. Remember that the battle against Iga struck a blow to the autonomy that the families enjoyed and practically destroyed them. A few managed to survive and took their abilities elsewhere into the service of other lords. There was a well-known atrocity that took place at the end of this terrible battle. One could presume it was for shame or pride that these facts were omitted from the record. However, after study of the document, it seems that there is another explanation.

As I mentioned earlier, the document in question belongs to the *Togakure-ryū* school. The founder of this school remained in the province of Iga where he learned *shinobu-hō* (ninjutsu). As it turns out, he was from the village Togakushi (another reading for Togakure,) which is in the current prefecture of Nagano. *Togakure-ryū* formed, in part, as the other schools of the province of Iga. However, after having received the teachings, the scrolls report that the founder returned to his native province well before the invasion of Iga by the troops of Nobunaga. We now must reconsider the battle of Iga with the foundation of *Iga-ryū ninjutsu*.

## The Origin of Ninjutsu According to the Togakure-ryū School

What follows is a comprehensive history of ninjutsu, with detailed explanations of the precursors, names of people and places, and so forth, including the interactions and the complexities involved in the origins of ninjutsu.

According to Takamatsu, the thirty-third successor of *Togakure-ryū ninpō*, Ninjutsu or *ninpō*, formerly called *shinobu-hō*, would have been born during the fifty years that separated the Manjū (1024–1028) and Jōhō (1074–1077) periods. This is well before the creation of *Togakure-ryū ninpō*, which dates from the Kamakura (1192–1333) period. Keep this mind when reading the following facts.

### The Prehistoric Period: Kesshi Jidai

The scrolls called *Ryūsen no Maki* (瀏潜之巻), report the following history:

> In full battle with the army of Shiki in the province of Iware, Emperor Jinmu was unable to turn the battle to his advantage and was in a difficult situation. One night, he had a divine revelation in the form of dream:
>
>> Tenkōguzan is a divine fortress. To seize his ground, ritual objects should be created. Then, with unshakable faith, offer your prayers to the gods.

In order to seize the divine ground that was in the midst of the enemy forces, Jinmu immediately ordered Shine Tsuhikō and Otōkashi to change their appearance to that of an old man for one and an old woman for the other. Then he said to them:

> The foundation of our country is in your hands!

From Tenkōguzan, both disguised ninja seized the sacred ground without incident. From this soil, it is said that Jinmu created a sacred sword, a jewel, and a mirror.

And for helping him to win this battle, he offered fervent prayers to the gods over the Niye River.

The Amenoshibi no Mikoto, Ōkume no Mikoto, and Ōtomo families sent the shinobi-jutsu.[16]

Although the existence of the Jinmu emperor is not historically confirmed, the Sino Japanese character, *hensō* indicates "disguise," "camouflage," and "imitation," and directly makes reference to the techniques of camouflage, concealment, and disguise called *hensō-jutsu*.

The use of these techniques was allotted early on to the historical ninja. Another point is that the ancient ninjutsu was called *shinobu-hō* or *shinobi-jutsu*. It was a practice of combat based on espionage and information gathering. Of primary importance was the concept of achieving invisibility and remaining incognito. Therefore, camouflage and disguise played a large role.

The Ōtomo family was a powerful clan, similar to the Abe and Kume. They were in the service of the imperial family and rendered many services towards the end of protecting the empire.

*Tsuki no shō, Kage-ryū Heihō-sho, Iran-ki, Iga fusa shuscho,* and *Ninjutsu hiden tōnin mokuroku.* Private collection.

These families compiled a significant number of documents on various subjects, disciplines, and sciences. One finds in their writings various disciplines, such as bujutsu, meteorology, divination, religion, history, geography, medicine, military strategy, espionage, ninjutsu, and so forth.

In the genealogy presented in various *densho* and *makimono*, many ninja families, starting with Momochi, Hattori, and Mochizuki, are presented as direct descendants of the Ōtomo family. The Ōtomo would have surely developed a fighting style that would have been transmitted within the family under the generic title of *Otome-ryū* (御止流).

The majority of the secret or technical family schools of combat had as a generic name *Otome-ryū*. That indicates that for a very long time secret knowledge was transmitted, to which only some members of the family had access.

*Jūjutsu* schools, like *Shōsho-ryū* (賞諸流) were presented under the name of *Otome-ryū*. Ninjutsu was also a very advanced form of secret techniques, and there is no doubt that a family as significant as the Ōtomo had a group of people indoctrinated with the methods of concealment, espionage, and swift action.

Note that the origin of ninjutsu is often associated with the final chapter of the military strategy treatise titled *The Art of War* by Sun Zi (Son-Shi in Japanese). Because *The Art of War* presents highly sophisticated combat survival methods, many see the influence of the theories preached by Sun Zi. The theories of Sun Zi, as well as traditional methods of espionage, would have been introduced to Japan by Kibi Makibi (693–775), who traveled twice to China as an ambassador.

On his return, he would have brought back with him many traditional Chinese concepts, as did many emissaries who returned to the country after having being immersed in Chinese culture. This was very evident during the Nara period.

Among these traditional concepts, one found the treatise of military strategy by Son Shi. Known under the generic label of *Bukei Shichisho* (武経七書), the principal treatises were: *Sonshi* (孫子), *Goshi* (呉子), *Shibahō* (司馬法), *Riei Komontai* (李衞公問対), *Utsu Ryōshi* (尉繚子), *Sanryaku* (三略), and *Rikutō* (六韜).[17]

Although Sun Zi is better known than other proponents of Chinese military strategy, the Japanese warriors initially rebuffed his ideas. Interestingly, the *Shoku Nihongi* was compiled in the year 747, and it contains several examples that curiously reiterate the lessons of Son Shi and the works other quoted above.

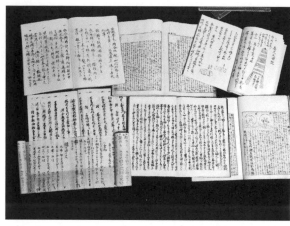

*Zokkin hisei-dan, Kōga nijū ichi-ke sensō-sho, Kōga-ryū shinobi no hō, Fukuda-ryū heihō,* **and so on. Private collection.**

Because Emperor Jinmu is a legendary character, and the history presented in the manuscript is the sort of tale invented to provide an origin, one cannot be certain of the exact origins of traditional ninjutsu.

The origin of this practice is mostly shrouded in ancient Japanese history. We can surmise simply that ninjutsu is an ancient Japanese combat technique. However, because of the inherent difficulty of determining its exact origin, the field is left open to various interpretations and possibilities.

## Period of the Korean Dynasty: General Ikai

In the first year of the Huang Du era (corresponding to the Kōyū era in Japanese, the year 1049), Ikai of the Sijang province, who was defeated by the armies of Ren Zong, Qidan (916–1125) and of Xia (1038–1227), was exiled to distant Japan.

He arrived in the province of Ise and lived in a cave in the province of Iga. The transmission document of the school indicates that Ikai was a general who excelled in hichō ongyo no jutsu (combat techniques based on "hidden kicks").

According to this document, the basis for ninjutsu was established by "naturalized" Chinese like Ikai, Yō Gyokko, and Chō bushō, who disseminated (among other things) *hichō-jutsu* (combat techniques based on the kicks), *tōte-koppō-jutsu* (art of unarmed combat based on Chinese bone-breaking techniques), and *Senban-nage-jutsu* (shuriken throwing techniques).

Specifically, the Gyokko-ryū kosshi-jutsu school spawned the following schools: Kotō-ryū koppō-jutsu, Gikan-ryū koppō-jutsu, and Gyokushin-ryū koppō-jutsu.

Moreover, if one considers the way that the fifty-three families of Kōga-ryū ninjutsu as well as the thirty-eight families of Iga-ryū ninjutsu developed *happō-biken-jutsu* (combat techniques based on the eight secret laws governing the art of the sword) from the Gyokko-ryū school, it can be argued that the aforementioned schools lie at the origin of Japanese martial-arts.

During the Jōho era (1074–1077), the document reports that Ikai had two pupils called Gamon Dōshi and Hōgen Tesshin. Ninjutsu was established during the fifty years that separate the Manjū and Jōho eras.[18]

This passage, which one also finds in the *Gyokko-ryū kosshi-jutsu* (玉虎流骨指術) and *Kotō-ryū koppō-jutsu* (虎倒流骨法術) schools' transmission documents, reflects the theory that immigrants bought about the genesis of ninjutsu.

*Kosshi-jutsu* (骨指術: combat techniques based on the use of the fingers to attack the vital points and break bones) and *koppō-jutsu* (骨法術: combat techniques based on breaking bones and use of the skeleton) were the basic techniques that jointly formed the foundation of combat practice for all of the ninjutsu schools in the provinces of Iga and Kōga.

These combat techniques were developed to be adaptable to any weapons. The ancient ninja was devoted to these two practical styles, *kosshi-jutsu* and *koppō-jutsu*, and they practiced them together with the study of anatomy and traditional medicines, as well as the various weapons of the ninjutsu arsenal.

*Isui onkō no sho, Iyō anmin-ki, Goke-ryū seitō hiden no sho, Iga gun-ki, Take no uchi-ryū gokui no uta,* and so forth. Private collection.

Indeed, these two combat sciences are based on a profound knowledge of the human anatomy and the meridian lines of the body and the flow of energy.

The study of anatomy spawned a science called *kassatsu jizai* (活殺自在: method to revive or kill, in any situation, by control of the meridian lines and various vital point of the body). This practice was born from *koppō-jutsu* and from *kosshi-jutsu*.

Another technique, resulting from aforementioned sciences, (破術之法: technique to tear ligaments, skin, and muscles) developed during the same time but only in a small circle of insiders. This method was born in the Japanese provinces of Iga and Kōga.

*Hajutsu no hō* is a very violent method of combat, which requires a deep understanding of the human anatomy as well as the ability to move with fluidity. *Hajutsu no hō* allows the practitioner, among other things, to incorporate the use of the various types of weapons. It encompasses the likes of *kosshi-jutsu* and *koppō jutsu*, the art of *kyūsho* (急所) and *kyūsho* (求所 or 救所). Here, the two words have the same sound, but the characters are different. They are complementary sciences, which shows why *kosshi-jutsu* and *koppō-justsu* were always transmitted together.

The first *kyūsho* (急所) is the generic term for vital points in general. The second *kyūsho* (求所 or 救所) means the vital points necessary to treat, revive, or save a person. It is a very old science resulting from ninjutsu, developed in Japan through a variety of fruitful exchanges of knowledge and direct application in real situations.

Therefore, the combat technique forming the basis common to all the Iga and Kōga schools of ninjutsu (particularly *Iga-ryū* and *Kōga-ryū*), was *kosshi-jutsu* and *koppō-jutsu*, because it allowed an unlimited and continual adaptation.

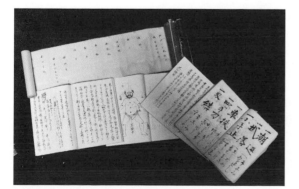

Scrolls from the Seigō-ryū, Shibukawa-ryū, Araki-ryū, Ittō-ryū, and so forth. Private collection.

Another interesting point is that if there was some Chinese influence in the creation and development of ninjutsu in the province of Iga, it was not a series of specific imported techniques. These would have undergone modifications over time. Rather it was an exchange of a great amount of knowledge and methods related to various fields of combat, strategy, medicine, and so forth.

The creation of ninjutsu is truly the result of collaborations within a Japanese province.

Japan was a land of exile for a great number of immigrants who fled their countries of origin for various reasons. Upon arrival in Japan, they adapted the techniques and practices of their former lands to their new environs and passed on their various skills.

Some decided to leave the bustle of society altogether and moved to the rural and less populated areas. The provinces of Iga and Kōga fit that description at that time in history. There, they lived with the autonomous families who had escaped the domination of the central authority and the exchanges of knowledge occurred naturally.

## Jireki Period (1066): Fujiwara Chikado

A general from the province of Ise raised a rebellion against the central government from Mount Takao in the province of Iga.

He fought admirably by using the techniques of concealment known as *Ongyo-ki* (隠形鬼), composed of *doki* (土鬼), *kaki* (火鬼), and *fūki* (風鬼) (methods of hiding using the natural environment and the five phases). But shortly after his victory, he became a hermit.

Reportedly he withdrew to a cave on Mount Takao in the village of Tanao in Taga-gun. However, it is also reported that a few years before, General Ikai fled to a cave of the same region.[19]

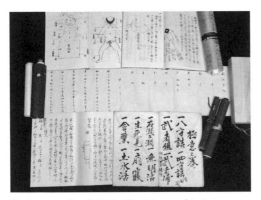

Various scrolls of *jūjutsu*, *kenjutsu*, and *taijutsu*. Private collection.

During the Heian period (782-1190), under the reign of the Emperor Murakami (who reigned from 946–967), one of the powerful autonomous families of Iga named Fujiwara Chikado rebelled against the imperial court. One also finds the names Senpō, Chikata, and Chorozu used to indicate the same family.

Precise details of this story are contained in the *Tenryaku Goki* (天暦御記). According to this document, the Fujiwara Chikado family had four members among its high-ranking warriors who were distinguished from the others by their mastery of a mysterious art.

They were specialists and masters of the following techniques: *fūki* (風鬼), *suiki* (水鬼), *kinki* (金鬼), and *ongyōki* (隠形鬼). Volume 16 of the *Taiheiki* (太平記) with the heading: "About the Enemy of the Court of Japan" (之朝敵之事) says the following:

Fūki: "To sweep the enemy as a powerful blast of wind," implying a manner of silent moving and fighting.

Suiki: "Like a flood–flood the enemy everywhere," referring to combat in groups, namely harassing the enemy on all sides in order to leave no chance of retreat.

Kinki: "The body is so disciplined that no arrow can wound it." The training of the body is the key to survival. To forge it, like the mind, with a discipline enabling one to face any situation.

Ongyōki: "To hide one's appearance and to surprise the enemy in order to crush them." Here, the ongyō term refers to the art of ninjutsu as the highest form of combat. "To become hidden." Surprise the enemy bycloaking one's intentions from the enemy.

Although here the information on the technical terms differs a little, it is evident that *Taiheiki* corroborates the indications of *Makimono.* It is possible that the writer of *Makimono* has read *Taiheiki*, but that is not certain.

The people of Iga province reportedly governed themselves for many years. Deposed warrior families called themselves *jizaimurai*—warriors of the soil—and created a federation against all external threats.

The majority of the inhabitants of Iga were not ninja or even warriors in the traditional sense. However, the significant families of the area had a vast information and spy network, allowing them to supervise the undesirable neighbors.

Iga, the cradle of ninjutsu, was a refuge for all the dissidents, deposed warriors, immigrants, and other rebels who sought to

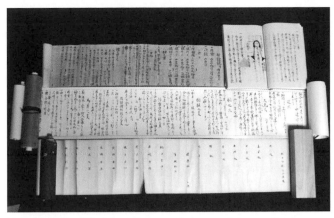

Various scrolls of Kenjutsu, sōjutsu, and ninjutsu. Private collection.

go "underground" in order to foment revolt. The geography, surrounded by a mountain range, made the location difficult to reach. Iga offered the ideal sanctuary to these dissidents who often worked in the shadows in order to sow disorder and confusion.

## Tenkyō Era (938-947): Tatsumaki Hōshi

During the Tenkyō era, Mochizuki Saburō Kanesada, the third son of Suwa Saemon Minamoto Shigeyori, lord of Shinano, who had been distinguished during the battle against the military leader Taira No Makasado, became the lord of a region southeast of the Ōmi province known as Kōga-gun, where he took the name of Kōga Ōmi no Kami Kaneie.

His son, Ōmi no Kaneie Iechika, excelled in the art of weapons as well as in that of letters, would have learned gen-jutsu (幻術: technique of conjuring) and ninjutsu from a Buddhist monk named Tatsumaki Hōshi, who lived in a place called Kōga Goryuso Tatsumaki. It is reported that this man founded Kōga-ryū.

The successors of the school were Iechika, Ienari, Iesada, Ienaga, Iekiyo, Iekuni, Ieto, Ieyoshi, and Ieyasu. Their descendants trained the five main families of the province of Kōga, and they were Kōga, Mochizuki, Ugai, Naiki, and Akutagawa.

To that, many warriors who had lost battles such as the Namboku-chō (battles for the legitimate authority between the Court of the North and the South, 1336–1392) came to dwell in the province and, thus, trained the fifty-three families of Kōga.

The continuation of the parchment reveals details starting as far back as the Muromachi period (1333–1467), when information relating to the ninja of Kōga is more reliable:

During the Hotoku era (1449–1451), the main successors of the previously cited families were: Kōga Saburō, Mochizuki Gorō, Ugai Ryuhōshi, Naiki Fujibe, and Akutagawa Kazuma.

During the Bunmei era (1469–1486), second generation Kōga Saburō , Mochizuki Yjirō, Ugai Chiaki, Naiki Gohei, and Akutagawa Tenpei gained victory for the Sasaki family by attacking the army of Shōgun Ashikaga Yoshihisa at the battle of Magari no Jin (1487).

Many of the deposed warriors (those who escaped from the battles of the Court of the North and the South) came to seek refuge with Kōga, where they constituted the fifty-three families of Kōga-ryū ninjutsu.

The surnames that follow are lumped under the title "Eight Tengu of Kōga" (甲賀之八天狗): Kōga, Mochizuki, Ugai, Naiki, Akutagawa, Ueno, Ban, and Nagano.

To these were added groups of hermits called Hiryu-gumi and Hakuryu-gumi, who excelled in ninjutsu and gen-jutsu.[20]

With regard to *Kōga-ryū* ninjutsu, the document reports that the second successor, Kōga Saburō, had three children, Tenryū Kōga, Chiryū Kōga and Aranami Kōga, who each created their own branch.

There are many documents and chronicles, *Iga Kunishi* (伊賀国志), *Isui Onko* (伊水温故), and *Iranki*, where facts relating to Kōga ninja and, in particular Kōga Saburō, are abundant.

Reportedly, the ninja families that constituted the fifty-three families of the province of Kōga consisted of *genin* (下人) and *chūnin* (中人) only, which is to say that they were only low to mid-level practitioners. They were not, as in Iga, *jōnin* (上人), head of the family or head of the line.

The "low ninja," or *genin*, was on the bottom rung of the ninja ladder. They were the first sent out on missions and often sacrificed. They did not have access to the science of the school, and what little training they had was done in the field.

*Chūnin* filled an intermediate position, being well elevated above the novices. Their role was to pass information—a very significant duty.

Finally, there was the *jōnin*, or the patriarch of the family, owner of the school, and master of the art of ninjutsu. It is this person who would choose the successor.

It is very interesting to note that from the very start ninjutsu was associated the practice of *gen-jutsu* (幻術), the art of conjuring and illusion. But it's just one of the many disciplines that the practitioner of ninjutsu had to master.

Moreover, the art of conjuring and illusion was not a collection of feats of skill to entertain crowds; rather, it was a matter of life or death. By necessity, to be effective with such skills, one needed to be able to use natural features and topography, as well as body flexibility, and other elements.

## Eichō Era (1097): Iga Heinaibe Yasukiyo and Iga-ryū Ninjutsu

Because he had supported Minamoto no Yoritomo (1147–1197), Iga Heinaibe Yasukiyo received permission to build a castle in the province of Iga Hattori as a reward.

There he taught Gamon Dōshi and strove to found *Iga-ryū ninpō*. Before the attack on the province of Iga by Oda Nobunaga's troops (the battles of Iga, 1579–1581), the genealogy of *Iga-ryū ninpō* was as follows:

| | | |
|---|---|---|
| In 1065–1068 | (Jireki era), | The foundation of Iga-ryū is attributed to Gamon Dōshi. |
| In 1074–1076 | (Shōho era), | The successor is Garyū Dōshi and, thereafter, his successor was Unryū Dōshi. |
| In 1096 | (Eichō Era), | Iga Heinaibe Yasukiyo. |
| In 1159 | (Heiji era), | Tozawa Hauubsai and his successor, Saburō Yoshimori. |
| In 1207–1210 | (Shōgen Era), | Togakure Daisuke. |
| In 1249–1255 | (Kencho Era), | Kasumigakure Genryu. |
| In 1288–1292 | (Shōho Era), | Tozawa Seiun. |
| In 1334–1335 | (Kenmu Era), | Tozawanyūdo Genmonsai. |
| In 1379–1380 | (Koryaku Era), | Kakun. |
| In 1394–1427 | (Oiei Era), | Kyūryuzū Hakuun. |
| In 1487–1488 | (Chōkyo Era), | Tozawa Ryutarō. |
| In 1532–1554 | (Tenmon era), | Momochi Sandayū and his successor, Heinaisaemon Ienaga. |

Invasion of the province of Iga by the troops of Oda Nobunaga.

Edo castle's east side view, picture taken
during the Meiji period. Private collection.

The twelfth generation of the succession descending from Heinaibe Yasukiyo boasted three
sons. The eldest one was called Kamihattori Heitarō; second, Nakahattori Heijirō Yasuyori;
and the third, Shimohattori Heijūrō Yasunori. According to the same document, it is said that
Hattori Hanzō was predecessor of the Kamihattori family.[21]

Later, the fifty-five ninja families of the province of Iga that emerged were divided into the
various historical lines listed here:

Tozawa, Fujiwara, Minamoto, Taira, Momochi, Hattori, Izumo, Ōkuni, Tsutsumi, Arima,
Hata, Mizuhara, Shima, Togakure, Ise, Sakagami, Narita, Oda, Mori, Abe, Ueno, Otsuka, Ibuki,
Kaneko, Kotani, Shindō, Iida, Kataoka, Kanbe, Sawada, Kimata, Toyota, Toda, Suzuki, Kashi-
wabara, Fukui, Iga, Kuriyama, Ishitani, Oyama, Sugino, Hanbe.[22]

In the ninth year of the Eiroku era (1558–1569), Oda Nobunaga invaded the province of Iga
and attacked the ninja families who lived there. In a few weeks the resistance was crushed and
the majority of the rebels, including the ninja, were all killed.

However, the bodies of certain heads of ninja families, such as Momochi Sandayū, were never
found.

With regard to the three Hattori families, they were completely crushed, and only twenty-four
survivors escaped. The surviving Kamihattori family, led by the famous Hattori Hanzō Masanari,
found refuge with the Tokugawa family.

The Shimohattori survivors found refuge with the Ochi family in the province of Yamato
(near the present-day Nara prefecture), and the Nakahattori fled into the Takano mountains in
the province of Kishū.

The rest of the survivors left to serve the lord of the province of Kawachi.[22]

It is very interesting to note that the names Iga Heinaibe Yasukiyo, Gaamon Dōshi, and Tozawa Haku
Unsai are all closely connected, and each appears in a different ninjutsu school genealogy. The schools
of *Gyokkō-ryū, Kotō-ryū, Gikan-ryū, Kumogakure-ryū, Shinden fudō ryū*, and *Gyokushin-ryū* all mention
the names of the people listed above in their genealogies.

Moreover, one also finds the names of Tozawa, Iga Heinaibe and Gamon Dōshi in the genealogy of
*Kurama-ryū*, a school of the famous Kurama temple in Kyōto.

Hattori Hanzō's house situated in Tokugawa Ieyasu's Edo castle. Picture taken during the Meiji period. Private collection.

Hattori Hanzō's father's grave in Iga, Mie prefecture. Private collection.

Hattori Hanzō Masanari's grave in Tōkyō's Shinagawa district. Private collection.

Marker in the Yagyū village area.
Private collection.

View of the Iga Mountains. Private collection.

So there is ample evidence that these schools were well formed and shared a common origin. This underscores the point that ninjutsu developed as a unique art distinct from other combat techniques that existed at the time.

In *Igakuni meisho-ki* (伊賀国名所記), one finds the entire genealogy of the Hattori family. The more than 100,000 Japanese people currently bearing the name of Hattori are not necessarily direct descendants of this famous ninja family.

According to the official genealogy,[23] there are two families, Ayahatoti (漢服部) and Kurehatori (呉服部), which descended from a noble family named Hatanosake no Kimi. In the famous chronicle of *Genpei jōsui-ki* or *seisui-ki* (源平盛衰記),[24] mention is made of one of the most famous members of the Hattori family, Iga Heizaeimon no Jyō Ienaga, the founder of *Iga-ryū ninjutsu*.

The Hattori family, as well as the Momochi and Fujibayashi families, were some of the most significant ninja families in the Iga province. They all entered into mutual alliances and many intermarried, strengthening ties.

The Hattori family would become famous thanks to Hattori Hanzō who rescued Tokugawa Ieyasu, became the head of *Iga gumi dōshin* (伊賀組同心), a group of two hundred people and received a salary of 8000 koku. He established his home at one of the entrances in Edo castle, which he guarded and which bears his name today, Hanzō Mon (Hanzō Gate).

Not far from his residence, while crossing the current district of Yotsuya, Akasaka denmacho, there were two districts that bore the names Kita iga-chō (northern district of Iga) and Minami iga-chō (southern district of Iga). These two districts were the permanent residences of the 200 Iga gumi dōshin and their families. A great number of *bujutsu* schools were born in this district.

The case of Momochi Sandayū is most interesting. When you look carefully at the genealogy of the Momochi family, *Momochi keizu* (百地系図), or *Iga musokunin Torishirabe-chō* (伊賀無足人取調帳),[25] the first name "Sandayū" does not appear at all. One finds many other first names like Kandayū, Tadasaburō, and Saburōei, but not that of Sandayū, which leads one to suppose that he was a fictitious character.

*Genkan*, or hall, in the Momochi family home. Private collection.

Stairs to a ninja house situated in the Iga province, Ueno city's suburbs. Private collection.

The entrance of the Momochi family home in Nabari, Mie prefecture. Private collection.

A different view of the Momochi family home. Private collection.

The name of Momochi Sandayū appears for the first time in 1797 in *Ehon Taikōki* (絵本太閤記), a romance on the life of Toyotomi Hideyoshi, written by Takeuchi Kakusai and depicted in the paintings *by* Ishida Gyokuzan. Sandayū appears at the side of a certain Ishikawa Goemon, a notorious robber who was scalded alive along with all his family. This history is reported with some alterations in another document entitled *Zokukin Hisei-dan* (賊禁秘誠談).[26]

Another document that is even more surprising is that of a report entitled *Nihon Oukuni-ki*

Mr. Momochi in front of family photos. Private collection.

(日本王国記: Chronicles of Greater Japan) written by a Spanish merchant living in Japan, named Abira Hiron. In it he mentions the date of execution of Goemon in 1594, who was scalded to death along with his wife, brothers and parents, and the name is written like this: "Ixicaragoyemon (Ishikawa Goemon)."

Even if the stories overlap, many points remain to be clarified regarding the character of Momochi Sandayū. What is sure is that the Momochi family had a house in the Village of Iga Ryūguchi (the current town of Nabari). The Momochi family gravesite is in Hoojiro (the current town of Ueno).

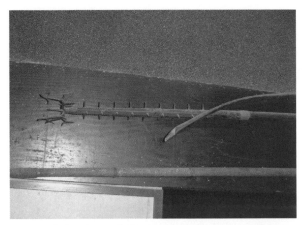

Weapons belonging to the Momochi family. Private collection.

The ancient armor belonging to the Momochi family, displayed in the *tokonoma* (alcove), inside the house. Private collection.

View of the Momochi house roof. Private collection.

The *Sankoku Chishi* (三国地誌)[27] twice mentions the name of Momochi Tanba. The most historically reliable chronicle is *Tamon in nikki* (多聞院日記), written in 1579, which mentions the Momochi family. Their skills in ninjutsu are recognized there. Of course, the *Iran-ki* and *Shinchō kōki* mention the acts of bravery by Momochi Tanba during the invasion of Iga by the troops of Nobunaga Nobuo. According to the *Shinchō kōki*, he fought valiantly, using firearms, bow and arrows, and swords.

Following the battle of Iga the village where the castle was built was destroyed. The records of Momochi Tanba's fate are unclear. Some say he escaped towards the province close to Kii from the Kōya Mountains, others say he fled towards Yamato, and still others say he died of his wounds.

Today still, the estate of Momochi Tanba keeps a genealogy, and weapons such as shuriken, muskets, and *kusari gama*. This suggests that the *Kotō-ryū* school had a curriculum in the technical arts of the *kusari gama*, *kayaku jutsu*, and *shuriken jutsu*.

This is logical because *koppō-jutsu*, just like *kosshi-jutsu*, are sciences that make it possible to use any type of weapon. This is the essence of ninjutsu—to be well founded in many disciplines in order to be able to use any of them to your advantage at a moment's notice.

Although the character Sandayū seems to be fictitious, the man behind this creation appears to be a genius without peer. One needed a very advanced form of *gen-jutsu* and anonymity in order to live in peace.

Stone that marks the entrance of the Momochi home. Private collection.

The secrecy remains impenetrable still today, because there are not enough historically reliable documents to enlighten us on this *Sandayū*.

This shows us how much the art of the ninjutsu balances on the edge of the blade that separates truth from deception.

## Ōho Era (1161–1163):
## Shima Kosanta Minamoto no Kanesada and Togakure-ryū Ninjutsu

The continuation of the text regarding the *makimono* of the *Togakure-ryū* school returns us to the account relating to its genesis. The school appears to have been founded during the Ōho era (1161) by Togakure Daisuke. Togakure Daisuke would have followed the teaching of a certain Kain Dōshi. In what follows, I present the remainder of the manuscript that I translated.

In translating this, I strove to be faithful to the original text. Naturally, this translation cannot duplicate the same "flavor" that one experiences with the original, for example, in the color of paper, the quality of the ink used, and especially the writing style of the author.

During the Ōho era (1163–1163), among the supporters of Kiso Yoshinaka, there was a member of a powerful warrior family in the province of Ise named Shima Kosanta Minamoto no Kanesada.

At that time, he was 16 years old. A member of the army of Kiso Yoshinaka, he was on the road with three thousand horsemen led by Fujiwara no Hidehira.

Abandoned by the fickle fortunes of war and wounded at several places, he lay in the mud in serious condition. Kain Dōshi rescued him, and together, they fled towards the province of Iga.

Subsequently, it is said that he followed the teaching of this Kain Dōshi and devoted himself to the practice of ninjutsu and bujutsu.

The second-generation disciple of Kain Dōshi, Togakure Daisuke, founded Togakure-ryū ninjutsu.

Various documents and chronicles mention the existence of other deposed warriors of the Fujiwara, Minamoto, and Taira families, which, like Shima Kosanta, were exiled in the mountains of the Iga.[24]

This section concludes by reporting the genealogy of the *Togakure-ryū* ninjutsu school. Note that Togakure Daisuke followed the teaching of Kain Dōshi. Thanks to this teaching, he founded the school. For this reason he is regarded as the second generation, even though he remains the sole founder of the school.

However, since the name Kain Dōshi is not found in the genealogy of the school, I conclude that the first place is reserved for the founder, who is known to be Togakure Daisuke. Here is the genealogy of the school according to the *densho* of the *Togakure-ryū* school:

*First generation*: Togakure Daisuke, Shima Kosanta Minamoto no Kanesada, Kōga Kisanta, Kaneko Tomoharu, Togakure Ryūhō, Togakure Gakuun, Kido Koseki.

*Tenth generation*: Iga Tenryū, Ueno Rihei, Ueno Senri, Ueno Manjirō, Iizuka Saburō, Sawada Gorō, Ōzaru Ippei, Tomata Hachirō, Kataoka Heizaemon, Mori Ugenta.

*Twentieth generation*: Toda Gobe, Kanbe Seiun, Momochi Kobe, Tobari Tenzen, Toda Seiryū Nobutsuna, Toda Fudō Nobuchika, Toda Kangorō Nobuyasu, Toda Eisaburō Nobumasa, Toda Shinbe Masachika, Toda Shingorō Masayoshi.

*Thirtieth generation*: Toda Daigorō Chikahide, Toda Shinyūken Masamitsu, Takamatsu Toshigutsu Yokuō, Hatsumi Masaaki Byakuryū (thirty-fourth generation of the school since the founder Togakure Daisuke.)[25]

Different views of the Edo castle, the shogun Tokugawa's castle.

✦ CHAPTER 4 ✦

# The Essence of Ninjutsu

So far, I've presented the history and practice of ninjutsu. Now we can finally address the core of this study, namely the essence of ninjutsu—the substance, form and thought of this special practice.

Now I'll present the art from the inside, from the eyes of a practitioner, Takamatsu Toshitsugu (1887–1972). Toshitsugu was a true ninja, descended from a ninja family of Iga, and heir of nine schools of ninjutsu, including *Togakure-ryū* ninjutsu which has roots in the Kamakura period.

Like most of those who came before him, Takamatsu recorded his life experience for the future heir to the nine schools, namely Hatsumi Masaaki. This account is titled *Ninjutsu Hiketsu Bun* (忍術秘訣文: Secret Ninjutsu Text), and the universal philosophical underpinnings of ninjutsu that are recorded therein impart to it a unique flavor.

Pictured: Master Hatsumi Masaaki (left), Don F. Dreager (center),
and Quintin Chambers. Private collection.

During my last stay in Japan, I was able to ask Hatsumi Masaaki about some difficulties inherent in the interpretation of this text. His answer was as short and to the point.

In his experience, a combination of physical practice and profound soul searching is the key to understanding the "mysteries of the soul." With that, he added that, as for religious practice, the value of interpretation depends on the depth of the practice.

A balance between spiritual and physical activity is the foundation to understanding the deeper essence of Toshitsugu's text. Be that as it may, the manuscripts of each school of combat in Japan were written so that only the heir can fully grasp the real meanings hidden behind the esoteric writing and illustrations.

**Statue of Tengu in the temple. Private collection.**

Ninjutsu is extremely esoteric. Indeed, for a shadow art like ninjutsu, its secrets are necessarily well hidden. It was necessary for an heir to go through various stages of initiation and deep soul searching, strewn with difficult tests designed to open "the eye of the heart" to the essence of the art.

This explains why in the history of the transmission of ninjutsu, the chosen successor was the sole representative of a tradition whose nature is balanced between the light and the shadow, power and helplessness, hunger and plenty, honor and humiliation, arising and descending, and so forth.

It remains, however, very difficult to directly approach the text *Ninjutsu no Hiketsu Bun* by Takamatsu, because it presents only the ultimate state to which the practice of ninjutsu leads.

Also, to understand this text, it is necessary to know more about the author. For that purpose I have recently studied the original copy of an autobiography written by Takamatsu when he was 78 years old, entitled *Shinden Shura Roppō* (神伝修羅六方).[1] This biography chronicles his youth and his experiences which were, without any doubt, his basis for writing the *Ninjutsu no Hiketsu Bun* text.

But, after a meticulous study of this biography, it appears that Takamatsu gave only snippets of information, particularly about his travels in China and Manchuria as a young man. It should be stated that this biography was written for a widely read Japanese martial arts magazine. It is, therefore, understandable that Takamatsu didn't mention his adventures in China.

However, there is another autobiography by Takamatsu, mentioning all his journeys, experiences, and motivations. It's titled *Meiji Mōroku Otoko* (明治毛六男). This document, as well as a number of other writings on subjects like religion, the Kami and the Buddha, and "happiness through the practice of ninjutsu," were all bequeathed to Hatsumi Masaaki along with the weapons, scrolls, and densho of nine schools of ninjutsu.

Only some anecdotes concerning Takamatsu's fights and combat experiences, as well as his personal practice, are reported here, but the whole account is distilled succinctly. Hatsumi Masaaki will one day bequeath *Meiji Mōroku Otoko* to his successor, if there is to be one.

The important question of this chapter and book is: how can one engage in a spiritual quest while also becoming a skillful fighter, one who is pragmatic and highly adaptable, and destined to survive all adversity?

Can there be compatibility between two practices that are, for most people, basically opposite?

Here is where we get the famous concept of "the way" (道: *dō*), which appeared during the Edo period.

Even if they did undergo training from childhood, as it is the case for Takamatsu, when warriors and soliders are confronted with the hard reality that is war, a shift takes place deep within.

This intimate confrontation with a frightening reality leads naturally to belief and connection with religion and a different view of the world.

However, before addressing this intimate experience that is the basis for the text by Takamatsu, I'll first present the spiritual and physical impetus of ninjutsu, "the awakening," or the opening, to which it can lead.

# Ninjutsu: Form and Spirit

All combat training is carried out via *kata* (型: kata, or 形: *katachi*):[2] preestablished sequences of movement. For all training, be it martial or not, a model, a diagram, a plan, or a form is necessary.

However, when learning, as is the case of ninjutsu, requires a form that is stripped of any unnatural mental or physical mechanism, allowing the practitioner to get a sense of his body without any reference to styles or of dogma, the form, the kata takes on another dimension.

I will explain ninjutsu katas, how they are perceived, and how they grow blurred from their original structure to a point where an infinite number of techniques are possible, springing forth in response to any situation, be they orthodox or not.

The forms (kata) and body postures (*kamae*) of ninjutsu did not undergo any change or "evolution," contrary to all those that we find in modern *budō*, which were born during the Meiji, Taishō and Shōwa periods (1867–present). They were never transformed or modified for the purposes of physical education or competition. Takamatsu bequeathed them just as they were to his single successor, Hatsumi Masaaki.

Portrait of Master Toshitsugu Takamatsu, 33rd *soke* of *Togakure Ryu ninjutsu.*

Even with the opening of the art to Westerners and the rest of the world, there have not been any modifications. The secret nature of ninjutsu and its transmission, made from master to disciple, and the, kata and kamae, remain even now, in full view of everyone, a secret.

They are like the images of the Holy Scriptures, the Torah, the Gospels, and the Koran. They are read throughout the world, yet palpable and comprehensible only for those who have a physical and especially a spiritual capacity.

It isn't simply a matter of an intellectual knowledge or a straightforward scientific practice of the techniques of combat by which one may arrive at a certain level of understanding.

They have eyes, but their hearts are blind.[3]

This sentence, on the subject, holds remarkable depth. It testifies, among other things, that the two bodies—the eyes and the mind—although connected together in the same body, do not function in unison, although we are tempted to believe so.

The essence of ninjutsu is difficult to grasp. There is no form, no technique, no name. Only action stripped of forethought. This unpremeditated action is the embodiment of the state in which the spirit and the body regain their unity, and where true body and spiritual flexibility is restored.

It is on this concept that the kata and kamae, of ninjutsu are built, which we will call (for lack of better terms), its mental and technical doctrine.

In connection with the forms in ninjutsu, Takamastu Toshitsugu taught his disciple Hatsumi Masaaki the *gokui* (極 意: essential points, teachings) according to the phrase:

The color of the water is the color of its vase.[4]

The spirit must be flexible, not fixed on any physical forms or attitude. The technical concepts of ninjutsu are based on the spirit of endurance and perseverance, of battlefield and combat survival. This also applies to the perpetual combat against oneself, where endurance and perseverance are again of primary importance.

The techniques of ninjutsu were conceived so that beginning with a posture, or a punch, the movement could be adapted on the fly for use with weapons, be they specific to ninjutsu or not.

From unity towards multiplicity; herein lies the form and thus the spirit of ninjutsu.

Natural, benign, and open, this spiritual attitude coalesces during a confrontation and, being versatile, one changes their combat posture.

*Nitō no kamae* performed by Master Hatsumi Masaaki. Private collection.

To be able to move naturally and flexibly, through any combat body posture, to use any weapons without conscious thought, this requires a rare and singular broad-mindedness. It is this idea that Takamatsu describes.

Movements reflect the motives and attitudes of the martial artist. Yet, how can a form of combat reflect a mental state where there is no premeditation? The closer the movements approach the pure unity of body and spirit, the more the intention is erased. Of course, this movement must initially be natural itself. What is a natural movement in the martial arts?

According to Takamatsu, true effectiveness is a natural movement that is done without brute force.[5] If there is body unity, then physical power is not necessary, because the body acts as a whole. Today, for a great number of martial art practitioners, power is conveyed by mainly the use of the hips or the shoulders, the "belly" or torso.

One may speak about total body force or *ki*, but if movement is always from the hips or the shoulders, the physical force created is based on a duality where only power reigns—and that will decrease with age.

However much some might insist that the hips form the engine of the body, in ninjutsu, the spirit is the source of power.

The hips are only part of the body and it is surely not, until proof to the contrary emerges, solely with the hips that we walk.

The feet, ankles and knees are the key drivers of all body movements. Movement starts with a succession of imbalances brought about by one's desire to walk.

All starts with a step. The form and, thus, the movement that follows are no exception. Any form of combat must be carried out starting from the natural walk of all human beings.

The movement must be natural, for several reasons:

First, we human beings have a body that consists of 70 percent water.[6] Thus all movements must be loose and flexible without rigid blocking, which can cause injury and prevent continued practice into old age.

Second, any movement reflects the mental state of the individual. If the individual is stressed, upset, aggressive, and so on, the movement will be an embodiment of such feelings or mental attitudes. Let's not forget that the "the body is the temple that houses the spirit," and, consequently, any psychological state has an effect on the body and vice versa.

Most of the movements, forms, kata, *kamae*, and the like that one finds in the martial arts today condition the body of the individual. Like dogmatic thinking cultivated during youth, they impose an unnatural way of moving on the body.

Indeed, if the movements are too rigid or jerky, too linear or too circular, too forceful, don't allow for enough flexibility or, instead, impose a flexibility that, far from being natural, is rather harmful for the body, then there must be a problem in the transmission of that martial art.

Or, it may indicate that the majority of such martial art forms were practiced during a particular moment in history that is very different from today. It can even be argued that they were not formulated to preserve physical and mental integrity. These kinds of positions, postures of combat, and other formative tools of the body do not develop the body, and thus the spirit, in the natural way.

A large majority of martial art practitioners have a body and spirit conditioned by their current or former practices, and those unnatural movements have become second nature.

Many practitioners have expressed doubts about their practice after many years of intense training, which, generally, has brought them more physical problems (and mental problems for some) than anything else. One thing is certain; now that such individuals know they need to make a change, there is hope! If we seek to move as naturally possible, it is necessary for us to alter our current way of moving and seek a way of movement that does not bring any harm or injury. Indeed, if we fail to make this a priority in our practice, it could have serious physical and mental health repercussions in the long run.

The third argument for natural combat movements is that spontaneous reaction requires a natural mental state in which the mind reacts to threats instinctively and without conscious thought, making it possible to defend and attack instantaneously and without hesitation. This is what is often meant by "invisibility" In reference to ninjutsu.

According to Takamatsu, this state of invisibility can be attained only when the body and the spirit do not exist as isolated entities anymore, and the practitioner has, in a sense, "forgotten the self." This requires profound soul-searching and an inner journey of the soul. This physical and mental process confers a quasi-religious depth to the practice. As the movements becomes second nature to the practitioner, the physical and mental postures do as well.

Most of the kamae postures of ninjutsu are positions where the body is seen in profile and on a line (feet on the same line). To have such a profiled posture carries with it a "spirit of profile," a spirit in which only half is allowed to show, what the practitioner decides to offer.

The spirit of this profiled posture is one of a state of hiding. In other words, the practitioner of

*Hyōen no kamae* performed by master Hatsumi Masaaki. Private collection.

ninjutsu doesn't appear directly vis-a-vis to his adversary but instead creates doubt about his real capacity. Is he really there? That's the question to create in the mind of the enemy.

For many practitioners of combat techniques, one of the basic strategies consists of probing the adversary's spirit through his posture and position. To probe the posture, is to probe the spirit—the attitude of the adversary. But how does one ascertain the mind of the ninja whose posture is "silent?"

This is not to say that such a posture does not offer any opening or that it is compact, rooted, or the like. No, this posture offers at the same time everything and anything. It is seemingly an open posture that invites the adversary to make the first move. What posture makes it possible to be at the same time protected and yet open to all attacks, present and absent, or rather both "dead and alive?"

Takamatsu said on this subject that when the ego is extinguished, then ineffective fighting stances are replaced with a unique posture, one of all possibilities and all openings, that which suggests and misleads at the same time. More than a simple technical illusion, it is at the same time real as it is false.

Other martial art practitioners favor an explosion of aggressive energy to show power through their respective forms. This kind of display is nonexistent in ninjutsu. To show aggressiveness is to give away information on oneself and one's practice, and in a certain manner, it shows a lack of humility.

A ninja's true effectiveness remains hidden to the eye. It's an attitude that can be felt only by the body. This unique spiritual posture cannot be explained by words—it must be felt.

The ninja never reveals what he is truly capable of; he passes unnoticed, even avoiding conflict in order to remain anonymous. A ninja intent on remaining undiscovered by avoiding confrontation will foster the impression that his adversary is in control of the situation.

All the *kamae*, whether they are offensive or defensive, have in themselves this characteristic that makes it possible, with the proper state of mind, to allow the adversary to believe that the fight is already finished before it even starts.

Certain practitioners could see here the simple concept of a lure or trick often called *kyojitsu* (虚実), but this is not so. Everyone, and especially the combat sports practitioners, understands the use of pretenses and tricks.

However, in this case, the posture corresponds to a state of mind and the concept of *kyojitsu tenkan* (虚実転換: to change truth into false and vice versa). Ninjutsu requires much more than simple knowledge of postures or unspecified tricks intended to mislead the adversary.

By *kamae* (構), it is generally understood to mean posture, attitude, or combat position. In fact, it is much more that a simple body position or posture, but it is also more an attitude of the spirit. Indeed, we can easily assume a physical posture, whereas assuming the proper spiritual posture is another matter. The aim is to open the mind to other combat possibilities. The actual posture, the proper *kamae*, is in fact in the mind or the heart.

Accordingly, one of the basic kata of attack and defense in ninjutsu, named the *san shin no* kata (三心之型), must be taken into account. It is very different from the famous *sanchin* that one finds in karate, with open hands for *Uechi-ryū* and closed hands for *Gōjū-ryū*, *Shōtōkan*, and *Shitō-ryū*. It is not

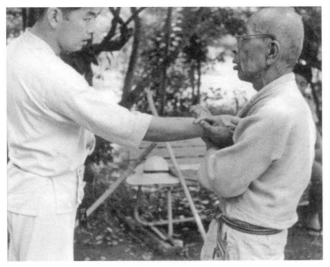

Master Takamatsu teaching the art of using the *tan bo* and the *eda koppo* to Sensei Hatsumi during an outdoor practice.

repeated more than three times and is sometimes exercised only once in the form known as *shinken* (真剣) or *jissen gata* (実戦型: real form for combat).

*San shin no* kata is defined as "form of the three hearts" (心 = *shin/kokoro* = spirit, heart, or thought.), but its meaning is deeper. Toda Shinryūken, grandfather and master of Takamatsu, taught that the major principle of the *san shin no* kata lay in the heart, the spirit of the practitioner rather than in the physical form, and that the rate/rhythm of the san shin no kata made it possible, for those who had the capacity, to grasp the merits of this kata.[7]

Three spirits (or hearts), three rates/rhythms, and three attacks in one–they're carried out by a succession of defensive positions. If physical and mental unity is achieved, then either the attack or defense is done with a natural smoothness that would surprise anyone, because the movements give the impression that three attacks are occurring.

This movement is easily transposed for use with weapons, such as the sword, shuriken, knife, rope, chain, gun and so on; the movement remains the same and the transition is natural. The *san shin no* kata illustrates the principle that from only one technique, only one form, multiple applications can be produced.

A different view of Yagyū village. Private collection.

The technique is an expression of the posture, and both in turn are a reflection of the practitioner's attitude and spirit. In this case, Takamatsu stated that, in the practice of ninjutsu, having the correct spirit is of primary importance. Having the proper spirit involves much more than simply the having the technical ability to carry out a superb technique or kata. Any practitioner in his discipline can, with daily practice, arrive at a refined level of technique.

Here, the right spirit springs forth from the right heart. It reflects what the practitioner has deep within. It is the nature of the heart, one's convictions and deepest motivations, that drives the practitioner's actions.

To defend, fight, and persevere, the heart of the practitioner is reflected in all his actions, and the postures and kata are no exception. Thus, this correct form and the kata become alive and real.

An imperceptible spark of life, the essence of all human qualities, it is the heart that remains secret in any posture or form, for ninjutsu and for anything else. Of course, the heart remains a great mystery to man, but through a physical form, it remains possible to feel the heart. According to Toda Shinryūken:

> The heart of the form is the sword of the disciple. It is with it that he fights his enemies and by it that he pushes back the calamities that threaten him.[8]

As others have said, the form is there, first and foremost, to shape the body. And, it is a question of training the body so that it can perpetually "listen" in order to answer any situation without hindrance.

The main entrance of the Hōtoku Zenji temple in Yagyū village. Private collection.

The forms of ninjutsu allow for introspection, where each detail has importance. It can be said that the formation and shaping of the body through the techniques of combat provide a necessary sanctuary for the development of the heart.

If we pour water into a vessel thought to have integrity, but there are holes, even very small ones, then liquid will leak out. Spiritual development remains the essence of the form because it depends on the heart of the practitioner, spirit and heart being synonymous.

All details have their importance in combat, and this is especially true for a form, because it makes it possible to confront the spirit and the heart with reality. Each detail of the form reveals the soul through internal introspection; the angles, the rates/rhythms, the distance, the breath, balance and imbalance, they all demonstrate the need to have a form that makes it possible to adapt.

"Adaptation" is a term that comes up often in the practice of techniques of combat, but who can claim to have succeeded in adapting to all dangerous situations or conflicts, especially ones dealing with emotion?

The form in ninjutsu makes it possible to react spontaneously, no matter the situation. Only the flexibility resulting from the integration of the form with the subconscious, awakening the original unity within us, can make it possible to find that.

For many, flexibility is more than a technique or a series of stretching exercises. Some say that to adopt a flexible attitude, one needn't also be physically flexible. But if physical and mental unity is truly sought, there should be no difference between the condition of the mental attitude and the physical body. If the attitude is flexible, then the body must also be so. Visualize the flexibility of young children.

Takamatsu spoke to this point when he said that to understand the essence of ninjutsu and of the martial arts in general, it is necessary to have a heart similar to that of a child—flexible and generous. I did not know Sensei Takamatsu as he died when I was still an infant. However, an old film recording of him exists, when he was 75 years old, where we can see him moving in an exceptionally neutral and relaxed way. His successor, Hatsumi Masaaki, has also attained a state of complete emptiness and is not directed by conscious thought in the execution of his combat movements.

When the angles, rates/rhythms, breathing, distance, balance, and imbalance merge with the form to become based in the heart, then the original unity emerges and all actions can be carried out effortlessly and without premeditation. Such is the foundation of the form coming from the spirit ninjutsu practitioner.

## Awakening in Ninjutsu

For many individuals, especially intellectuals and academics with no practical knowledge of combat techniques, the practice of martial arts consists of breaking wooden boards with shrill cries, demonstrations of physical prowess, and shows of force awkwardly mingled with "philosophical" concepts from Taoism and Zen Buddhism.

This ignorance is due mainly to several factors that prevent one from distinguishing truth from fiction. Misinformation combines with fragmentary and erroneous knowledge of the practice itself and of its current sociocultural context. This is then conveyed by practitioners who emulate a flawed model, that of a "master" who does not always conform to social and cultural reality. These are the principal causes of continued ignorance.

The confusion caused by composite martial arts and hybrid combat practice, which combine various techniques and central ideas from Taoists, Zen Buddhists and other mystical philosophies, makes it very difficult, even impossible, to approach what we call an awakening in the practice of martial arts. In the following section, I will define what "awakening" is in ninjutsu (which can be applied to all martial arts), without resorting to any esoteric ideas of Taoism, Buddhism, and the like, but rather by looking at the many spiritual lessons that our Western culture holds.

This calligraphy means "know the importance of living in the moment." Private collection.

By doing this, I intend to show how the universality of some of these lessons can be applied to ninjutsu as to other martial arts, and that according to the motivations and beliefs of each individual, there lies the essence of very practical training, be it martial or not.

This calligraphy, "*Yume*," means "dreams." Private collection.

For followers of Buddhism, enlightenment is a state achieved through the gradual passage of tests or suddenly during a spontaneous act, depending on the originating school of thought. This state of being allows one to achieve an intimate understanding of Buddhist law and to also understand more fully one's circumstances. Many books written by experts brilliantly illustrate the different stages of enlightenment and the different ideas of awakening from the different schools of Buddhism. With the simple definition quoted above, I hope to avoid any confusion regarding the concept of awakening in ninjutsu and the martial arts.

In this case, to be "awoken" in the martial arts means to be attentive, on guard, to be alert in any situation, whether it be a physical or emotional conflict. To be attentive to all things, it is necessary to be sufficiently perceptive in order to recognize and respond to all possible attacks, physical or otherwise.

For the spirit to be awoken, the body must be also. The logic of fighting techniques shows us that body and spirit must be one if they are to respond appropriately to an attack. As the mind is alert and sensitive to even the subtlest change, the body must also be responsive and flexible.

Among the lessons some great saints taught, certain maxims wonderfully coincide with the practice of ninjutsu. For example:

> The body is the Temple that shelters the Spirit.[9]
> The true Holy War is against oneself.[10] (i.e., the ego)

If the physical body of the martial artist can be distinct from the spirit as these two maxims preach, one's spiritual orientation is then revealed by the motivations and beliefs of the individual.

Combat experiences, like any confrontation, remain vividly in the memory. Not unlike problems within a marriage, stress at work, a disappointment in love, the death of a close relative, and the like, there are many different kinds of combat where only the "weapons" and the situations differ.

However, the result remains the same. The two maxims quoted above are simple, and everyone can comprehend them. But to understand them on a mental level only scratches the surface; the full meaning is much deeper.

The first maxim quoted above indicates that, to control the spirit, it is necessary for us to pass through the training of the body. This is logical, as the spirit is, in a sense, the element of central control within the body where all communications converge. When one is thirsty, one tightens the arm, deploys the fingers, and seizes the glass.

Training, thus, allows one to polish the spirit, and the body is the sole vehicle for this training. In all warrior cultures, this maxim was funda-mental to the training regimen.

This calligraphy means "patience." Private collection.

This stage is the first in the warrior's training, but it doesn't boil down to a simple technical profi-ciency that many could reach through daily practice. No, for the body to be "the Temple that shelters the Spirit," much more than simple practice is required, and it is here that the second quoted maxim cannot be dismissed.

The second maxim resembles the first but brings a precision that illuminates the true heart of the practice. The fight is, this time, against oneself. How does this relate to ninjutsu?

Ninjutsu is an elaborate and adaptable means of defense and attack developed to detect and neutralize threats before they can overwhelm. To be able predict danger in all its forms before it occurs requires an intimate understanding of the nature of threats.

Indeed, to know danger, it is necessary to live with it, to feel it. It is when our life hangs by a thread that all the details, even the most trivial, become vitally important. A lapse in attention means death.

However, even if the practitioner cannot perceive it, the greatest dan-ger comes from within, from the ego. A lack of vigilance in any situation, be it a conflict or not, can prove to be deadly in certain cases, for our families or ourselves.

The kanji *"nin"* or *"shinobi"* writ-ten by Hatsumi Masaaki. Private collection.

In the practice of ninjutsu, one understands from the start that the ego remains the principal source of danger and is at the base of all con-frontations. The suppression of the ego is the basis for the body/mind unity that makes it possible to avoid gathering danger.

In ninjutsu, in the instructional documents of technical knowledge (*densho*), the term *sacchi suru* (察知)[11] which means to guess, predict, or sense, is often used to indicate the ability to anticipate danger. This ability can be obtained only when there is unity between the body and the spirit. This harmony, like enlightenment, is always characterized by flexibility; a flexibility, vigilance, malleability, openness, and the like, and, in a certain manner, by an in-ternal peace which brings the unity of the body (a deep knowledge of one's own physiology and anatomy) and of the spirit (sense of control and behavior in any situation).

When this harmony is disturbed, because both are closely bound, one will sense the disturbance im-mediately.

It should be stated that all people have experienced this feeling in an abnormal situation. But being able to effectively respond to the feeling remains very difficult. For most people this unity, and the har-mony which goes with it, remains elusive. Only when a person feels threatened or when a situation spirals

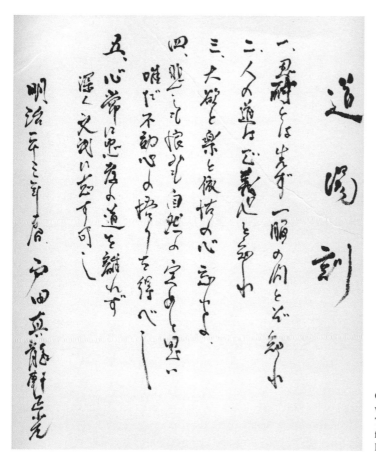

**Copy of the *Dōjō-kun*
written by master
Takamatsu Toshitsugu
for Hatsumi Masaaki.
Private collection.**

out of control does it spring forth from the depths of being. If it is not developed, it will often coexist with, and be smothered by, the ego.

How can we claim to detect danger in the world around us if we cannot detect it even in ourselves? One can say that to understand the nature of danger is to understand the nature of man, who, when not disciplined, is but a reflection of impermanence. Self-knowledge through the death of the ego is at the heart of ninjutsu.

Self-knowledge is the only weapon that makes it possible to sense danger in time to avoid it. Without this knowledge, the practice of the combat techniques is largely stripped of its usefulness, as it is then merely the reinforcement of our own self-centeredness.

This state of ultimate self-knowledge is necessary to understand the famous statement by Sun Zi cited earlier:

If you know the enemy and know yourself, you need not fear the results of a hundred battles.

The true strategist is before all a strategist of his own being, his ego. In the same manner, a doctor should be his own doctor. How can we cure others, if we are not even able to see the disease and first cure it in our own bodies?

Self-diagnosis relies on internal introspection that comes with practice. All strategies start with a knowledge of ourselves and, thus, of our own abilities. This includes the knowledge of all our defects and weaknesses, particularly the most hidden.

**The view from the Hakuho castle in Iga's Ueno city. Private collection.**

It is in this vein that there exists a true holy war; it does not have any set duration like a battle. Indeed, each battle with an adversary knows an end, and afterwards there is a celebrated rest for the warrior. But in the case of the "war against oneself," there is no rest; from when we wake in the morning until we sleep at night, there is perpetual combat against oneself.

In this combat, the aim is to overcome all the contrary practices and reactions that have become "second nature." Unrestrained, this second nature mingles with our original mind/body unity, preventing spontaneous movement that is free from distracting thought. If we allow it, our fears, prejudices, resentments, and the like will block us and prevent the freedom we seek. This combat against oneself, which leads to intimate self-knowledge, cannot be carried out without sincerity and faith.

Sincerity is stripped of any fear, because it is tested and found to be true by the body/spiritual unity. Pain makes it possible for fear to be transcended and to feel things as they really are. It is often from pain that awareness is born. Indeed, it is after the "cold shower" that one awakes and that one reaches an enlightenment. In connection with pain, Toda Shinryūken said this to Takamatsu Toshitsugu:

> If it lasts, make it a friend. The real practice of ninjutsu consists in being accustomed to misfortune, so much so that he (misfortune) becomes a friend (ally). And through the persistent use of resignation you will get stamina. [12]

Here, the grandfather and master of Takamatsu wanted him to grasp a truth that remains key to the practice. The power of this truth, of "resignation," lies in patience, an essential quality for all real practitioners. It is for this reason that it is necessary to understand the terms *uke* (受) and *ukemi* (受身).

The first term is often translated as "blocking," as in blocking a strike, and the second is translated as "to fall," "break fall," "rolling," and the like, as in to fall and hit the ground safely. However, the correct translation of the term *uke* is actually "to receive." In order to receive, it is also necessary to be able to give or rather to learn how to give.

The Ittō seki in Yagyū village, situated in the place where Yagyū Muneyoshi was doing his solo practice. According the story, he cut the big rock in half because in the darkness he mistook it for a Tengu. Private collection.

The correct translation of the term *ukemi* is then the body, the flesh (身: *mi*), which receives (受: *uke*). It is thus a question of knowing how to receive in order to avoid injury, which is very important for many practitioners who cannot carry out a proper fall because of age or because their body, having been poorly educated, "receives" badly.

If the body receives badly, then the spirit receives badly as well and, thus, does not accept things. Thus, the practitioner has fallen into a bad practice even if he doesn't realize it—in addition to all the injuries that he's likely to receive.

When one sincerely embraces all that is offered by the practice, a "gift of oneself," then one enters into truth; where there is a sincere gift of oneself, there is no ego. It then becomes easy to feel and envision danger from wherever it comes.

The gift of oneself in practice is closely linked to the idea of acceptance. It brings with it an opening of the heart that makes it possible to react instinctively and appropriately to any attack, whether it be a physical attack or not.

Fighting techniques and combat training are not enough to survive a battle. Because it is only about one technique even if it is secret or perfectly executed.

Without conviction, without faith, nothing is attainable. It is what makes the difference between an "alive" technique and a "dead" technique, even if the latter is sometimes effective.

History shows that a great number of saintly men, who inevitably did not have knowledge of the combat arts, still succeeded in overcoming the combat techniques of adversaries through their faith alone. For these unskilled and unarmed holy men, it was their inward convictions—their faith—that enabled them to find the weaknesses in these hard and savage warriors. Their combat technique may not have been impressive, but they held a sincerity and faith that could only be achieved through body/spirit unity.

Many warriors succeeded where others failed thanks only to their convictions. Soldiers on a battlefield are confronted with a life-changing experience that leads to discovering the depths of man. Without going to such extremes (and in order to avoid injury) the pursuit of self-knowledge can bring the same

Another entrance to the Yagyū village. Private collection.

enlightenment without requiring the hazardous trip to the battlefield.

It is very easy to wound, malign, destroy, attack, and the like. But to seek peace, while knowing that one is capable of carrying out appalling acts of violence requires a state of mind that understands the terrible outcome of violence and that is free of all encumbrances.

In this case, the practice of combat techniques, and ninjutsu in particular, take on another dimension. What is important about the role sincerity in the practice of ninjutsu?

This concerns the passage from "natural" hypocrisy to spiritual sincerity. The criteria for spiritual sincerity include flexibility, adaptability, and humility (the master of humility will often go unnoticed by an adversary), to show bravery and resignation.

Sensei Takamatsu taught that the result of the persistent practice of awareness, of ninjutsu, is the inner transformation of the subconscious and the building of reflexes that adapt to any given circumstance.

A mystic of great piety who died in Baghdad in ninth century said "to seize the truth, it is necessary to confront false perceptions of reality."[13]

This is the path that leads to ultimate self-knowledge, from which the famous moment of truth arises, requiring us to commit all that we are, in all sincerity, to the simplest of truths. Ultimate self-knowledge is the attainment of a purity that requires the practitioner's total commitment. It is towards this goal that famous swordsmean of Japan practiced their art—with enthusiasm, sincerity and faith.

Dousing with cold water was a ritual found not only in Japanese religious practices but also in Judaism, Christianity, and Islam. It is physically and spiritually valuable, and was often done to prolong the state of purity brought about by religious practice combined with the practice of combat. Curiously, the ritual was performed at the time in the life of the warrior when they endeavored to be divorce themselves from all that was not real.

Peace, stillness of the spirit, an unflappable nature; none of these states can be attained through simply training in a multitude of combat techniques with the aim of simply having the most effective methods. No, combat begets combat, hatred begets hatred, and the savage animal within man that wallows in self-love will suffer an unexpected and early demise.

Master Takamatsu demonstrating the art of *tai-jutsu*.

Master Hatsumi Masaaki performing the *mutō-dori* techniques
in his personal dōjō in Noda city. Private collection.

The opening of oneself, and thus one's heart, brings self-knowledge and also knowledge of others since, in the end, we human beings are not very different from each other. The practice then penetrates the surface and goes deep within. While the weapon may be an extension of the arm and hand, its true connection lies with the spirit.

This intimate and unquestionable experience of the faith is more important than the wide array of combat techniques that have no connection to the spirit.

> If you don't control your ego, it will control you.
> Your body threatens to overwhelm your spirit, and if it does, it will kill you.
> Kill your heart (or ego) to make it live again.[14]

There are many such maxims left by men who had the joint experience of combat against oneself and against others for their own survival, and from other men who knew only the combat against oneself and who still succeeded against others who'd only mastered the physical aspects of warfare.

These individuals managed to find the perfect balance between the original unity of body and spirit, and the warrior techniques that they used when there was no way to avoid conflict. For those who attained this ultimate state, and there were very few, they were able to eliminate threats before they could overwhelm.

In conclusion we can say that any physical doctrine or practice is tied to a mental practice. But in the case of ninjutsu, or *ninpō* as it is also known, which translates as the science of combat through an enduring and persevering spirit, it it calls for transcendence.

Perfect balance between the body and spirit depends on the harmonious union of the internal and external intentions of the individual. From there, the vision and direction of one's life, one's attitude with respect to people, and one's acceptance of conflict and chaos are perceived differently.

To be conscious of danger and to know it comes from a self-knowledge that makes it possible to predict it and intervene. One must be able to synthesize effective, adaptable physical techniques with sincere spiritual practice.

This state is attainable and history provides many examples where the practitioners of the combat arts were deeply committed to spiritual practice. It all comes down to the heart of the practitioner; within this resides impetus for every kind of practice.

By its very nature ninjutsu is esoteric. Like any state of enlightenment that cannot be seen or felt, but rather must be *lived*, it contains truths that are revealed slowly over time, unlike scum that arises immediately to the surface.

Painting of Daruma by master Hatsumi Maasaki. The kanji written are "*kaze,*" which means "the wind," and "*nintai jisei,*" which means "self-control and endurance" or "capacity to control one's endurance and patience." Private collection.

# CHAPTER 5

# Autobiography of a Ninja Master

This is the autobiography of Takamatsu Toshitsugu: Shinden Shūra Roppō.

## Seventy-eight Candles[1]

It seems that I have just turned seventy-eight years old this year (1966). It is not that I do not know my age or that I forgot to count since I was two or three years old, but quite simply I did not desire the knowledge. I know only the year of my birth, the twenty-third year of the Meiji era (1888).

Also, I deduce my current age only by counting the years that have passed since my birth. Just as I do not know what I resemble because I have not seen myself in a mirror for more than thirty years. If I looked in a mirror, the reflection of my face would say to me: "But who are you?" But otherwise, I feel magnificently well!

Indeed, whereas for an ordinary person it takes one hour to traverse 4 kilometers, 30 minutes are more than enough for me. I lie down without fail at nine o'clock in the evening. Jirō, a Siamese cat given to me by Kobe Ichirō via Hatsumi Masaaki of the Chiba prefecture, sleeps close to me. I rise each morning at 6:30 and do *reisui masatsu* (冷水摩擦: cleansing consisting of washing the body with a cold wet towel), a ritual that I have not ceased doing for these last forty years. Thanks to it, I never fell sick.

I like to paint and do calligraphy, and although I am not a naturally gifted artisan, I always take pleasure in painting.

## The Crybaby[2]

When I was child, I was called the crybaby. At school, my "friends" from classes made me go on my hands and knees, while they rode atop my back as if on a horse, thus causing me to cry loudly because of the pain that they inflicted on my back.

Before I was one year old, I was separated from my real mother, and by my twentieth year I would know nine different mothers. My father was a well-known contractor and continually moved from job to job. He started by working on the construction of Sanyō Tetsudō (the Sanyō Railway) in the town of Kobe, and then opened a match factory in the town of Akashi, being thus devoted to other many trades.

With each time he took up a new vocation, my "mother" also changed. However, I do not think that the source of my tears was in the successive change of mothers.

## Disciple in the Dōjō of Sensei Toda[3]

At that time, in the town of Kobe, there was a man named Toda Shinryūken who, while teaching the techniques of combat that he exemplified, also ran a private clinic of osteopathy. He was a master in techniques of combat originating from the province of Iga, and in his dōjō, he taught *Shinden Fudō-ryū* (神伝不動流).[4]

Because he was family, my father consulted him in connection with my future when I turned 9 years old.

"I would like my son to become a soldier, but he is very timid and the others call him 'the crybaby.' How would you advise me to resolve that?" asked my father.

"The practice of combat techniques of would be best. A strict discipline will make him a strong and courageous person," replied Toda Shinryūken.

On this advice, my father ordered to me to go to the dōjō the every day after school. I was completely distraught and cried even more, but I went to the dōjō meekly, as a lamb is led to the slaughterhouse.

Usually, the assistant of the master would teach beginners. But with regard to me, Sensei Toda taught me directly. The lessons that I followed were very unusual.

Normally, in the beginning of training, one starts by teaching a form (kata), either how to throw or be thrown. But, at nine years old, Sensei Toda would freely throw me in all directions, from right to left, without seemingly taking any method into account.

Even when my knees were scratched and my elbows started to bleed, he did not stop and hardly lessened his pace. "No matter what happens, tomorrow I will not return!" I thought.

Young disciple practicing *kenjutsu* in a temple. Private collection.

I regarded the dōjō with a glare of animosity as I washed off the blood which ran from my hands and knees, and returned home where nobody comforted me. After a good night of sleep, however, I had already forgotten all the pains I'd received the day before in the dōjō, and I continued to attend.

I was only a child with a short memory. It was only after an entire year, during which I had only been constantly thrown, that Sensei Toda began the ordinary technical lessons.

## End of the Crybaby[5]

At age ten, during my fourth school year, our professors made us take part in a sumō competition. I shrank back in order to hide behind the others when the professor called me and said: "Takamatsu, go ahead!"

Timidly, I went out on to the *dohyō* (土俵: sumō combat surface, raised above ground) and without any intention to beat them, I naturally started to throw my opponents.

After throwing seven or eight people, I left the *dohyō* without a loss, to which the astonished professor exclaimed: "Oh! Strapping man, that small one."

After this demonstration, everyone treated me differently (out of fear), and I said to myself: "Well, they are quite weak. I do not have reason to fear."

Quickly, my confidence grew, and the weak crybaby who I had been up until then disappeared entirely.

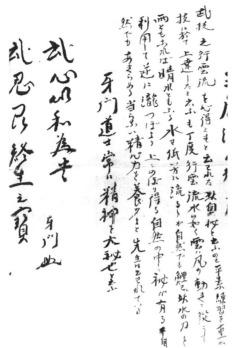

Copy of the *Togakure-ryū budō hiden-sho*, written by Takamatsu Toshitsugu. Private collection.

Part of the *Togakure-ryū budō hiden-sho* that deals with ninjutsu's history, the Sarutobi sasuke, Gyokko-ryū, and Kotō-ryū's school. Private collection.

## Kotengu[6]

At the age of twelve years, thanks to the training regimen, my body weight had increased considerably and, thus, my power also increased. I could, in only one blow, raise a rice bag of approximately 4 *to* (72 liters or 19 gallons).

In the dōjō, I put forth great effort and I was called Kotengu. I saw, thus, the attraction of the dōjō. Although Sensei Toda's inscription in front of the dōjō indicated that it taught *Shinden Fudō Ryū taijutsu* (神伝動流体術), Sensei Toda was an expert in *Shinden Kotō ryū tōte* (神伝虎倒流唐手)[7] and in *Togakure ryū ninjutsu* (戸隠流忍術).

At 13 years of age, after I had already studied all the techniques of *Shinden Fudō ryū*, Sensei Toda started to teach me *Kotō ryū tōte* and *Togakure ryū* ninjutsu. I preferred the practice of *tōte* to that of the ninjutsu, which hardly interested me.

With regard to ninjutsu, my principal daily exercise consisted of running vertically up a board six centimeters wide, which was positioned upright against one of the walls of the dōjō.

At that time, as it was impossible to earn one's living by teaching the techniques of combat (because of the politics of the era), so I didn't see the use in learning something like ninjutsu. But Sensei Toda, who by no means paid any attention to these arguments, didn't offer the chance for me to quit."

## Against Sixty[8]

This is another story of mine from when I was 13 years old. At that time, there were many bands of delinquents in the town of Kobe who, like nowadays, remained close to women and children with the simple aim of provoking fights with other men.

Calligraphy for "Bushin" or "Mushin," which means "warrior's thought, warrior's heart and warrior's attitude." Private collection.

One evening, as I walked along the Arima road in order to return to the religious festival of Ikuta temple, three boys from one of these bands, around the age of 17 or 18 years old, grabbed me and said: "Takamatsu, come here!"

They brought me to a vacant lot that had once been Lake Gorō and started to beat me. I do not know how, but I threw the first boy a distance of approximately two ken (approximately 3.6 meters/12 feet). The two others jumped on me and suffered the same fate. After dealing with these delinquents, I returned home.

The following night, I left with a friend to go to the public pool but the boys from the other evening ambushed us in the same vacant lot. They whistled and other members of their band also arrived. Among them, there was one who had a sword.

This one stepped forward and said: "We came to make you pay for what you did the other evening. If you do not want to fight, then get down on your knees and ask for forgiveness!" Thinking that it would be stupid to be wounded by the sword, I pretended to go down to my knees in front of him to apologize. Then, attacking them by surprise, I picked up a stone and smashed it on his foot.

He collapsed in pain and the others attacked me. One by one I threw them to the right and to the left. I don't know how many I threw, perhaps 5–8 of them. The others fled. The following morning, a senior police officer from the Kiryubashi district in Kobe was sent to bring me to the police station.

There, an officer questioned me: "Yesterday evening, at the time of a brawl, you wounded several young delinquents. How many were with you?" I answered that I fought all alone and he replied: "Do not say silly things! That miserable band was made up of 60 delinquents among of whom at least 10 were wounded!"

"I do not know how many were there, but as one of them held a sword and was dangerous, I dealt with him first. Then, I threw the others as they advanced. But as for knowing if I wounded them or not, I couldn't say."

Skeptical, the officer brought in and questioned my friend, Osaka-kun who was with me at the pool the previous evening, in order to understand more clearly what happened. But Osaka-kun attested: "It is true, there was the two of us, and I simply watched."

The officer was really astonished. Then Sensei Toda, who had learned the news, arrived and declared: "He is only 13 years old but is very gifted and has the level of a *menkyo* (免許: diploma attesting to accomplishment in the techniques of combat), so it does not matter the number of those with whom he deals!" The next morning, my name was on the first page of Kobe's newspaper, the *Kobe Shinbun*: "13 year-old *jūdō* expert easily demolishes band of 60 delinquents!"

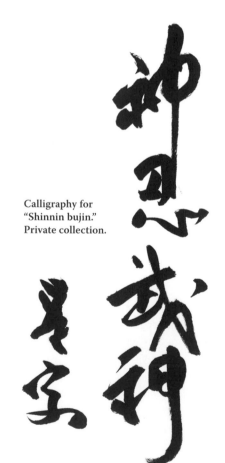

Calligraphy for "Shinnin bujin." Private collection.

## Confrontation with *Musashi-ryū*[9]

In the spring of my thirteenth year, after having finished my second year of school, I attended the English classes at an English school as well as courses in *kanbun* (traditional Chinese) at a school in Kobe.

As it was more convenient, I moved into my father's match factory in Akashi. There, I nightly attended the dōjō of Mizutani Yoshitarō Tadafusa, a master of *jūjutsu* of the *Takagi Yōshin-ryū* (高木揚心流) school.[10]

As I already had a *menkyo-kaiden* (免許皆伝: certificate of complete transmission of the knowledge of a school) of *Shinden Fudō-ryū*, after hardly one year of practice, I was taught the deep principles and secret techniques of *Takagi Yōshin-ryū*.

One day, when I was fifteen, I returned to visit Sensei Toda in his dōjō in Kobe. When I arrived, Sensei said: "You came just at the right moment! Two *bugeisha* (two experts in techniques of combat from one or more schools) of *Musashi-ryū* (武蔵流) are here to test themselves against us. Shinbō-kun takes on the first, you take the second."

Calligraphy for *"Bushidō shoshinshū."* Private collection.

Of course, I accepted and watched the first match attentively. Shinbō-kun was, at 25 years old, at peak form, and he had a *menkyō* in the school. I thought that he would not have any problem winning the match against his adversary of the *Musashi-ryū* who seemed to be 27 or 28 years old.

But the match had hardly started, when Shinbō lost on a *gyaku-otoshi* (reverse crushing throw). It was a disappointing match. I was to follow. Thinking that I was only one simple 15 year-old child, my opponent dropped his guard, and in no time I threw him and won the match with a *gyaku-nage* (reverse throw).

The next opponent was more formidable and seemed to be about 30 years old. He had observed my first match and was on his guard. For approximately 30 minutes, dripping sweat, we pushed ourselves without being able to apply a technique, and during a moment of carelessness I immediately entered for a *gyaku-dori* (reverse capture) in order to throw him. However, even though I threw him, I lost consciousness.

In fact, at the time when I threw him, he struck me on my right ear with the palm of his hand. As I had not been able to avoid this attack, my defeat seemed obvious.

My opponent came forward and said: "No, it is I who lost. He had already begun the winning throw."

He asked Sensei Toda my age. When he learned that I was 15 years old, he was astonished and declared: "If he is this skillful at 15 years, he must be very gifted. He will surely become a master."

From its origin, the principal technique of *Musashi-ryū* has been the use of a strike as one is being thrown. Once he had seen my technique, I couldn't use it against him again.

Since then, I've had a painful right ear because my tympanum was damaged. Because of this trauma, I was not allowed to take the examination for entry into the military academy, and at 21 years of age, I was excused from military service because of hearing loss.

## Techniques of *Kuki Happō Biken*[11]

When I was 17 years old, an old man by the name of Ishitani Matsutarō, who used a wooden sword as a cane, came to my father's match factory. He was a splendid *budōka*, but as it was difficult to earn a living by the teaching of *budō*, he sought other work.

My father hired him as a guard. He transformed the warehouse into a dōjō and started to teach me his vast knowledge.

This Master taught me the techniques of *Kuki happō biken*[12] (九鬼八方秘剣: the eight secret directions and orientations of the *Kuki* sword technique), that is, the techniques of bujutsu such as the shuriken, *bō-jutsu*, *ken-jutsu*, and so forth. He taught me also ninjutsu. Unfortunately, he died unexpectedly and breathed his last in my arms.

## One Year on Nourishing Brown Rice[13]

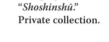

Calligraphy for *"Shoshinshū."* Private collection.

It is surely not only because of the heavy water buckets that I carried for my father (for nothing could keep me at home), that during the summer of my twenty-first year, I left the factory. I withdrew myself to Mount Maya of the town of Kobe to a place there called Kame no Taki, and lived there with only brown rice for food for one year.

During this year, I studied only new techniques that were added to the ninjutsu that I had studied up until then. In these mountains, I became acquainted with an old man whose name and appearance were completely strange to me. Was it really a man or a kind of spirit of the mountains called a *tengu*? I do not know for sure. But he taught me various things. And thus, I lived one year in the mountains of Kobe.

Realizing that I could do nothing without making some money, I decided to seek my fortune in China. I wandered between Manchuria and the north of China for ten years.

As fate would have it during this time, I engaged in combat with an expert in *Shorin-ryū* (少林流):[14] Zhang Zhu Rieu.

As the match finished on a draw, I was promoted to president of the Nihon Kokumin Seinen Butokukai (日本国民青年武徳会).[15]

My years spent in China were very turbulent, and both good and bad memories return to mind. I cut off heads fighting against gangsters, and I used Japanese ninjutsu.

Suddenly, the ninjutsu became terribly necessary, and thanks to my command of it, I acquired 200,000 yen, which represented a sizable sum at that time, and with it I left to return to Japan.

While reminiscing about these experiences, I've found that it is important to be able to measure the power as well as the attitude of the enemy who faces me. I can apply this principle to the use of the sword, to jūdō, to sumō, and to all aspects of life.

You must be able to measure your enemy instantaneously; otherwise, you will not be able to avoid the danger. Any human being, using all the senses, must be able to feel the deadly intent of an enemy.

You must be able to feel this hostility as if it were radar. If you cannot accurately detect deadly intent in others, then you do not have "the right stuff" to become a master of the techniques of combat. It is through my experiences on the path between life and death that I could sense the intent of others within my innermost being."

## Commentary

This last part of the autobiography is very interesting. We find there the basic principles on which Takamatsu will write the text *Ninjutsu no Hiketsu Bun*. This autobiography is built on the same model as that text of Takamatsu, where he relates his journey and all his experiences while he developed his practice of ninjutsu.

However, before approaching the text of Takamatsu, let us study the autobiography starting from the part that I think is at the heart of the text. This part is divided into five sections related to each other by historical events that dominated Takamatsu's psychological development.

In the first section, the author approaches his life on the mountain, a strange meeting, and his practice as a recluse. In the second section, he explains the reasons for his departure towards the Asiatic continent. The third section quickly presents one of his many fights, which remains the least bloody, and his promotion to president of the Nihon Kokumin Seinen Butokukai, (which translates to: "Grouping of Japanese youth for the techniques of combat and virtue"). The fourth section returns to his actions in China and in Manchuria and in the fifth section, he approaches, through his many experiences, the state that leads to the practice of the martial arts.

The strangest section for most Westerners is the one where he tells of his sudden meeting with a kind of hermit at Kame no Taki on Mt. Maya in *Kobe*. Takamatsu had withdrawn to the mountain for his personal practice after giving up a home that was only an illusion. He was just twenty years old, and his grandfather, Toda Shinryūken, who had made him the successor of the seven schools that he had, giving all the documents and weapons of those schools to him, had died recently.

His retirement to the mountain is to be put in parallel with the initiatory voyage of any follower of martial arts.[26] This withdrawal to the mountain, to practice and to look further into the techniques and principles of the schools, was an essential stage for the formation of Takamatsu. There is no doubt that his grandfather influenced his in this choice at the beginning of his initiation into ninjutsu.

When he had withdrawn to the mountain, Takamatsu was, at twenty years, the sōke, chief of nine schools of traditional martial arts. Seven schools came from his grandfather, one he inherited from Ishitani, *Kukishinden-ryū Happō Biken-jutsu*, and the other, *Takagi Yōshin-ryū Jūtaijutsu*, he inherited from Mizuta Yoshitarō.

The latter was taught for a long time jointly with *Kukishinden-ryū*, because, after a meeting between two masters, one of *Takagi Yōshin-ryū* and the other of *Kukishinden-ryū*, they had reduced overlapping and overrepresented techniques while improving techniques, and concepts that they felt were poorly represented and weak.

Note also that the ninja were famous for their gift of mimicry; they were able to take any technique or form they had seen and re-work it to make it more efficient and effective.

In addition, Takamatsu had begun his training in ninjutsu at a tender age and, thus, it was child's play for him to identify the weakness of a given technique or a movement and then to improve it.

That explains why the techniques of *Takagi Yōshin-ryū* and *Kukishinden-ryū* that Takamatsu transmitted to its single disciple, Hatsumi Masaaki, are different from those practiced before, when it was more of a traditional form of *jūjutsu* like many others.

As he explains it, he practiced, improved, and sharpened all that he had received from his masters and innovated new techniques. This year spent as a recluse in mountains, when he was twenty years old, was, for Takamatsu, an experience that surely affected him profoundly. However, the famous meeting with a strange hermit remains a total mystery.

Did Takamatsu want to return to the tradition that is found in the other martial art origin chronicles and romance stories that were popular during the Edo period?

On one hand, this is a geographical area associated with the ninja of Iga and Kōga who once rented their services to rival *daimyō*, and also one associated with legends concerning dangerous exiled fugitives and fearless warriors. On the other hand, this is a mountainous area, where *shugenja* and others carried out mystical and esoteric practices of *Shugendō Yamabushi*.

In other words, this is the perfect combination of ingredients for an origin account concerning a ninja and the ninjutsu of the Edo period.

On this subject, in his autobiography, he uses the following sentence to describe the strange hermit:

天狗ではないけれども...[16]
It was not a *tengu*, but . . .

In the collective imagination of the Japanese, the mountains are the places where all kinds of spirits, demons, ascetics, and, of course, ninja reside. Mystic and mystery, are words with an evil connotation.

Indeed, they are forebiding because they allude to the unknown and hidden, and are unwelcome terms to the man who hates to accept what he does not know or does not understand.

A great number of phenomena cannot be explained scientifically, even nowadays, simply because they escape commonly allowed "logic," just as the cerebral capacities of human beings as well as states like enlightenment remain a mystery to science.

Mystery and secrecy form an integral part of the essence of ninjutsu. When a man does not understand, does not perceive, then there inevitably seems to be a mystery or secrecy. In fact, it is quite simply about a lack of opening of oneself combined with a misunderstanding of what surrounds us.

Regarding the meeting with an old hermit, whom one finds in many of the origin stories of martial art schools, we can only adopt a position of neutrality. Because it is not ours to judge a 78-year-old man whose experience speaks for itself, especially since he survived the fire of war and died at the ripe old age of 85 years without ever ceasing his practice.

The reason for his departure to the Asian continent, which he explains in the second section, was money. To a 21 year old, money is vital to be able to live, especially when one has, like Takamatsu, cut ties with a family that was not much of one in the first place.

In 1909, Japan invaded Korea, and its influence overflowed into China and Manchuria, where it set up a puppet emperor, Pu' Yi, in 1932. China, Manchuria, and Korea were, at this time in the history of imperialist Japan, the destinations for many young Japanese who felt cramped and tied down in Japan, as well as adventurers and gangsters in search of fortune and glory.

These countries resembled a virtual El Dorado, where all could go and succeed. This image of the colonist who successfully settled foreign ground, of course, was advertised by a whole slew of propaganda. Thus, like a great number of other young Japanese at the time, Takamatsu embarked for the continent in order to make his fortune.

His life in Manchuria and in the north of China, where, according to another source in 1919,[17] he wandered for ten years before returning to Japan, was not peaceful. Takamatsu, when he arrived on the continent, was just one unknown among so many others, which suited him just fine, however, as this was the aim of any traditional ninja.

Indeed, nobody was aware of his physical and mental capacities, because Sensei Toda had taught him to always conceal his abilities. We find here, all the logic of ninjutsu, which always consisted of hiding power.

There is no doubt that he knew how to benefit from his knowledge. One need only turn to all the brawls and fights he had with gangsters and local "warlords," where he had to use his knowledge to survive. We have some of these anecdotes, and for the sake of completeness, I will simply say that with each time he was confronted by this kind of individual, it inevitably resulted in the death or maiming of the attacker.

Remember, Takamatsu had nine schools, each of which taught how to kill or incapacitate, and also conveyed medical knowledge about how to heal internal organs and injuries to the human skeleton.

Because of that, one sees that ninjutsu concerns two ends, namely life and death. To be able to destroy but also to have the capacity to cure–life and death are intimate aspects of the essence of ninjutsu, because it concerns survival.

The fight with a Chinese master of the *Shorin-ryū* school is very interesting because it anchors the history with corroborating details. The match was with a master who, according to another source, was an important member of the Nihon Kokumin Seinen Butokukai. The result of the fight was never in doubt, but it was stopped by one of the organizers.

The name of Master Takamatsu Toshitsugu (of the nine schools) written by his successor, Master Hasumi Masaaki. Private collection.

An instant friendship bound the two fighters and, certainly thanks to his competency in the martial arts, Takamatsu was promoted to be the president of the group, all when he was only 27 years old.

This promotion brought a lot of knowledge and support in the world of business, politics, the military, and so forth. But it also allowed him to observe the practice of other martial arts, regardless of the style or the school.

The phrase "the techniques of combat and virtue" originated from the Japanese Dai Butokukai of Kyōto, the imperial organization set up to develop the patriotic spirit through the practice of martial arts. Manchuria, as a colonized country, had the same organizations and associations as Japan.

These groups and associations allowed the Japanese colonists who practiced or taught martial arts to find each other and practice together. If the practice of martial arts were proposed, these associations and groups contributed by gathering information, spying, and, in certain cases, with the direct action.

There is no doubt that all these groups were closely associated with the espionage services of the Nakano school about which we'll speak later.

It celebrated all kinds of events that made it possible to reinforce the Japanese presence in Manchuria, as in the 1942 celebration of the tenth anniversary of the founding of the state of Mancukuo. It is on this occasion that Ueshiba Morihei (1883–1969), the founder of aikidō, carried out a demonstration in the presence of Emperor Pu' Yi.

This group was dependant on the University of Kenkoku,[18] established in Manchuria, like others, for the education of the young colonists. Tomiki Kenji (1900–1979), a pupil of Ueshiba, was there as an instructor and taught jūdō, *jūjutsu* and *aiki-budō*.

Takamatsu does not hide the fact that he performed decapitations, fought until the death of his attackers and, of course, used ninjutsu. But, he never reveals specific details in this account. Note that he had been unable to carry out his military service because he had hearing problems because of an old injury.

Thus, he did not work in an official capacity. But, he was a ninja, trained from an early age to survive and operate silently, and as he states, there came a time when the ninjutsu was in great demand. His combat experience and knowledge would bring him enough money to return to Japan.

What else could he have done? It is difficult to guess, because the truth of his 10-year tour on the continent was consigned entirely and in detail to the *Meiji Mōroku Otoko*, which he bequeathed to his successor, Hatsumi Masaaki.

That work only reveals some anecdotes and, as it reveals nothing very specific, its direct implications and its nationalist enthusiasm remain difficult to prove. Many think that Takamatsu was a spy/assassin, because the behavior of Japanese in Manchuria, in China, and elsewhere was certainly similar to that of ninja.

Ian Nish[19] reported about a study of information from a British observer, which explains why a great number of itinerant Japanese patrolled under various disguises from one end to the other of Manchuria,

*"Hiken"* means "secret sword" or "hidden sword."
Private collection.

collecting any type of information, so that when the war against Russia broke out in 1905, the Japanese state was in possession of very detailed information.

However, Takamatsu did not participate in any spy network, and it seems that his activities were limited to his own survival.

The famous school of espionage in Nakano was an establishment founded in Tokyo in 1938 to train and lead secret agents skilled in the various methods of espionage, sabotage, assassination, and sedition. It was often associated with the teaching and practice of ninjutsu.[20]

The image of the school's spies and of their training has inspired many authors to attribute a link between the school and ninjutsu. However the differences between the curriculum of the spy school in Nakano and ninjutsu are manifold.

Indeed, ninja, in the true sense of the term, always acted without any external influence, led only by their own convictions. They operated without any net or cover and managed even the most extreme situations without the assistance of anybody.

The center for training these agents was established in 1944 in Futamata.[21] Many were trained and sent to the Pacific Islands that had been captured by American soldiers, where they were to continue the fight.

Some were deployed throughout Japan in various places, in preparation for an enemy invasion. The documents related to the Nakano school were always burned, and all the agents went "underground" before and after committing their activities.

One may point tellingly to the agent's use of ninja methodologies, but keep in mind that any spy organization uses these types of methods.

In the autobiography of Hirō Onoda, a soldier in the Second World War who remained hidden in the island jungle of Lubang until 1974 when he was found by the American army and was returned to Japan, we have a good example of the training given by the school of Nakano in Futamata relating to the methods used by certain specialized intelligence and espionage units:

> ...The training given to us was very different from that given to officers, where, one was taught not to think but rather to lead troops in the battle, and if necessary to die there. Their sole purpose was to attack enemy troops and to kill as many as possible before being killed themselves. But in Futamata, our goal was to survive and to continue the guerilla warfare as long as possible, even if that led to outrageous conduct.[22]

This might suggest the practice of ninjutsu, but it is a false lead. The training of spies on this large scale and in record time (particularly after the attack of Pearl Harbor on December 7, 1941) is contrary to the principles of ninjutsu.

In contrast, the teachings of ninjutsu are addressed only to one single heir. In addition, the teaching at the school was primarily geared toward spying: the techniques of information gathering, misinformation and infiltration. When the techniques of combat were studied, they accompanied the ordinary military service and they covered ordinary techniques of *jūken-jutsu* (bayonet), karate, jūdō and in certain cases, *jūjutsu*.[23]

In the same chapter, Onoda explains the details of their actions, which bore a striking similarity to what one finds in the teaching of Sun Zi:

> . . . We were taught that it was not a disaster to be made a prisoner. When made prisoner, we understood that we were in a good position to feed false information to the enemy.
>
> On certain occasions, we actually allowed ourselves to get captured deliberately... Only our colleagues (at the Nakano school) knew that we were engaged in a secret war. We endured the taunts of the other soldiers as best we could.
>
> Almost no one was aware of what we did for our country. Such is the fate of those engaged in the secret war.[24]

We cannot say if, like Onoda, Takamatsu was an unwavering patriot. Contrary to Onoda, who acted towards the victory of "Greater Japan" and put aside the need for money, Takamatsu makes no secret of his motivations and convictions.

Takamatsu did not undergo intensive military training in any military school nor did he get preparation at the Nakano school, where it was necessary to become an officer to enter. With regard to the motivations that drove Onoda, he exposes the "philosophy" of the teachings put forth by the Nakano school for us:

> In what do those who engage in this type of war put their hopes?
>
> At the Nakano school, one answered this question with this simple answer: in a secret war, integrity is what's important.
>
> That is true, integrity is what is most necessary for a man when he has to deceive not only his enemies but also his friends. Integrity, with which I included sincerity, honesty, a sense of the duty as well as a sense of the morality that enables us to face the tests and to surmount them and finally to be victorious.[25]

This combat "philosophy" can be related to the essence of ninjutsu in the sense that it is a question of keeping to one's own convictions and fighting for them. But given the situation in which Japan found itself, one rather acts more out of a nationalist indoctrination than anything else.

Let us not forget that the Nakano school was built in 1938 during a period when Japan was deeply touched by the militarism coupled with rampant nationalism. Takamatsu returned to Japan in 1919, well before the Manchurian incident and the desire for independence by those colonized. Why?

He does not mention the reason. Once back in Japan, he withdrew to the town of Kashihara in the Nara prefecture, where he opened an inn and a restaurant, Maru no Ichi (丸の一). According to Hatsumi Masaaki, his successor, when he returned to Japan, Takamatsu was at the head of a circle of practice, the *Shobu kyoku*, but, like any ninja, he hardly spoke about his practice and his real qualifications.[26]

Takamatsu never publically taught his practice, especially on his return to Japan, where disciplines like jūdō, karate, and *Ueshiba-ryū* developed and were an instant success.

The teachings received by Takamatsu focused on immediate results; he could not open his school or teach ninjutsu to the public without changing the essence of the pragmatic practice that is ninjutsu.

Far from the capital, he was a complete stranger and as a ninja, he did not seek to draw attention to himself. Hatsumi Masaaki adds that the woman and the children did not even know about the number of schools of combat and the real value of Takamatsu. It is not surprising that a practitioner of ninjutsu at that time knew that discretion was synonymous with survival. Of course, Takamatsu met many people eager to learn and receive diplomas, *densho*, *makimono* and other *menkyo kaiden*.

The practicioners Iwami Nangaku, Kimura Masaji, and Akimoto Fumio, of the Shobu kyoku group, which aimed to promote the techniques of the Kuki family, practiced with him for a time and accepted their diplomas. But to practice for a time, to attend for a time does not mean a lifelong commitment, let alone being chosen by Takamatsu to be his successor.

Also, what was the nature of the relationships with these passing disciples? Were they also deep and close friendships like the relationship that bound Takamtasu to his grandfather and master, Sensei Toda, or the one he had with Sensei Ishitani?

Sensei Takamatsu was a ninja trained in the deep culture of body and mind that leaves no room for compromise. The relationship between master and disciple was to be of the same nature as that demanded by the practice of ninjutsu, that is, one master and an exclusive practice.

Thus, one understands well why Takamatsu offered many manuscripts and other valuable documents to people eager for a title. Art requires sincerity, as everyone knows.

However, the master always tests this sincerity, and above all, it is tested by *time*. Because to be sincere one day, two days, two years, five years, that is nothing in the practice ninjutsu, and Sensei Takamatsu was fully aware of that. It is about a sincerity that comes with the continuity of the practice.

The signature, the seal, the stamp, or having the *densho* or other documents of Takamatsu do not mean anything without the practical knowledge and especially the life experience.

Thus the *kuden*, *shinden* and *taiden* cannot be enrolled without having had a previous intimate experience of this transmission through the exchange with the master and the personal practice.

To receive the immense knowledge of Takamatsu, it was necessary to forget. To forget what one had learned, to be a virgin, unpolluted by other practices so that the mind and body are imbued with ninjutsu. Because ninjutsu is like a precious fluid, it is offered to only one single container.

Thus, for Takamatsu, one could not be a person seeking to pad their martial curriculum vitae; one had to be a disciple who was not afraid to start all over again and get rid of all past knowledge (in other words, to be an individual willing to learn to unlearn).

Among the people claiming to be authentic disciples of Takamatsu are found the late Ueno Takashi and Sato Kinbei.

Master Takamatsu teaching the *shuriken-jutsu* to Hatsumi Masaaki. Private collection.

Master Takamatsu teaching how to control the *sankejo* (wrist lock technique) to Hatsumi Masaaki.

Both were well known in Japan; they were part of a group called the *Kenyukai* (拳友会), where practitioners of high rank gathered to practice together. Famous names like those of Kenwa Mabuni (*shitō-ryū*), and Miyamoto Hanzō (*Tenshin shinyō-ryū*) appeared in it. All the techniques practiced were carefully noted in writing.

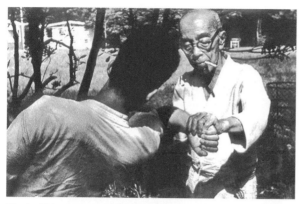

Master Takamatsu teaching how to control the *sankejo* (wrist lock technique) to Hatsumi Masaaki.

Master Takamatsu demonstrating the *uke waza*.

Master Takamatsu demonstrating the art of *naginata* and *bisento* in his home.

Master Takamatsu and his disciple, Hatsumi Masaaki, in the front of Takamatsu's restaurant, the Maru no Ichi.

Apart from the documents and diplomas sent through the mail, there was no evidence of an authentic encounter between Takamatsu and Takashi Ueno and Sato Kinbei—not even one photograph in the company of Takamatsu or his family.

However, when one studies, on the one hand, the impressive technical curriculum of the latter, and on the other hand, the number of photographs that Ueno and Sato Kinbei have with various masters of extinct Chinese martial arts, one can only remain skeptical about the nature of their relationship and of their meeting with Takamatsu. Of course, there will be always somebody who says that everything was burned in a fire or that that the evidence was stolen . . . so there is no tangible proof on their side.

But one can always find evidence to the contrary. For example, at the time of Sensei Takamatsu's funeral, none the people mentioned above were present in the photographs of the event.

If he has a relationship with a master, whatever it is, and especially with a master of Takamatsu's caliber, how is it that the disciple or the so-called successor is not present at teacher's funeral? Hatsumi Masaaki was the only one there throughout the whole funeral, from beginning to end and even after the end. . . .

Once again, there is always a master and a practice. The master is master for life. Takamatsu was master through this principle because he was a ninja. This principle is inherent in all the disciplines of *budō*, *bujutsu*, *kōryū*, *Nō*, *kabuki*, dance, *sadō* (tea ceremony), *shodō*, and so on.

**Master Takamatsu demonstrating the** *kuji kiri*. **This photograph shows how his fingers were extraordinarily conditioned during his lifetime.**

To break with that tradition is to break with one's roots and, of course, to close the door that was opened by the former masters and their knowledge.

Of course, Takamatsu had three masters, but in succession. Moreover, it is necessary for us to understand that Takamatsu is included in a very special category of master.

He belongs to those who one names the *denshosha* (伝書者), that is, a person who will be the prism in which an incredible amount of knowledge and technical ability will converge. He became the holder of a knowledge that must be protected and transmited to the person who will be elected to be the next *denshosha*. That shows how truly rare real ninja were in the true sense of the word, and that the *jōnin* (上 忍)[27] were very precious indeed.

In the same manner, in *Asayama Ichiden-ryū taijutsu* (浅山一伝流体術)[28], Okura was the "prism" of this school. We met the Sakai family whose grandfather was the only pupil of Okura and who have the *chi no maki* (地之巻) written by the hand of Okura.

At the funeral of Takamatsu on April 2, 1972 in Kashihara, all the people who knew him, from near and far, were surprised to learn that he was a ninja and also the head of nine schools. Takamatsu, being disciplined in ninjutsu from childhood, had withheld the true state of his knowledge and abilities in accordance with ninja ideals.

**Master Takamatsu demonstrating the** *kosshi-jutsu* **and** *koppo-jutsu suwari gata* **in his home. Private collection.**

# CHAPTER 6

# The Secret Text of Ninjutsu[1]

In the early 1960s, the encounter with his future successor, Hatsumi Masaaki, marks a watershed moment in the life of Takamatsu. He finally found someone worthy to succeed him as head of the nine schools. At the request of Hatsumi, Takamatsu, at seventy years of age, would put in writing the technical and psychological concepts of ninjutsu.

I believe that it is around this time that he wrote the *Ninjutsu no Hiketsu Bun*, but it is not certain. The autobiography that I presented was written around the time he was 68 years old.

A little earlier, a 30-minute long 8mm film was recorded by Hatsumi during a training session in Kashihara, showing the then 65 year old master executing armed and unarmed techniques with a grace quite surprising for his age.

In 1969, three years before his death, he made Hastumi his sole successor, giving all the documents of transmission to him, as well as all the weapons of the nine schools, which represents a considerable historical and technical heritage. Included among the scrolls was the one containing the *Ninjutsu no Hiketsu Bun*.

As mentioned, the text that we present in this book represents only part of the original text where various subjects like medicine, religion, faith, the Buddha, and the kami are discussed. The scroll on which the text is written measures 1.8 meters (6 feet) in length and is approximately 45 centimeters (18 inches) wide. It is covered with a green velvet fabric sheath with gold stripes. On it is affixed a vertically oriented label where the words "*Ninjutsu no Hiketsu Bun*" (Secret Text of Ninjutsu) are written. A thin cord binds the scroll, and one wraps it around the manuscript to close it. To open it, one simply withdraws the fine cord to let the scroll unroll to its full length.

The text starts with the following inscription:

of Takamatsu Toshitsugu Yokuō thirty-third sōke, to Hatsumi Masaaki 34th sōke.

A blank space appears following the name of Hatsumi Masaaki, so that he may write the name of his successor if he finds one. In the photocopy of the document that we have, a date does not appear there, so it is difficult to pin down the date that the text was written.

As is typical of traditional Japanese paper, the document is a little yellowed. The same handwriting is used throughout. The author's style of writing is cursive, and the characters are, at certain points in the text, almost illegible. The penmanship is very beautiful and testifies to the character of the author and his control of the brush.

This is not a text written in *kanbun* (classical Chinese), but rather uses grammatical forms such as *nari* and *beshi*, which suggests that the classical language was used to lend a solemn tone to the author's words. The text does not pose major difficulties for translation; however, the interpretation is a different matter.

With regard to this study, there are two parts. The author adopts a logical tone from the start, which is reminiscent of his autobiography.

Indeed, he begins with discipline and training, followed by his experiences and examples that illustrate his remarks. The reader is left with, according to the author, the ultimate goal of ninjutsu.

In the text, Takamatsu's desire is to get across the deeper meaning of this practice called ninjutsu. This is also illustrated through his life experiences, which were recorded like those of the successors of each school before him.

The first part discusses the mental state required for the practice of ninjutsu and how it applies to various human actions. The second part discusses what will emerge from the practice of ninjutsu when it is carried out with the proper state of mind coupled with a period of profound introspection; a sort of enlightenment that is not unlike a religious experience.

Here I present the text in this English version directly translated from the Japanese without omitting with the profundities that were so important to Takamatsu.

## *Ninjutsu no Hiketsu-bun* (Secret Text of Ninjutsu)[42]

The way of combat and military strategy consists in protecting the body. The essence of this protection lies in ninjutsu, because ninjutsu also aims to protect the mind of the practitioner. In other words, when the mind is not engaged in the practice of the way of combat, sometimes death is the result.

For example, we say that medicine is the way to save life, but if medicine is used improperly, it becomes a poison. Food and drinks are used for the development of life. But to drink and eat in excess destroys the body.

Similarly, the mission of politicians must be to protect the people and to govern the country correctly. However, when politicians become power-hungry, ignorant, and cowardly, they sow confusion across the land and torment its people.

The same concept applies to religion. When it is based on sincerity and truth, the faithful are protected, the families thrive, and the community benefits from it. However, when it goes down a bad path, it then brings destruction to the people and jeopardizes the state.

This is why when a master of martial arts [a *budōka*] practices ninjutsu, he can gains access to its important hidden knowledge. The essence of this secret is the spirit and the Divine eye.

In other words, it is necessary to understand ninjutsu as knowledge of the Celestial Way.

What one calls the sincerity of Heaven is a righteous thing without any malice. This principle, which one finds at the same time in Heaven and in man, is unique. For example, the five phases cannot be generated without the earth, just as by the action of the interposed periods (*doyō*), the four seasons move. Then, when there is no doyō for the four seasons or there is no earth for the five phases, it is like Heaven devoid of sincerity.

When a person is motivated by a sense of justice and genuine sincerity, then he conforms to the Celestial Way. And, when he is conforms to the Celestial Way, then he satisfies the Purpose of Heaven. Herein lies the spirit and the Divine eye. That is why the ninja must be a person who knows justice.

I call ninjutsu the art of awareness. Thus, always at peace, the ninja does not know surprise. Such is the practical philosophy of *Togakure-ryū*.

Takamatsu Toshitsugu Yokuō thirty-third successor of *Togakure-ryū Ninpō*.

## Commentary

The first four sentences of the text set the tone for the entire passage. Ninjutsu is, according to Takamatsu, the practice that makes it possible to protect the body and the mind and which extends to all military sciences and strategies. Thereby he says that a correct practice maintains the body and, thus, the mind.

Indeed, we must consider the fact that in ninjutsu, physical training is done in harmony with mental training. However, how can one avoid the mental and physical after-effects of combat training?

From his experience and his own practice, which came from the teachings of his masters and the successors of each school, Takamatsu concludes that the control of the mind goes hand in hand with physical discipline that borders on asceticism. Indeed, the body is the vehicle that makes it possible to control the mental element through physical training.

This practice is present in all combat practices throughout the world, but in Japan, with the appearance of the concept of "道: *dō*" during the period of Edo and its crystallization in Meiji, this mental discipline through the practice of the combat was developed at the highest level. In ninjutsu, for Takamatsu, this concept is of primary importance.

In the majority of the practices known as "martial arts" or combat sports that were created in the Meiji period (1868–1912) and restructured after the Second World War under the influence of occupying troops, the practitioner's upper age range typically falls around the age of forty. Why?

It is because the practice of martial arts, such as jūdō, karate, kendō, and the like, was built around movements intended for physical education. One inevitably reaches a certain age when these movements can no longer be performed comfortably. These movements, which condition the behavior of the individual, are unsuited to natural human biomechanics.

The forms are rigid and lack flexibility. Long-term practice causes frequent injuries such as osteoarthritis, fractures, joint problems, and other injuries.

For example, if the practice is composed of rigid, jerky, inflexible movements that demand great physical force, the body, which consists mainly of water, will wear out little by little as its members weaken.

In Japan, as in other countries, many leading practitioners have noted with concern the early cessation of practice as well as the obvious bodily after-effects.

Indeed, it is true that most of the Okinawan masters who created the principal styles of karate died at relatively young ages, when typically one advances and increases in skill into the ninth decade of life, like Uehara Sekichi of the *Motobu-ryū Udonti* (本 部御殿手).[2]

Karate is a practice of exaggerated movements that do not conform to the natural shape of the body and that imposes a rigid form and little flexibility. The unnatural hardening of metacarpus and phalanges as well as other parts of the body, not to mention the excessive sparring, is harmful to the body, and causes long-term decalcification of bone marrow.

Currently, in the United States, Japan, and the rest of the world, it is not uncommon to see a great number of injuries in high-level martial arts experts, which prevent any possibility of further progression.

In jūdō and in aikidō, the injuries are similar; they generally relate to the back and the joints, which are stressed during falls. This shows that the practice is misguided and, therefore, unwelcome.

Additionally, the legacy of the practice is often mental disorders that are difficult to categorize. Just look at the trauma caused by repeated blows on the body or head in boxing.

It is during this period of practice that spiritual search is generally felt. After sustaining successive injuries, the practitioner begins to question the nature of the practice and seeks a solution. It is the beginning of the opening of oneself and the search for peace of mind through natural movement that is not harmful in the long run.

In general, the practice of martial arts is exhausting, and the example of Takamatsu in his autobiography shows it well. As a child, he underwent hard discipline inflicted by his grandfather. However, as a long-term practice, the principle of energy regulation must prevail. This energy regulation goes hand in hand with learning the movements that allow for flexibility in the body. One of the basic tenets of ninjutsu is flexibility, which allows for adaptation to all situations.

Indeed, the ninja could cleverly liquidate its enemies thanks to an emphasis on adaptation. It is true that in ninjutsu, the adept must work to gain strength as they age, being careful not to lose flexibility.

Although it is unlikely that Takamatsu paid much attention to his health in his youth, once he reached a certain age, he understood that this component was essential to the practice.

Note, however, that Takamatsu followed the training of his grandfather, Toda Shinryūken, a descendant of a ninja family. The techniques of ninjutsu that were taught to him, for instance, not imposing a predetermined form in order to be as natural as possible and not getting locked into a rigid dogma, had in themselves the underlying theme of belonging an art that's practice was designed to promote survival and longevity.

It is evident that the practice that he underwent in his youth and the deprivations he experienced when he lived in the mountains certainly strengthened Takamatsu right up to the end of his life.

The beginning of his biography where he explains that he can easily traverse 4 km (2.5 miles) in 30 minutes even at the age of 78 is the proof of his hardiness. Add to that how, until Takamatsu's death at the age of 82, he continued to teach to his successor.

> . . . Ninjutsu also aims to protect the mind of the practitioner. In other words, when the mind is not engaged in the practice of the way of combat, sometimes death is the result.

Into these two sentences, Takamatsu implicitly introduces the necessity of having a proper mental attitude.

The practice is violent and could really be deadly for those who did not follow the correct teaching–especially if the practitioner approached the art with the wrong mindset.

According to Takamatsu, the practice of ninjutsu protects the mind, that is to say, it is not harmful to the spirit and it protects the body as well. But, the meaning goes deeper. Ninjutsu involves a spiritual quest, making its practice much more introspective than a simple military education concerning the techniques of combat.

In most schools of combat, and in the practice of various martial arts that have emerged recently, one finds a regimen that makes it possible to develop a strong body and "the mind of a warrior." However, these programs often prove harmful for the body and the spirit.

We generally notice only external wounds on the body, but what of the "wounds of the spirit," the mental strains that go unnoticed? In ninjutsu, it is patience that protects the mind and the body.

Every physical and mental detail is meticulously polished through self-study and independent practice, while at the same time immersing oneself in an introspective spiritual quest. To protect the body and the mind of the practitioner requires more than just a range of techniques, various combat strategies, and philosophical concepts borrowed from here and there.

Only an unceasing practice, coupled with deep introspection, makes it possible to acquire the patience that, in turn, makes it possible to protect the mind and the body.

It is this patience that leads to clarity of the senses, the correct functioning of which protects of the life of the practitioner. Developing patience takes time, often resignation, but especially faith, which makes it possible to persevere.

The protection about which Takamatsu speaks in his text is against oneself, that is, against all excess, physical and mental. It is in this sense that Takamatsu explains that without the proper mental attitude, without uprightness, the practice is unfair and, therefore, allows the mind of the practitioner to become vulnerable to various dangers. The state of mind as well as personal motivations and beliefs are the driving force behind every practice.

Just let us not forget that the master, at the creation of the school, transmitted his knowledge to the worthiest pupil. That implies a deep confidence and, thus, an endorsement of a certain perceived "purity" in the motivations and convictions of the disciple. Indeed, though a great many would relish possessing such power, each master knew that he could not widely distribute such dangerous knowledge without it leading to great loss of life. Therefore, there was only one heir. The continuity of the initiatory chain of masters with disciples until Takamatsu, and now Hatsumi Masaaki, testifies to this.

Ninjutsu is a science of combat where life and death are intimately linked. One should not expose his life to mortal danger lightly. Thus, the significance of life that hangs in the balance is realized through just acts and right intentions.

It is important to exercise patience so that you may know when and how to act, and make the wisest choice possible, because all actions have consequences. Lethal actions should not be taken lightly, on an impulse, or as an emotional reaction.

The proper state of mind allows for patience, which in turn will make it possible to act at the at the best time. Thanks to his practice in ninjutsu, Takamatsu survived many brawls, many fights, and yet he still avoided many others. He patiently weighed when and where it was necessary to act, and for which reasons.

Indeed, the knowledge that he possessed could not be used under the influence of a sudden desire; it was necessary for him to always exercise restraint in order to avoid disaster. Understanding and subduing his own ego enabled him to understand his adversaries and sense when they would act. In this way he was able to avoid confrontations. And when he had no other choice, he chose to survive.

It is through self-denial that he honed his senses, as he grappled with a reality that changed him profoundly.

On this subject, Antara, mystical poet and soldier who lived during the end of 6th and the beginning of the 7th centuries, taught his son the following:

> . . . war sharpens the senses, strengthens the will, improves the body, and swiftly brings combatants into close combat. It is there where one can find the measure of a man.[3]

As I explained in Chapter 4, "The Essence of Ninjutsu," it is when a man is directly confronted with a harsh reality, like war or fighting, as well as asceticism, that a profound change takes place.

Of course, not everyone will benefit from this experience; some will go insane; others will suppress the memory of the experience, and it will return to haunt them. It is in the crucible of this experience, in the center of this reality, that the convictions, the faith of the individual will know a moment of truth that will make it possible to reveal their righteousness, if such righteousness exists.

The word righteousness contains the notion of rectifying, correcting, adjusting, and the like. Takamatsu understood the concept of righteousness, which leads to a fair spirit and self-correction. In other words, to rectify what is not natural in us—our inner threat.

During the Pacific War and other bloody conflicts, many soldiers became intimately familiar with Takamatsu's vision of the stark reality of war and the shifting winds of fortune. But as mentioned previously, most became physically and psychologically affected or, given the horror of the situation, some even deeply suppressed the memory of those terrible moments spent under fire of the opposing army.

In his book *The Thin Red Line*,[4] a James Jones, former U.S. Marine who fought at Guadalcanal in 1943, recounts the wartime experiences of several of his comrades, most of whom died in combat. Deeply indoctrinated, they fought for the ideal of freedom, and later, when they arrived at the front, they realized that they had to kill or die. Aghast, and unnerved, they lost part of themselves.

It is in this morbid atmosphere, where death confronts the individual, that something else is born from the depths within after idealism and bravado are extinguished. James reports that after having felt that, after having lost oneself completely, one becomes aware of the value of life. Many turned to religion and faith to overcome war's horror. Faith enabled them to withstand and endure the war.

It is difficult to conceive of the suffering of others without actually having felt it oneself, according to Jones. However, the difference with the soldiers of Jones' book lies in practice. Takamatsu was involved from his youth with highly effective martial arts, even though he had not experienced the battlefront. Despite his martial experience, Takamatsu's introduction to warfare at such a tender age engendered the same feelings to him as it did to the soldiers in Joyce's book.

The terrible experiences of the struggle to stay alive as well as the ups and downs of a hard-knock life, made it possible for Takamatsu to feel this state of self-loss.

Takamatsu was already predisposed to feel this state through the practice of ninjutsu, in which he had to constantly exercise the essential qualities of patience and perseverance. Indeed, ninjutsu is a practice dedicated to emotional control, that is, to fight without telegraphing intent, which requires a certain level of mental fitness that is not easily attained.

Let me stress that the ninja of old were displaced warriors who had survived painful experiences in war. In developing ninjutsu, and by devoting body and soul to it, they sought to avoid more of this type of experience and, thus, at least a few of them became ninja.

Because they had once experienced defeat on the battlefield, the ninja knew a death of sorts and, thus, were "reborn." Because of this, the introspective ninja was able to analyze his actions and behavior in order to avoid repeating the mistakes of the past. From there, is the ninja was more open and had an early awareness of the first hints of a battle, a threat, a disease, or the like. well before they become life-threatening.

Harsh, dog-eat-dog reality certainly left its mark on Takamatsu. Twenty-five years old at the time when he was in China and Manchuria, he was surely well aware of all the evils of the colonies.

The Japanese colonists were not all cut from the same cloth, that is, they did not all behave as crude racists, as was the case of some in Korea, the Philippines, and the like.

However, as he says himself, he thoughts were of survival and his primary goal was, without any doubt, to grow rich by selling his services.

But what use is uprightness of spirit in a practice such as the ninjutsu where "survival by any means" is the watchword? Survival is not a sport, and no one is keeping score.

Uprightness of spirit applies to various fields like medicine, religion, and politics, where it is necessary to first be able to cure one's own diseases. To know how to care for the body and mind, to understand the workings of a policy failure or how to govern cultivates a sincere heart through practice, which at the very least requires vigilance.

It all begins with the heart of the individual, because if personal demons are not conquered first, it is difficult to undertake another endeavor without killing, wounding, misleading, and so forth.

It is in that sense that Takamatsu counseled students to start with a sincere heart; everything that follows will also be sincere and straight. It is a question of applying one's interior world to that which lies outside.

This is equivalent to the application of sword strategy that both Miyamoto Musashi (1584–1650)[5] and Yagyū Munenori (1571–1646)[6] taught in their writings. Through intense practice with the sword and fighting techniques, they had arrived at a level where they could apply their knowledge to various fields that required deep personal commitment.

The experience taken from their deep involvement in the way of the sword was compatible with everything that was related to self-discipline. Munenori, unlike Musashi, really applied his practice in the form of political savvy by assuming the important position of instructor to the shōgun, which he occupied during the Edo.

We find this application in jūdō, where Kanō preached that the "way" was a unified concept, and that when one educated the body and the spirit through jūdō, the way of the flexibility, one could apply the principles to any field. But when one looks at what has become of modern jūdō, one can only question if the application of the way of flexibility to any situation in life really exists in the current practice.

However, ninjutsu is distinguished by that the way that it remains unchanged and how the essence of this practice judiciously mixes spiritual and physical components. With the technical arsenal of ninjutsu being very dangerous, only one heir—with the necessary spiritual qualities—was needed to guarantee the continuation of art in future generations to come.

The fact that Takamatsu was the last ninja in a long, uninterrupted tradition transmitted from master to disciple shows that he had something extraordinary in his heart. It was surely righteousness.

In the tribulations that he knew, Takamatsu bore witness to many things that left an impression on his heart. During his travels, he was often without medicine and food. He was certainly familiar with the plight of the less fortunate in contrast with the affluence of others, and the lack of sincerity in many.

In the same way that bitterness can cause disorders of the body and the spirit, ignorance, excess, and avarice can also be harmful to both the individual and those close by. It is in this sense that uprightness should be understood, and thus the righteousness of spirit in the practice of ninjutsu; that is, the invisible substance that brings meaning to the life of the practitioner. And if this uprightness is beneficial to the practitioner, by extension, it will also be to everything that surrounds the one who is devoted to it.

> This is why when a master of martial arts [a *budōka*] practices ninjutsu, he can gains access to its important hidden knowledge. The essence of this secret is the spirit and the Divine eye.

These two sentences mark the transition to the second part. The author discusses secrecy and thus the essence of ninjutsu. The speech of Takamatsu blends with that of religious discourse. After having experienced so much conflict, often deadly, to be drawn to religion is logical, especially when death is approaching. Let us note that Takamatsu uses the term of *tatsujin* (達人: the man who achieves a certain level of skill), which I translated as "master."

He explains why the practice of ninjutsu is not for everyone but only the most elite; one must already be a master to approach the practice of ninjutsu. This also suggests that to understand the history and essence of ninjutsu, it is necessary to already understand the history and essence of other fighting techniques, whether they are Japanese or not.

More importantly, this shows that is it necessary to have an open mind, and to be able to accept the history and the characteristics of other disciplines, and thus other individuals, in order to understand them.

It is a matter of relinquishing prejudices, because in practicing combat techniques, having prejudice is synonymous with over confidence (in one's technique and knowledge), and this prevents one from understanding and adapting to an evolving situation.

Therefore, it is necessary first to be an expert in combat techniques, after which there is a remote possibility, probably one in a hundred, that one may even ascertain the principal secret insight that the practice of ninjutsu brings. But how should we define knowledge of "the spirit and the Divine eye?"

For Takamatsu, does this text represent the ultimate state that the practice of ninjutsu makes it possible to achieve?

Or is it that in the past, ninjutsu was a practice where, through the erasure of self, it was possible to foresee and respond to danger before it occurred?

The mystical component attributed to the ninja of the Edo period surely existed long ago. Indeed, because ninjutsu is a "wild" practice, being born of a natural environment, this return to the "primordial nature" is logical for the spirit of Takamatsu. Thus, it is easy to believe that certain historical ninja were very religious and had succeeded in balancing pragmatic, survival-oriented practice with religious asceticism. Of course, there always were excesses: pseudo-practitioners, insignificant warriors, robbers, gangsters, and the like, who, under cover of black clothing, acted in their own interests. The reputation of the ninja was used to cover a multitude of sins. History abounds with examples of this kind, but should we condemn the art itself because of a few men who were unaware of its true teachings and used it for their own ends?

During my last stay in Japan, I asked Sōke Hatsumi Masaaki about the problem posed by attempting to translate and understand the phrase: "the Spirit and the Divine eye" (神心神眼). I sought clarification because the concept of "divinity" in Japan is different from that preached by the monotheistic religions with which I am more familiar.

He answered that the implications of the remarks of his predecessor were not limited to Japan or any Asian religious dogma, but rather had to do with the scope of the practice of the ninjutsu, unbound and free of dogma. By "the Spirit and the Divine eye" he was referring to a singular, high principle.

Hence the choice of a capital letter for the translation. This interpretation seems plausible, because when one looks at the combat techniques of ninjutsu, one realizes immediately that it is fluid, flexible, and adaptable. This principle of "formlessness" calls for a certain state of consciousness where the body and the spirit are one.

This state brings one closer to that which certain mystics attain while erasing their ego through gradual and profound combat against the same.

To arrive at this state, they had the ability to feel and perceive things and be in harmony with nature. Fusion with nature, the quest for harmony, and the detachment of the ego is not restricted to esoteric Buddhism, Zen, and the like. One also finds it in monotheistic and Gnostic religions.

One finds this idea of introspection in sword practice during the Edo era. It is during this period that the state of the war changed. Because the incidences of large-scale battles were decreasing, the goal of the practice adapted to, and coexisted with, Confucian ethics and spiritual practices resulting from various religions like Zen, esoteric Buddhism, and others.

The way of the combat being open to interpretation, a concept evolved in certain martial circles where, rather than to try to kill an enemy, one tried to simultaneously avoid dealing an injury and avoid being a victim. This school of thought reached a high level of development with certain followers.

In several cases, like that of Yagyū Munenori who jointly practiced *kenjutsu* and Zen Buddhism, there was a kind of fusion between the art of the sword and Buddhist thought. One could suppose that ninjutsu also had similar examples.

However, the technical teachings and the essence of ninjutsu did *not* undergo this modification. The practice remains pragmatic and its applications as deadly as ever, which explains the exceptional level of Takamatsu, and that of his successor, Hatsumi Masaaki, who is able to administer extreme pain and even death, without hesitation.

As with a surgeon, precision is paramount, and thus the self-knowledge is infinitely deep. The ninja deals with the fine details of life and death. This part of the text is a beautiful example of "spiritual transformation." The question is: how does one arrive at this point?

Like all the techniques of combat in the world, ninjutsu is concerned with situations where the outcome is either life or death. For those involved, the paramount concern is determining if they will survive or not.

Like Takamatsu, many masters exposed themselves to danger and violence to master combat techniques, and ultimately arrived at a solution that contradicted their original destination.

They all discovered that they had actually committed to a spiritual or religious endeavor. All religions speak of the high value of human life. Based on this, they try to give us confidence in the face of the death that we must all someday experience.

However ninjutsu is, in essence, a science of survival based on the experience of the "death," which rises from defeat and thus brings rebirth. One who survived by avoiding the many internal threats to his being (understood as those caused by his ego) was then entitled to be a ninja.

For this reason, we see that ninjutsu represents an extreme. If, like Takamatsu, one reaches a deeper understanding of oneself through fighting techniques and by unreserved spiritual devotion, then everything changes. The practice of combat techniques becomes a "religious" practice.

Ueshiba Morihei (1883–1969), a contemporary of Takamatsu, had the same type of spiritual experience. However, he did not hide his ties to *Omoto-kyo* (a Shinto-based religion). It is reported that he often said, "*Budō* is love." He also witnessed the terrors of combat.

From experience, Takamatsu reports that in a real struggle, as in the fight against one's ego, we are always on "the edge of the blade." The spirit faces daily challenges from the practice of asceticism, which is employed to subdue undesirable behavior patterns. One needs to have a certain philosophy in order to keep internally balanced and at peace.

For this reason a kind of religious attitude is required, in the same way that through fear and pain on the battlefield, the deepest beliefs resurface to bring courage to the combatants. The techniques of ninjutsu are concrete. They use deception, illusion and other techniques to determine the outcome of combat.

But the technique is not an absolute thing; it is relative because it can, with daily practice, be controlled and be applied by anyone. All the same, let me add that ninjutsu techniques remain special and unique. Of course, some principles are common to all the world's combat practices, but it is in their application and practice that the difference dwells.

The art of predicting and neutralizing threats remains at the heart of ninjutsu. Ultimately, to sense and predict danger, and to avoid being taken by surprise are the conclusions to which the scroll's author leads. But, Takamatsu was not limited to a simplistic definition of "surprise."

More profoundly, a ninja can sidestep an enemy's element of surprise by rooting himself in nature and his basic principles. By doing so, he is only responsible to the higher authority that is within, and thereby he enters into unity with totality. In so doing the ninja is no longer taken by surprise by the random events of history and the fickle whims of men.

To the ninja who empties his mind, the unforeseen no longer exists because he does not presuppose. In the same way, one is physically most flexible when relaxed and free of tension. Consider the flexibility of the bamboo; which is attributable to its empty interior. Likewise, when we are open, we are sensitive to all things, in any situation.

This place where one feels unity with nature even in one's slightest gestures implies the extinguishing of one's own desires and, thus, the ego. This place cannot be reached without sincerity and rectitude of the soul. It inevitably implies a unity between the body and the spirit that can only be obtained by a practice that leads to the abandonment of the self.

The treatment where Takamatsu refers to nature with words like the "Celestial Way," recalls the famous saying "Wherever you turn is the Face of God." It is certainly a simplistic interpretation, but it remains in the reality of what Takamatsu wanted to convey in his text.

The place of all things, whether they are of a spiritual nature, natural, or human, cannot be reached by a person who has no zeal for justice. When the balance between the spirit and the body is broken, then the balance of one's harmony with the Celestial Way and Heavenly Intention and all that depends on it is broken.

Justice serves then, according to Takamatsu, to restore this vital balance for the ninja as it does for all humanity. He refers to a universal justice, which is not restricted to Japan.

> I call ninjutsu the art of awareness. Thus, always at peace, the ninja does not know surprise. Such is the practical philosophy of *Togakure-ryū*.

Takamatsu plays here with the Sino-Japanese reading of the characters forming the term of ninjutsu (忍術) with two other characters that are also read as ninjutsu (認術), but for which the meaning is different. The first character (認), whose reading *kunyomi*, *nin*, is the same as that of (忍) is used to write ninjutsu or ninja; however, it has as another meaning: to recognize, acknowledge, or attest.

Thus, for Takamatsu, ninjutsu is the art of recognizing one's own flaws and abuses, which are against nature, and the ability to recognize what is and must be. Part of ninjutsu is to recognize defeat and know when to resign oneself to the real battle within.

According to Takamatsu, the essence of ninjutsu remains an amazing fusion between adaptable, practical survival techniques and a spiritual search for profound self-knowledge that allows the sincere practitioner to anticipate and neutralize threats within and without.

**Master Takamatsu demonstrating a *bo-jutsu kamae* (stance), namely *hira ichimonji*.**

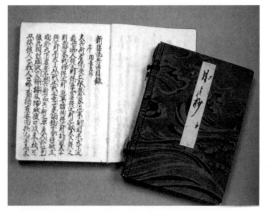

A different view of the *Tsuki no shō, densho* written in 1642 by Yagyū Jūbei. Private collection.

Portrait of Tsukaraha Bokuden, founder of the Kashima *shintō-ryū*. Private collection.

The *Hokushin Ittō-ryū Heihō Shinan no sho*, a scroll written by Chiba Chūsaku's son, Ciba Ryūtarō, in 1897. Private collection.

The *Nen-ryū Seihō Heihō Miraiki Mokuroku*, scroll written in 1596 by Tonomatsu Rokusaemon. Private collection.

Samurai wearing the traditional armor. Picture taken in Meiji era. Private collection.

Picture showing (in the center) Sakakibara Kenkichi, master of the Kashinma *Shinden Jiki-shin Kage-ryū*, founder of the Gekken kōgyō-kai during the Meiji era. Private collection.

Picture taken in middle of Meiji era showing different types of armor.

Mochizuki's grave in Inaba, a suburb of Iga's Ueno city. Private collection.

Warriors floating on wood as done by Rappa's ninja of Takeda. Private collection.

A view of the Sawamura home in the Nabari suburb of Mie prefecture. Private collection.

Warriors waiting for the right moment to launch a raid. Private collection.

A scene with ninjutsu warfare tactics in use. Private collection.

A battlefield spear-fighting scene. Private collection.

Warriors observing the enemy's movement. Private collection.

Warriors using the art of *kisha no jutsu*. Private collection.

A samurai battlefield scene. Private collection.

A cavalry maneuver known as a triangular raid. Private collection.

A view of the Iga's Ueno city's castle, the Hakuho in Mie prefecture. Private collection.

A view of Iga's Ueno city from the Hokuho castle in Mie prefecture. Private collection.

Entrance of the temple that used to be the last fortress of the Iga no mono during the last war against Oda Nobunaga's army during Iga's riot. Private collection.

A view of the village of Inaba east of Iga's Ueno city. Nowadays it is the Mie prefecture. Private collection.

Entrance of the Sawamura family home in Iga, Mie prefecture. The Sawamura family still keeps a few old scrolls and handwritten documents about ninja and their practice. Private collection.

Presumed grave of Fujiwara Chikado and his family in Iga. Private collection.

Fujibayashi family graves in Kôga province, nowadays Ōmi prefecture. Private collection.

Entrance to the Nabari village that was the birthplace of the Momochi family, a prominent ninja family of Iga. Mie prefecture. Private collection.

Waterfall situated in the suburbs of Iga where Shugenja and other hermits used to practice ascetism and *shugendō*. Private collection.

The entrance of the temple in the Yagyū village in Mie prefecture. Private collection.

Spear that belonged to Hattori Hanzō, who was famous for his skills in the art of spear. Private collection.

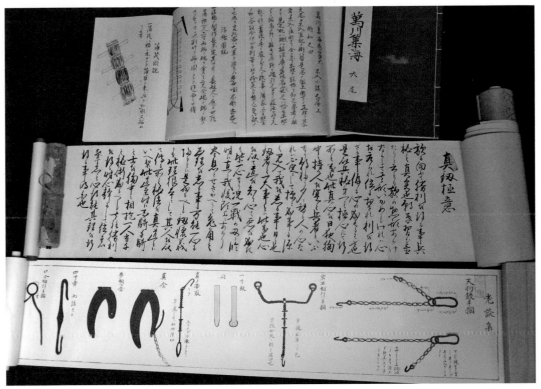

A few *densho* from the Bansen shūkai and *makimono* such as the *Ninpiden* and *Ongyō-ryu ninjutsu*. Private collection.

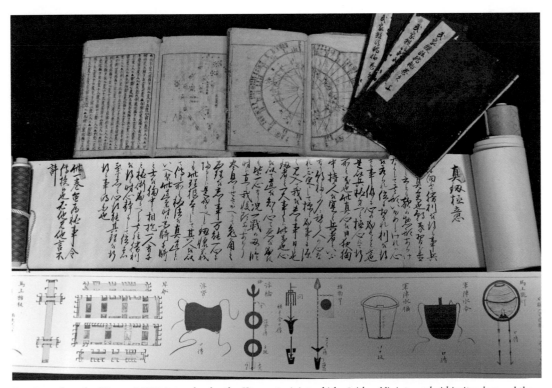

*Densho* such as the *Kōga-ryū Hōjō-jutsu densho*, the *Kōga-ryū ninjutsu hisho ōgiden*, *Ninjutsu gokui himitsu-kan* and the *Gunpō taiyō shūchū settō no maki*. Private collection.

Various scrolls (*makimono*) from different ninja schools such as *Gyokko-ryū*, *Gikan-ryū*, *Gyokushin-ryū*, *Kumogakure-ryū*, *Yasuda-ryū*, etc., as well as *densho* from *Tengu-ryū* and *Kōgan-ryū*. Private collection.

*Bansen shūkai, Shōnin-ki, Ninpō Ikkan, Hontai yōshin ryū jūjutsu, Takagi yoshin ryu shuki, Koshijutsu chu-gokui oboegaki*, etc. Private collection.

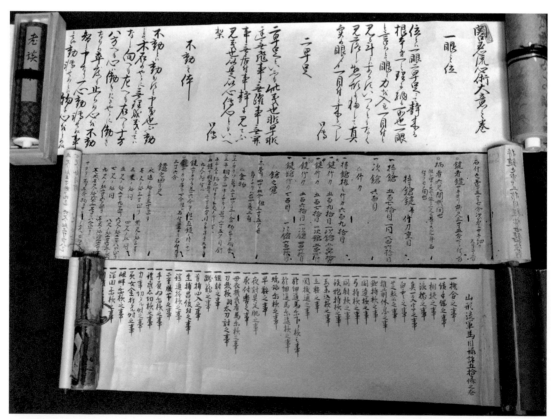

A scroll from *Kusunoki-ryū, Masaki-ryū* and *Kage-ryū*. Private collection.

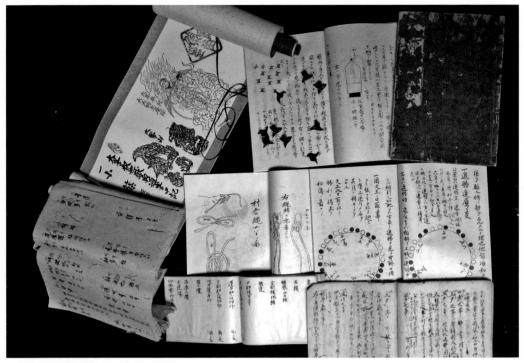

Muhen-*ryū, Kage-ryū, Ninjutsu ōgi hisho, Isshi sōden tōryū shinobi takoku-hi, Ninichi-ryū missho no maki*, etc. Private collection.

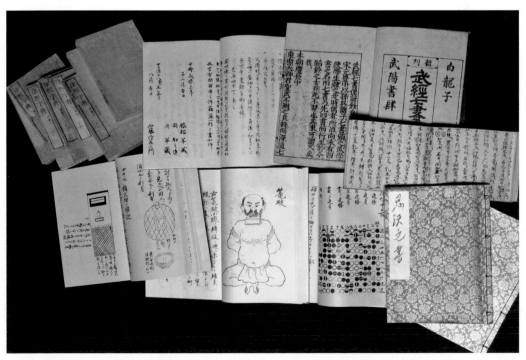

Various *densho* from *Yōshin-ryū, Hogan-ryu, Yagyū-ryū, Gikan-ryū, Kumogakure-ryū, Kusunoki-gunpō-sho, Ninkoku hiden-sho*, etc.

A print showing an example of the art of *mutō-dori*, an empty-handed technique against a weapon. This technique is also called *yari tori* or *yari-tome*. Private collection.

A print showing an example of a ninja using a bamboo stalk as a shield while drawing his sword. Private collection.

A statue of the monk Takuan (1573-1645), master of Yagyū Munenori, and the third shogun, Tokugawa Iemitsu. Private collection.

Weapons belonging to Momochi Sandayū or Kandayu. These weapon were passed from generation to generation in the Momochi family that still lives in a very old house in the Mie prefecture, Iga province. Private collection.

A temple situated in Yagyū village, Mie prefecture. Private collection.

The Momochi Tamba no kami, This monument marks where the castle of the Momochi family was constructed before the Riot of Iga. Private collection.

Master Hatsumi Masaaki, headmaster of *Togakure-ryū ninjutsu*. Private collection.

Demonstration of *Takagi yoshin ryū jū-taijutsu's* high level technique by Master Hatsumi Masaaki in Tōkyō Ayase Budōkan. Private collection.

The *kenjutsu* posture called *seigan no kamae* performed by master Hatsumi Masaaki. Private collection.

*Tsuki* in the art of *taijutsu*, performed by Ishizuka Tetsuji shihan, currently Master Hatsumi Masaaki's most senior disciple.

Painting depicting Fudōmyō. Private collection.

# ✦ CHAPTER 7 ✦

# Conclusion

The essence of ninjutsu cannot be fully explained in a few hundred pages. However, we can conclude a number of things from our study of this exclusive practice that so deftly balances truth with falsehood, and virtue with vice.

To put too fine a point on ninjutsu would be to misrepresent it, something that's been done in so many accounts that describe it simply as a practice of guerilla warfare and espionage. It seems more appropriate to offer various aspects of the practice from the experiences of Takamatsu Toshitsugu, who was introduced in Chapter 4, "The Essence of Ninjutsu."

Although I've faithfully reconstructed what ninjutsu is (and is not), I did not discuss esoteric Buddhist practices like the *kuji kiri* (九字切). In the past, the link between ninjutsu and esoteric Buddhism has been exaggerated, as if esoteric Buddhism was the seminal influence in the origins of ninjutsu.

It is true that the ascetics, hermits of the mountains (*yamabushi*), had ties to the ninja. Considering the fact that both groups lived in the mountains where few others ventured, the relationships were inevitable. However, it would be erroneous to believe that in the beginning there were only *shugenja* and other *yamabushi*. I was careful to avoid associating our logical discussion of ninjutsu with fantasy imagery of the wizard conducting mystical rites and manipulating reality.

In Japan, and in many other countries, the practitioners of various martial arts, and ninjutsu in particular, often know very little about the history and practice of their art. What dubious information they do have generally filters through many layers of translation. Based on these limited resources, it's easy to understand the ignorance of these so-called practitioners, some of whom attain very high rank.

Montesquieu once said, "One knows only what one practices."

The practice is a reflection of the individual, and what's more, for those with eyes to see it, of the practitioner's hidden character. For Takamatsu, the practice of ninjutsu revealed a true vision of the practitioner's heart.

This heart is formed with enduring patience and thus acquires faith. Endurance is half of faith, the other half being patience. To have the faith, is to believe. One must believe in victory in order to fight against oneself and to sense danger when it comes.

The practice does not only consist of going to the dōjō to slip on a kimono and have fun with friends, although that aspect can be enjoyed by many, as this kind of activity supports social and cultural exchanges. The practice of ninjutsu, as you can see in Takamatsu's text, is a lifelong, sincere, and profound internal practice, where each moment has significance.

The heart is the engine of all practices, just as the physical heart needs "to practice" or the body dies. Indeed, if the heart "forgets" to beat, what remains? The practice requires a spiritual heart that is beating and living.

If the practice only consisted of footwork, chambering, punches, and kicks, then everyone would be a ninja: boxers, Muay Thai fighters, jūdō players, and so on.

Even to prepare for a boxing match, jūdō, Muay Thai, or karate competition one needs drive, sweat, and dedication, all for the victory. Isn't it an incredible effort?

Then imagine for a moment a practice against yourself, your ego. The practice is constant, without a physical trainer, coach, doctor, practical training course, strategy, technical staff, federation, and so forth;

the challenger is much more powerful and crafty than any other adversary you have faced, because this adversary (your ego) knows you inside and out, and specifically all of your flaws and weaknesses.

That's why I wrote earlier that endurance is half of faith, and patience is the other half. There are degrees in faith, and they exist in the individual's practice and in the effectiveness sought by many practitioners. The insight of Takamatsu was absolute; he concentrated his faith in each thought, each inclination, action, fear and hope. Through the practice of ninjutsu he sought to eradicate anything that could exist outside of that perfect concentration. It was an ongoing effort to return to harmony.

I didn't translate all of the available ninjutsu texts because they would fill several volumes. The interpretation of some texts is so difficult that I preferred to limit the scope of this discussion.

However, the written works of Sensei Takamatsu are monumental. There are many paintings, letters, *densho* and other *makimono* that he transmitted to Hatsumi Masaaki.

All these splendid documents are written in a secret style. Their language is so dense that they are difficult to

Master Takamatsu shows a stance from *bōjutsu*, in this case, *jōdan no kamae.*

understand for someone who is not familiar with this way of thinking, practicing, teaching and living. This exquisitely beautiful language veils more than it reveals of the true significance of the practice of ninjutsu.

The struggle against oneself, a constant analysis of the most secret motives of the heart, is really the basis of a practice known as the art of remaining unseen. In any event, we must accept the secrecy and understand that we cannot grasp its deeper meaning, especially because this is a language of lived experience, based on dedicated practice.

The secrecy of the heart and of the practice is at the core of man. Who can claim to know himself to the last detail?

This presentation raises many questions whose answers can only be discovered within oneself and through sincere and solitary practice. It is to delve into our own shadows that we practice; it is in this way that the practice of ninjutsu reveals its significance.

This is why the true master must teach how to distinguish the truth from vanity and a serious statement from a joke. If your instructor teaches you how to be wise and urges you, by their behavior, toward righteousness, then your practice becomes practical.

Nothing prevents the realization of the goal as much as neglecting the fundamentals of practice. It is up to the follower to define the foundation of their practice by remaining open and receptive to everything, good or bad, that could help their practice. With regard to the practice of ninjutsu, it remains the secret of those who devote their body and heart to it.

# Appendix A: History and Definition of *Jūjutsu*

*Jūjutsu* (柔術)[*] is a generic term used from the very start of the Edo period to define a whole series of empty-hand combat techniques. Indeed, although the term is recent, it indicates a specific use of the body rather than a specific technique of combat. In fact, *jūjutsu* is inherent in all arts that require a flexible body, making it possible to demolish an enemy whether armed or not, to control the body of the enemy (articulations, tendons, muscles, etc.), and, of course, to do so with the weapon used. Therefore, that which is called *jūjutsu* and that has been called by various names during the history of the Japanese martial arts, is an attitude, a way of being and of being driven that allows one to adapt to all situations and weapons, rather than a type of technique used to demolish the enemy. What one calls *sōgō bujutsu* (総合武術), or composite techniques of combat, uses the art of *jūjutsu* as the central axis for using various weapons in combat.

The origin of the Japanese techniques of bare-hand combat is far back in the history of Japan. One of the very first references on these types of body techniques or system of combat, including hand-to-hand combat, is found in two prominent Japanese historical works: *Kojiki*[†] (古事記 *Chronicle of the Old Facts*, written in 712) and *Nihon Shoki*[‡] (日本書記 *Historical Chronicles of Japan*, 720) which tell of the mythological creation of Japan as well as the establishment of the imperial family. One can find other references in various Japanese chronicles and in paintings and drawings showing *Sumai no sechi* (相撲節)[§], a rite that was practiced at the imperial courts of the Nara and Heian, where skilled fighters competed.

According to *densho* of various schools of *jūjutsu*, in particular the pioneering schools of *Shoshō-ryū* (諸賞流) and *Takeuchi-ryū* (竹内流), these systems of empty-hand combat combined with the use of various weapons, made their appearance during the Muromachi period. However, I should add an interesting fact: the use of the body in the art of *kenjutsu*, *sōjutsu*, and the like in the writings of prominent masters of Kamiiizumi of the Shinkage-ryū and Tsukahara Bokuden of the Shintō-ryū shows that they developed a deep and subtle understanding of the use of all types of weapons, and is a testament to the ultimate technique of *Mutō-dori* (無刀捕り). In one of the more striking examples that is reported in *Shuki* (手記), containing all the anecdotes relating to Kamiizumi, we see one disguised as a monk in order to come to the aid of a child taken as an hostage by a fanatic armed with a short sword. The document reveals how, by gaining the confidence of the fanatic, the "monk" was able to disarmed him in a flash. How had this sword-wielding fanatic, considered in all of Japan to be a master of *kenjutsu* without equal, been disarmed with so little effort? The art of holding and handling the sword requires coordinated flexibility, suppleness, and strength of the arms, forearms, wrists and fingers, and therefore, the body as a whole. It's similar to holding a brush for calligraphy. Thus, it goes without saying that Kamiizumi was a master of movement and knew how to disarm any type of enemy because of his training in the art of flexibility. He had the ability to flow, like water, in his movements; a skill that is necessary to the art of *kenjutsu* and the use of other weapons.

## Various Terms

The term *jūjutsu* means to use flexibility and "flexible techniques," and thus to *use* flexibility it is necessary to *have* flexibility, to develop a flexible body, and to know how to use this flexibility. The use of the body remains the keystone of all the forms of *jūjutsu*. This is apparent in all of the various names given to the various schools that claim to use *jūjutsu*.

- In the *Sekiguchi-ryū* (関口流), *Araki-ryū* (荒木流), *Seigō-ryū* (制剛流) schools, the techniques of *jūjutsu* used the following names: *hade* (羽手), *hakuda* (白打), *jūjutsu* (柔術), *kenpō* (拳法), *torite* (捕手)
- In the *Takeuchi-ryū* and *Yagyū Shingan-ryū* (柳生心眼流) schools: *koppō* (骨法)[¶], *gōhō* (強法), *kogusoku* (小具足), *yawara-jutsu* (和術), *koshi no mawari* (腰之廻), and *yoroi kumiuchi* (鎧組打).

---

[*] One finds also the following kanji (十術) for the term *jūjutsu*. Many believe it relates to the influence of Japanese practitioners converted to Christianity, a feasible assumption because the cross represents at the same time a mystery and a protection. However, in many cases, in particular in ninjutsu, there is another interpretation. Indeed, the use of the character *jū* (十) here refers directly to *jūppō sesshō no jutsu* (十方折衝之術), but also with *jūji ron* (十字論) theories concerning various fields like *tenmon* and *ch mon* (the use of angles, degrees, fractals, etc., to measure time and distances), *koppōjutsu* and *kosshijutsu* (systems of bone and body, muscles and blood), and *kyōmon* (religion and philosophy) in which the *jūmonji* attitude (十文字) is directly present. The schools using *koppōjutsu*, *kosshijutsu*, *hajutsu no hō*, *dakentaijtsu*, and *jūtaijutsu* have this guiding principle for the use of different weapons, for example, in the application of individual strategy in combat on a large scale, *gunryaku heihō* (軍略兵法).

[†] In *Kojiki*, it is about the combat between Takemikazura no Kami and Takeminakata no Kami. The term used is *chikara kurabe* (力くらべ).

[‡] In *Nihon shoki*, it is about the combat between Nomi Nosukene and Taima Nokehaya in front of the Suinin emperor. Here also, the term *chikara kurabe* is used. Others share only the description, but the techniques used, such as blows and strikes, throws and locks, show that it is indeed a form of *jūjutsu*.

[§] The *sumai no sechi* is ancient sumō. This form of fighting was an occasion to celebrate the gods, and it was very popular during the end of the Nara period and into the Heian period under the reign of Emperor Murakami (946–966/7).

[¶] The terms *koppō*, *kowami*, *hakuda*, *shubaku* and *kenpō*, refer to types of *jūjutsu*, where the blows and strikes, known by the generic term, *atemi*, occupy a dominating place. The term *gōhō* refers to a type of *jūjutsu* where one uses a broad range of short weapons in the style of *kogusoku* or *koshi no mawari*. However, this range is far from being limited only to the short weapons. Longer weapons are not excluded because there was the question of dealing with longer range weapon attacks. All the same, the essence of the use of all these characteristics resides in the controlled use of the body, termed *taijutsu* (体術), which one finds written with different characters.

- In the *Tenshin Shōden Katori Shintō-ryū* (天真正伝香取神道流), *Tatsumi-ryū* (立身流), and *Shoshō-ryū* (諸賞流) schools: *kumiuchi** (組打), *shubaku* (手縛), *tōde*(唐手), *torite* (捕手 or 取手, both ways exist), *wa-jutsu* (和術), *yawara-jutsu* (和術), and *kowami*(剛身).

These names were used throughout the various periods, areas and successors. Each one of these names refers to appreciably different design features some of which apply to the use of the body as a whole, and some apply to the use of just part of the body.

### Blows, Strikes, Dodging, Absorption, the Use of the Center and Other Techniques

Among all these various schools of *jūjutsu* one finds three approaches to the use of various techniques for the use of the body. One, jointly uses the techniques of arterial blows and strikes, blood controls, and tendon attacks, applying a very broad palette of *kyūsho* (急書), significant and vital points of the body. The other style uses very few blows and strikes, but they remain present all the same. Finally, the last style uses no or almost no blows or strikes. However, we should add that the ultimate state of this practice is to not have to use blows and strikes; this is known as *atemi* (当身). Indeed, the goal is to achieve the most judicious use of the body in its entirety (control of the centerline, *seichūsen*, 正中線), of a subtle displacement, absorption and joint dodging with the various angles of exit and timing of dodging. All this makes it possible not to use *atemi*.

The schools that use the terms of *hakuda*, *shubaku*, and *kenpō*, frequently use *atemi*, revealing that these techniques of combat were subject to the influence of different styles, in particular the use of the hands as weapons, which came from China.[†] Without limiting themselves to just the Chinese-influenced techniques, these techniques of striking were also used when the warrior wore armor, because they were essential in order to be able to apply twists, throws, and various locks. That shows that this approach was not about brutal strikes, as presumed, but rather it was an art of striking that made it possible not to be wounded by contact with the armor that would have been covering critical parts of the body. We cannot categorize all the *jūjutsu* schools into systems where 50% of the techniques are throws, twists, locks, and controls, and 50% are blows and strikes. What the large majority of *densho*, *makimono*, *shuki*, and the like, reveal is that all known *jūjutsu* started as an art that, at its core, has to do with the use of the entire body, through subtle movements that can be adapted to the use of various weapons.

The use of blows and strikes developed individually within each school, some making less balanced use, an occasional few making a balanced use, and others not using them at all. That does not mean that the blows and strikes are not effective. It simply reveals that the use of body flexibility, positioning, movement and dodging were employed with a high level of efficiency. The other reason that *atemi* is of less importance is that the majority of the schools, which were born during the Edo period, favored controlling the attacker rather than bringing about his destruction. Indeed, during this period, rather than killing one's enemy, he had to be controlled so he could not use his weapons or disarming techniques. One finds this principle of control in the kata (*kime no kata*, *nikikata* and *kiri oroshi*) of the *Tenshin Shinyō-ryū* school, which one still finds certain traces of in modern *jūdō*. However, when there are kicks used of the *mawashi geri* type, *yoko geri*, or *oi tsuki*, *gyuka tsuki*, *uraken*, *jōdan uke*, or the like, such as one sees in the different schools of karate, or from the circular motions, which come from other styles, whether that is being used as traditional Japanese *jūjutsu* is not in question. Karate was introduced for use in summer in Japan during the twenties by Gishin Funakoshi (1868–1957), and, thus, well after the birth of the majority of the schools of *jūjutsu* or schools that use *jūjutsu*.

### *Jūjutsu*: a Multidisciplinary Art:

For many *jūjutsu*[‡] practitioners in the world, there is only one approach for close combat: using bare-handed techniques to overcome or control an opponent. These are "flexible techniques" used in hand-to-hand combat. As I noted throughout my

---

  * The term *kumiuchi*, also called *senjō kumiuchi* (戦場組打) when used in the context of *yoroi kumiuchi* or *kaichū kumiuchi* (介冑), or the use of *jūjutsu* in armor, comprises *heifuku kumiuchi* (平服組打: fights in ordinary clothing) and *suhada kumiuchi* (素肌組打: fights without armor). The name *suhada musha* (素肌武者), indicates a type of warrior who fought on the battlefield without armor. It surely referred to a warrior with little wealth, who thus used a type of technique that was appropriate for him.

  † Custom notes that this influence is not very clear in the documents of transmission. Even a very detailed analysis of techniques only shows a resemblance to adaptations from commonly known biomechanics. Thus, there were years when there was some unquestionable influence, but it was over very shorts durations. Schools of *jūjutsu* that have close links with China through the Chinese master Chingenpin (陳元賓, who arrived in Japan as a translator and remained there from 1615 to 1624) are the *Ryōi Shintō-ryū* (良移心当流) of Fukuya Shichirōemon, *Miura-ryū* (三浦流) of Miura Yojiemon, *Isokai-ryū* (磯貝流) of Isokai Jiemon. These three rōnin (浪人: samurai without a Master) accepted the teaching of Chingenpin and diffused it within their schools. *Yōshin-ryū* (楊心流) was founded by Akiyama Shirōbe (秋山四朗兵衛: 1680), who was a rich person teaching a fusion of technical combat and Chinese traditional medicine. The founder imported his knowledge from China, where he traveled to study and he learned a form of *jūjutsu*. The current *Yōshin-ryū*, had schools break from it, in particular the *Shin Shintō-ryū* (真神道流) of Yamamoto Mizaemon, and *Tenshin Shinyō-ryū* (天神真楊流) of Kiso Mataemon (1789–1870). The latter influenced the founder of jūdō, Kanō Jigorō, who always refuted the assumption that Japanese *jūjutsu* derived directly from Chinese *wushu*.

  ‡ A special note should be devoted here to Brazilian *jūjutsu*. However, after a meticulous study of this discipline, one notices that it does not have any relationship to traditional Japanese *jūjutsu*. Indeed, it seems that it is closer to *kōsen jūdō* (高専柔道), a form of judo developed for combat on the ground only when the practice of *waza* (寝技) failed. The majority of Brazilian *jūjutsu* stylists practice boxing and kicking, which shows that there is no science of *atemi* nor any use of weapons.

explanation, *jūjutsu* is the foundation of a whole series of combat techniques with various weapons. It includes various techniques of blows and strikes, blocks, deflections, dodging, twists, locks, chokes, and stances, as well as a method of controlling the body during falls, knowledge to neutralize the attack before it happens, and so forth. But the most significant skill lies in developing a deep understanding of body physics, making it possible to control the transfer of body weight to manipulate the state of imbalance. This is known under names such as *musoku no hō* (無足之法), *suri ashi* (摺足), *yoko aruki* (横歩), *ninsoku* (忍足), and so on, and is the foundation of the use of all the weapons, as well as one of the secrets of *mutō dori* or *shinken shirahadome* (真剣白刃留).

According to another point of view, based on the nomenclature of the traditional techniques of Japanese combat *ryū-ha*, the techniques of using short weapons such as *jutte*, *tantō*, *kakushi buki* (hidden weapons), *kusari fundō* (ballasted chain), *tetsuken* (iron fist), *bankoku choki* (glove in form of hatchet), and the like, against armed or unarmed adversaries, are all a form of *jūjutsu*. The term *jūjutsu* is also used to refer to a tactic or a movement inherent in the use of the major weapons like the *ken* or *tachi* (swords of various lengths), the *yari*, the *naginata*, the *bō*, and the *jō*. These particular combat techniques were preeminent in the different *ryū-ha* that were developed for the battlefield. Still, one distinguishes between the *kaichū bujutsu* or *yoroi kumiuchi* (combat in armor with or without weapons) from the Kamakura, Muromachi and Sengoku periods, and the *suhada bujutsu* (techniques of combat developed for use in everyday clothes) developed for the Edo period. During the latter period, the introduction of peace, free moving clothing, and the prohibition of duels and fights to the death provided a new dimension to *jūjutsu*. Many schools, like *Tenshin Shinyō-ryū*, *Kitō-ryū*, *Yōshin-ryū*, and the like, abounded and worked out a more appropriate form of *jūjutsu* for the time and manners of the Edo period. In addition, a great number of manuscripts propose two different views. The first explains that *jūjutsu* was a whole series of techniques created in rural environments by warriors of low rank. Warriors of high rank felt reluctant to use their hands to fight. The second explains why *jūjutsu* was transmitted like a secret technique among the warriors of high rank, like a survival technique, to control and disarm an adversary in the confines of a castle, or in order not to soil the sword blade.

# Appendix B: History of *Daitō-ryū Aiki-jūjutsu*

### History of an Uncommon School: *Daitō-ryū Aiki-jūjutsu*:

*Daitō-ryū aiki-jūjutsu* (大東流合気柔術) is a famous school of Japanese *jūjutsu* that was formed relatively recently. It has a rich history of personalities, with a confusing mix of legendary, mythological figures and histories that raises many questions regarding the authenticity of the lineage prior to *Takeda Sokaku* (1860–1943). For clarity's sake, the term *aiki-jūjutsu* is also known by the names *aiki no jutsu* and *aiki-jutsu*. The associated controversies do nothing to quell the opinions of enthusiastic and impassioned practitioners or other interested parties. It is by meticulous study of newly discovered historical documents that I propose a more concrete approach to the history of this current, typical Japanese *jūjutsu*.

### A Remote Disputed Origin

According to *makimono* of the *Daitō-ryū* and *Takeda-ryū* (武田流), the style goes back to the end of the Heian period (782–1190). In these two schools that refer to *aiki-jutsu*, the style is a whole set of techniques for self-protection, transmitted secretly from generation to generation of emperor Seiwa Genji's (858–876) heirs. The 5th generation heir, the shogun Minamoto no Tomoyoshi, would have transmitted this knowledge to his third son, Shinra Saburō Minamoto no Yoshimitsu (between the eleventh and twelvth centuries). He compiled and gave form to this method of pragmatic combat, which he named after the place where he lived, Daitō no yataka (大東之館) in the province of Omi (today's Shiga prefecture).

According to these same sources, the brother of Yoshimitsu, Yoshi-Ie, largely contributed to the development of this method by adding techniques from an art named *geki-tō* (撃刀: technique for using the *daito* or large sword). At the time of the defeat of the battle "*ato san nen no yaku*" in 1083, Yoshimitsu started to develop control of precision techniques, blows, strikes, and chokes derived from meticulous observation of corpses on the battlefield.

After this battle, he left for the Kai province (in the area of the Kantō) and adopted the name Takeda. His son, Kanja Takeda continued the tradition. One of the descendants of this family, Takeda Shingen (1521–1573), is listed as a warlord of note during the period of Sengoku jidai (1480–1600).

This method of combat was transmitted in the greatest secrecy within the family as a *hi-kaden* (秘家伝), secret family transmission. The terms of *aiki-jutsu* (合気術), *aiki no jutsu* (合気之柔術), and *aiki-jūjutsu* (合気柔術) were not really used. The documents relating to the school mention the name *oshiki uchi* (御式内, also referred to as *oshiki nai*, the shape of combat) which was transmitted inside the castle where the warriors of high rank resided.

However, the term *oshiki uchi* does not translate as the shape of combat; its literal translation would rather make one think of the forms and labels, customs and habits to be respected within the castle walls. Thus, the technical contents, the form that *oshiki uchi* proposes remains very vague, and remains unknown to this day because there are no historical manuscripts or chronicles that present a precise reference.

Right before the destruction of the Takeda family by the army of Oda Nobunaga (1534–1582) in the battle of Nagashino in 1575, a certain Takeda Kunitsugu supposedly carried all the notes of the late Takeda Shingen and fled to Kyushu, where the stronghold of Aizu was located. There he supposedly established the Takeda family where the style *oshiki uchi* was transmitted secretly from generation to generation until Takeda Sokaku, the first to reveal it officially. According to another version of the history, it would be about a faithful vassal of Shingen, Daitō Hisa Nosuke, who fled secretly towards the stronghold of Aizu. There are still many stories and anecdotes that mixed into the official history, and many doubts remain.

First of all, the *makimono* and *densho* that present the history, as well as the genealogy, of the school all date from the Meiji period. Before that, there is no mention of the name *Daitō-ryū aiki-jūjutsu*, the term *aiki-jutsu* or *oshiki uchi*. In the strongholds close to Aizu, like that of Shimazu, prominent schools of *bujutsu*, like *Jigen-ryū* (自現流) and *Taisha-ryū* (タイ捨流) exist, whose technical and historical lineage are proven back to the beginning of the sixteenth century. This training was transmitted to the elite of the warlike class, but there is no family history nor do any historical notes relating to these schools mention the name of *Daitō-ryū* or the terms *aiki-jūjutsu*, or *oshiki-uchi*. There is no document that makes even the smallest mention of the term *aiki-jūjutsu* or *oshiki-uchi*.

Another detail deserving attention is that the techniques of *Daitō-ryū* are very numerous; some say more than 2,000. One must question the ability to faithfully transmit such a great number of techniques, yet have them remain "secret." The techniques of *Daitō-ryū* are not unique, and by studying their forms well, one immediately notices obvious similarities with those of other *bujutsu* and *jūjutsu* schools from the Meiji period (1868–1912).

The Meiji period is marked by a significant societal upheaval in Japan. During this cultural shift in Japanese society it became possibile for the common man to learn *bujutsu* or have a career in the army, while he was still prohibited from carrying of *dai-shō*, or double swords, as distinctive signs of the samurai class; all of this was happening, of course, while the whole country was opening up to foreign powers.

The prohibition against carrying the double swords by the samurai class helped support the emergence and the development of a new type of school, whose teachings were primarily centered on techniques of self-protection. It is in this context that the following schools emerged: *Okura Asayama Ichiden-ryū taijutsu* (浅山一伝流体術), *Takeuchi-ryū* (unrelated to the ancient *Takenouchi-ryū kogusoku* which goes back to the 15th century), *Nakazawa-ryū* (中澤流), *Bokuden-ryū* (卜伝流), *Daitō-ryū* (growing out of the *Araki-ryū*), *Hakkō-ryū* (八光流), and *Isshin-ryū* (一心流).

The prohibition against carrying the double swords, the adoption of new methods of combat to form the Japanese army, the threat exerted by the Western powers of the time, and the insecurity related to the urban development of major cities, such as *Tokyo*, are many of the factors that permitted the emergence of these types of schools, whose techniques were based on pragmatic self-protection. These all arose from the old schools of *bujutsu*.

When one thoroughly studies all the information that one can find on the *bujutsu* training by Takeda Sokaku, one does not find any instance of him receiving a *menkyo kaiden*, attesting to the total transmission of any *jūjutsu* or *bujutsu* school. Indeed, the technical curriculum vitae of Sokaku starts under the tutelage of his father, Takeda Sokichi (1819–1906), an expert in sumō and in the use of several weapons, such as the sword and halberd. Sokaku's mother came from the Kurokuchi family, famous for their various *bujutsu* experts who trained the Aizu family.

Very early on, the young Sokaku began *bujutsu* training in the stronghold of the Aizu family. However, in 1871 he was initiated into the art of *kenjutsu* under the tutelage of Shibuya Toma of the *Ono-ha Ittō-ryū* (小野派一刀流) school. Sokaku received the *menkyo kaiden* from Shibuya in 1877. Of course, this *menkyo* shows that Takeda Sokaku was proficient in the art of *kenjutsu* to a high degree; however, receiving a *menkyo kaiden* does not give one the ability to be the style's successor nor to open his own school. Moreover, it should be noted that this was not a *menkyo* from a traditional school of *bujutsu* where the *bugei jūhappan* was taught.

*Ono-ha Ittō-ryū* is the current principal style that arose from *Ittō-ryū* (一刀流). It was jointly taught with *Yagyū Shinkage-ryū* (柳生新影流), the *kenjutsu* school of the Tokugawa family during the Edo period. The current *Ono-ha Ittō-ryū* techniques are presented in the teachings of *Daitō-ryū*, not only in the form of use of the body and balance displacement, but also in the use of *kenjutsu*, the teachings of which testify to the skills of Takeda Tokimune, son and successor to Sokaku.

At the same time, during his time in Tokyo, (1872–1876), Sokaku studied at the dōjō of the famous Sakakibara Kenkichi (1830–1894) of *Jikishin Kage-ryū* (直真影流), as well as with another world-famous *kenjutsu* expert of this period, Momoi Shunzō (1825–1885) of the *Kyōshin Meichi-ryū* (鏡心明智流) school. The *kenjutsu* dōjō of these two masters was located near the site of another dōjō that sheltered another famous school of *bujutsu*, *Kiraku-ryū* (気楽流).

Since the middle of the Edo period until the middle of the Meiji period, public demonstrations of martial arts, under the generic title of *gekiken-kai* (撃剣), were very widespread. A great number of these demonstrations took place not far from the *Kenkichi* dōjō of Kenkichi where Sokaku enthusiastically devoted himself to the art of the *kenjutsu*. Of course, a great number of experts came to present certain facets of their school, and among these masters and experts, was the *soke* of the *Kiraku-ryū* school, Okusawa Shichisai.

The results are very easy to guess. For a genius on a scale of Sokaku, who came to Tokyo to be trained near the best masters of *bujutsu*, nothing could be easier than to quickly glance and copy the techniques of a master or expert from an unspecified school, and then to extract the essence from it in order to perfect it in another form or with another name. One would not be astonished when Sokaku begins the teaching of *Daitō-ryū* that he continued to say, "The technique should be stolen because I cannot teach it!" One of his famous pupils, *Mr. Sagawa* (1902–1998) said this in the same way.

*"To steal the technique at a glance,"* is, however, not a small matter. Indeed, that requires that one have exceptional faculties in order to be able to reproduce the technique or movement in the most perfect way possible and in sufficient depth. These skills are not learned. In fact, any successor or creator of a school has this gift of perfect imitation.

It was to prevent the movements or techniques from being "stolen" or copied, that engagements between schools, much like the demonstrations being done at the time, were prohibited in all the traditional *bujutsu* schools. Moreover, Sokaku was an expert in *sōjutsu*, the art of the spear, from the famous *Hōzoin-ryū* (宝蔵院流槍術), the art of the shuriken, and he had learned the art of *yō-yari*, or small lance, one of the weapons from the arsenal of *Kiraku-ryū*.

*Kiraku-ryū jūjutsu* (気楽流柔術) came from the *Toda-ryū* (戸田流), whose lineage back to the beginning of the Edo period is attested. It is closest to the *Daitō-ryū* school in the field of form and technique. It is enough to see the basic forms that even if the names of the techniques differ, the wrist holds such as *ikkyō*, *sankyō* and *kote gaeshi*, are very similar, perhaps too similar.

Let us add that the first character that forms the name of the school itself, *Ki-raku*, is none other than the character *ki* (気) of *aiki-jūjutsu*. The second character, *raku* (楽), is defined as a direction: easy, without effort, comfortable, light, and thus, by extension, free and flexible. Thus, the name of the school evokes an approach where the *ki*, or vital energy, must not only circulate freely and easily in the body, but also applied in various fields as in the techniques of combat and the use of the weapons.

This implies great body flexibility, which goes hand-in-hand with flexibility of the spirit. One can easily advance the idea that the concept of *aiki* already existed in the movements and techniques of the schools of Japanese *bujutsu*, but the term itself is very recent. It went from being something real without a name, and, little by little, with the rise of many "pseudo-masters," has become a name without anything real behind it.

The first mention of the term *aiki*, but with a different first character from that of *aiki-jūtsu* or *aikidō*, is in the *densho* entitled *Tomoshibi Mondo* (燈火問答: *Enlightened Conversations*) of the *Kitō-ryū jūjutsu* (起倒流柔術). Written in 1764 during the last part of the Edo period, the definition given for *aiki* was, *"to control and master the attack, or provide a very standard defense posture before the attack becomes insurmountable."* Thus, the term of *aiki-jutsu*, such as we know it today, is very recent. The first use by Sokaku himself dates from the middle of the Taishō (1912–1926) period when he changed the name of his art of *Daitō-ryū jūjutsu* into *Daitō-ryū Aiki jūjutsu*.

However, the first appearance of this term, as it is used today, comes from a work entitled *Budō hiketsu: Aiki no jutsu*, (武道秘訣合気之術: *Secret text of Budō: Aiki no jutsu*) published in twenty-fifth year of the Meiji era (1892). Only the pen name of the author is known: Bukotsu Kyoshi.

After reading this book, one immediately sees that the author, although impassioned about *bujutsu*, is not a practitioner, but rather a journalist providing an insightful glance into the Japanese society of his time. This explains why *aiki no jutsu* is the quintessential principle of *bujutsu* and that its essence can be translated as *"Anticipating the enemy in his intentions and movements"* or by *"The art of distinguishing the intentions and feelings of the enemy."* For the author, the first appearance of this term, as well as the most fitting application, harkens back to Uesugi Kenshin (1530–1578).

Uesugi Kenshin was supposedly the eternal rival of another famous warlord, Takeda Shingen, heir to the Takeda family and thus, according to manuscripts of the *Daitō* school this same Takeda is reputed to be one of the very first holders of *aiki no jutsu*! This anecdote leads one to think critically about the work mentioned above and how it came to be the first to make the wholesale mention of *aiki no jutsu*.

I'm not targeting anyone, only trying to reveal the true nature of a martial art. One must keep an open mind and investigate all possible reasons for an art's development, look at all the facts, without blindly swallowing the heresay and pseudo-truth from purported masters or experts.

The nature of the movement of *Daitō-ryū* that focuses on the use of the sword is very similar to that of the *Ono ha Ittō-ryū* school founded in first half of the sixteenth century. There are, of course, unique *Daito-ryū* characteristics, made famous by the use of the principle of *aiki-jūjutsu*, which is inherent in the incredible personality of Sokaku.

## A Genius Master:

Sokaku was born the same year as another master, whose creation is universally known: Kanō Jogorō, the founder of jūdō. However, there is a difference between these two characters. Sokaku was a born combatant, who spent his time practicing any martial art that was extremely effective. There is no doubt that he achieved a great level of skill.

Born in Aizu in Kyūshū, an area known for the ferocity of its warriors, he began his study of martial arts under the tutelage of his father in the cramped family dōjō. In spite of the new prerogatives resulting from the Meiji Restoration, such as the prohibition on carrying double swords, he did not cease acting like a warrior of feudal times. Indeed, all his life, he lived at the edge of society, going from one end of Japan to the other in order to perfect his combat techniques. He met various masters and never refused to show his skill while measuring his own progress.

In 1877, he intended to join the forces rebelling against the Meiji government led by Saigo Takamori (1827–1877) in Kyūshū, but this plan fell through because the revolt was crushed before he could join in. The meeting with Tanomo Saigo (1872–1922), enigmatic *aiki-jūjutsu* and *Kōshū-ryū* (甲州流), schoolmaster of *Mizoguchiha Ittō-ryū* (溝口派一刀流), of course, led Sokaku to reconsider the practice of *bujutsu*. Tanomo transmitted all the secrects of *oshiki uchi* to Sokaku, as he had done for another former protégé who became famous in *Kodokan jūdō*, Saigo Shiro. Sokaku worked out *Daitō-ryū* starting from the teachings that he had received from Tanomo Saigo and from his *kenjutsu* skills, supplemented by techniques he drew from his incomparable experiments in combat.

Sokaku did not have a dōjō and moved across Japan, teaching primarily high-level police officers, soldiers, politicians, and the rich, who were interested and fascinated by his astonishing technical skill. He was not at all well educated, however, he kept two notebooks, *Eimei-roku* (英名録), which contained all the names of the people attending his courses, and *Shamei-roku*, which contained his accounts and expenses. Sokaku was one of the, if not the only, martial arts masters at the time to be paid very high sums for his lessons. He knew his value and did not hesitate to increase prices.

Prestigious names like that of Ueshiba, Takeshita, and Asano appear in these notebooks. Although Sokaku was said to have taught with more than 3,000 pupils, the number receiving *Kyōjū-dairi* (教授代理) certificates making it possible to teach and to have a dōjō, did not exceed twenty. The more well known certificate recipients are Sagawa, Ueshiba (1883–1969), Hisatakuma (1895–1979), and Yoshida (1871–1947). It was necessary to complete a certain number of courses and, moreover, to be gifted to be able to receive *Kyōjū-dairi* (教授代理).

With this certificate, the *makimono* entitled *Daitō-ryū Aikijūjutsu Hiden*, (大東流合気柔術秘伝: *Secret transmission of the Aiki-jūjutsu of Daitō-ryū*) was given. This cerificate contained all the techniques studied in the order of training, but with names that did not have clear meaning, just as in the *makimono* and *densho* of other traditional *bujutsu* and *jūjutsu* schools. Although the name of the technique does not tell anything about the control itself, it is interesting to note that, for a system that goes back to an emperor, the fact that no technique has a name remains very strange.

Sokaku did not follow a step-by-step curriculum or a particular technical progression. Each technique was shown once, never several times. He would offer a course only on *kote gaeshi* or *ikkajō*. This demonstrated his great skill, innovation, and creative spontaneity. He showed the technique based on the skills of the pupil, his size, weight, force, and function. He showed techniques on the left, on the right, in front, and behind, proving that the practice of *Aiki-jūjutsu* must conform to and be used with the body in its entirety, so that the *ki* circulates on the two sides in a single way allowing the practitioner to be ambidextrous, flexible, adaptable, and thus free. Sokaku was not one for filling time with speeches on technical or philosophical concepts. He was only interested in real and pragmatic application.

One can say that Sokaku did not teach, he demonstrated…showing an incomparable talent to demystify, while enchanting the audience fascinated by his technique. With regard to the teaching of weapon use, he kept this private and personal. Some elected officials saw Sokaku using various *bujutsu* weapons. He demonstrated his skills bare-handed against various armed attackers or against another expert with swords and spears, without ever losing. This shows how much he had mastered the practice of weapons, understanding the angles of attack, balance, and especially the distance that makes it possible to measure the partner. Let us not forget that there would be nothing to discuss without the famous principle of *aiki*, which remains the heart of everything having to do with combat.

Only rare initiates, such as Sagawa, or his son, Tokimune, had *makimono* concerning the weapons techniques, such as *aiki no daitō* (合気之太刀), *aiki nitō-jutsu* (合気二刀術), *aiki-sōjutsu* (合気槍術), and *aikibōjutsu* (合気棒). He also transmitted teachings on *kusari fundo-jutsu* (鎖分銅術) and *shuriken-jutsu* (手裏剣術) to both Sagawa and Tokimune. Today, Katsuyuki Kondo has the only copy of the technical curriculum vitae for weapons with the documents of transmission given to him by Tokimune before his death. Thus, the practice of weapons still remains the prerogative of the current *soke*, who, just like Sokaku, Tokimmue or Sagawa, only reveals it to a few selected individuals.

Sokaku, although very small (4'6" tall), was of a robust constitution, with a very piercing glance, and a face that reflected a very hard, violent core. Anyone who saw him for the first time would want to avoid him, with his defiant and challenging demeanor. He maintained a sharp sense of those around him, and possessed a deep understanding of human nature. He did not trust just anybody to prepare his tea, draw his bath, or even prepare his meals. These activities he did himself or relied only on a trusted few. It is easy to see how the character of Sokaku developed. His attitude was a reflection of his technical application of his martial character throughout his daily life. He evolved and moved as a living weapon.

But, according to the testimony of those close to him, he could be very soft and pleasant to those he cared for. This was definitely the case with certain pupils like Sagawa Hisatakuma who was the only one to receive the *menkyo kaiden* of the school from the hands of Sokaku, and Yamamoto Kakuyoshi (1914–1982), who received the *Daitō-ryū aiki-jūjutsu hiden* as well as the sword of Sokaku.

Like an itinerant warrior continuing his eternal *musha-shugyō* (warrior's quest or pilgrimage), he taught where he was, and he used anyone as a training partner, including sumō wrestlers or other martial arts styles. It was no problem, for he was so skilled in the concept of *aiki* that, although he was of a slight stature, he was able to overcome all who came against him.

Two years before dying, he was paralyzed on the right side of his body, and in spite of his family and son, Tokimune, trying to control the wanderlust living within him, Sokaku found the means of escaping to go to give courses to the police force. In spite of his handicap, he could still demonstrate his skills, and even made the headlines of the newspapers of Hokkaidō to the great surprise of his family. Sokaku died in an inn during his last trip in the town of Aomori. He was eighty-six years old.

### The Changing

The succession of *Daitō-ryū* was ensured by Sokaku's son, Takeda Tokimune who was trained in the discipline of *aiki-jūjutsu* from an early age. An anecdote reported by sensei Katsuyuki Kondo demonstrates this in Tokimune's early training. Sokaku inflicted certain drudgeries upon his son, including cutting logs in below freezing temperatures, using a very small saw. The purpose of this exercise was to forge the tendons of the knees, ankles, and hips as well as develop the flexibility of mobility of the spinal column, all in one movement. This was also to allow him to learn to heat his body and to feel all the energy flow throughout his body. Owing to the fact that he was the son of famous Sokaku, he showed a tireless energy and a true devotion to the practice that everyone admired.

He slackened his training in later years in order to develop *Daitō-ryū aiki-jūjutsu* in all Japan, and he did not hesitate to travel throughout the country. Tokimune was very different from his father, a softer, and more accessible character, and very diplomatic. He was a career police officer, which provided him with combat experience and allowed for the real-life application of the techniques and teachings of his father. He built a dōjō, *Daitō-kan*, and started to provide structure to his father's teaching, bringing to it a great number of notable innovations. The first was the classification of the technical terms with a technical progression in a more logical form than those used by his father in the first *makimono, Daitō-ryū aiki-jūjutsu Hiden*. He replaced the old names with more logical terms for training. He created a system of ranks and diplomas that did not exist during his father's lifetime.

To have a system in which only *kyōju-dairi* and *makimono* are awarded was very tedious. Often Sokaku would only practice one set or group of techniques for months on end, which by today's standards, would not interest new pupils. The students stopped training, and Tokimune often reported that many stopped after the long practice sessions or after just having received their rank. The options were clear: either continue practice as a recluse, and stop giving seminars, and the like, or reform the program and go to the dōjō in order to teach. Giving up on the art, and denying the popularity of *Daitō-ryū* was not what his father had transmitted to him. Tokimune was very astute about what to do, drawing on his experience and on that of a number of people who came to see his father.

A system of ranks made it possible to give rewards to those who attached more value to the fiction of recognition than to sincere, practical, continuous training. With regard to teaching, although he was a man of a great kindness, he did not teach the secret techniques of *Daitō-ryū* or the techniques he had received from his father. Indeed, he reportedly said:

> *One never should teach one's true techniques nor to show them, because they can be used against you one day. It is necessary to be sure of the person to whom you will transmit them. Therefore, there is always only one successor. Also, it is necessary to know the true effectiveness of a demonstrated technique without showing that effectiveness....*

Providing a major shift in the training presentation and style from what his father had bequeathed to him, Tokimune maintained the secrecy of his father's art, while presenting the more visible and attractive portions of *Daitō-ryū aiki-jūjutsu*. One can see the major changes to the approach by attending some publically-offered seminars.

The meeting with Katsuyuki Kondo would change the course of the life of Tokimune. Katsuyuki had already trained under Yoshida Kotarō (1871–1947) who introduced Ueshiba to Sokaku while living in Hokkaidō. Kotarō had received a *kyōju-dairi* from Sokaku, and he had taught among others, Mas Oyama, the founder of *Kyokushinkai*. It is with the introduction from Kotarō that Katsuyuki began to practice under the tutelage of Tokimune. Katsuyuki did not hesitate to live for a long time as *uchi deshi* (apprentice in residence) in the *Daitō-kan* in Hokkaidō to follow the teaching of Tokimune.

Showing a thirst for research, and exceptional skills, little by little he worked his way into Tokimune's heart. Katsuyuki received a *kyōju-dairi* from Tokimune, and opened a dōjō in Chiba, very close to Tokyo. During the inauguration of the dōjō, prestigious practitioners such as Kisshomaru Ueshiba, Gozō Shioda, and Tokimune, among others, were present.

In conjunction with his assiduous practice of *Daitō-ryū aiki-jūjutsu* (and not hesitating to invite Tokimune himself for particular courses), Katsuyuki collected any document or manuscript on *Daitō-ryū* that had belonged to Sokaku or his first pupils. He even acquired weapons and personal effects of Sokaku. Katsuyuki has the *densho* and first photographs showing Sokaku practicing *Daitō-ryū*, including him practicing techniques with Hisatakuma. Hisatakuma asked Katsuyuki to take over his school, but since Katsuyuki was already committed to the teachings of Tokimune he had to refuse this immense honor. This shows that already some of the pupils of Sokaku thought of him as a possibility for the resumption of their dōjō.

Katsuyaki also has all the technical notes and calligraphy of Admiral Takeshita and Asano, who both compiled all the techniques they studied under the tutelage of Sokaku. These documents are very estimable historical sources, containing a comprehensive view of one of the many facets of the art developed by Sokaku. Sensei Katsuyuki stores all of this material in a museum-like room, located in a soundproof, private part of his dōjō in Chiba. At the time of our conversation, I had the immense privilege to review all of these splendid documents and objects that are witnesses to the incredible history of Sokaku and *Daitō-ryū aiki-jūjutsu*. Katsuyaki also has a very beautiful collection of calligraphy by Yamaoka Tesshū (1836–1888).

After having lost his wife to disease, Tokimune felt his time was near, and decided to offer the succession of *Daitō-ryū aiki-jūjutsu* to the one person who had the values, morals, and the technical skill, and who achieved the unanimous support of the oldest pupils of Sokaku still living, Katsuyuki Kondo. Katsuyuki Kondo occupies the rank of *sōke dairi* (someone who temporarily teaches in place of the main instructor) of *Daitō-ryū* and represents the technical and historical reference point, making it impossible to circumvent the study of authentic *Daitō-ryū aiki-jūjutsu*.

Bibliography (only in Japanese language):
- *Daitō-ryū Aiki-jūjutsu Hiden Mokuroku*, private collection, 1869.
- *Aizu Han Kyoiki KB*, (*Historical Reflection on the Physical Education of the Aizu Family*), 1765
- *Budō Hiketsu: Aiki no Jutsu*, 1892.
- *Nihon Budō Taikei*, 1970.
- *Hiden Nihon Jūjutsu*, 1979.

# Appendix C: Timeline of Japanese Martial Arts

| | |
|---|---|
| 10 世紀後半 (tenth Century) | The *nihontō* (日本刀) made its appearance. The curved blade differentiates it from a Chinese sword. *Kashima no Tachi* (鹿島之太刀) and the eight schools of Kyōtō (京の八流). |
| 1159 | *Yoshitsune* (1159–1189) receives the teaching of the art of the sword from a certain Kiichi Hōgan of the Kurama temple. |
| 1160 | Creation of the *Ogasawara Gen-ryū kyūjutsu* (小笠原原流) school by Ogasawara Enmitsu. |
| 1180 | - The names of the following combat techniques, *kakujō* (角縄), *chichūshu* (蜻蛛手), *jūmonji* (十文字), *tonbō kaesu* (蜻蛉返す), *mizu guruma* (水車), and others, are used to indicate a type of technique from a particular school.<br>- Creation of *Chikujō Shima-ryū bōjutsu* (竹生島流) by Nanba Heiji. |
| 1200 | Creation of *Shoshō-ryū jūjutsu* (諸賞流和術) by Mori Chūhei Okunitomo. |
| 1350 | Creation of *Nen-ryū* (念流) by the monk Jion, who started teaching in various temples. |
| 1384 | Chūjō Hyōgonosuke Nagahide of *Chūjō-ryū* (中條流) enters to the service of the shōgun Ashikaga Yoshimitsu (1358–1408) as an instructor of *bujutsu*. |
| 1387 | Birth of Iizasa Choisai Yamashiro no Kami Ienao |
| 1408 | The monk Jion (慈音), builds Jōfuku-ji (長福寺) and takes the name of Nendai washō (念大和尚). |
| 1430 | Creation of *Tenshin Shōden Katori Shintō-ryū* (天真正伝香取神道流) by Iizasa Choisai Yamashiro No Kami Ienao |
| 1466 | Aisu Ikōsai (1441–1538) begins the teaching of the *Kage-ryū* (陰流) |
| 1467 | Beginning of the disorders of the Onin era (1477) |
| 1470 | Creation of *Toda-ryū* (富田流) by Toda Nagaie |
| 1480 | Creation of the *Heiki-ryū kyūjutsu* (日置流弓術) school by Heiki Dansei |
| 1485 | Founding of *Kashima Shin Kage-ryū* (鹿島新陰流) by Matsumoto Bizen no kami Masanobu (1468–1524) |
| 1489 | Birth of Tsukahara Bokuden (1489–1571) |
| 1508 | Birth of Kamiizumi Nobutsuna (1508–1582) |
| 1520 | Creation of *Shintō-ryū* (新当流) by Tsukahara Bokuden |
| 1521 | Birth of Hōzoin Inei (1521–1607) |
| 1529 | Birth of Yagyū Sekishūsai Muneyoshi (1529–1606), successor of Kamiizumi |
| 1530 | - Creation of *Shinkage-ryū* (新影流) by Kamiizumi Ise no kami Nobutsuna<br>- Creation of *Takeuchi-ryū kogusoku* (竹内流小具足) by Takeuchi Hisamori |
| 1549 | Tsukahara Bokuden (1489–1571), becomes the *bujutsu* instructor for shōgun Ashikaga Yoshiharu (1511–1550), Yoshiteru (1536–1565) and Yoshiaki (1537–1597). |
| 1550? | Birth of Ittō Itōsai, founder of *Ittō-ryū* (一刀流) |
| 1558 | Kamiizumi writes *Kage mokuroku* (影目録). |
| 1560 | Creation of *Hōzoin-ryū sōjutsu* (宝蔵院流槍術) by Kakuzenpō Inei (1521–1607) |
| 1561 | Birth of the founder of *Jigen-ryū* (示現流), Togo Chūi (1561–1643), in Satsuma |
| 1565 | Yagyū Sekishūsai Muneyoshi (1529–1606), receives *ikkoku hitori inkajō* (一国一人印可状) from the hands of Kamiizumi Nobutsuna (1507–1582). |
| 1574 | Higuchi Matashichirō (1550?–1600?) receives *Mokuroku* (目録) of the *Nen-ryū* (念流). |
| 1575 | Battle of Nagashino, defeat of Takeda Katsuyori (1546–1582) by Oda Nobunaga (1534–1582) |

| 1576 | Ittōsai forms his school, *Ittō-ryū* (一刀流). |
|------|------|
| 1580 | Creation of *Tendō-ryū* (天道流) by Satō Denkipō |
| 1585 | Toyotomi Hideyoshi (1536–1598) becomes *Kanpaku* (関白). |
| 1587 | Higuchi Matashirō receives the *inka kaiden* (印可皆伝) and becomes the 17th successor of the *Nen-ryū*. |
| 1588 | Toyotomi Hideyoshi (1536–1598) spearheads *katana-gari* (刀狩), dismantling the factions of armed peasants. |
| 1590 | - Hideyoshi launches out in the unification of the country, Tokugawa Ieyasu is established in Edo<br>- Creation of *Jigen-ryū* (示現流)<br>- Creation of *Hayashizaki-ryū* (林崎流抜刀術) by Hayashizaki Jinzuke (1542?–?) |
| 1591 | Onojirōemon Tadaaki receives the transmission of having the *Ittō-ryū* from Ittōsai |
| 1594 | Yagyū Sekichūsai enters his son, *Yagyū Munenori* (1571–1646) into the service the Tokugawa family. Ieyasu writes a pact, *kishōmon* (起請文), for submission to Sekishūsai |
| 1600 | - Battle of Sekigahara<br>- Creation of *Tamiya-ryū* (田宮流抜刀術) by Tamiya Shigemasa<br>- Creation of *Hokki-ryū* (伯耆流) by Katayama Hokki Hisayasu |
| 1602 | Death of Okuyama Kyuga-sai, instructor of *bujutsu* to Tokugawa Ieyasu |
| 1603 | Tokugawa Ieyasu establishes his *bakufu* within Edo. |
| 1610 | Creation of *Niten Ichi-ryū* (二天一流) by Miyamoto Musashi |
| 1612 | Miyamoto Musashi (1584–1645), wins his fight against Sasaki Kojirō on the island of Funajima in Okura. |
| 1615 | - Summer campaign against Toyotomi cut off in their castle in Osaka<br>- Establishment of *Bukesho hōdō* (武家諸法度) |
| 1620 | Creation of *Shintō Musō-ryū* (神道夢想流杖術) by Musōken nosuke |
| 1621 | Yagyū Munenori teaches the ultimate technique of the *Yagyū Shinkage-ryū* (柳生新影流) to the shōgun, Iemitsu. The shōgun writes a pact of recognition. |
| 1630 | - Creation of *Yagyū Shingan-ryū* (柳生心眼流) by Hayato Kanetsugu<br>- Creation of *Asayama Ichiden-ryū Taijutsu* (浅山一伝流体術) by Asayama Ichidensai (1609?–1687?) |
| 1632 | Yagyū Munenori writes *Heihō kadensho* (兵法家伝書) |
| 1637 | - Revolt of Shimabara, Shimabara no Ran (島原の乱).<br>- Ibaragi Mataemon writes *Kitō-ryū ran mokuroku* (起倒流乱目録). |
| 1639 | - The shōgun, Iemitsu, famous amateur of *bujutsu*, organizes a meeting between the best practicioners of Japan, *Gozen-shiai* (御前試合).<br>- Creation of *Sekiguchi-ryū* (関口流) by Sekiguchi Ujimune (1597–1670) |
| 1641 | - Miyamoto Musashi writes *Heihō Sanjūgo Kajō* (兵法三十五箇条) at the request of Hosokawa Tadatoshi (1586–1641).<br>- Ikeda Mitsumasa forms the first school where one teaches both letters and *bujutsu* in the stronghold of the Okayama family. |
| 1642 | Yagyū Jūbei (1607–1650) writes *Tsuki no Shō* (月之抄). |
| 1643 | Miyamoto Musashi writes *Gorin no Sho* (五輪書). |
| 1648 | Prohibition on craftsmen and tradesmen carrying a *wakizashi* or a *tachi* |
| 1660 | Creation of *Yōshin-ryū* (揚心流) by Akiyama Shirobei |
| 1664 | Kotoda Heii writes *Ittōsai Sensei Kenpōsho* (一刀斎先生剣法書). |
| 1680 | Creation of *Shibukawa-ryū* (渋川流) by Shibukawa Bangorō Yoshikata |
| 1682 | Ibaze Suiken begins the teaching of his *Shingyōtō-ryū* (心形刀流). |
| 1686 | Oda Kiri Ichiun writes *Sekiun-ryū kenjutsu sho* (夕雲流剣術書). |
| 1702 | The *Akōgishi* (赤穂義士) victory led by Ōishi Yoshio. |

| | |
|---|---|
| 1716 | Publication of *Honchō Bugei Shōden* (本朝武芸小伝) |
| 1727 | Publication of *Inaka Sōshi* (田舎荘子) of Issai Chōzanshi, including *Neko no Myōjutsu* (猫之妙術) |
| 1728 | Publication of *Tengu Geijutsu Ron* (天狗芸術論) of Issai Chōzanshi |
| 1729 | Terada Shiemon writes *Tōkashū* (登假集), which recalls the history of *jūjutsu* up to the creation of *Kitō-ryū*. |
| 1754 | Hosokawa Shigekata opens the *Jishūkan* (時習館) in the stronghold of Higo (Kumamoto prefecture). The following year, the founder of the *Unkō-ryū* (雲弘流), Ijima Kageun, becomes the chief instructor of this school. |
| 1755 | Nakanishi Chūbei, legate of *Naka Nishiha Ittō-ryū* (中西派一刀流), uses the *shinai* in kenjutsu practice. At the same time, Yamada Saemon opens a *dōjō* and teaches the school *Jikinshin kage-ryū* (直心影流) there, where one also uses *shinai* and various defense techniques. <br> From this date, the use of the *shinai* and the creation of new defense techniques will help give birth to a great number of new schools. |
| 1759 | Birth of Hiryama Kōzō (1759–1828), future founder of *Kōbu Jitsuyō- ryū* (講武実用流) |
| 1767 | *Nippon Chūkō Bujutsu Keifu Ryaku* (日本中興武術系譜略) is written by Shiga Yoshimoto after having compiled a great deal of information on the most important schools of Japanese *bujutsu*. |
| 1773 | Momoi Hachirōsaemon, founder of *Kyōshin Meichi-ryū kenjutsu* (鏡新明智流剣術), establishes the *Shigakukan* (士学館) very close to Nihonbashi. |
| 1778 | Togasaki Kumatarō opens a *dōjō* in Edo and teaches the techniques of *Shintō Munen-ryū* (神道無念流). Okada Tōmatsu, his pupil, succeeds him in the order of the school and establishes *Gekiken-kan* (撃剣館) in the district of Kanda. |
| 1787 | A tournament between masters of various disciplines focusing on *kenjutsu* and *sōjutsu*, in particular, are organized in the stronghold of Tsuyama (Okayama). |
| 1789 | Birth of Satō Yakurō (1789–1871) |
| 1792 | Promulgation of a law to encourage the warriors with the practice of letters and *bujutsu* |
| 1805 | Promulgation of a law aimed at prohibiting the practice of *bujutsu* by the peasants |
| 1810 | Creation of *Tenshin Shinyō-ryū jūjutsu* (天神真揚流柔術) by Kiso mataemon (1786–1863) |
| 1818 | Foundation of *Fuji Shin-ryū* (不二心流) by Nakamura Isshinsai who passes on his teaching in the areas around Mt. Fuji |
| 1822 | Chiba Shūsaku (1794–1855) of the *Hokushin Ittō-ryū* (北辰一刀流) establishes his *dōjō*, Genbukan (玄武館), in Shinnagawa. |
| 1825 | Birth of Momoi Junzō (1825–1885), who will become the fourth successor of *Kyōshin Meichi-ryū* (鏡新明智流剣術) |
| 1830 | Birth of Sakakibara Kenkichi (1830–1894) |
| 1833 | - Oseki Susumi organizes the first combat with protective armor. <br> - Birth of Kondō Isami (1833–1868), member of *Shinsengumi* and fourth successor of *Tennen Rishin-ryū* (天然理心流) |
| 1836 | Birth of Yamaoka Tesshū, future founder of *Ittō Shōden Mutō-ryū* (一刀正伝無刀流) |
| 1838 | Satō Yakurō opens a *dōjō* with Kudan (Ichiōji) and diffuses the teaching of *Shintō Munen-ryū* (神道無念流). |
| 1842 | The school education of the children of the families of warriors, *Kōdōkan* (弘道館) established in the stronghold of Mito. |
| 1853 | Arrival of Commodore Perry |
| 1854 | Rōjū Abe Masahiro receives the order of the *bakafu* to catalogue the number of establishments where various *bujutsu* are taught. The same year, a very new type of establishment, named *Kōbusho* (講武所), where *bujutsu* is taught is opened. |
| 1855 | Opening of a *bunbu gakkō* (文武学校)—School for Literary and Military Arts—in the stronghold of Matsudai, with a teaching of several disciplines like the *kyūjutsu, sōjutsu, kenjutsu, jūjutsu*. |

| 1856 | The *bakufu* establishes a network of *Kōbusho* (military academies) throughout Japan. Otani Nobutomo, leader of the *Jikishin Kage-ryū* (直心影流), becomes the first tutor of the *Kōbusho* located at Kanda Ogawachō. |
|------|------|
| 1860 | Birth of Kanō Jigorō |
|  | Birth of Takeda Sokaku, founder of *Daitō-ryū Aiki-jūjutsu* (大東流合気柔術) |
| 1864 | Shinsen Gumi (新選組) attacks the Ikeda residence in Kyōto |
| 1865 | Tokugawa Iemochi (1846–1866) fixes the directives for the practice of the *kenjutsu, sōjutsu, hōjutsu* of the *Kōbusho* in the town of Osaka. |
| 1866 | - The dōjō *Kōshikan* (倣士館) of the traditional *Maniwa Nen-ryū* is built in the prefecture of Gunma in the Maniwa village.<br>- Period when the proliferation of *bujutsu* practice within the dōjō of *Bugakkō, Enbujō* is increasing in all the strongholds of Japan |
| 1868 | War of *Boshin* (戊辰戦争).<br>*Gokajō no seimon* (五箇条誓文). Restoration of *Meiji*. |
| 1870 | Birth of Funakoshi Gichin (or Gishin) |
| 1871 | Removal of the strongholds and installation of the prefectures |
| 1872 | Installation of the imperial education system |
| 1873 | Sakakibara Kenkichi organizes great demonstrations of *bujutsu* named *gekiken* (撃剣). |
| 1879 | Dialog to incorporate the practice of *kenjutsu* within the training of the police force |
| 1880 | *Kōdōkan jūdō* (講道館柔道) of *Kanō* |
| 1883 | - An investigation by the Ministry for Education is carried out to uncover the advantages and disadvantages related to the practice of *gekiken, jūjutsu*, and the like<br>- Birth of Ueshiba Morihei |
| 1895 | *Japanese Dai Butokukai* (大日本武徳会)—Greater Japan Martial Virtue Society—created |
| 1896 | An imperial law allows the inclusion of the practice of the *gekiken* in the schools. |
| 1899 | Construction of Butokuden (武徳殿) is completed. |
| 1900 | Creation of *Daitō-ryū* by Takeda Sokaku |
| 1911 | - Creation of the *Butokukai* school<br>- Competition in kendō introduced |
| 1912 | Opening of the school specializing in the training of the masters in *bujutsu* |
| 1915 | Meeting between Takeda and Ueshiba in Hokkaidō. |
| 1919 | The school specializing in the training of *bujutsu* masters takes the official name of *Budō Senmon Gakkō* (武道専門学校). |
| 1920 | Beginning of the teaching of aikidō (合気道) under the name of *Ueshiba-juku* (植芝塾) |
| 1923 | Official introduction of karate, then named *Okinawa tōte* (沖縄唐手), during a demonstration of *Funakoshi* to *Kōdōkan* by Kanō. |

# Appendix D: Alternative Names for Ninja

As I discussed in Chapter 2, *The Public Record of Ninjutsu*, the term "ninja" is very recent. Studying the historical documents relating to the actions of those individuals who could be called ninja, one finds a great number of names associated with them. These names, varied according to the times, places, lords, families, and other factors, but they always clearly pointed out the express function or skills of the ninja. Here is a list of the important names that one consistently finds in supporting historical documents.

**The Earliest Names**

The names of kanchō (間諜), kansai (姦細), yōkan (用間) and gokan (五間) were the first names to indicate the ninja. One finds these four in the majority of the great treatises of military strategy and of espionage of China, particularly, *Sonshi no Heihō, Rikutō Sanryaku* and others. One can legitimately propose that those terms originated in China. The ideograms *hosoi* (細) and *chō* (諜) show a clear indication of the manner of this type of warrior. Indeed, *hosoi* (細) means, "work meticulous, fine, delicate, precise," and *chō* (諜), means: "information, the adviser, to listen to the hidden words." Thus *kansai* (姦細), can be translated as: "One who finds vital information in the conflict" and *kanchō* (間諜) can be translated as, "One who dissects and controls information."

The ideogram *kan* (間), means: "time, interval, duration, or space." This shows us that the ninja was a person who was in the middle of the things, of people, political actions, economic situations, and soldiers of the time. Thanks to very highly developed skills in using their bodies and a sharp sensory acuteness, the ninja had been able to maximize the use of time and space. The ideogram *yō* (用), means: "to use, use, need, or employ." The ideogram *go* (五) means the figure five.* Together with the ideogram *kan*, *yōkan* can be translated as, "One who makes good use of time, of space."

*Gokan* (五間) can have several levels of meaning. The first refers to the military treatise on strategy and espionage by *Zun Zi* where the *gokan* is a spy sought out for his skills in listening and abilities to manipulate information. Another interpretation stresses that the figure five is significant. Indeed, the value has broad symbolic appeal: the five continents, the five elements, five phases, the five fingers of the hand, the five directions, and so forth. Combined with the ideogram *kan*, it shows one with a deep knowledge of the natural laws, a human who has mastered perfect control of the body and is able to claim the name *gokan*. The names of *kanchō, kansai, yōkan* and *gokan* slowly evolved into the term *mono mawashi* (回者).

**The Asuka Period (592–710)**

Under the reign of the prince regent Shōtoku Taishi (574–622), the term used was that of *shinobi*, which communicates something different from *shinobi* (忍). The ideograms used were (志能便). The first ideogram (志) has as a reading *kokorozashi* and means, "to aspire to something," "to have the intention," "to aim to do something." The second ideogram (能) is pronounced *no*, and means "the talent" or "skill." Finally, the third ideogram, (便) has several pronunciations: *bin, ben, bi*, and means, "chance," "occasion," or "mail." By associating the three ideograms, one finds the following significant representations of the skill of the ninja, "One who has the talent or skills to achieve their goal through information" or "One who has the talent or the skills to carry out their goals by seizing the right time" Under the reign of Tenmu Tennō (673–686), one finds the names *kanchō* (間諜) and *sokkan* (側間). The indication remains the same, namely, "One who dissects and controls information," but *sokkan* was also used to mean a spy or assassin.

**The Nara Period (710–784)**

During this period, one finds several ideograms that are different but are all are read with the same pronunciation: *ukami*. The ideograms are: (斥候), (候), (間諜), and (窺見). The first ideogram, (斥), has as a reading *seki* and means: "to spy, to watch for, draw aside, or push back." The second character, (候), means: "expectancy, makes an attempt, sign, season, or time." One can clearly see the direction of the words *ukami* which means "one who watches for a sign" or "one who pushes back time (quietly, patiently)." The term *ukami* slowly replaced the old term *kanchō* and ended up indicating any type of action relating to a particular type of warrior native to the areas of Iga and Kōga. *Ukagami* evolved from the term *uka gamiru* (窺見), which means spy, to supervise, watch for movements of the enemy, watch for the favorable occasion, and so forth. It remains one of the more general terms indicating the ninja and his art.

The *Taihei-ki* mentions the term *ongyō no mono* (隠形之者). The first two ideograms immediately reveal one of the technical characteristics essential to the practice of ninjutsu, namely: dispersion, invisibility in combat as a driving force. Indeed, the first ideogram (隠), means: "to hide, conceal, disperse, secrete, to cover up." The second ideogram, (形), means: "form." One can translate *ongyō* along the lines of "Those whose appearance is dispersed, hidden, concealed, and the like" or "That which is hidden, covered up." One will find the term *ongyō no jutsu* (隠形之術) in various *densho* and histories.

**The Kamakura (1192–1333) and Muromachi (1333–1467) Periods**

From the Kamakura period, when the warriors seized power until the end of the Edo period, in the provinces of Ōshū† and Kyūshū, one finds the term *tandai* (探題), which indicated a very particular type of active spy. This indicates the skill to supervise remote provinces. The first ideogram (探) means: "deep, intense, to deepen;" the second ideogram, (題), means: "topic,

---

    * The figure five, refers also to the five groups of *musoku-nin* (無足人). During the Sengoku period, the inhabitants of *Iga* were divided into five distinct groups under the generic name *musoku-nin*. The five groups were made up in the following way: *Soge no Shū* (組外之衆), *Boi soshū* (母依組衆), *Teppō Soshū* (鉄砲組衆) *Ryūshū Kyoshū* (留守居衆), and finally *Shinobi no shū* (忍之衆). Each one of these groups had a well-defined function such as the guarding of a fortified town for the *Ryūshū Kyoshū* or forming the militia of a city or castle for the *Teppō Soshū*.

    † In modern-day Japan, this includes the departments of Fukushima, Aomori and Iwate.

subject, title." The function of the *tandai* can be translated as "That which looks further into the problem" or "That which controls the problem deeply."

In the annals of the Muromachi Bakufu entitled *Nochi Kagami* (後鑑), we find the terms, *saisaku* (細作) and *kagimono-kiki* (嗅物聴). The first ideogram of *saisaku*, is *hosoi* (細), that we already discussed in relation to the term *kansai*. The second ideogram, (作), means: "to manufacture, make, build, work, or harvest." One can translate *saisaku* as, "One who manufactures (creates) with meticulousness (a plan)" or "One who collects what is fine, delicate (quietly perceives essential information)." *Kagimono-kiki* is composed of three ideograms. The first (嗅) means "to feel, to sniff, to breath in, or to smell." The second (物) means "things, object, or articles." The last (聴) means "to hear, listen, learn, to get information, or to inquire." *Kagimono-kiki* can be translated as: "One who feels and hears the things (quietly, which cannot be heard by anyone but him)." This name shows yet another facet of the ninja, they listen to all things, seeking information. This skill was also used personally, that is, to listen to one's own body, having the knowledge to feel danger and to quell disease.

The terms *Iga no mono* (伊賀之者) and *Kōga no mono* make their appearance during this period at the battle of Magari no jin (鈎の陣) in 1487. This battle took place at the end of an event of great importance in the history of Japanese warriors, the Ōnin (1467–1477) wars. *Iga no mono*, along with *Kōga no mono*, of course, designates the natives of the provinces of Iga and Kōga; but it especially shows that very early inhabitants of these provinces were known for their unorthodox methods of combat and espionage.

*Nochi Kagami* also mentions the term *Yatō* (夜盗). The first ideogram, (夜), means "the evening, nightfall, or the night." The second ideogram, (盗), means "to fly or conceal." *Nochi Kagami* explains that this type of spy had the skills to infiltrate enemy castles, in secrecy, and conceal himself in the linens in order to hide his plans, weapons, and information. *Yatō*, correctly translated means "that which is concealed under the cover of night." However, the history does not reveal if this type of spy originated in Iga or Kōga. It surely relates to a type of warrior whose techniques were connected with those of the ninja, but who may have had a different origin.

Lastly there is *sansha* (三者) whose ideograms are the same ones as those used for *mitsumono* (三者), but with a different pronunciation. *Mitsumono* refers to the three types of spies used by Takeda Shingen. *Sansha* is known under the various pronunciations and the following ideograms: *kenmi* (検見), *kenbun* (見分), and *enkō* (遠候). These names, in particular *kenmi* and *kenbun*, all have the same meaning and were used during the Kamakura and Muromachi periods. Their definition translates into the role of a type of spy sent by the *bakufu* for espionage or to uncover the situation in a province. Thereafter, the terms moved toward *ukami* or *monomi*, and during the Edo period, they moved toward *monogiki* (物聞) or *metsuke* (目附).

## The Sengoku Period (1477–1603)

This period in the history of Japan is very rich in documents on the activities of the ninja. It is during this period of history that they were most active, because of the confusion and the chaos that reigned then. One finds a great number of names that vary according to the places, lords, and people involved. A historical chronicle, which is appeared in a newspaper known as *Tamon-in Nikki* (多聞院日記) gives a variety of names. In the same way *Kōyō Gunkan* (甲陽軍鑑), *Mikawa Fudō-Ki* (三河後風土記), *Hōjō Godaiki* (北条五代記), and the like, give us a great number of terms: *kanja* (間者), *kyōdan* (饗談), *kikimono-yaku* (聞物役), *kusa* (草), *mitsumono* (三者), *shinobi no shū* (忍之衆), *Iga shū* (伊賀衆); *Kōga shū* (甲賀衆), *kobu shinkata* (小普請方), *suppa* (素破), *grated* (乱破), *inu* (犬), *daigo-retsu* (第五列), *tan* (擔猿), *toppa* (突破), *nusumi gumi* (盗組), *negoro-gumi* (根来組), *mawashi mono* (回者), *mittei* (密偵), *monomi* (物見), and *sansha* (三者).

The term *kanja*, with the ideogram *ja* (者) meaning: "nobody," remains by far the term that best shows the technical merits and the aspect of invisibility characterized very early in the practice of ninjutsu and the attitude of the ninja. *Kanja* (間者) can be translated as "that which is between the things, between the men, entering the actions," the man of the intersection, the man in the middle. That shows how much the true direction of the real ninja was to be a person free of any external pressure and was sensitive to the order of the things.

*Shinchōkō-ki* (信長公記), a chronicle relating to the life of Oda Nobunaga (1534–1582), reveals that he called upon a certain a type of spy called a *kyōdan* (饗談). The first ideogram (饗), means: "resonance, echo, to sound, reverberate, resound," and the second ideogram, (談), means: "matter, conversation, discussion." Thus, this type of spy was famous for combining the ability to track enemies and the ability to collect vital information in secrecy. This term can be translated as "one who seizes the nature of the discussion." Indeed, it is a question of knowing which type of information would likely be of interest to the lord. In this case, the lord was Oda Nobunaga, and when his formidable rise and his various military successes are studied, one cannot help but presume he had a deeply acute knowledge supplied by an accurate source of information. This information was revealed to him by a *kyōdan*, a spy whose skill to measure the nature and value of information was unequaled. However, the hatred of Oda Nobunaga towards the ninja of Iga, and the bloody battle of 1583 which followed (*Tensho Iga no Ran*), shows well that the *kyōdan* did not act as a native ninja of Iga and Kōga.

*Kikimono-yaku* (聞物役), was a type of spy like *kgimono-kiki* (嗅物聴), who had the function of listening to the conversations of the enemies. The ideogram *kiki* (聞) means "to hear or listen," the *mono* ideogram (物), means "thing," and the ideogram *yaku* (役), means "function, role, service, battles, or drudgery." The direction of the ideograms is very clear, "one whose role consists in hearing specific things."

*Kusa* (草), which means "grass, plants, or vegetation," is often mentioned in *Hōjō Godai-ki* (北条五代記), many passages of which where translated in Chapter 2, *The Public Record of Ninjutsu*. This name refers to a type of ninja who was an integral part of the warlord's army. This ninja's role was to sow disorder in the enemy's lines. Their particular ability was to blend into the vegetation, trees, and grasses. *Kusa* always acted in groups; therefore, they functioned as teams rather than as singular commandos like the *rappa* and *suppa*. The titles of *rappa* (乱破) and *suppa* (素破) are also mentioned in *Hōjō Godai-ki*. The ideograms that form the word *rappa*, is made up of the terms *ra* (乱), "disorder, rebellion, to put in disorder, or to be in disorder," and *ha* (破) "to tear, break, or lacerate." This name wonderfully illustrates the function of *rappa*, namely to cause disorder and to break up the enemy lines by furtive actions. The two ideograms of *suppa* are made up of the characters, *su* (素), which means "simple, natural, or unbleached," and *ha* (破), which means "vague." One can, thus, translate *suppa* "that which simply infiltrates." According to the *Hōjō Godai-ki*, it seems that this type of warrior had the reputation of being able to easily infiltrate enemy lines and that this skill was natural for him. The names of *kusa*, *suppa* and *rappa* formed *mitsumono* (三者), literally "the three people," also known as the three types of spies that Takeda Shingen (1521–1573) used at the time of his battles.

Another type of warrior spy is mentioned in the same chronicle, called *toppa* (突破). The first ideogram (突), means "to break in, strike, push, bore, or attack." The second ideogram, *ha* (破), means "to tear, break, or lacerate." It, thus, refers to a group of warriors whose skill was to find or to create a breach in the enemy lines.

The military chronicles, such as the *Taihei-ki* or *Kōyō Gunkan*, often mention the term of *daigo-retsu* (第五列), literally meaning "*the fifth column*," identifying a group of warriors who used unorthodox fighting methods similar to those of the ninjutsu of Iga and Kōga. The armies of the warlord were divided into four groups, with the fifth group consisting of warriors who acted in the shadows, acting outside the accepted codes of combat and who sowed disorder and confusion in the enemy's army. These warriors, even if they had exceptional skills in traditional combat, were not regarded as *bushi* in the real meaning of the term. They were, however, included in the warrior classes, but normally at the lowest of social levels.

The rival of Takeda Shingen, Uesugi Kenshi (1530–1578) used of a type of spy connected to the ninja tradition that was called *tanzaru* (擔猿) or *nokizaru* (軒猿). The name *tanzaru* (坦猿) is also one of the synonyms. The *tan* (擔) and *in* (猿) ideograms indicate a type of spy who has the skills to move from roof to roof with the agility of a monkey.

The *Tamon-in Nikki* (多聞院日記) mentions the terms *Iga-shū* (伊賀衆), *Kōga-shū* (甲賀衆), *shinobi-no-shū* (忍之衆) and *musoku-nin* (無足人). The ideogram *shū* (衆) means "mass, multitude, or crowd." Coupled with the name of the provinces of Iga and Kōga, it means the group from Iga or group from Kōga. In the same way *shinobi-no-shū* (忍之衆) indicates that the members of this group all are trained with the combat methods and techniques of ninjutsu. The name *shinobi-no-mono* (忍者), which one can translate as "those who see and hear without being seen," or "those who endure all things," also appears along with *shinobi shū*.

The *musoku-nin* has a significant meaning because it reveals a characteristic in the manner of movement by followers of ninjutsu. Indeed *musoku* (無足) means "without the legs," which translates as action in which people cannot see the legs moving because the motion is too fast. A deeper look at the meaning reveals that there is a method of body displacement in ninjutsu schools that makes it possible to obscure the transfer of the weight of the body in the execution of combat techniques, as well as in the use of the body in everyday life.

It is a question of relaxing muscular tension, not of using brute force or movement that could telegraph the combat technique to be used or the intention of movement to the enemy. This method, called *musoku-no-hō* (無足之法), is unquestionably used in all reputable martial arts schools, and if one adds the mental state of this technique to the physical practice, it makes it possible for one to reach a state in which movement seems to disappear from the enemy's field of vision. This method of displacement is used in almost all the traditional *bujutsu* schools of Japan, such as *Kage-ryū* (影流), *Shinkage-ryū* (新影流), and *Nen-ryū* (念流). We can also find examples in *Nō* theater, wherein such subtle and focused movements and displacements also manifest. During the middle of the Edo period, the term *musoku-nin* ended up indicating the lower level of the warrior class. The underlying principle of body movement and displacement inherent in the translation of this name was mostly forgotten, except for a small number of followers who kept it alive.

The record entitled *Isui Onko* (伊水温故), written in 1706, mentions how the Maeda family, in order to establish a firmer position in the stronghold of Kaga, used a group made up of 50 warriors from Iga, who answered to the name of *Nusumi-gumi* (盗組). Once the Maeda family's position was firmly established, the use of ninja was no longer required and the group dispersed, disappearing into nature. The ideograms show that this was a group who used hiding-places, and moved in secrecy. The ideogram *nusumi* (盗) means "to fly, secretly, or in hiding place," and *gumi* (組) means "a group, class, to be linked, or to join."

This record reveals most of names of the principal types, with particular mention of *kobu shinkata* (小普請方). This was someone who had the occupation of a maintenance engineer, specializing in the construction, development, and repair of various buildings, objects, weapons, and so forth. The services of *kobu shinkata* were highly prized, and they were always under the direct orders of the chiefs of the main households in the province of Iga. The ideograms *ko*, meaning "small or detailed," *bu*, meaning "general, broad, or universal," *shin*, meaning "to solicit, answer, require, claim, or a support," and *kata*, meaning "person," clearly shows that a *kobu shinkata* was a person who constructed and built a variety of things with a great meticulousness.

The record entitled *Zokkin Hisei-dan* (賊禁秘誠談), written in 1788, mentions the following terms: *Negoro-gumi* (根来組), *mono mawashi* (回者), *mittei* (密偵), and *monomi* (物見). *Negoro-gumi* was a group of *sōhei* (僧兵), or warrior monks. The Negoro temple was built in 1130 in the province of Kii. The province of Kii was always a haven for pirates, dissidents, and renegades. Naturally, ninja also lived there. Thus, relations between ninja and the warrior monks of Negoro temple were very probable, especially when one knows the reputation of the temple and that the warrior monks were trained in the use of the *teppō*, powder, and explosives. After the destruction of the temple by Oda Nobunaga in 1585, it was rebuilt during the Keichō era (1596–1615) by the Asano family. A great number of the survivors from Negoro temple were recruited by Tokugawa Ieyasu and they fought under the Tokugawa banner during the battles of Sekigahara and the two campaigns of Osaka.

*Mittei* (密偵) were secret agents who monitored the actions and movements of the different warrior families. They were also known by the name of *tantei* (探偵), which translates today as "detective," but originally had a significantly different meaning. The ideograms in *tantei* are broken out as follows: *tan* (探), meaning "deep, intense, or to deepen," and *tei* (偵), meaning "soothsayer, spy, to spy upon, or one who spies upon." Thus *tantei* was "one who deduces the depth of issues, the screening of facts" or "one who is an in-depth spy." This meaning is closer to that of *mittei* whose ideogram *mitsu* (密) means "dense, tight, detailed, or secret," and *tei* (偵), which means "soothsayer, spy, to spy upon, or one who spies upon." One can translate *mittei* in this manner: "one who spies intensely in secrecy." This is not the translation of *tantei* today, which is "a detective."

## The Edo Period (1603–1867)

Tokugawa Ieyasu gained a great victory at the decisive battle of Sekigahara, where his army was opposed by a coalition of lords faithful to Toyotomi Hideyoshi, gathered around Mōri Terutomo. In 1603, in dedication for this victory, Ieyasu accepted that which his two predecessors had never managed to obtain from the Goyozei emperor, the title of shōgun. He set up new a *bakufu* in the town of Edo. During nearly 260 years the Tokugawa family controlled Japan until the arrival of Commodore Perry. This era was characterized by a long period of peace where, in spite of two great battles,[*] the status of *shinobi* changed. All the skills in guerilla activities and other secret warrior arts in which ninja excelled no longer had any justification. With their change of status, a great number of names for them changed. The most used were: *onmitsu* (隠密), *oniwaban* (御庭番), *teppō hyakunin-gumi* (鉄砲百人衆), *metsuke-yaku* (目附役), *akeya shikiban* (明屋敷番), *ohiro shikiban* (御広敷番), *yokome* (横目), *ongyō-no-mono* (隠形之者), *Iga-shū* (伊賀衆), *Kōga-shū* (甲賀衆), *Iga dōshin* (伊賀同心), and ninja (忍者).

The term *onmitsu* (隠密), was used for the first time by Toyotomi Hideyoshi (1537–1598), the successor to Oda Nobunaga. This term indicates the controlling spy network on the various strongholds and their lords set up by the *bakufu* of Tokugawa. The first ideogram (隠) means "to hide, one who hides, conceal, to be concealed, or to bury." The second ideogram (密) means "dense, detailed, secretly, furtively, or clandestinely." Onmitsu correctly translates the nature of the secret activities of the ninja during the Edo period. *Oniwaban* (御庭番) was the name given to the ninja who had the responsibility of securing the private locations in the castle where the families and concubines lived. The ideograms (御), (庭), and (番), show that this person was to supervise the private sectors of the Edo castle or the living quarters of the shōgun's family. *Teppō Hyakuningumi* (鉄砲百人衆), the name of the armed body, also known by the name *Teppō-tai* (鉄砲隊), was established by the military government of Tokugawa during the Edo period. This armed body consisted of four groups: the first group was *Kōga-gumi* (甲賀組), the second, *Iga-gumi* (伊賀組), the third, *Negoro-gumi* (根来組), and finally the fourth, which did not carry specific name. This describes a group that is closely related to what we would call "reservists" today and that was mostly made up of rōnin (masterless samurai).

Among the *Hyakunin-shū*, the most well-known groups were the *Okubo hyakinin-shū* (大久保百人衆) and the *Hachiō-ji sennin-shū* (八王子千人衆). Nowadays, one still finds great demonstrations where groups will parade and use the *teppō* in memory of these first groups who were so armed and in charge of protecting the shōgun, Tokugawa. *Okubo*, just like *hachiō-ji*, are districts of Tokyo where these annual demonstrations are celebrated. In the temple of the Okibo district, just as with *hachiō-ji*, one finds tombs and memorials set up in honor of the memory of the first such armed groups in the town of Edo. The majority of the members of these groups were survivors of the Negoro temple who had entered into the service of Tokugawa. Among them were a great number of *genin* (下人 or 下忍) native to Iga and Kōga.

*Metsuke-yaku* (目附役) was a function started at the beginning of the Edo period by Tokugawa to supervise and control the movements of the various families and monitor traffic throughout all the country. *Metsuke-yaku*, "one who sees all," were divided into three groups. At top of the hierarchy, one finds the *ometsuke* (大目附), tasked directly by the shōgun. The second rank is that of *nin-metsuke* (忍目附), and the third rank is *on-metsuke* (隠目附).[†] The ideograms *nin* (忍) and *on* (隠) show that these two functions were given only to ninja of Iga or Kōga. The role of these *metsuke* was of capital importance to the *bakufu* of Tokugawa, in particular at the time when the country was closed to outsiders. Indeed, the control and monitoring of the various strongholds and the families far away from the capital prevented rebellion from fomenting. It was necessary to also have warriors able to convey precise information and in place to act quickly without making waves.

*Akeya shikiban* (明屋敷番) was a name of a type of ninja who had a quite specific function. Created by Tokugawa Iemitsu (1604–1651), *akeya shikiban* supervised the residences of the shōgun and the lords when those homes were unoccupied. The group of *akeya shikiban* consisted of a hundred ninja of Iga with three distinct leaders. *Ohiro shikiban* (御広敷番) had the exclusive function to protect part of the Edo castle. *Gojō-guchi* (御錠口) had responsibilities strictly focused on the shōgun's close relations. This group consisted of ninja from Iga to whom Tokugawa Ieyasu (1542–1616) had already entrusted many parts of the castle and to whom responsibility fell for the protection of certain doors like that entrusted to Hattori Hanzō (1543–1599).

---

[*] An uprising against the Osaka castle in 1614 and the battle of Shimabara in Kyūshū in 1637, which I mentioned in Chapter 2.

[†] *Yagyū Munenori*, master of martial arts of the Tokugawa family, accepted the title of *Ometsuke Kansatsu* (大目附監察) in 1632. Very early on, Munenori succeeded in setting up a vast spy network in which a great number of ninja of Iga played a dominating role. Moreover he delivered many transmissions of *Shinkage-ryū* to pseudo-instructors who went under cover to teach the method to the family of the shōgun, and observed the every action of the various lords among whom they were sent.

*Yokome* (横目) were a special police force created by Tokugawa to control the town of Edo and to deal with crime. *Yokome* literally means "the eye on side" therefore, it indicates parallel groups for investigation and crime prevention. This was the beginning of the future police force for investigation and information, which sadly became the infamous *Kenpei-tai* (憲兵隊).

The names *ongyō-no-mono* (隠形之者), *Iga-shū* (伊賀衆) and *Kōga-shū* (甲賀衆) were always used during the Edo period, as testified to in the *Amakusa-gunki* (天草軍記) record relating to the battle of Shimabara in 1637. The names *Iga dōshin* (伊賀同心) or *Iga-gumi dōshin* (伊賀組同心) were well known throughout all Edo. The latter had been very early in the service of Tokugawa Ieyasu and Hattori Hanzō (1543–1599) was their most famous leader. Their role, in addition to espionage, consisted of protecting certain parts of the Edo castle. The members of *Iga dōshin* had established their residences not far from that of Hattori Hanzō. While crossing the current districts of Yotsuya, Akasaka Denmacho, there were two districts which bore the names Kita Iga-chō (northern district of Iga) and Minami Iga-chō (southern district of Iga). In these two districts lived permanently the two hundred *Iga-gumi dōshin* and their families. A great number of *bujutsu* schools came from this district.

Lastly, the name most famous remains that of ninja (忍). The name ninja and ninjutsu are quoted for the first time in the *Buyō Benryaku* (武用弁略), compiled in 1684 by Kinoshita Gishun. This work gives us the following definition:

*"The ninja were people who could be hidden on their premises, as well as in the other provinces. Among them, some knew secret techniques and could infiltrate an enemy castle in full safety. They were native to the provinces of Iga and Kōga, which were for a very long time the source of this type of warriors excelling in this art. It is told that they transmitted their knowledge from generation to generation...."*

The ideogram *nin* (忍) covers several levels with significance. It can be read *shinobu* or *shinobi*. When it is pronounced *shinobu*, it has the meaning "to endure, to support, or tenacity," and when it is pronounced *shinobaseru*, it has the meaning "to hold hidden, to hide, furtive, or secret."

In a great number of cases, the ideogram translates into the concept of patience, endurance and perseverance, sometimes even the idea of resignation, a kind of patience in the face of all tests. By breaking up the ideogram "*nin,*" one finds two other ideograms: "the heart, feelings, or spirit" (心),* and the edge of the blade (刃).

One can interpret the meaning of the ideogram *nin* in several ways. Indeed, the meaning depicts the state of mind of one who suffers, endures misfortune, and must moreover hide, to hide one's pain. In other words, to hone to one's thoughts and ego like the edge of the sword, to be constantly vigilant, forming one's heart to endure. Such is one of the many meanings of the word *shinobu* (忍ぶ).

The meaning of this ideogram also refers to a way of practice in which the will becomes as sharp as the edge of the blade (the body, terribly effective, will be the tool of expression for this will) and evokes, consequently, the control of the spirit in the body. One already can, using the meaning of the character *nin*, understand that the ninja is a person who acts with great patience in the greatest of secrecy.

It is possible to push interpretation more deeply, drawing from the depth of the practice of one devoted to ninjutsu. The term ninja translated as the permanent state of ultimate patience towards all things. It is about one existing in a permanent state that falls under the continuity of things in the cycle of life, regardless of religious dogma. One may include, and better understand the name *jōnin* (上忍), which means that the person lives in an ultimate state of endurance, perseverance, and permanent patience.

Therefore, one can say that the name ninja translates as the permanent state of a person (者) who endures and perseveres over all the evils encountered. The fruit of one's experience that rises from survival includes understanding the profound reality that masks the heart of an enduring person.

# Appendix E: The Aiki-kai Foundation

The History of an Institution Devoted to the Teaching and Spread of the Authentic Aikidō of Morihei Ueshiba

The Tōkyō *Aiki-kai* (合気会), collectively known as the *Hombu* dōjō, remains in the eyes of aikidō practitioners the incontestable reference that ensures the loyal and authentic transmission, the world over, of the art of the founder: Morihei Ueshiba (1883–1969). The history of the creation of the Aiki-kai Foundation is none other than the remarkable materialization of a life dedicated entirely to aikidō, that of the second *dōshu*; Kisshomaru Ueshiba (1921–1999). The creation of the *Aiki-kai* is the cornerstone that represents the link between two periods in the history of aikidō: that from before the war and that from after the war. We will look at the key events that led to the creation of the *Aiki-kai* and its functions.

---

* This ideogram indicates the functions of the spirit, sentimental and intellectual. This concept is used in many cases in opposition to the body and the object. Five great types of significance are distinguished in the martial arts and in particular in ninjutsu. These are: keep thoughts or feelings secret, within the spirit; spiritually adapt to every situation; accept the truth, even when it is contrary to one's presuppositions; always stay mentally engaged (this has a major relationship with human behavior); focus primarily on essential things. The left central line of the human body is where it was traditionally thought that the spirit resided: the heart, the chest.

## A Nomadic Practice

Situated in the Ushigome district, within Tōkyō, the current building that houses the *Aiki-kai* foundation (in Japanese: *Zaidan Hojin Aiki-kai*) is today a three-story building with the reception area on the main floor, the beginner's room on the first floor, the regular training room (first kyu and above) on the second, and finally a small room for private classes along with locker rooms on the third. There is also a small storage area for the *keiko-gi* (uniforms) located under the roof and a supplementary "half-floor" to the building.

Even though the area where this building evolved was always home to the practice and instruction of aikidō, the building itself saw a great deal of change. First of all, there was no permanent location for the teaching of aikidō in Tōkyō before 1927. Basically, before this time Morihei Ueshiba taught in Ayabe, fief of Onisaburō Deguchi, the charismatic leader of the Omoto religion, in a room that had been converted into a dōjō in his home. The dōjō was called Ueshiba-juku (植芝塾: the class of sensei Ueshiba). The Ueshiba-juku was not open to the public but was restricted to those close to Deguchi as well as many devotees of *Omoto-kyō*. This dōjō measured approximately thirty-two square meters and was more of a dōjō office reserved for the personal practice of Ueshiba. During this period (1919–2021) the art was known as *Daitō-ryū jūjutsu* (大東流柔術).

Before this period, Master Ueshiba had already practiced *Yagyū Shingan-ryū* (柳生心眼流) in Osaka, *Tenshin Shinyō-ryū* (天神真楊流) in his childhood, and much later on he very closely followed the teaching of Takeda Sokaku (1860–1943) in *Daitō-ryū jūjutsu*, while he was in Hokkaidō, the northern region of Japan. This was, therefore, a period where teaching was not the priority for Ueshiba, it was only his personal practice that counted. Setting up a dōjō and the structure necessary for the training of instructors was far from being his focus.

Moreover, the reigning political climate of this prewar period was very conducive to the practice of the martial arts. Military expansion, along with the search for raw materials created a demand in all of the institutions like the navy, army, secret service, military and political police, and the like, for competent martial arts instructors. The structure of *Kōdōkan-jūdō* founded by Kanō Jigorō (1860–1938) was distorted from its primary function to one that fed the warlike and militaristic spirit. Instructors from the *Kōdōkan* as well as *Kōsen-jūdō* (高専柔道: jūdō where only ground techniques are practiced) could be found throughout Japan.

The practice of these two systems of sport, along with karate at the time of its popularization in 1929, were the only ones that someone could easily learn during this period. In fact, the practice of *ko-bujutsu* (古武術), the traditional martial arts, was still extremely restricted to a small circle of initiates, numbering ten at the most, and where the succession of the school would be given to a single student. This system of practice and transmission of knowledge continued right up until the pre-war period and after the war for a few rare individuals in the midst of the massive expansion of jūdō, kendō, karate, and aikidō. The practice, as well as the teaching, of Master Usehiba grew out of this world of *ko-bujutsu*; it is the reason he did not have a dōjō, and the reason he frowned upon mass instruction to a certain degree.

## Settling Down to Teach

Among the followers of the Omoto religion are numerous personalities from the realms of politics, finance, and the military. Thanks to the intervention of these prestigious members, such as Admiral Asano Seikyu who introduced Ueshiba to Admiral Isamu Takeshita, who was a martial arts fanatic, the teaching of Ueshiba's art would move from the shadows into the spotlight. It was at this time, and surely thanks to the connections of Admiral Takeshita, that master Usehiba carried out a series of seminars and demonstrations during the next two years in Tōkyō. During this period, 1926 or 1927, the entire Ueshiba family relocated to Tōkyō in order to support the founder who was still in the process of making his art known, which was called *Ueshiba-ryū Aiki-budō* (植芝流合気武道), *Aiki-Budō*, or *Aiki-Jūjutsu*.

Restricted to a group of prominent personalities, the teaching of master Ueshiba between 1927 and 1931 still did not take place in a dōjō and was always done in private residences. However, with the growing number of people interested in devoting themselves to the discipline of the master, even in spite of the draconian conditions, the necessity to build a dōjō that could support both current and future students was starting to be felt.

In 1931, thanks to some generous financing, a dōjō with an area of 160 square feet for practicing *aiki-budō*, an extraordinary feat at the time, was constructed in the district of Ushigome in Shinjuku. The home of the Ueshiba family served as the dōjō, and was quite large (290 square meters or 3122 square feet). At the inauguration, Ueshiba's very first students were present, among them: Hajime Iwata, Hisao Kamada, and of course Noriaki (Hoken) Inoue, who was Morihei's cousin. Known by the name Kobukan (皇武館), this dōjō rapidly became the hub for the teaching and training of many *uchi-deshi* (内弟子), who would later become instructors and spread the art of *aiki-budō*.

The majority of the most important *uchi-deshi* of this period are already well known to us, among them are Minoru Mochizuki, Kenji Tomiki, Aritoshi Murashige, Gozo Shioda, others are less known such as Hisao Kamada, Hajime Iwata, Shigemi Yonekawa, Rinjiro Shirata, Zenzaburo. The practice of *aiki-budō* at the Kobukan was reputed to be very rough, and soon it became known as "the dōjō from hell." In 1932, at the behest of Deguchi, the Budō Senyo-kai (武道宣揚会) organization was created for the purpose of promoting the art of master Ueshiba on a national scale. We can see here that the Kobukan and the Budō Senyo-kai were merely the seeds from which the Aiki-kai foundation of today would later grow. In effect, the art, location, and desire for a loyal and authentic diffusion of the founder's art remains the heart of what the Aiki-kai represents in the eyes of all practitioners, and at the same time guarantees the legitimacy of one art, one group, and one location.

The hazards that the charismatic Deguchi faced with the political power, his connections throughout the Budō Senyo-kai and in his close relationship with Ueshiba—all of this combined with the climate of war during this troubled period of Japanese history would be both an inexhaustible source of experience crucial to the finalization of aikidō by Master Ueshiba and a story rich in examples of what not to do for the Aiki-kai foundation that Kisshomaru would later magnificently forge.

## An Obscure Historical Context

In 1937, Japan went to war with China and, in so doing, turned down a dead-end street that would eventually lead to the tragic bombings of Nagasaki and Hiroshima in 1945. During this black period in Japanese history, the ranks of *uchi-deshi*, old and new, would thin as several among them who were called to duty for their country would never return. At the height of the Pacific War the dōjō was almost deserted, and Master Ueshiba was absorbed in teaching at various military institutions. It was during this period (1939–1940) that Koichi Tohei and Osawa Kiburō started to train at the Kobukan and the use of the term aikidō to designate their practice became official. In addition, in 1939 the Kobukan was restructured into a foundation, and in 1940 it was officially declared the Kobu-kai (皇武会) foundation and Takeshi Isamu took office as its first president.

The air raids of the American bombardiers devastated the principal cities of Japan, and daily life in Tōkyō was quite seriously disrupted. One of the direct consequences to the Kobukan was that it sheltered victims who had lost their homes to the deluge of incendiary bombs showered by the bombardiers. On more than one occasion, Ueshiba had to fight fires that attacked the building that housed the Kobukan itself, the home of his family, or that of his neighbors. Luckily none of the fires seriously damaged the dōjō, and given the diminished number of students, Ueshiba, with the help of Tohei and Osawa, continued the administration and teaching.

It was this period that marked the transition between the old training that took place in the Kobukan and the modern practice in the Aiki-kai foundation. From the beginning of 1943, the health of Master Ueshiba began to deteriorate because of his many occupations, lack of rest, deficiencies linked to the lack of food and surely to the nosiy and polluted atmosphere, as well as the general climate of insecurity that reigned over Tōkyō. To this we must add two very important points that influenced Ueshiba's decision to take up residence in the country, in Iwama within Ibaraki prefecture, approximately 120 km (75 miles) from Tōkyō. The first is that Ueshiba was perpetually absorbed in the quest for the most profound essence of the martial arts, which demanded the complete devotion of his entire being. The second is that he was not attached to teaching his practice, or at least for no more than short periods at a time. From the beginning, he held the deep conviction that teaching and all of his other responsibilities, such as the expansion of the art, training, and managing and administering a dōjō represented sizable obstacles to his personal quest.

For the following twelve years, right up until his death, the founder secluded himself in Iwama and devoted all of his time to the culture of the ground, religious introspection, and his personal practice. Moreover, it was during these years, far from the distractions and tumultuousness of the city, that he would perfect his art and explore new spiritual dimensions that would give birth to the concept of *Takemusu Aiki* (武産合気), the highest level of technical excellence in modern Aikidō.

## A Choice: The Beginning of a Succession

It was his son, Kisshomaru, who took on the most thankless work, as he already had a career in a brokerage firm. A graduate in economics from the prestigious Waseda University, his professors could only imagine the future of this young financial prodigy. However, he was driven from within, and felt obligated by his duties as incumbent technical and administrative director of the Kobu-kai. He confessed this to Kaku Kozō several years ago:

> *I, who didn't have the talent for the role which my father had bestowed upon me, in addition to the fact that I already had responsibilities with a business, had to manage first and foremost my work and the restructuring of the Aiki-kai... this was very hard and my family suffered because I was seldom at home even though it also played the role of principal dōjō. What was I to do? It would seem that it is the most appropriate vocation that chooses us and not the reverse....*

After the war and the defeat, came the American occupation that prohibited, among other things, the practice of *budō* in all its forms, which resulted in a long standoff between the authorities of the SCAP (Supreme Command of Allied Power) and the members of many groups supportive of the practice of *budō*. Under the pressure of the occupational authority, it was necessary to restructure and change the orientation of *budō* to one that was either geared towards learning such as physical education or towards sport like boxing or escrima. Almost immediately, Kisshomaru undertook a restructuring of the Kobukan to respond to this new development.

## The Postwar Years: Creation and Development

A preparatory reunion was held on November 22, 1945 at Tokiwa's manor in the Maru no ichi quarter in Tōkyō. Fifty-three people attended, including Prince Konoe, the former prime minister. It was during this reunion that the foundation adopted the name "Aiki-kai". On February 9, 1945 the new Aiki-kai Foundation received approval, and this marked a new period of growth for aikidō. In 1948, the government, through the Ministry of Education, officially recognized the new structure, the

Aiki-kai Foundation (財団法人合気会: Zaidan Hojin Aiki-kai), as the sole national organization to promote aikidō.

This postwar aikidō had an unprecedented boom in Japan at the beginning of the fifties thanks to the efforts of several long-time practitioners, such as Gozō Shioda, Tohei Koichi, and, of course, Master Ueshiba. The administration of the Hombu-dōjō and the Aiki-kai Foundation, technical programs, the issuance of grades, the training of instructors and the diffusion of aikidō throughout the archipelago was in the hands of Master Ueshiba, senior students who were technical experts of the art, and members from the administrative counsel of the Aiki-kai Foundation. After disassociating from the other emerging groups as well as from Daitō-ryū, Master Ueshiba created a technical program loyal to the art founded by his father and exams for the attainment of grades, and wrote technical books that are still essential references.

Master Ueshiba involved himself in the training of young instructors who would, in turn, help to promote aikidō throughout the Japanese school system. Starting in 1955, he put into place an effective organization that would allow the expansion of aikidō throughout every layer of Japanese society. In 1999, the number of aikidō groups in Japanese universities numbered 120, and the organization officially recognized over 500 dōjō in Japan, and this did not included those affiliated with the Japan Aikidō Association or the Student's Aikidō Association. The number of centers across Japan are in the range of 1,400. The principal center of all these organizations, in the eyes of all practitioners of aikidō, is still the Aiki-kai Foundation, and its main training center is the Aikidō Hombu dōjō (合気道本部道場).

The foundation saw a massive influx of students flocking from the four corners of Japan, and other countries, and had to adapt in order to accommodate new practitioners as well as to facilitate practice. In 1968, the wooden structure of the old dōjō was replaced by a larger five-story building.

At the same time, aikidō was undergoing spectacular development on the international scene, in many countries on every continent. Aikidō was initially introduced to the United States via Hawaii by the founder himself, and in France by Minoru Mochizuki, Aritoshi Murashige, and Noro Masamichi. Following this, many instructors were sent by the Aiki-kai Foundation in order to help other countries to have a better understanding of aikidō, and some even made these countries their homes, like Noro Masamichi and Tamura Nobuyoshi in France.

In 1975, a committee gathered in Madrid representing thirty countries to discuss the creation of the International Aikidō Federation. The federation was officially inaugurated and opened its doors for business in 1976. In 1984, more than forty federations and national organizations came together under the aegis of the Aiki-kai Foundation of Tōkyō.

The foundation regularly sends teachers abroad and maintains regular relations with all of the dōjō through an internal unit called the "foundation for cultural and international exchange." The Aiki-kai Foundation centralizes registration, the standardization of grades, and the delivery of diplomas. Black belt diplomas must be approved by the Dōshu himself, Moriteru Ueshiba, who succeeded his father, Kisshomaru.

## The Dōshu

The role of the *dōshu* (道主), the master of the way, is at once precise and complex. In addition to maintaining classes at the *Hombu-dōjō* as well as seminars throughout Japan, his presence is always highly solicited at various reunions, symposia, and at cultural, sporting, and martial arts events.

The term *dōshu* is not limited merely to technical mastery, or to the knowledge of the history and deeper principles of aikidō. It must be understood here that there is a subtle dimension where the mastery of the way is applied to every domain, even those that may seem less obvious. It, therefore, encompasses coming to terms with the modern world and all of its necessities, as well as being able to discuss a broad range of subjects, even those that do not seem to have any direct relation to aikidō.

In this sense, the responsibility of the *dōshu* goes much further than that of the founder, as it doesn't only mean remaining loyal to the authenticity of that which he was transmitted but also remaining diligent in his own personal practice, all the while nurturing the imaginative and creative aspects of the art and still staying within the boundaries set forth by the founder: a constant evolution through time.

More than a simple location for practice and apprenticeship, the *Hombu-dōjō* of the Aiki-kai Foundation is in essence the materialization of the sincere devotion of one man, Kisshomaru Ueshiba, who committed himself throughout his lifetime to the creation of a solid and serious structure for the art of aikidō, which deserved nothing less.

## Bibliography of Japanese Language Documents

- *Sekai no Aikidō wo Tsukutta Otoko Tachi*, These Men Who Built the World of Aikidō, by Kaku Koso, consists of a series of articles and interviews realized since 1990.
- *Budō, Nihon Budōkan*, a monthly magazine on all of the *budō* that relate to the major events of the Aiki-kai Foundation.
- *Nihon Budō Taikei*, Vol. 7, Imamura Kayū, 1980.
- *Aikidō Kaiso Ueshiba Morihei-den*, Kisshomaru Ueshiba
- *Ueshiba Morihei Tanjyo Hyakunen Aikidō Kaiso*, Kisshomaru Ueshiba

# Appendix F: *Densho* and *Makimono* of Ninjutsu

One still finds a great number of documents on the ninja and his practice, ninjutsu in Japan. However, for a great number of people, consulting these documents remains rather difficult. The majority are often preserved within private collections; the most well known, such as the *Bansenshūkai* or the *Shōninki*, are preserved at the Diet Library in Tokyo. In the family collections that we could consult, the vast majority of the documents are bequeathed from generation to generation. Most of the members of the family do not read them any more and do not practice ninjutsu or, in many cases, martial arts in general. After reviewing a great number of manuscripts, I humbly undertook the task of classifying them into two groups.

The first group lists historical chronicles and memories. The second group lists the *densho* or *makimono* of ninjutsu which concern only techniques, methods, weapons, uses, principles, and strategy of combat. Simultaneously, within these two groups, there are two sub-groups. One contains the *densho* and *makimono* of various schools of *bujutsu* that have a connection to ninjutsu or that mention certain principles of ninjutsu like the *Kage-ryū*. The other contains all paintings, prints, and the like showing ninja.

All the documents that I consulted for the drafting of this work, just as for our research on ninjutsu and *bujutsu* in general, are written in *kanbun* (漢文). One also finds certain manuscripts written in *bungo* (文語), but these are not numerous. The writing, as in the great majority of these manuscripts, is cursive, of *komonjo* type (古文書). Thus, major knowledge of the ideograms, the language, penmanship, and the historical and sociological framework in which these documents of transmission were compiled is very important. In the study of this kind of document, it is always necessary to take into account several factors that can clarify their meaning.

One can still find copies today of some documents, such as the *Bansenshūkai*, *Shōninki* or *Iranki*, but they are often incomplete. Certain very old and invaluable originals can only be consulted on microfilm in the libraries of Japan as well as in the Diet Library, and in the towns of *Ueno* and *Shiga*. In the part that follows, I present all the manuscripts that one can find in the largest libraries of Japan, in the Diet, in the library of the town of Ueno, and in certain private collections.

However, I must note that there are still a great number of manuscripts that we did not register in this list, respecting the people who did not wish their family collection to appear here. I must also note that there are surely some manuscripts that we do not know exist. Certain family manuscripts appear in the text, notes, and references of our work. The presentation of the manuscripts follows this order: manuscript title in italics, title in kanji, type of manuscript (booklet, scroll, etc.), date of writing, name of the author. All the documents are ordered by their date of writing. Those whose date of writing and whose author were unknown have been placed at the end.

Lastly, among the manuscripts that we did not consign to this list, it is necessary to give special note to the work of Takamatsu Toshigutsu, who gathered a little more than two hundred documents and whose totality—*densho* and *makimono*, *shuki*, paintings, and so forth—were bequeathed to Hatsumi Masaaki. I had the chance and the rare privilege to be allowed to read some of the original works on the nine schools. I also read *densho* where Takamatsu Toshitsugu explains technical, philosophical principles, concepts, and other aspects, of ninjutsu and the martial arts. The work is considerable and is truly the keystone of this work and the associated research.

## First Group: Historical Documents Concerning Family Histories

- *Iga Fused Shucchō* (伊賀附差出帳), a booklet, written in 1637 by Ishitaka Kanshi
- *Ōgen Bukan* (江源武鑑), nineteen booklets, written in 1657 by Araki Rihei
- *Kochigi Hyōgoki* (闕疑兵庫記), a booklet, written in 1668 by Hikō Sane Shimanobu
- *Zokkin HiseidaN* (賊禁秘誠談), a booklet, written in 1668 by Tobu Zankō
- *Iranki* (伊乱記), four booklets, written in 1679, Kikuoka Nyōgen
- *Asai Sandaiki* (浅井三代記), fifteen booklets, written in 1684 by Yama Unshi
- *Okazaki Monogatari* (岡崎物語), a booklet, written in 1685 by Kikuoka Nyōgen
- *Isui Onkō* (伊水温故), four booklets, written in 1687 by Kikuoka Nyōgen
- *Iga Kuni Ninjutsu Hiden* (伊賀国忍術秘伝), a booklet, written in 1699 by Kikuoka Nyōgen
- *Ii Kaden Gunki* (井伊家伝軍記), a booklet, written in 1703 by Katsuno Uji
- *Washū Sho Shōgunden* (和州諸将軍伝), six booklets, written in 1704, unknown author
- *Kitabatake Monogatari* (北畠物語), seven booklets, written in 1706 by Tetsuya Shichirōhei
- *Isui Onko* (伊水温古) five booklets, written in 1706 by Kikuoka Nyōgen
- *Ninja Kansho Tsūgyō Shōjuryō Bunsho* (忍者関所通行証受領文書), a booklet, written in 1711 by Hattori Hanzō Masakatsu
- *Gundan Kinchō Ikkai* (軍談勤恐懲一階), a booklet, written in 1716, unknown author
- *Nanajō Kahara Ishikawa Monogatari* (七条河原石川物語), a booklet, written in 1716 by Kuniko Dayū
- *Hattori Hanzō Shoyōsō onikirimaruzu* (服部半蔵所用槍鬼切丸図), a scroll, written in 1718 by Hattori Saemon Masatake
- *Ise Gunki* (伊勢軍記), a booklet, written in 1734 by Matsuoka Gentachi

- *Ise Kuni Shisho Shikeizu Fusho Taifuchō* (伊勢国司諸司系図普諸待附帳), a booklet, original written in 1583 by Oshima Naizō, recopied in 1748 by Nakauchi Hisarō. There is also the version of Takizawa Bakin written during the Edo period
- *Iyō Heiteiki* (伊陽平定記), three booklets, written in 1753 by Kubei Kōshi
- *IgaKB* (伊賀考), three booklets, written in 1772 by Gankatsu Akira
- *Iga Ninshi Seiji Daiyū Daidai Yushosho* (伊賀忍士城大夫代々由緒書) a scroll, written in 1774 by Seishi Jūrō
- *Inkōryū Ninpō Chūsho tsuke Nagai Kaden* (引光龍忍法註書長家伝), four booklets, written in 1775 by Beihara Kosaemon
- *Zokkin HiseidaN* (賊禁秘誠談), three booklets, written in 1788 by Nagai Yoshigan
- *Kika Kage Hazama Gosen* (木下蔭狭間合戦), a booklet, written in 1789 by Fuki Sengyū
- *Kusunoki Masanari Ikkansho* (楠正成一巻書), a booklet, written in 1789, by Osaka Yahei
- *Kōga nijū ichi ke* (甲賀二十一家), a sheet, written in 1789, unknown author
- *Iga Mono Taiyu Shoki* (伊賀者大由緒記), a booklet, written in 1798 by Kōgi Kude
- *Kōga Ninshi Yushosho* (甲賀忍士由緒書), a booklet, written in 1816 by Wada Hachirō
- *Sankō Iyō HeBudan Yōroku* (武談要緑), a booklet, written in 1818 by Yamamoto Hisakei
- *Iteiki* (参考伊陽平定記), two booklets, written in 1830, unknown author
- *Bugei Hyakunin Isshu* (武芸百人一首), a booklet, written in 1830 by Hasekō Senka
- *Budan Yōroku* (武談要緑), a booklet, written in 1818 by Shimazu Nadanobu
- *Seiyō Sekichōsō* (青陽石庁礎), eight booklets, written in 1844 by Ifuchiyear
- *Ihon Ise Kuni Shigo Keizu Fusho Taiyaku Fuchō* (異本伊勢国司御系図普諸待役附帳), a booklet, written in 1846 by Uji Hayashizaki
- *Zokkin HiseidaN* (賊禁秘誠談), three booklets, written in 1847 by Tobu Zankō
- *Zadenga Shits Kasōka* (座敷知恵可下層加), two booklets, written in 1848 by Kura Wanka Tengawa
- *Honchō Kagushoku Yushosho* (本朝香具職由緒書), a booklet, written in 1860, unknown author
- *Iga Mono Goyūsho no Oboegaki* (伊賀者御由緒之覚書), a booklet, written in 1861, unknown author
- *Bukyo Zensho* (武教宝書), two booklets, written in 1864 by Yamaka Kangoemon
- *Iranki* (伊乱記), three booklets, written in 1898 by Momochi Orinosuke
- *Iyō Anminki* (伊陽安民記), a booklet, rewritten from the original in 1935 by Tanaka Eijirō
- *Kōga no Minyō* (甲賀之民謡), a booklet, written in 1938 by Kōga machi Kyōikukai
- *Iga Gunki* (伊賀軍記), three booklets, dates and author unknown
- *Kōga Samurai Fuchō* (甲賀侍附帳), a booklet, dates and author unknown
- *Ōmi Kōga Ryūhōshi Mochizuki Uji Baiyakunōsho* (近江甲賀龍法師望月氏売薬能書), a booklet, dates and author unknown
- *Kōga Nijū ichi ke Sensosho* (甲賀二十一家先祖書), a booklet, dates and author unknown
- *Kōga Koshi Yushosho* (甲賀古士由緒書), a booklet pertaining to the Udono family, dates and author unknown
- *Kōga Gun Koshiden* (甲賀郡古士伝), a booklet, dates and author unknown
- *Butoku Seigyō* (武徳成業), ten booklets, written by Shirai, date of writing unknown
- *Iga Kuni Kūdaison Momochike Yushosho* (伊賀国喰代村百地家由緒書), a booklet, dates and author unknown
- *Ninke Zakki Bunsho* (忍家雑記聞書), a booklet, dates and author unknown
- *Hisho Mudaishi* (秘書無蹄子), a letter, dates and author unknown
- *Kōga Gumi Yushosho* (甲賀組由緒書), a booklet, written in 1840, unknown author

## Second Group: Documents Concerning Techniques, Strategies, Weapons, and Transmission of Ninjutsu

- *Fukushima-ryū Neinin no Chūsho* (福嶋流寧忍之註書), a booklet, written in 1560 by Behara Kosaemon
- *Hattori Hanzō Ninpō Menjō* (服部半蔵忍法免状), a scroll, written in 1561 by Hattori Hanzō Yasunaga
- *Ninpiden* (忍秘伝), a booklet, written in 1561 by Hattori Hanzō Yasunaga
- *Bubishi* (武備誌), eighty booklets, the original is written by Bōgengi in 1615. The copy preserved nowadays was rewritten in 1665 by a member of the family of Aisu Ikōsai, founder of *Kage-ryū*
- *Tōyaku no Hō* (筒薬之方), a booklet, written in 1620 by Kobayashi Kurōhei
- *Seishō Ikkansho* (清詔一巻書), a booklet, written in 1623 by Miuchi Zenkan Chōbo
- *Iga Ninka no Maki* (伊賀忍火之巻), a scroll, written in 1624 by Hattori Hanshō Yasumasa
- *Iga Mono Kajutsu Hisho* (伊賀者火術秘書), a booklet, written in 1624, unknown author
- *Unki no Zu* (雲気之図), a booklet, written in 1627, unknown author
- *Gunki no Maki* (軍気之巻), a booklet, written in 1637, unknown author
- *Tōdō Shinshichirō Gunpō Kaidensho* (藤堂新七郎軍法皆伝書), a booklet, written in 1639, unknown author
- *Takeda-ryū Tenmon no Kuden* (武田流天文之口伝), a scroll, written in 1642 by Koman Kanei
- *Shajiki-ryū Teppō Densho* (柘植流鉄砲伝書), a booklet, written in 1646 by Yamada Nagasaemon Masaji
- *Ninpō Hikan* (忍法秘巻), a booklet, written in 1653 by Inue Shosaemon Masayasu
- *Gunpō TaiyōShū* (軍法待用集), five booklets, written in 1661, unknown author
- *Jikan Kokin no Sho* (自鑑古今之書), a booklet, written in 1661, unknown author

- *Heihō Hiyōsho Shinobi no Maki* (兵法秘要書竊盗之巻), a booklet, written in 1664 by Koike Hachirō
- *Yoshitsune Heihō Tora no Maki* (義経兵法虎之巻), three booklets, written in 1664, unknown author
- *Yoshitsune ShūkaShū* (義経袖下集), a booklet, written in 1666 by Taneda Yoshitomo
- *Shibayashi Shōmei* (士林正名), a booklet, written in 1675 by Tsuyama Bunko
- *Bansen Shūkai* (萬川集海), twenty six booklets, written in 1677 by Fujibayashi Masatake
- *Bō Hiya Ōgi Gokui Hiden* (棒火矢奥義極秘伝), a booklet, written in 1669 by Kabe Saemon
- *Ninpōsho* (忍法書), a booklet, written in 1716 by Shimiya Morisumu
- *Iga-ryū Ninpō Goku Hikan* (伊賀流忍法極秘巻), a booklet, written in 1717 by Inue Shosaemon
- *Shinobi no Gokui Mokuroku* (忍之極意目録), a booklet, written in 1720 Heigan Yoshijirō Nobumi
- *Shinobi Daii* (忍大意), a booklet, written in 1722 by Sabane Jieimon
- *Onmitsu Hiji Shinobi Daii* (隠密秘事大意), a booklet, written in 1725, unknown author
- *Shinobi Kokyō no Maki* (忍小鏡之巻), two scrolls, written in 1727 by Fukuchi Arimasa
- *Isshi sōden Tō-ryū Shinobi Daigokuhi* (一子相伝当流忍大極秘), a booklet, written in 1732 by Takano Mataemon
- *Shinobi no Mono Gunyō Kajutsu* (忍者軍用火術), a booklet, written in 1741 by Sakai Tadaei
- *Hattori-ryū Ninpō Hiden* (服部流忍法秘伝), a scroll, written in 1761, unknown author
- *Gunyō Hika* (軍用秘歌), a booklet, written in 1763, unknown author
- *Seki Kasen Chōtan Shukyō* (石火箭長短手鏡), a booklet, written in 1768 by Iji Dayū
- *Yoshitsune Tora no Maki* (義経虎之巻), two booklets, written in 1779, unknown author
- *Kurama Yama KotenguHō* (鞍馬山古天狗法), a booklet, written in 1789, unknown author
- *Iga-ryū Kōgaryū Shinobi Hidensho* (伊賀流甲賀流忍竊盗秘伝書), a scroll, written in 1789, unknown author
- *Heigu Yōhō* (兵具要法), a booklet, written in 1789, unknown author
- *Man Kudensho no Maki* (萬口伝書之巻), a booklet, written in 1789, unknown author
- *Gunkan Yōhō* (軍鑑要法), a booklet, written in 1789, unknown author
- *Kōyō Gunkan Tora no Ryakuhin* (甲陽軍鑑虎之略品), a scroll, written in 1790, unknown author
- *Yoshitsune Kōgun Hyakushu* (義経公軍百首), a scroll, written in 1795, unknown author
- *Ninpō Suikyō* (忍法水鏡), two scrolls, written in 1799 writing by Fuki Shinjūrō Masanaga
- *Teiyō-ryū Kayaku Hōsho* (提要流火薬方書), a booklet, written in 1801, unknown author
- *Komori-ryū Kajutsu Yakuhō Hidensho* (小森流火術薬方秘伝書), a booklet, written in 1803 by Omori Masatsune, fifth generation
- *Goshinhō no Maki* (護身法之巻), a booklet, written in 1804, unknown author
- *Kōga-ryū Ninjutsu* (甲賀流忍術), a booklet, written in 1804, unknown author
- *Shinobi no Maki Shukyō* (忍之巻手鏡), a scroll, written in 1804 by Aoki Hachirō
- *Kōga Shinobi no Den ReflectedKi* (甲賀忍之伝未来記), a booklet, written in 1806 writing by Mizuno Tadayū
- *Gōbu Santōshū Senyōhō* (合武三島舟戦要法), ten eight booklets, written in 1807 by Morishige Kenin
- *Kurama Heihōsho* (鞍馬兵法書), two booklets, written in 1818, unknown author
- *Iga Mondō Ninjutsu Gashisei* (伊賀問答忍術賀士誠), a booklet, written in 1818, unknown author
- *Dakkō Shinobi no Maki Ryakuchū* (奪口忍之巻略註), a booklet, written in 1830, unknown author
- *Kōshū-ryū Ninpō Densho RōdanShū* (甲州流忍法伝書老談集), a scroll, written in 1831 by Yamamoto Kanzuke
- *Fueki-ryū Hōjū Sōden* (不易流放統相伝), a scroll, written in 1840 by Fueki Ichigyō
- *Kasen no Jidai* (火箭之次第), a scroll, written in 1843 by Aio Sessai Sairen
- *Sonshi Dōkanshō* (孫子童観抄), fourteen booklets, written in 1865 by Katō Kenji
- *Kusunoki-ryū Kajutsu* (楠流火術), a booklet, written in 1867, unknown author
- *Tenmon Shōgi Shūken* (天文象儀験), eight booklets, dates and author unknown
- *Rikutō* (六韜), three booklets, see the note for Sonshi no Sonbu
- *KorinKei* (虎鈴経), four booklets, dates and author unknown
- *Chōryō Ikkansho* (張良一巻書), a booklet, dates and author unknown
- *Gunki Hiden* (軍記秘伝), two booklets, dates and author unknown
- *Yoshitsune-ryū Ninjutsu Densho* (義経流忍術伝書), a booklet, document of the Fukui family, dates and author unknown
- *Tō-ryū Shinobishū Kakugo no Shō* (当流忍衆覚語之抄), a booklet, dates and author unknown
- *Yoshimori Hyaku Shūka* (義盛百首歌), a booklet, dates and author unknown
- *Kōgen Gunpō Hikan* (甲源軍法秘巻), a scroll, written by Koyama Denshin, date of drafting dubious
- *Tō-ryū Dakkō Shinobi no Maki* (当流奪口忍之巻), a booklet, dates and author unknown
- *Kusunoki-ryū Ninpō Dakkō Shinobi no Kanchū* (楠流忍法奪口忍之巻註), a booklet, dates and author unknown
- *Ningu Zue* (忍具図), a scroll, dates and author unknown
- *Shinobi no Mono Gunyō Kajutsu* (忍者軍用火術), a booklet, dates and author unknown
- *Ninjutsu Densho* (忍術伝書), a booklet, written by Dōbei Hansaemon, date of writing unknown
- *Gunzui Ōdōki Shinobi no Maki* (軍随応童記忍之巻), a scroll, written by Natori Sanjūrō Masazumi, date of writing unknown

- *Ninjutsu Hiden Shinobi Mokuroku* (忍術秘伝竊忍目録), a scroll, *densho* of the Akutagawa family, dates and author unknown
- *Matsumei Yōshū* (松明要集), six booklets, dates and author unknown
- *Monomi Hidenshō* (物見秘伝抄), a booklet, dates dates and author unknown
- *Iga-ryū Ninjutsu Onka no Maki* (伊賀流忍術隠火之巻), a booklet, dates and author unknown
- *Shinden Ninjutsu Hisho* (神伝忍術秘書), a booklet, dates and author unknown
- *Shi Koppō* (使骨法), a booklet, dates and author unknown

# Appendix G: Historical Chronology of the Ninja

| Period | Date/Era | Historical Events | Connection with the Ninja and Ninjutsu |
|---|---|---|---|
| **Jōmon** | - - 10,000 | | |
| **Yayoi** | - - 221<br>- +57<br><br>- 265<br><br>- 369<br><br><br><br>113–179<br><br>- 574 | - Seal given by the court of Han to the king of the Na country.<br>- Embassy of Wa in Jin.<br>- Kofun, time of the funerary hillocks.<br>- Manufacture of the sword with seven branches deposited with the sanctuary of Isonokami.<br>Seven embassies of Wa in China of the South.<br>- Birth of Shōtoku Taishi. | |
| **Sendai** | - 587<br><br><br><br>- 604<br>- 607<br><br><br>- 645<br>- 672<br><br><br>- 694<br>- 699<br><br><br>- 700 | - Creation of the 17 Article Constitution.<br>- Founding of the Hōryū-Ji temple.<br><br>- Taika Reform<br>- The disorders of the Jinshun year.<br>- Tenmu becomes Emperor.<br><br>- Founding of Fujiwara-kyō. | - Otomo Sainyū (大伴細入) is employed, under the name of *shinōbi* (志能便) by the prince regent Shōtoku. Otomo Sainyū worked for the conquest of Mononobe Moriya.<br><br>- The strategies and methods of combat of Yōkan (用間) arrive in Japan in the province of *Kii*.<br><br>- Bito Takobi, a warrior of Yamato is employed as *shinōbi* (志能便) by the Tenmu emperor to attack Otomo Kōshi (Kōbun Tennō) in the province of Omi.<br><br>- The founder of *Shūgendō* (修験道), Otsune (小角, 637–701), arrives in the province of Izu after having been accepted at the Court. |
| **Nara** | - 710<br><br><br><br><br><br>- 712<br>- 720<br>- 734<br><br><br>- 752<br><br>- 758 | - Foundation of Heijō-kyō (Nara).<br><br><br><br><br>- Completion of Kojiki.<br>- Completion of Nihon shoki.<br>- Return to the Court of the emissary sent to China.<br>- Completion of the great Buddha of the Tōdai-ji temple.<br>- Compilation of the *Man Yōshū*. | - In order to prevent the confrontations between various religious factions, some *shūgenja* (修験者) develop the *Yamabushi-Heihō* (the strategies and methods of combat of the mountain hermits and ascetics) from different combat strategies from China.<br><br>- Kibi Makibi brings back from his voyage to China the *Sonshi* (孫子), a military strategy spy's treatise. |

| Heian | - 794 | - Transfer of the Capital to Heian-kyō (Kyōto). | - Abe Seimei (921–1005), master of *Onmyōdō* (陰陽道), creates his own version of *Omyōdō*.<br>- Methods from *Mikkyō* (密教) and *Onmyōdō* are included in the *Yamabushi-Heihō* (山伏兵法). This method is propagated little by little through the families of warriors and becomes a purely Japanese method of combat. |
| | - 801 | - Campaigns against the Emishi. | |
| | - 804 | - The monks Saichō and Kūkai leave for China. | |
| | - 805 | - After a nine month stay in China, Saichō returns to Japan and establishes the *Tendai-shū* school at Hiei-zan. | |
| | - 806 | - Kūkai returns from China after two years and establishes the *Shingon-shū* school at Kōya-san. | |
| | - 935 | - Beginning of the disorders of the Tengyō era. | |
| | - 936 | - Fujiwara Sumitomo rebels against the Court. | |
| | - 1063 | | - Death of Fujiwara Sanetori, lord of the province of Iga. |
| | - 1086 | - Emperor Shirakawa inaugurates the system of the withdrawn Emperor, or *insei*. | - Fujiwara Chikado, Kōga Saburō, and Hattori are the first families of ninja that appear in the province of Iga. |
| | - 1126 | - Foundation of the Chūson-ji temple. | |
| | - 1156 | - Civil war of the Hogen era. | - Minamoto no Yohitsune creates his school, *Yoshitsune-ryū ninjutsu*. Supposed drafting of the *densho* entitled *Yoshitsune-ryū ninjutsu* (義経流忍術), by Ise Saburō Yoshimori. |
| | - 1159 | - Civil war of the Heiji era. | |
| | - 1167 | - Taira no Kiyomori becomes Minister for Supreme Affairs. | |
| | - 1175 | -The monk Hōnen founds *Jōdo-shū*, "The Sect of the Pure Earth." | |
| | - 1184 | | - Yoshitsune demolishes the army of the Taira at the battle of Ichi No Tani. |
| | - 1185 | - Battle of Dan no Ura, the fall of the Taira, establishment of the *jitō* and the *shugo*. | - Supposed death of Hattori Heisaemon Ienaga at the time of the Dan no Ura battle.<br>-The *Ninke* (忍家), families of ninja, Hattori and Momochi rise in influence in Iga. |
| Kamakura | - 1192 | - Minamoto no Yoritomo becomes *Seii tai shōgun* and establishes the *bakufu* at Kamakura. | - Zen is imported from China and will exert a great influence on Ninjutsu as it does in the warrior class.<br>- The influence and competencies of the great ninja families, Momochi and Hattori, are growing. The bonds with the families of warriors are woven. |
| | - 1219 | - Assassination of Minamoto no Sanetomo, political power passes to the Hōjō, the regents, *shikken*. | |
| | - 1221 | - Disorders of the Jōkyū era. | - Diffusion of the science of *Heihō* (兵法: Ninjutsu, *bujutsu*, *Heigaku*) among the *Ji-samurai* of the province of Kōga. |
| | - 1224 | - Shinran begins the diffusion of his doctrine, the "True Sect of the Pure Earth," *Shinjōdo-shū*. | |
| | - 1227 | - Return to Japan of Dōgen, founder of the *Sōtō* school (Zen). | |

| | | | |
|---|---|---|---|
| **Kamakura cont'd.** | - 1253<br>- 1274<br>- 1281<br>- 1321<br>- 1331 | - Nichiren and the Lotus sect, *Hokke-shū*.<br>- First attack of the Mongols.<br>- Second attack of the Mongols.<br>- The Godaido Emperor takes power. | - War between the families of Hōjō and Kusunoki Masashige. |
| | - 1333 | - End of the Kamakura *bakufu*. | - A prominent family of Kōga province, the Sasaki, uses the *Kōga-shū*.<br>- From his castle, *Kusunoki Masashige* confronts the *Hōjō* army.<br>- Creation of *Kusunoki-ryū Ninjutsu* (楠流忍術). Under the influence of *Kusunoki*, *ninjutsu* will be used as a political instrument. |
| | - 1334 | - Government of the Kenmu era. | - *Kusunoki Masashige* uses a group of forty-eight *ninja* of *Iga* called *Yonjū hachi Shinobi-shū* (四十八忍衆).<br>- Kusonoki Masashige gives the name of *suppa* (透波) to the ninja of Iga, factions are located in three important cities, Nara, Heian and Osaka. |
| | - 1336 | - Schism between the court of North and that of the South, *Nanbokuchō*. | |
| **Muromachi** | - 1338<br><br>1397<br><br>- 1401<br><br>- 1428<br><br>- 1457<br>- 1467<br>- 1485 | - Ashikaga Takauji becomes shōgun, beginning of the Muromachi bakufu.<br>- Construction of Kinkaku ji monastery by Ashikaga Yoshimitsu.<br>- Ashikaga Yoshimitsu enters into relations with the Ming.<br>- Farmer revolts of the Shōchō and Eikyō eras.<br>- Construction of the castle of Edo.<br>- Civil war of the Onin era.<br>- Revolt of Yamashiro. | - On the eleventh day of the twelfth month, Nishi Tsuneo recovers the castle of the Tomita family by using a science called *Yama-biko no jutsu* (山彦之術). |
| | - 1487 | | - The Kōga province warriors join the army of Rokkaku Sasaki and attack the army of Ashikaga Yoshihisa. Magari No jin (鈎の陣). |
| **Sengoku** | - 1495 | - Hōjō Sō takes the castle of Odawara; beginning of the period of the fighting provinces, Sengoku. | - Period of apogee of Ninjutsu, proliferation of the schools, the knowledge, and the techniques. Drafting of the first manuscripts of transmission of the technical and practical knowledge of Ninjutsu. |
| | - 1543 | - The Portuguese arrive in Tanegashima; introduction of firearms. | |
| | - 1544 | | - On the fifth day of the third month, after learning the trade secrets of guns in Tanegashima, Tsuda Kenmotsu overturns the province of *Kii*. He transmits his science in Negoro temple and founds his school, the *Tsuda-ryū Hōjutsu* (津田流砲術). |
| | - 1549<br>- 1551 | - Saint Xavier arrives in Kagoshima. | - On the first day of the ninth month, General Oouchi Yoshitaka kills himself after having rebelled against Sueharu Kata. |
| | - 1555 | | - The armies of Takeda Shingen and Uesugi Kenshin fight at Kawanaka-jima. |

| Sengoku cont'd. | | | | - On the first day of the tenth month, Sueharu Kata dies during the battle of Ganjima against the army of Mori. |
| --- | --- | --- | --- | --- |
| | - 1560 | - Battle of Okehazama. | | - The nineteenth day of the fifth month, Oda Nobunaga crushes the army of Imagawa Yoshimoto; he is decapitated.<br>- The names of the ninja used by the *daimyō* of this time are as follows:<br>*Hōjō*—Kuma Kōtarō.<br>*Mori*— the Sada brothers<br>*Murakami*—Abe Jirōsaemon<br>Takeda Shingen—*rappa* (乱波) and *mitsumono* (三者)<br>Uesugi Kenshin—*Nokizaru* (軒猿)<br>Oda Nobunaga—*Kyōdan* (饗談) |
| | - 1561 | | | - On the tenth day of the ninth month, the armies of Takeda Shingen and Uesugi Kenshin fight yet again at Kawanaka-jima. |
| | - 1562 | | | - 170 (?) warriors of Kōga are used by Tokugawa Ieyasu for the attack on the Sumpu castle. |
| | - 1563 | | | - Japanese pirates (*wakō*) plunder Nankin. One of the things that was lost was the *Mokuroku* of *Kage-ryū* (影流), founded by Ikōsai. |
| | - 1566 | | | - Nobunaga crushes the resistance of the Kitabatake family and invades the province of Ise, very close to the province of Iga. |
| | - 1569 | - Oda Nobunaga enters Kyōto. | | - On the eleventh day of the tenth month, Oda Nobunaga forces Kitabatake Tomonori to take Nobuo Nobunaga as his adopted son. |
| | - 1570 | | | - On the nineteenth day of the fifth month, Sugitani Zenshubō, a ninja of Kōga, tries to assassinate Oda Nobunaga.<br>- On the twenty-eighth day of the sixth month, the armies of Oda Nobunaga and Tokugawa Ieyasu crush the army of Asai Nagamasa in the province of Omi.<br>- At the time of this battle, Hattori Hanzō Masanari becomes known as an expert of *sōjutsu* (槍術). |
| | - 1571 | - Fire of the Enryaku-ji temple. | | - On the twelfth day of the ninth month the battle of Ishiyama begins.<br>- On the twelfth day of the fifth month, Oda Nobunaga crushes the resistance of Nagashima in the province of Ise. Nagashima Ikki (長島一揆).<br>- The great ninja families during the Sengok period were:<br>1) Iga Jōnin (伊賀上忍)<br>Katō Danzō<br>Fujibayashi Nagamon<br>Fujibayashi Yasutake (Bansen Shūkai author)<br>Momochi Tanba<br>Hattori Ienaga Hanzō<br>Hattori Hanzō Masanari<br>2) Kōga-shū was constituted of fifty-three families, which were collectively called *Kōga gojūsanke* (甲賀五十三家). Most were known as follows:<br>Kōga, Mochizuki, Ugai, Naiki, Akutagawa, Ueno, Ban, Nagano. |

| | | | |
|---|---|---|---|
| **Sengoku cont'd.** | - 1573 | - End of the Muromachi *bakufu*. | - In the ninth month, Sugitani Zenshubō dies under the torture of the men of Nobunaga. |
| | - 1576 | - Oda Nobunaga enters the castle of Azuchi. | - On the nineteenth day of the fourth month, Kitabake Tomonori dies. |
| | - 1579 | | - On the twenty-fifth day of the seventh month, warriors of Iga and ninja in Tendōsan gather and attack the army of Takizawa Kazumasu in Maruyama castle. Beginning of the battle of Iga. |
| | - 1580 | - Surrender of the monk warriors of Hongan-ji. End of the Ishiyama war. | - Golden age of ninjutsu, records of activities of the ninja. |
| **Momoya-ma** | - 1581 | | - In the third month, Fuma Kotarō and his group, under the banner of Hojō Ujinao, attacks the army of Takeda Katsuyori camped in Ukishima-gahara.<br>  On the twenty seventh day of the ninth month, Oda Nobunaga with an army of 40,000 men, attacks the province of Iga (last phase of the battle of Iga).<br>- On the twenty-eighth day of the tenth month, the Iga province is completely under the control of Oda Nobunaga's army.<br>- The survivors of the Iga battle find new lords. The ninja of Kōga work for Toyotomi Hideyoshi. The Maeda family gather 50 ninja of Iga, which will form *Nusumi-gumi* (盗組). |
| | - 1582 | - Disorders of the *Honnō-ji*. | - On the second day of the sixth month, assassination of Oda Nobunaga in the Honnō-ji. Toyotomi Hideyoshi takes power.<br>- On the sixth day of the sixth month, Tokugawa Ieyasu receives the assistance of Iga ninja to return to his stronghold in Mikawa. |
| | - 1582–98 | - Reforms known as of *Taikō kenchi*, freezing of the social classes. | - On the fourteenth day of the sixth month, Tokugawa Ieyasu creates the *Iga-gumi* (伊賀組), Hattori Hanzō Masanari becomes the chief of this group. |
| | - 1584 | | - On the first day of the first month, the Saga brothers and Negoro-shū attack the soldiers of Toyotomi Hideyoshi. |
| | - 1585 | - Hideyoshi becomes *Kanpaku* (chief advisor to the emperor). | - On the twentieth day of the third month, Hideyoshi, with an army of 100,000 warriors, crushes the rebellious factions of the Negoro temple. |
| | - 1587 | - Hideyoshi prohibits Christianity. | |
| | - 1590 | - Reunification of the country under the authority of Hideyoshi. | - On the third day of the fourth month, Hideyoshi attacks Hōjō Ujimasa in Odahara.<br>-On the first day of the eighth month, Tokugawa Ieyasu which controls eight provinces of Kantō, settles in his castle in Edo.<br>- Hattori Hanzō takes up residence close to the one of the gates of the castle of Edo. Creation of *Hanzō no Mon* (半蔵門). |
| | - 1591 | - Census takes place in the entire country. | - The *Iga-gumi* or *Iga-Dōshin* (伊賀組同心) settles very close to the castle of Edo, creation of *Iga machi* in *Kōji machi*.<br>- On the eighteenth day of the eleventh month, Iga-gumi receives from Tokugawa land of a value of 1000 koku. |
| | - 1592 | - First attempt at invasion of Korea. | |

| | | | |
|---|---|---|---|
| **Momoya-ma Cont'd.** | - 1594 | - Construction of the castle of Momoyama. | - Supposed drafting of the *densho* entitled *Ninpiden* (忍秘伝) by Hattori Hanzō Masanari. |
| | - 1596 | | - On the fourteenth day of the eleventh month, death of Hattori Hanzō Masanari (57 years old). |
| | - 1597 | - Second attempt at invasion of Korea. | |
| | - 1598 | - Death of Toyotomi Hideyoshi (63 years old). | |
| | - 1600 | - Battle of Sekigahara. | - On the first day of the eighth month, death of several Kōga ninja during the battle in Fushimi. |
| | - 1603 | - Tokugawa Ieyasu becomes shōgun, beginning his bakufu in Edo. | - Tokugawa Ieyasu takes into his service the ninja families from places where some died during the battle of Sekigahara. |
| | | | - He entrusts the command of 100 Kōga warriors to Yamaoka Michihei. |
| | | | - He names Tōdō Takaō as lord of Iga province. Tōdō Takaō had to manage the Iga ninja families. |
| | | | - Creation of *Musokunin* (無足人). |
| | | | - Creation of *Shinobi machi* (忍町). |
| | | | - Drafting of the *Iga Fusa Shuchō* (伊賀付差出帳). |
| | - 1604 | - Confirmation of the boats under license, shuinsen. | |
| | - 1605 | | - On the second day of the twelvth month, Hattori Hanzō Masao, Masanari's son, becomes the chief of the *Iga-Dōshin*. |
| | - 1609 | - The Hirado harbor is opened to the Dutch. | - A group of Kōga ninja dies in combat for the Toyotomi family in the castle of Fushimi. |
| | - 1614 | - Winter Campaign against the castle of Osaka, end of the Toyotomi family. | - On the sixth day of the fourth month, the *Iga-Dōshin* and *Negoro-shū* participate in the Summer Campaign under the command of Hattori Hanzō Masao. |
| | - 1615 | - Summer Campaign. | |
| | | - Laws for the families of warriors, Buke sho-hatto. | - On the seventh day of the fourth month, death of Sanada Yukimura dies (49 years old). |
| | - 1616 | - Death of Tokugawa Ieyasu (75 years old) | |
| | - 1622 | - Deaths of fifty-five Christians in Nagasaki. | |
| | - 1635 | | - In the third month, the residence of *Iga-Dōshin* is moved to Kōji machi in Yotsuya. Creation of the districts Minami Iga-machi and Kita Iga-machi. |
| | - 1637 | - Revolt of Shimabara. | -10 Kōga ninja are placed under the command of Matsudaira Nobutsuna and infiltrate the castle of Hara in Shimabara. It is the last great feat of arms of the ninja. |
| | | | - Supposed drafting of Shimabara Ninki (島原忍記). |
| | - 1639 | - Closing of the country, sakoku. | - Period when the progressive dismantling of the groups of ninja starts. |
| | | | - The technical science and knowledge of ninjutsu, little by little will disappear. |
| | | | - Installation of the network of information as well as the control and the reinforced monitoring of the various strongholds. Appearance of Onmitsu (隠密). |
| | - 1641 | - The Dutch can trade only in Dejima. | |
| | - 1643 | - Prohibition against changing arable land. | |
| | - 1657 | - Large fire in Edo. | |
| | - 1688–1705 | - Genroku era. | |
| | - 1709 | - Arai Hakuseiki assumes his responsibilities. | |
| | - 1716–35 | - Tokugawa Yoshimune becomes new the shōgun. | - The Negero-shû takes the name of Negoro-Dôshin (根来同心) and will take residence in the district Dôshin machi in Edo. |
| | | - Reforms of the Kyōhō era take place. | |

| | | | |
|---|---|---|---|
| **Momoya-ma Cont'd.** | - 1724 | - Death of Chikamatsu Monzaemon. | -The formation of Onmitsu is controled by the only school Kishû-ryû (紀州流), all the methods of the ninjutsu are forgotten little by little. |
| | - 1733 | - Revolt over rice in Edo. | |
| | - 1774 | - Sugita Genpaku publishes his *Kaitai Shinsho* (解体新書), a treatise on anatomy translated from Dutch. | |
| | - 1778 | - A Russian boat arrives at Ezo (Hokkaidō). | |
| | - 1783 | - Great famine of the Tenmei era. | |
| | - 1787 | - Matsudaira Sadanobu becomes *rōjū* (老中 —senior member of the shogunate). <br> - Beginning of the reforms of the Kansei era. | - Families of ninja on the decline, the practice of ninjutsu becomes forgotten. <br> - Drafting of Iran-ki (伊乱記). |
| | - 1800 | - Ino Tadayoshi draws a map of Ezo (Hokkaidō). | |
| | - 1808 | - Mamiya Rinzō explores Sakhaline. | |
| | - 1815 | - Sugita Genpaku publishes *"Introduction to the Dutch Studies."* | |
| | - 1825 | - Order to destroy the foreign ships issued. | |
| | - 1832–37 | - Farmer famines and revolts. | |
| | - 1853 | - Commodore Perry enters the bay of Edo. | |
| | - 1854 | - Treaty of Kanagawa between Japan and the United States. | |
| | - 1858 | - Commercial Treaty with the United States. | |
| | - 1864 | - Bombardment of the town of Shimonoseki by the Westerners. | |
| | - 1866 | - Secret agreement between the clans of Chōshū and Satsuma. | |
| | - 1867 | - End of the Edo *bakufu*. | |
| | - 1868 | - Meiji Restoration, "imperial Promises in 5 Articles" | |
| | - 1871 | - Abolition of the *han* and establishment of the departments. | |
| | - 1873 | - Establishment of the conscription. <br> - Adoption of the Gregorian calendar. | |
| | - 1877 | - War of Satsuma. | |
| | - 1879 | | -With the development of the policy imperialist and a more consequent military force, broad studies are undertaken in order to create a structure mixing at the same time military police force and spy network. <br> - The technical and practical concept of Onmitsu and the Ninja will be used as model to create a new type of spy organization equipped with a modern technology, more adapted to this century. |
| | - 1881 | - Rules for the military police force, *Kenpeitai*, are fixed. | - Establishement of the Kenpeitai (憲兵隊), military police force which exerced the repression, the censure, the control of the thoughts, narrow monitoring of the population. <br> This type of action is similar to the action of the Onmitsu organization set up by the Bakufu during the period of Edo. |
| | - 1882 | - Creation of the Bank of Japan. | |
| | - 1889 | - Promulgation of the Constitution, *Dai nihon teikokukenpô* (大日本帝国憲法). | |
| | - 1890 | - First session of the Diet (Japan's parliament). | |
| | - 1894–95 | - Sino-Japanese War <br> - Treaty of Shimonoseki | |
| | - 1898 | - Okuma-Itagi Cabinet, first of a political party. | |
| | - 1902 | - Treaty of alliance with England. | |

| | | | |
|---|---|---|---|
| **Momoya-ma Cont'd.** | - 1904–05 | - Russo-Japanese War. | |
| | - 1905 | - Treaty of Portsmouth. | |
| | - 1906 | - Creation of South Manchuria Company of the railroads. | |
| | - 1910 | - Annexation of Korea. | |
| | - 1912 | - Death of the Meiji Emperor. | |
| | - 1914 | - Declaration of war against Germany. | |
| | - 1918 | - Sending of troops in Siberia. | |
| | - 1919 | - Treaty of Versailles. | |
| | - 1922 | - Treaty of Washington on the limitation of warships. | |
| | - 1923 | - Big earthquake of Tokyo. | |
| | - 1925 | - Law on the maintenance of law and order.<br>- Male vote. | |
| | - 1927 | - Financial Crisis. | |
| | - 1930 | - Conference of London. | |
| | - 1931 | - Incident of Manchuria. | |
| | - 1932 | - Incident of Shanghai.<br>- Assassination of Inukai Tsuyoshi. | |
| | - 1933 | - Japan abandons the SDN. | |
| | - 1936 | - Attempted coup d'etat of February twenty-sixth. | |
| | - 1937 | - Beginning of the Sino-Japanese war. | |
| | - 1940 | - Treaty of the Axis: Japan, Germany, Italy.<br>- Foundation of the military academy Nakano (中野学校) for the training of the officers. | - The Nakano school was established to train spies in order to support the Japanese imperialism in the Asian sphere. Largely presented like a school forming of the spies similar to the ninja, of many novel, film and news, have in fact a legend. |
| | - 1941 | - Attack of Pearl Harbor, beginning of the war of the Pacific. | |
| | - 1942 | - Battle of Midway. | |
| | - 1943 | - Establishment of the Ministry in order to administrate Asia. | |
| | - 1945 | - Declaration of Potsdam.<br>- Atomic Bomb on Hiroshima and Nagasaki.<br>- Entry in war of the Soviets.<br>- Surrender of Japan. | |
| | - 1946 | - Declaration that the Emperor is not divine.<br>- Promulgation of the Constitution .<br>- Land reforms. | |
| | - 1947 | - Prohibition of the monopolies (*zaibatsu*).<br>- Fundamental labor law. | |
| | - 1948 | - End of the international military tribunal of the Far East. | |
| | - 1949 | - Yukawa Hideki receives the Nobel Prize for physics. | |
| | - 1951 | - Signing of the peace treaty of San Francisco.<br>- Signing of the defense treaty the United States. | |
| | - 1953 | - First television broadcast for the NHK. | |
| | - 1954 | - Law on self-defense. | |
| | - 1956 | - Japan becomes a member of United Nations. | |
| | - 1960 | - Renewal of the defense treaty with the United States. | |
| | - 1961 | - Fundamental law on agriculture. | |
| | - 1962 | - Liberalization of trade. | |
| | - 1964 | - Opening of the high-speed line at Tokaidō.<br>- Tōkyō Olympic Games. | |

| Momoya-ma Cont'd. | - 1965 | - Tomonaga Shin Ichirō receives the Nobel Prize in Physics. | |
|---|---|---|---|
| | - 1967 | - Creation of the Economic Committee of the Pacific. | |
| | - 1968 | - Kawabata Yasunari receives the Nobel Prize in Literature. | |
| | | - Retrocession to Japan of Ogasawara island. | |
| | - 1969 | - Students' Demonstration. | |
| | - 1970 | - Launching of the first artificial satellite. | |
| | | - Osaka World Exposition. | |
| | - 1972 | - Retrocession of Okinawa island to Japan. | -Death of Takamatsu Toshitsugu, 33rd *soke* of *Togakure-ryū ninpō*. |
| | | - Visit of Prime Minister Tanaka to China. | |
| | - 1973 | - Ezaki R. receives the Nobel Prize in Physics. | |
| | - 1974 | - Lockheed scandal, *Miki* cabinet. | |
| | | - Satō the Nobel Prize of Peace. | |
| | - 1978 | - Opening of the Narita airport. | |
| | - 1979 | - Summit of Tokyo. | |
| | - 1981 | - The Pope visits Japan. | |

# Notes

## Chapter 1: What Is Ninjutsu?

1. In a passage of the *Suikoden*, the term *bugei jūhapan* appears as follows:

> *Day after day, Shishin received the transmission of his master. He was devoted to the practice of the 18 disciplines of Bugei. These 18 disciplines are as follows: the spear, archery, espionage and methods of infiltration, the sword, the chain and the sickle, the stick, moving with the body, horsemanship, and so forth.*

In the illustrated dictionary, *Sansai Zue* (三才図会), written in 1607, just as in *Gozasso* (五雑狙),* written in 1619, the term *bugei jūhapan* is presented and explained in a very precise way with certain differences from the disciplines presented in the *Sukikoden*. With regard to the meaning of the term, in Japan one finds several assumptions. First, in the history of Japan, one finds that the figure 18 is associated with various terms such as *Jūhakke* (十八家), the 18 great daimyō that have land, *Jūhachi Matsudaira* (十八松平), the 18 families that constituted the great Matsudaira family, *Jūhasshū* (十八宗), the various currents of Japanese Buddhism, *Jūhachi Danrin* (十八檀林), the 18 schools of the Buddhist sect *Jōdo* (浄土), and so on. In the Buddhist lexicon one finds, among other things, the terms of *Jūhakkai* (十八界), the 18 Worlds, *Jūhatten* (十八天), the 18 heavens, and so on. The figure 18 in the term *bugei jūhapan* is often thought to have resulted from the influence of a passage of a Buddhist text. Indeed, in the *Daichi Doron* (大智度論), a large dictionary of Buddhism in 100 volumes, one finds the term of *Jūhakkū* (十八空), 18 spaces or voids. The *kū* in *Jūhakkū* is found in the sentence "shiki sokuze kū (色即是空)" from the sutra *Hannya Shingyō* (般若心経). Some centuries later in a similar fashion, when Funakoshi Gichin (1868–1957) introduced *Okinawa tōte* (沖縄唐手) to the Japanese archipelago by the invitation of Kanō Jigorō (1860–1930), the characters for *tōte* (唐手) were changed to *karate* (空手).

2. In *Nihonshi Kohyaka budō*, 日本史小百科 (*Small Encyclopedia of the History of the Japanese Martial Arts*), chapter 9: 鎌倉武士と武芸 (*Warriors of the Kamakura Period and Practice of Bugei*), p. 28, Tōkyōdō Edition, Tokyo, 1994.

3. The *inka* (印可), is the first form of a certificate of the comprehension of knowledge that the master gives to his disciple within the framework of an esoteric or exoteric transmission. One finds this type of certificate in Buddhism, as stated in the *Injin Koka no Ryaku* (印信許可之略). There is no doubt that the mode of transmission found in traditional *bujutsu* emerged from Buddhism, which was widespread among the warlike class of the Kamakura period. Within a school, the framework of transmission of knowledge of the martial arts, the *inka* is a certificate that combines different documents, such as the *heihō-mokuroku* (兵法目録), the index of techniques of the school), the *densho* (伝書) and *makimono* containing transmission secrets, ultimate techniques, and of course the care created by the founder of the style. This is the reason for the famous statement (一国一人之印可相伝): "Only one act of transmission for a disciple in each province" decreed by Kamiizumi Isenokami (上泉伊勢守 1508–1577) the founder of *Shinkage ryū* (新影流) is notorious. The *kirigami* (切紙), known also under the generic title of *kirigami mokuroku* (切紙目録), is a diploma which attests level of practice of a disciple in various disciplines, *bujutsu*, *geinō* (芸能), and so forth. It acts as the first diploma accepted before entering into the higher levels of transmission of the school, where the techniques studied until the handing-over of the *inka* are registered. The paper used is known under the generic title of *Sugihara gami* (杉原紙), or *sugiwarashi*, or of *Bōshoshi* (棒書紙). In *bujutsu*, this type of certificate of control of a transmission already appears during the Sengoku period in the Shinkage-ryū school, whose *kirigami* were signed hand of the founder, Isenokami, as are those of the *Takeuchi-ryū* school (竹内流), and others. The influence on this type of certificate in *bujutsu* would come from *Denpō kanjō* (伝法灌頂), a certificate of transmission delivered in the esoteric Buddhist shingon (真言). However according to another source, it seems that the use of the *mokuroku sōden* (目録相伝) or sometimes called the *hijidenju* (秘事伝授) as the act of transmission already existed in the Ashikaga period (足利時代).† During the Edo period, with the diffusion of the techniques and the multiplication of the schools of *bujutsu*, the system of recognition of the level of a disciple in the schools, was as follows:

> *Sho mokuroku* (初目録), *chū mokuroku* (中目録), *dai mokuroku* (大目録), *kaiden* (皆伝), *or shoden* (初伝), *mokuroku* (目録), *gokui* (極意), *menkyo* (免許), *inka* (印可).

Heihō Michi shirube (兵法未智志留辺; written in 1833) gives the following definition:

> *What one names kirigami mokuroku is a certificate where the first conditions observed by the disciple are consigned. Thereafter, it will be able to begin the practice of the higher techniques of the school.*

Also let us add that the definition given by *Nippo Jiten* (日葡辞典: a Portuguese dictionary written in 1630, known under the title of *Vocabulario da Lingoa of Iapam*) indicates that the *kirigami* was also used like a simple letter or missive.

---

\* This work belongs to a literary type called *zuihitsu*, 随筆, "following the brush," very much in vogue during the Edo period.

† This source is reported by the work *Kendō no Hattatsu*, 剣道の発達, pp.132–150, ED. *Zaidan Hōjin Dainihon butokukai*, Tokyo, 1926, by Shimogawa Yoshio, a man of letters and practitioner of a high level *kendō* who occupied a high rank within the *Nihon butokukai*.

Ibid, chap. 66: 武 芸 伝 書 (*Works of Transmission of the Bugei*), p. 162, also in, *Nihon Budō Jiten*, 日 本 武 道 事 典, Sasama Yoshihiko, p. 489, ED. Kashiwa shobo, Tokyo, 1982, and in *Budō Kotoba Gogenjiten*, 武 道 言 葉 語 源 辞 典, p. 80, ED. Tōkyōdō, Tokyo, 1995.

4. The term *budō* (武 道)\* is an old one, which one finds already the use in the work *Rigi Shishū* (李 義 詩 集) by the poet Rishōin (李 商 隠 812–858) who lived at the end of the Tang dynasty. Indeed, the formula *bunbu ryōdō* (文 武 両 道), the joint practice of the martial arts and the letters, is presented there by Rishōin. This statement will be used again by the majority of the prominent masters of Japan. In Japan, the time when the use of this term first appears is unclear; however, one finds the term *budō* in a great number of notable literary works such as *Taiheiki* (太 平 記) or *Heike Monogatari* (平 家 物 語 巻 十 二). This leads us to us suppose that the term had a connotation stressing warlike duty, courage in front of the adversity, uprightness, fidelity, and the like, but it seems like it refers to more than a warlike attitude, and uncommon courage, rather than being a generic term indicating a particular practice of weapons.

Nowadays the idea of *budō* is very different, it includes all the ideology grafted onto the *bushidō*, the culture of the movements that developed in the Meiji period, a patriotism, and the like. Consequently, it easy to understand that with the passing of time, the term has defined an attitude, a way of living, a cultural movement, and a way of thinking resulting from the warlike culture. In *Budō Bunka no Tankyū*, 武 道 文 化 探 求, chap. 1, 武 道 論： 武 術、武 芸 と 武 道 (*budō ron: bujutsu, bugei to budō*), p. 15–17, ED. Fumaido, Tokyo, 2003.

5. Kamiizumi Isenokami Nobutsuna, 上 泉 伊 勢 守 秀 綱 (1508–1577), invented the *shinai*[†] 竹 刀, exercises using bamboo armor. Before that, the practice of the kenjutsu was carried out mainly with the *bokken* or *bokutō* (木 剣 木 刀 a wooden saber). However, exercises with the *bokken* resulted in many accidents as soon as combatants turned to dueling. Wanting to avoid such accidents, Kamiizumi developed the *fukuro shinai* (袋 竹 刀) or *hikihada shinai* (引 肌 竹 刀), composed of a whole piece of bamboo attached to the handle, split into fine plates along the part that corresponds to the blade of the saber and threaded into a leather sleeve. Lacquer reinforced the leather, making it narrow and giving it the aspect of frog skin, from which it gets its name: *hikihada shinai*. The length of the *shinai* was that of a saber. This type of *shinai* is still used today in the traditional school *Yagyū Shinkage ryū* (柳 生 新 影 流). The *shinai* used in kendo (剣 道) currently is a derivative of this. About the middle of the eighteenth century, the followers of various schools introduced the use of the *shinai* with protective armor. The most well-known of these are Yamada zaemon and Naganuma Shirōzaemon of the school *Jiki Shinkage ryū* (直 心 影 流), an offshoot of the current *Kashima shikage ryū* of Matsumoto Bizen no Kami, and Chūsei Chūbei of the school *Chūseiha Ittō ryū* (中 西 派 一 刀 流), founded by Itō Ittōsai, mainly using the saber in the sixteenth and beginning of the seventeenth centuries, whose style is today dominated by the practice of the kendo. One calls *shinai uchi* (竹 刀 打), *kenjutsu* (剣 術), or *gekiken* (撃 剣) or *gekken*, the thrusting with the saber with the *shinai* and the protective armor. This form became dominant during the nineteenth century, the techniques diversified and become increasingly subtle. In, *Nihonshi kohayka Budō*, op. cit., chap. 29: 柳 生 新 影 流 剣 術 (*Yagyū Shinkage-ryū Kenjutsu*), p. 29 and chap. 49: 竹 刀、防 具 道 場 (*Shinai, Bōgu, Dōjō*), p. 125, and In *Nihon Budō Taikei*, 日 本 武 道 大 系, Imamura Yoshio, Vol. 1, p. 5–10, ED. Domeisha, Tokyo, 1982.

6. *Shinage ryū* (薪 陰 流), school of saber founded by Kamiizumi Isenokami Nobutsuna (上 泉 伊 勢 守 信 綱, 1508– 1577), starting from the school *Kage-ryū* (陰 流) of Aisu Ikōsai (愛 洲 移 香 斎, 1441–1538).[‡] The techniques of these two

---

\* If one refers to the etymology of the term, the implication expressed by the contrived ideogram (武): combat where "one attacks with his lance," is not supported by recent history. In current usage, the character incorporates at least the idea of a search for peace. In old times, the character was a pictogram before it was transformed into an ideogram. The translation of the original term was "*shika*" (止 戈) and contains the implication of retaining the lance to put an end the war. Iron had succeeded stone, giving weapons a fatal force that frightened at the same time that it allowed users to overcome their enemies. The bitterness related to the loss of many valorous warriors gave birth in antiquity to an eminent wisdom: this lance, the instrument of death that they had in their hands, they associated with the various nuances of the character "*todome*" (止): "to remain upright," "to stop," "to be satisfied with." War, something that has always generated fear and inspired humanity's deep hope for peace, was expressed with the birth of this ideogram. However, reality is very different. The violence of such engagements caused a regression to the idea of retaining the weapon, "*shika*," and anthems rose to the glory of the victors. The evolution of the language represents changes that come with the passage of time. In the recent past, in particular during the last great war, the character (武) emphasized bravery. After the Japanese defeat, the implication again changed abruptly in regard to retaining weapons by integrating the concept of "the way." In conclusion, the combination of the two characters represents the integration of two practical elements that encompasses a great number of contradictory concepts. For the history of the etymology of the ideograms see Akatsuka Tadashi, *Shinjigen* (新 字 源), ED. Kadogawa Shoten, Tokyo, 1972, p.41 and 595.

† While it is certain that the invention of the *hikida shinai* took place in Isenokami, it is unclear if other schools developed a type of *shinai* and other protections before Isenokami invented its *shinai*. I think that the Tsukahara *bokuden* of *Shintō-ryū*, just like the *Nen-ryū* school, which Isenokami had deeply studied, also uses a form of *shinai*, certainly different in manufacture but similar in concept, which is to avoid needlessly wounding students during practice. One can also quote the school *Asayama ichiden-ryū*, *Niten ichi-ryū*, and others, where a type of shinai is also used. All that shows that very early, a non-lethal material for use in practice already existed and that many high-level masters, such as Isenokami, were already working with it.

‡ Aisu Ikōsai, his true name being Tarō Saemon Nōjō Hisatada, was renowned for his mastery of *kenjutsu*, *sōjutu* and ninjutsu. According to documents of the Higuchi family of the *Nen-ryū* school, Shirō Yoshimoto, known under the name Jion, the founder of *Nen-ryū*, had fourteen disciples, one in each province of Japan, who excelled in the art of *Nen-ryū* and other *bujutsu*. Among the fourteen disciples of Jion, one was Aisu Ikōsai. He was with the head of a powerful family of the area of Ise, known to be the cradle of Shintō, not far from the area of Kōga and Iga. Taiheiki, mentions the name of Aisu Isenokami. Ikosai had been a pirate in his youth. According to various documents that one finds on him, it seems that he went several times on the Chinese coasts and that he accumulated considerable combat experience there. In 1478, after being forced to withdraw in a cave of the south of Japan, he had an illumination, following which he founded his school, *Kage-ryū*. One of the oldest *makimono* of the art of the sword is *Kage-ryū Mokuoroku* (影 流 目 録), which one finds the illustration of the transmission in the bulky

schools come from *Nen-ryū* (念 流) founded in the fifteenth century by the monk and legendary master of saber, Jion (慈 恩 1351?–1409?). In fact, *Nen-ryū*, *Kage-ryū* and *Shintō-ryū* are regarded as the three principal schools of the art of the *kenjutsu* and various disciplines of combat, the famous *bugei jūhapan*, having influenced the great majority of the schools that were born in the Edo period. The work of Kamiizumi is incomparable. Having to work on a large manuscript, he remains by far, in this period of the history of martial arts, the ultimate master, who gave up directing his stronghold as a feudal lord to become a simple follower. He undertook a tour of personal initiation, wishing to propagate the art of his school, *Shinkage-ryū*. Many researchers think that it is from him that one starts to speak about fusion between the art of the saber and Zen. One of the most outstanding episodes in the life of Kamiizumi was included in an epic film by Akira Kurosawa: *The Seven Samurai*. It is the episode where one of the warriors saves a child taken hostage by a brigand. In his youth, Kamiizumi was a gifted pupil, and very early he was initiated into the secret techniques of *Nen-ryū* and *Shintō-ryū*, before being taken as disciple by Ikōsai of the *Kage-ryū* school. The latter developed in the province of Ise, and the tumultuous past of Ikōsai is legendary. It seems that the *Kage-ryū* school was a school practiced by pirates, *wakō* (倭 寇) or *kaizoku* (海 賊), and a relationship with the ninja is not excluded given the geography and the distance between the province of Ise and the provinces of Iga and Kōga, cradle of ninjutsu. Here is how Kamiizumi summarizes its practice in the first act of transmission, 一 国 一 人 印 可 相 伝, (a *transmission for a single pupil by province*), which he gave in *Yagyū Sekishūsai* (translated from the kanbun):

> *I practiced the way of the martial arts since my youth, and it is with unbound enthusiasm that I looked further into the ultimate techniques of various schools. Practicing night and day without slackening, I accepted an inspiration from the gods and named my school, Shinkage-ryū.*
>
> *Wishing to transmit my school throughout all the country, I went to Kyōto and it was on this occasion that I met you. I thank you for all the sincere attention that you have lavished on me and am grateful for your passion for the practice. I have transmitted to you all the knowledge of my school without omitting a single detail.*
>
> *May I be punished by the gods, Marishisonten, Hachiman Daibosatsu, Tenman Tenjin, Kasuga Daimyojin and Atagoyama, if what I write here is not the truth.*
>
> *If, in the future, you find a disciple impassioned (and serious), the nine principal techniques will have to be taught to him. And, depending upon the character of the disciple, you may judge it necessary to transmit everything to him.*
>
> *If you develop several hundreds of pupils, it is advisable to conform to the rule that consists in delivering only one act of transmission by province. Such is the condition of the transmission of our art.*
>
> *Kamiizumi Isenokami Fujiwara no Hidetsuna (seal)*
>
> *For the Lord Yagyū Shinzaemon*
>
> *The first day of the 8th year of the Eitoku era (1565).*

Kamiizumi had many pupils; finally he showed his art to many warriors eager to learn, preferring to give a lesson rather than to accept a combat or a duel. He showed his art to elites, as well as the shōgun, always refusing the honor and position of instructor in techniques of combat that would have ensured a comfortable future to him. The ultimate technique of the school is the *mutō dori* (無 刀), which follows the principle of *Maroboshi* (転), that is, to primarily guard one's adversary and to become his shadow to be able to follow his movement in order to disarm him without force.

One can count many schools formed by disciples of Kamiizimu, the *Hikida Shinkage-ryū* (疋 田 新 陰 流), of Hikida Bungoro (疋 田 豊 五 郎 1550-1630), the *Taisha-ryū* (タ イ 捨 流) of Marumeku Krando (丸 目 蔵 人: 1540–1626), the *Komagawa kaishin-ryū* (駒 川 改 心 流) of Komagawa Tairō Zaemon Kuniyoshi (駒 川 太 郎 左 衛 門 国 吉), and others, but only one disciple accepted the final transmission and the succession of the school: Yagyū Muneyoshi (柳 生 宗 義, 1528–1606).

Each transmitted the school to his children. The most notorious inheritor Yagyū Munenori (柳 生 宗 矩: 1571–1646), he founded the school *Yagyū Shinkage-ryū* (柳 生 新 陰 流), which became the school of Shōgun Tokugawa during the Edo period. Thereafter, this school evolved while diversifying. Muneyoshi, feeling that the practice of his school in Edo had moved away from the essence of the art, which to him had been transmitted by Kamiizumi, transmitted his art in its finest detail to his young son Yagyū Hyōgonosuke Toshitoshi (柳 生 兵 庫 助 利 厳: 1579–1650), who became the instructor in the stronghold of Owari, thus, allowing the art of Kamiizumi to be transmitted without any losses. Of the two principal branches of the school *Shinkage*,

---

Chinese treatise entitled *Wu EIB Zhi* (武 備 誌), or *Bubishi* in Japanese, an encyclopedia that was the result of fifteen years of work and that comprises the classification of two miles of documents. In addition to an illustration that shows monkeys handling swords, one also finds the presentation of *Mutōdori* (無 刀 捕). According to Selon Mao Yuanji, the author of *Wu Bei Zhi* in 1621, the scroll of *Kage-ryū* was lost by the Wakō (倭 寇), Japanese pirates at the time, in combat against the army of the General I. Q. Jiquang, who obtained it. The general worked out techniques of combat, starting from this document, to counter the techniques of the Wakō. In connection with the techniques of combat of the Wakō, there is the following passage in *Ji Xiao Xin Shu*, a treatise written by General I. Q. Jiquang in 1584:

We know for the first time the art of of *daitō* (long sword) of the Wakō during their invasion. They moved while leaping with their *daitō*, which disabled our soldiers. The Wakō were so skillful in leaping ahead to attack that they were able to make a jump of more than 3 meters with only one step. They used a long sword, that makes a deep penetration with each blow. A great number of our soldiers were slashed and perished with only one blow. Their sabers were short, and when they used a long weapon, they could not move quickly....

The name of the school, *Kage-ryū*, or School of the Shade, refers to the one of the first characterisitic arts to be included in ninjutsu. The relationship between this school and the schools of ninjutsu of Iga and Kōga is, thus, not in doubt.

the school of Edo and that of Owari, the first tended to slacken the practice by developing a sophisticated theorization,* while the second remained faithful to the tradition of the founder. The school then evolved and the techniques changed. The current the *sōke* of the school is Yagyū Nobuharu (柳生信治), who is the fifteenth successor of the school, and who has the documents transmitted in the Yagyū family as well as the acts of transmission of the art. In *Nihon Budō Taikei*, op. cit., Vol. 1, p. 5–10.

7. The school *Ittō-ryū* (一刀流) carries on the current tradition of *kenjutsu*, which finds its roots in the school *Chūjō-ryū* (中條流), founded in the fifteenth century by Chūjō Hyōgono Nagahide 中條長秀, who was one of the disciples who received the certificate of control (*inka*) from the founder of the *Nen-ryū* school. This branch would appear at the end of the Muromachi period (1333–1467), and remains today in various forms such as *Onoha Ittō-ryū* (小野派一刀流), *Chūseiha Ittō-ryū* (中西派一刀流), *Hokkushin Ittō-ryū* (北辰一刀流), of Chiba Chūsaku (千葉周作: 1794–1855), and *Ittō Shōden Mutō-ryū* (一刀正伝無刀流) of Yamaoka Tesshū (山岡鉄舟 1836–1888). Details relating to the life of the founder, Itō Ittōsai (1560?–1653?), remain very undefined and a great number of stories circulate about it. His school began at the end of the time of the feudal wars (*Sengoku Jidai*) until the beginning of the Edo period (1603–1868). According to various documents of the school, Ittōsai was born in the province of Izu and as a very young person he began the practice of the martial arts as a recluse in the mountains. Thereafter, he became the disciple of Kanemaki Jisai (鐘巻自斎), who was the founder of *Kanemaki-ryū* (鐘巻流).

Kanemaki Jisai was a disciple of Toda Seigen (富田勢源: 1520?–1590?), celebrated master of the saber of the *Chūjō-ryū* school, one of the specialities of which was the handling of the *kodachi* (小太刀 short sword) against one or more adversaries using a large saber (*tachi* or *daitō*). Kanemaki Jisai taught the handling of the saber of an average size (中太刀 *nakadachi*). Ittōsai was accepted thereafter in the *menkyō kaiden* (免許皆伝), which included the five secret techniques (秘伝) known as the following: *the myōken* (妙剣), the *zetsu myōken* (絶妙剣), the *shinken* (真剣), *kinshinchō O ken* (金翅鳥王剣), and the *doku myōken* (独妙剣).

After having arrived at the ultimate level of the teaching of Kanemaki, he undertook his initiatory journey throughout Japan to perfect his combat techniques. He fought many times with various warriors and always left victorious. Among the stories known about him, one recounts that he reached the ultimate state of *kenjutsu* and became most significant by far because of his level of control in the art, and this especially shows how much one finds this type of history in the great majority of the schools of techniques of traditional combat of Japan.

> *Ittōsai went to the divine temple of Hachiman in Kamakura, in the Kantō region, and he remained there seven days and seven nights, during which time he devoted himself to the practice of kenjutsu, and he also fasted and meditated. At the end of seven days, nothing occured. Despairing, he was at the point of leaving when, behind him, he sensed a will intent on killing him (sakki). Instinctively, he struck horizontally behind him with his saber. He discovered that the source of this premonition was a saber-weilding attacker, and he realized that this man's animosity was what caused his instinctive reaction. He named this technique the musō no ken (the saber of no thought). It became the highest technique of the Ittō-ryū school.*

After having taught his art to two disciples, Onozenki and Mikogami tenzen Yoshiaki, he withdrew to a temple where he became monk. Neither the cause nor the date of his death are certain. Mikogami Tenzen became the successor of Itōsai as the head of *Ittō-ryū*. He was the instructor of the Tokugawa house, as well as Yagyū Munenori, but with lower rank. *Ittō-ryū* is the school that most influenced modern kendō with its technical contents and its philosophical approach, which arises from a contemplative view of combat that has attracted generations of followers.

In *Ittō-ryū Heihō shikō*, 一刀流兵法史考, Morita Sakae, pp. 8–85, ED. NGS, Osaka, 1980.

In *Ittō-ryū gokui*, 一刀流極意, Sasamori Junzō, pp. 26–41, ED Reirakudō, Tokyo, 1986.

In *Ittōsai sensei kenpo sho*, 一刀流先生剣法書, of Kotoda Toshisada, written 17th century.

8. See Appendix A.

9. *Tenshin Shinyō-ryū* (天神真楊流) was founded at the beginning of the nineteenth century by Kiso Mataemon (1789–1870) (the reading of Iso Masatari is also possible), which had made the synthesis of two other schools, the *Yōshin-ryū* (楊心流) of Akiyama Shirobe, and the *Shin no Shintō-ryū* (真神道流) of Yamamoto Mizaemon, while making some personal modifications. It is an approach that finds its source in the *Yōshin-ryū* school of Akiyama Shirobe. This approach is subject to Chinese influence, because the founder accepted the teaching of a Chinese *wusgu* at the time of his trip in China to look further into traditional medicine. The founder created a fusion between *jūjutsu* and medical knowledge such as *sekkotsu-jutsu* (接骨術: form osteopathy) and the *keiraku-gaku* (経絡学: the science of the meridian line and the flow of energy or *ki*). The famous

---

\* This attitude allowed for the development of *Yagyû-ryû* of Edo as a result of the drop in the level of practice. Thereafter, the *Yagyû-ryû* of Edo developed this tendency, whereas the *Yagyû-ryû* of Owari (Nagoya) preserved the traditional severity. A difference in quality as well as in the level of the movements in the techniques was thus established during the Edo period between the two branches of the same school, *Shinkage-ryû*. One finds this evolution in several schools during this period of history. On this subject, Yagyû Jubei Mitsutoshi, teacher of Ygyû Munenori, writes in his *densho Tsuki No shô* (月之抄): "Munenori, my father said to me that he could teach all his knowledge to his own lord, his children, people of a great virtue (implying rich persons) and those who have great perseverance. To teach all of the art to these people does not pose a problem. If I say that I teach those who pay well, some will say that I am miserly. However those who learn while paying will never become our enemies, and they will reveal the secrets of the school reluctantly. It is necessary to make people pay gold for teaching…." This sentence may be a bit shocking, but it is known that the function of Munenori had exceeded by far that of a simple instructor. He was *Ometsuke* and held all the information, thus under cover of demonstrating his technique, he controlled people, provided them with diplomas and another testamonials.

*kappō* (活 法), methods of resuscitation, transmitted in the school *Tenshin Shinyō-ryū* are an offshoot. It is a school specialized in strikes and blocks. The techniques were conceived for combatants in everyday dress, which dissociates it from *Kitō-ryū* (起 倒 流), where the techniques were conceived for combatants in armor. In *Nihon Budō Taikei*, op. cit., Vol. 6, pp. 393–436.

10. The identity of the founder of *Kitō-ryū* (起 倒 流) remains heavily debated. Ibaragi Toshifusa (1579–1672) and Fukuno Masakatsu Shichirōemon, two close relations of the Yagyū family, are at the origin of the creation of another school of *jūjutsu*, *Ryoi shintō-ryū* (良 移 心 当 流), which leads one to think that Tadafusa changed the name into *Kitō-ryū* at the beginning of the seventeenth century. The first *densho* of the school that we have, the *Kitō-ryū Ran Mokuroku* (起 倒 流 乱 目 録), written in 1637, is signed by Toshifusa, it does not mention, however, the name of the *Ryoi shintō-ryū* school. Toshifusa taught Shōgun Iemitsu, who had at the same time as fencing master the very famous Yagyū Munenori (1571–1646), of *Yagyū Shinkage-ryū* (柳 生 新 影 流), whose masters were going to be of service to the shōgun until the end of the bakufu. Like Munenori, Toshifusa had as a mentor the Zen monk, Takuan Sōhō (1573–1645) of the Rinzai sect (臨 済 宗), and advocate of the application of the Zen thought to arts of combat. He wrote in particular for submission to Munenori, *The Book of the Mysteries of Motionless Wisdom, Fudōchi Shinmyō Roku,* (不 動 智 神 妙 録). Takuan played a major part in the choice of the name of the *Kitō* school, literally *ki* (起) "to rise" and *tō* (倒) "to fall." Takuan wrote two works for the attention of Toshifusa, *Hontai* (本 体) and *Seikyō* (性 鏡) in which one finds an explanation of the character *ran* (乱), which will become *randori* thereafter (乱 取). Thus, in the beginning, this school was obviously influenced by the *Yagyū* school and the lesson of Takuan, which brought the influence of Zen thought to him. The very first techniques of the school numbered 15 and were classified in the following way: five basic techniques: *Tai* (体), *Sha* (車), *Sei* (請), *Sayū* (左 右), and *Zenkō* (前 後). Then are followed by the higher level techniques: *ōgi* (奥 技): *Yuki-tsure* (行 連), *Yuki-chigai* (行 違), *Yuki-ate* (行 当), *Mikudaki* (身 砕), and *Tani-suberi* (谷 辷), and finally the techniques that supplement the total transmission: *Inraku* (引 落), and *Sei-hojō* (生 捕 縄). During the middle of the Edo period, the third generation of the school, Yoshimura Heisuke Sukenaga restructured the techniques of the school while adding to it new forms, such as the *omote katachi* (表 形), comprising fourteen techniques like *Tai* (体), *Yume No uchi* (夢 中), *Ryokuhi* (力 避), and *will ura*, and then *katachi* (裏 形) comprising seven techniques like *Mikudaki* (身 砕), *Kuruma gaeshi* (車 返), and *Mizu-iri* (水 入). Among the schools of *jūjutsu* that use a great number of techniques of blows and very violent strikes, the techniques of the *kitō-ryū* were conceived for combatants in armor and the speciality of the school was techniques of projection like the *yoko-sutemi* (横 捨 身). The most important documents of the school were written by Yoshimura, and number three, *Ten no maki* (天 之 巻), *Chi no maki* (地 之 巻) and *Jin no maki* (人 之 巻). In the *Ten no Maki* one finds the following sentence, which explains the significance of the name of the school: "When the enemy appears, he should be faced as if one is looking into a mirror, without showing the least emotion. Such is the attitude of our school." The *Chi no Maki*, among other things, presents the nine ultimate secret techniques of the *Zenkō Saidan no Koto* (前 後 際 断 之 事), and the principle of the *Mubyōshi no Koto* (無 拍 子 之 事), or the absence of rate/rhythm (the way to make an enemy lose all his capacities, in other words, to destroy the enemy's concentration). And finally, the *Jin no Maki* gathers the names of the Twenty-one forms. It was one of the schools that experienced great development during the Edo period. In 1735, during the fifth generation of the school, Ryūno Senemon Sadakata had a dōjō in the district of Asakusa attended by approximately 3000 students, which testifies to the popularity of this style. Kanō Jigorō studied this school and imposed the practice of *Koshiki no Kata* (古 式 の 形) on the students of his new school *Kōdōkan Jūdō*. In *Nihon Budō Taikei*, op. cit., Vol. 6, pp. 367–383 and in *Nihonshi kohayka budō*, op. cit., chap. 58, pp. 145–146.

11. *Nihon Budō Taikei*, op. cit., Vol. 10, pp. 204–219 and in Katō Jinpei, Kanō Jigorō, 嘉 納 治 五 郎, collection *Shin Taiikugaku Kōza* (新 体 育 学 講 座), ED. Shōyō Shoin, Tokyo, 1964, vol. 35, pp. 41–44. Kanō's school (*Kōdōkan Jūdō*) was open to boys of secondary university age, and provided general training in three fields: physical education, martial arts and moral training. The approach was conceived as research and practice aimed at applying the principles of *jūdō* to the whole life of the student. It is in the course of morals and the rules of the life of his school that the ideology and the practice that Kanō sought to set up have continued most clearly. He formulated the essence of his school of morals in the following way:

- *Study by completely investing yourself and having a goal in your life.*
- *Advance towards great future success without letting yourself be distracted.*
- *Work with confidence in yourself and bear in mind your own potential to make progress for your country.*
- *Think of the position of Japan in the international community and become a pillar of the state.*

Kanō expresses here all the dominant ideology of the time, namely a new capacity, resulting from a movement born in the warlike class to answer the threat of the Western powers. This new capacity tended to reinvest in the image of Japan, represented by the dual figure of the emperor of the state and the potential for devotion inherent in the old feudal bonds. Whatever the difficulty, to undertake the practice of the self-control, work, and the effort to contribute to many others with courage, here is a brief description of the state of mind expected of the students who will have to build the Japan of the Meiji period. The life of the pupils who attended the *Kōdōkan* of Kanō was governed by a strict discipline, and here are the rules:

- *To wake at 4:45 AM, to go to sleep at 9:30 PM. In turn, each student is charged with awakening the others because, as was the custom in the education of the warriors; Kanō thought that a man must be able to awaken himself at the hour of his choosing.*

- *Upon waking, the pupils clean their sleeping quaters and the school's garden.*

- *Daily jūdō practice is compulsory, and the hours of studies, practice and rest are precisely fixed.*
- *While they study, the pupils must always maintain the correct traditional posture; that is, seated in seiza, on the heels, with the back straight.*
- *Simple traditional clothing must be worn, which will be worn until complete worn out.*
- *Equitable treatment must be given to each pupil, regardless of whether they are from a rich family or a humble one.*
- *Students may not come and go as they please. However, pupils whose families reside in Tokyo may visit home twice a month. Group departures are done under the supervision of the senior members responsible for group. For this reason, only they are entitled to pocket money.*
- *Each pupil in turn takes a meal with the master in order to have a direct conversation with him.*
- *Every Sunday morning at 6:00 AM, Master Kanō teaches a class on morals to all of the pupils.*

12. ibid Chap. 1: Kanō Jigorō no konsei (嘉納治五郎の恨性), p. 10–12.

13. "the *soft one (flexibility, flexibility) easily defeats the hard one (the force, power)*" is the translation of the quotation *jū yoku sei gō* (柔能制剛) of the Chinese military treatise *San ryaku* (三略: *San Lue* in Chinese), very much inspired by the Taoist thought. This treatise is often ascribed to the legendary character Kōsekikō (黄石公), who would have completed it in Chōryō (張良: ?–161). This work of military strategy was highly valued by most warlords over the course of Japanese history, and was read jointly with *Rikutō* (六韜), from which the generic title of *Rikutō san ryaku* (六韜三略) arises. Heavily used in many *densho* of schools of *bujutsu*, it shows the influence of this traditional philosophy on the warrior elite, whose aim it was to embody the principle of this sentence. Kanō surely knew the work in its entirety, because one finds the instructions there to lead troops into combat and all qualities necessary to be a perfect leader. Likewise, the *densho* schools, *Kitō-ryū*, *Yōshin-ryū*, *Tenshin shinyō ryū* and others, also take this sentence as a central creed to promote the use of the flexibility against force in any situation.

14. In *Kindai karatedō no Rekishi wo Kataru, Discussion on the Modern History of Karate*, (近代空手道の歴史を語る), Gima Shinkin and Fujiwara Ryozō, ED. BB, Tokyo 1980, chap. 2, p. 25.

15. In Francine Hérail, *History of Japan*, ED. Horvath, Paris 1986.

16. Gima Shinkin and Fujiwara Ryozō, op. cit., Chap. 9, p. 91. In 1892, Ankō Itosu (1830–1920), one of the two masters of Funakoshi, and some of its pupils gave a demonstration in front of Ogawa Shintarō, the Chief of Police, who was visiting Okinawa. Following this demonstration, he asked that karate be taught in the first public college of Okinawa and the school of civil service candidates. In 1901, karate was included in the physical education program in the schools of Okinawa. The techniques of *Tōte* being deemed too dangerous for young schoolboys, they were modified so that they fell within the framework of physical education like jūdō.

17. The two sanctuaries of *Katori* (香取) and *Kashima* (鹿島) are located on opposite banks of the *Tone* river (利根). The gods of water, the river, and the tides are venerated there. With regard to the practice and the worship of the martial arts, the traditions of the two sanctuaries are shrouded in mythology. From the fourteenth century on, several schools of bujutsu were founded by their priests. A school was founded by Iizasa Chōisai Ienao (飯笹長威斎), a warrior attached to the sanctuary of *Katori*. Having experience in battle and knowledge of the sword and various other weapons, Chōisai lived in the field of the sanctuary of Katori, seeking to improve his sword technique. To please the martial god of the sanctuary, he practiced sword-fighting against the trees night and day. At the end of three years of intense research as a recluse, he accepted the illumination of the martial god and founded the swordfighting school *Tenshin Shōden Katori Shintō-ryū* (天真正伝香取神道流). This school is usually called *Shintō-ryū* (神道流 or 新当流). Iizasa Chōisai died at one hundred and one years of age in 1488 (in the fifteenth day of the second year of the Chōkyō era). This traditional school was classified as a national treasure and continues to operate in Chiba prefecture. The ritual of admission for the applicant was to make an incision in the index finger and to sign the *makimono* in blood. This ritual is doubtlessly a reason for the school's very restricted number of pupils. In *Nihon Budō Taikei*, op. cit., Vol. 3, pp. 5–8.

18. Matsumoto Bizen no kami Masanobu (松本備前守政信 1468–1524) was of a family who had taken up the duty of monks to the sanctuary of *Kashima* for several generation. He studied *kenpō* (剣法 laws and rules governing the practice of the *kenjutsu*) under the cane of his master Iizasa Chōisai, and from his personal practice, he worked out the techniques of combat for various weapons like the *bō-jutsu*, the *yari-jutsu*, and the *naginata*, and thus founded his school that he named *Kashima shin-ryū* (鹿島神流) whose *gokui* or *higi* (極意秘義 technical ultimate, quintessence of the school) has the name *Hitotsu no tachi* (一之太刀 the single sword). Bizen nokami died at fifty-seven, on the battlefield where he was, formerly, on several occasions illustrated taking the heads of many lords and warriors. However, long before his death, he transmitted the essence of his teaching of which the famous *Hitotsu No tachi* became famous thereafter with two masters: Tsukahara Bokuden (1489–1571) and Kunii Kagetsugu (1491?–1580?), expert of the school Nen-ryū (念流). In *Nihon Budō Taikei*, op. cit., Vol. 3, pp. 9–20.

19. *Yagyū Shingan-ryū* (柳生心眼流) is a school specializing in several disciplines of combat founded during the Edo period (1603–1868) under the shōgunate of Iemitsu (1604–1651), student of Tokugawa Ieyasu (1542–1616). Although it developed primarily in the stronghold of a family of warriors in the town of Sendai, a branch developed in the area of the Kansai that still remains ignored. According to manuscripts of the school, such as *Heihō Will Denrai Yūsho Ryaku* (兵法伝来由緒略) written in 1790, at the genesis of the school, there was no name; a certain Ushūtate waki (羽州帯刀), also known under the name of Tozawa Waki (戸沢帯刀), accepted the post of teacher of the *yagyū-ryū kenjutsu* (柳生流剣術) through Yagyū

Gorōemon Munetsugu, student of Yagyū Sekishūsai Muneyoshi (1527–1606) and brother of Yagyū Munenori (1571–1646). He added new techniques, which he worked out himself and propagated his knowledge under the name of *Shingan-ryū* (心 眼 流). However, reliable documents about this founder are very rare, and thus, nothing is known for certain about this individual. Some generations later, a certain Takenaga Hayato Kanetsugu (竹 永 隼 人 兼 次), a rōnin born in Sendai, established the school. Indeed, according to the same *densho*, after gaining possession of the technical knowledge of the *Shintō-ryū* (伸 道 流), *Shingan-ryū* (神 願 流), *Shuza-ryū* (首 座 流) and *Toda-ryū* (戸 田 流) schools, he went to Edo where the reputation of Yagyū Tajima No kami Munenori (1571–1646) was widespread. He became the pupil of Yagyū and after much sincere practice, he accepted the certificate of control (*menkyo kaiden*, 免 許 皆 伝) of the school *Yagyū shinkage-ryū* (柳 生 新 影 流). With all the knowledge that he had accumulated, he created his own school that he named *Yagyū Shingan-ryū* and taught without regard to social status. On return to his hometown Sendai, he primarily taught among the *ashigaru* (足 軽, warriors that form the first lines during the confrontation on a battle field). Of all the schools of jūjutsu that specialized in the teaching of *Suhada bujutsu* (素 肌 武 術 combat without armor), the school *Yagū shingan-ryū* is one whose teaching is based on the use of various weapons when one is armored, it taught *Kachū bujutsu* (甲 冑), techniques of combat in armor. One of the notorious characteristics of this school is its form of *jūjutsu*, named *Kachū-yawara* (甲 冑 柔 術) and especially a form of *kenpō* (拳 法), that is, an art of strikes and percussions, used against other warriors in armor. It is about a method of *kenpō* particularly precise and devastating. Today, *Yagyū Shingan-ryū* still exerts a very rich teaching through the following disciplines: *Yoroi Kumiuchi* (鎧 組 打), *Jūjutsu*, *Kogusōku* (小 具 足 art of short weapons, including a form with *jūjutsu*), *Torite-jutsu* (捕 手 aspect of *jūjutsu* focusing on the control of the joints), *Torinawa-jutsu* (捕 縄 術 technique of binding), *Tessen-jutsu* (鉄 扇 術 long-range techniques), *Daitō* (大 刀 large sword), Nakadaitō (中 大 刀 average sword), (小 太 刀 sword runs), *Iai-jutsu* (意 合 術), *tansō-jutsu* (短 槍 術 short lance), *naginata-jutsu, bō-jutsu, kusari gamma-jutsu*. In *Hiden Nihon Jūjutsu* (秘 伝 日 本 柔 術), Matsuda Ryūchi, ED. Sōjinsha, Tokyo, 1978, Chap. 2, pp. 73–80.

20. Takeda Sokaku (1860–1943) founder of *Daitō ryū jū-jutsu* (大 東 流 柔 術) or *aiki-jūjutsu* (合 気 柔 術) at the beginning of the twentieth century, seems to have been one of the greatest martial arts masters of his time. He had acquired his frightening skill by engaging in combat throughout all Japan, in the dōjō as well as in the street. He was born in Aizu, an area known for the ferocity of its samurai. His father, Sokichi, (1819–1906) was a champion of sumō as well as a master in the art of the sword and of the halberd, and even from his Sokaku childhood had learned how to fight in the rustic dōjō of the family. Even after the Meiji Restoration in 1868, he did not cease acting like a warrior of the feudal days. He embarked on a long journey that took him all around Japan: he still wanted to be involved with the best masters of *budō* and to challenge them, but he also wanted to determine his value while being measured against his predecessors. In 1877, he intended to join the rebel forces of Takemori Saigō in Kyūshū, but this plan fell through, because the revolt was crushed before Takeda could join the fight. Sokaku learned, under the direction of Saigō Tanomo (1872–1923), the secret techniques *oshiki-uchi* (御 式 内) from the clan from Aizu. This lesson stressed the will of the samurai as much as the techniques of combat. He also studied the *Ono* approach of the school of *kenjutsu* named *Ittō*, for which he received the certificate of mastery of the style. Sokaku worked out his own style by combining the fundamental elements of the *oshiki-uchi* with the *kenjutsu* of the *Ittō* school, as well as the techniques derived from the incomparable experience which he had with the traditional techniques of combat and the practice of actual combat. He named his style *Daitō-ryū Aiki-jūjutsu*. Without actually having a dōjō, he carried on a wandering life, often on the margins of the community. His reputation, however, attracted a significant number to him, including high-ranking officers and influential civil servants. In 1915, Takeda was teaching in the village of Engaru in Hokkaidō, in a dōjō established in an inn, when Yoshida Kotarō (1886–1964) introduced him to his future disciple Ueshiba Morihei (1883–1969). In, ibid Chap. 4, pp. 151–170.

21. See Appendix B.

22. Deguchi Onisaburō (出 口 王 仁 三 郎 1871–1948) was the main proponent of the sect *Omoto-kyō* (大 本 教) founded by Deguchi Nao (出 口 ナ オ 1836–1918), a very poor country-woman with the shamanic abilities. Onisaburō married Nao's daughter, Sumi, and ended up taking control of the entire organization, which he reorganized according to his own designs. Guided by his brilliant imagination and strong sense of esthetics, he developed quite a talent for prophecy. He taught his disciples that "art is the essence of religion" and had in addition developed a certain number of techniques of meditation as well as powerful incantations based on the theory of *Kotodama* (言 霊). The followers of *Omoto-kyō* believed that all religions emanate from the same source and that all the nations of the world would eventually unite. The meeting between Onisaburō and Ueshiba took place within the headquarters of Omoto-kyō based in Ayabe in December 1919. The nature and the depth of Onisaburō's teaching transformed Ueshiba's spiritual worldview and provided him with the basis of his ethical vision, one that thereafter was going to permeate aikidō deeply. The spiritual training of Ueshiba Morihei at Deguchi Onisaburō had as much importance in the development of modern aikidō as his study of the techniques of combat of Daitō-ryū. In Nihon Budō Taikei, op. cit., vol. 8, pp. 323–328.

23. Kanō, a tireless researcher, had created a division dealing exclusively with the study and the practice of *kobudō* or *kobujutsu* (old techniques of combat). Only certain hand-picked pupils were accepted into this division. Being keenly interested in all of the old Japanese combat techniques, after having attended a demonstration of *aiki-jūjutsu* in October 1930, he declared to Ueshiba: "*It is my ideal of the budō there; it is truth and pure jūdō.*[*]" Kanō sent three of his best disciples to the

---

[*] The content of the discussion between the two masters, Ueshiba and Kanō, is not known. However, it is very easy to understand that Kanō was filled with wonder to see such technical control, which exceeded by far what Kanō had been able to see, because he wrote a letter to Ueshiba where he made the statement that I translated here. This letter still exists, and it is preserved at Aikikai of Tokyo.

division on the *kobudō*, Tomiki Kenji (1900–1979), Mochizuki Minoru (1907–2003), and Sugino Yoshiō (1904–1994), to study *Ueshiba-ryū* at his expense. They were, in return, to submit a detailed report of all that they had learned. In Kanō Jigorō, op. cit., vol. 35, pp. 50–54.

24. See Appendix C.

25. The first mention of the term *aiki* (合 気), but with a first character that differs from that of aiki-jūtsu or aikidō, is found in the *densho* entitled *Tomoshibi Mondo* (燈 火 問 答: *Enlightened Conversations*) of the school *Kitō-ryū jūjutsu* (起 倒 流 柔 術). The term *aiki-jūtsu* (合 気 柔 術), as we know it today appears very late. The first use by Sokaku itself dates from the middle of the Taishō period (1912–1926) when the name of the practice of *Daitō-ryū jūjutsu* was changed to *Daitō-ryū Aiki jū-jutsu*. However the first appearance of this term as it is used today, comes from a work entitled *Budō hiketsu: Aiki No jutsu*, (武 道 秘 訣: 合 気 之 術, *Secret Text of Budō: Aiki no Jutsu*) published in the twenty-fifth year of the Meiji era (1892). Only the pen name of the author is known, Bukotsu Kyoshi. When reading this book, one immediately sees that the author, although impassioned about *bujutsu*, is not a practitioner but rather a journalist casting an incisive glance on the Japanese community of his time. However, he explains why the *Aiki no Jutsu* is the quintessence of all the principles of *bujutsu* and that its essense can be restated as "preceding the enemy in his intentions and movements" or by "the art of distinguishing the intentions and feelings of the enemy." For the author, the first appearance of this term, as well as the most perfect application, returns in Uesugi Kenshin (1530–1578), the constant rival of another famous warlord, Takeda Shingen (1521–1573), heir to the Takeda family. In *History of an Uncommon School: Daitō-ryū aiki-jūjutsu*, Kacem Zoughari, an article for the 20 excerpt series of special Bushido Karate Aikidō, ED. European of Magazines, 2004.

26. *A Sufi Saint of the Twentieh Century*, Martin Lings, Ed. Georges Allen & Unwin Ltd., 1971.

27. *Ninja no Seikatsu*, 忍者の生活, Yamaguchi Masayuki, Ed.Ozan kyakan, Tōkyō 1962, pp. 62–90.

28. *Kabuki*, Genji Masakatsu, Ed. Kōdansha, 1985, pp. 50–70.

29. ibid.

30. ibid.

31. ibid.

32. Ibid.

33. It is about an integral translation sourced from original manuscripts of Rene R. Khawam, the *Book of the Tricks: Political Strategy of the Arabs*, ED. Phébus, Vichy, 1982. This has to do with Abd Al-Malik, teacher of Salih Al-Hâchimî, grandson of Abdallah ibn 'Abbâs (cousin of the prophet Muhammad 570–632). He was the companion of Khalife Al-Rachid and had vast properties with Mannbidj (anc. Hiérapolis). He died in 199/815, ibid pp. 42–43.

34. The Council coming from the Al-Mouhallab will, governor of Khourassâne, a politically active general. He died in 199/815. Ibid Chap. 7: Tricks of the Viziers, the Governors and People of the Administration, pp. 214–216.

35. The Council coming from a letter written by Mou' âwiya, Arabic general who took part in the conquest of Syria and became governor of Damas. He died of the plague in 18/639 and was replaced by his brother Mou' âwiya, teacher of Abou-Soufyâne, who became the khalife in Damas (Omayyades dynasty) of 40/661 to 60/680. This letter was addressed to Marwâne ibn Al-Hakam, young nephew of Khalife Othmâne of the Omayyades family, for whom he was an assistant. As part of the Omayyades family, he later became khalife of Damas in 64/684 to 65/685. Ibid pp. 44–46.

36. In Yamaguchi, op. cit., chap. 6, p. 139.

37. Accounts of Takamatsu Toshitsugu were written in a series of articles published as *Tokyo Spotsu*. The newspaper goes back to 1963 and was published by the Tokyo Supotsu Shinbunsha. The company does not exist anymore, and the only copies were lost. The originals as well as the photographs showing Takamatsu Toshitsugu are in the possession of Hatsumi Masaaki.

38. Here, I wish to give some additional information on two subjects:

A) The number eight (八) for *hakkei* (八 景), *hachi mon* (八 門), is not arbitrary. This is not a question as much as a belief that there are a definite number of disciplines established. In fact; this figure hides the study of the immense knowledge that deep introspection reveals, and that the practice of the art of ninjutsu requires. It is also what the term *kihon happō* (基 本 八 法) translates or *happō biken* (八 法 秘 剣), and not just eight basic techniques that should be known to pass an examination as many believe. One finds it in the *kamae hachimonji* (八 文 字) of the school *Togakure-ryū ninjutsu* (戸 隠 流 忍 術) or again in the *hachi No kamae* (八 構) of the school *Nen-ryū* (念 流). The figure eight is also associated with the secret transmission, *hiden* (秘 伝), contained in all the traditional schools of *bujutsu*. The figure can either hide the form of movement, or a particular behavior of a weapon, a posture, an angle of reception or of attack, etc. It is very interesting to note that the term *jūhakkei* (十 八 景), or *jūhappan* (十 八 般), is only the association of two postures (*jūmonji no kamae, jūji no kamae, hachi-monji, hassō no kame*, or the like) or attacks which contain multiples of the figure eight (*hachi* 八) and ten (*jū* 十). One finds here a link that very closely connects the *sanshin no kata* (三 心 之 型) of the school *Gyokko-ryū kosshijtsu*, the *sanbyōshi* (三 拍 子) of the school *Kotō-ryū koppō-jutsu*, and the like, with the inherent principle which contains the figures one, eight, or ten. It forms a kind of triad whose secrecy is contained in the *ichi*, one or single. From where still the principle of *hitotsu No tachi* (一 之 太 刀), which one finds in many schools of *bujutsu* and of kenjutsu. *Maboroshi* (転) created by Kamiizumi, founder of the *Shinkage-ryū* school, is the ultimate principle of movement, which made it possible to pass from one guard to another, and thus, to pass subtly between the *ichi*, the *hachi*, and the *jū*. Thus, we can easily advance that ninjutsu proposed a form of numerology and that many prominent masters were versed in or very sensitive to this type of knowledge, because for these masters, each character, blow, and lesson concealed a hidden direction that the future successor or chosen pupil must find by practice. Thereafter, the reading of any document of transmission, regardless of style, became luminous and vivifying.

B) Takamatsu Toshitsugu's term *ninja no kiai* (忍 者 之 気 合) refers to a sound that must be vocalized during combat. He divides the *ninja no kiai* into three sounds, which resound in the whole body and not only in the belly. The three sounds are, *A* (ア), *KA* (カ) and *IE* (エ イ). Different *densho* from the nine schools that Takamatsu accepted and those that he transmitted to his only heir, Hatsumi Masaaki, which discusses these three breathings under the title *Mitsu Kudaki* (三 砕). The first is used to destroy the intention and the will of the enemy, the second to cancel the technique of the enemy, and finally the third, to destroy the body of the enemy. The final stage being to reach the state of *kage kiai* (影 気 合) or *kage no kiai*. Also, here as in other places, the figure three (三), is not arbitrary. It refers, as I showed earlier, to the *sanshin no kata, san byōshi, sanpō*. It is thus about a basic knowledge that comes before the basic technique. This led the wise ones to name this "the secret of secrects" or "the secret within the secret."

## Chapter 2: The Public Record of Ninjutsu

1. *Ehon Futami-gata* is allotted to Hokusai; *Ehon Takaragura* was created circa 1800; *Eimei Nijuhachi Shūku* was published in 1866, *Ehon Taikō-ki,* a love song based on the life of Toyotomi Hideyoshi by Takeuchi Kakusai and illustrated by Okada Gyokuzan, published in 1802 in Osaka by Kobayashi; *Nise Murasaki Inaka Genji*, "A Country Genji by a Fake Murasaki," written by Ryūtei Tanehiko and illustrated by Utagawa Kunisada, published in Edo between 1828 and 1842; *Ehon Toyotomi Kunki*, a love song based on the life of Hideyoshi by Ryūsuitei Tanekiyo, illustrated by Kuniyoshi and published between 1857 and 1884, and so forth.

2. The four authors who follow have studied and have undertaken deep research on ninjutsu, the ninja and the history of Japan. Their works are exhaustive and very difficult to find. Moreover, the relevance of their comments, and their concern about only reporting the most authentic facts is enhanced by the rigor with which they present proof, clearly places their work above all the other works on the same subject. It is interesting to note that the dates that I used for this part are the same ones in the four works that I have chosen, and they coincide with the various historical chronicles that I used to check each date and the facts concerning the ninja and his practice. In Yamaguchi, op cit., chap. 1, p. 19 and 91.

3. In Koyama Ryūtarō, *Shinsetsu Nihon Retsuden Ninja*, 真 説 日 本 忍 者 列 伝, ED. Arechi, Tokyo 1964, Chap.1, p.7 with 102.

4. In Tobe Shinjūrō, *Ninja to Ninjutsu*, 忍 者 と 忍 術, ED. Mainichi, Tokyo, 1996, chap. 22, 37, 52, 67, 82, 96, 110, 124.

5. In Sugiyama Hiroshi, *Nihon No Rekishi*, 日 本 の 歴 史, Vol. 11, 5th edition, Shōgakukan, Tokyo, 1980, chap. 11, p. 205.

6. To undertake a whole qualitative and rigorous study on the history of the ninja and its practice, it was necessary to consult a very vast library of works, the majority very old, that have a quotation or any relationship with the different kanji that constitute the words ninjutsu, ninja, and its practice. Here is a table with all the terms that I reconstructed to conclude this study:

- *Chūgoku Heijutsu Ninsho* 中 国 兵 術 忍 書), manuscript on the tactics and warlike strategies of China mentioning the ninjutsu or a form of ninjutsu.
- *Minamotoke Heijutsu Ninsho* (源 家 兵 術 忍 書), manuscript on the tactics and warlike strategies of the Minamoto family mentioning the ninjutsu.
- *Kusunokike Heijutsu Ninsho* (楠 家 兵 術 忍 書), manuscript on the tactics and warlike strategies of the Kusunoki family mentioning the ninjutsu.
- *Iga Ninjutsu* (伊 賀 忍 術), manuscript on the ninjutsu of the province of Iga.
- *Kōga Ninjutsu* (甲 賀 忍 術), manuscript on the ninjutsu of the province of Kōga.
- *Chihō Ninjutsu* (地 方 忍 術), manuscript on the ninjutsu of areas other than that of Iga and Kōga.
- *Kajutsu Kankei* (火 術 関 係), manuscript related to the use of the powder and be explosive (*kayaku jutsu*).
- *Juhō Ketsuinhō* (呪 法 印 法), manuscript related to the magic and *kuji*.
- *Unki, Sakki, Tenmon* (雲 気、察 気、天 文) handwritten in relation to the preaching of time, of the intention of the enemy, for predicting victory or defeat in a future war.
- *Gunki nor Arawareta Ninjutsu* (軍 記 に 現 れ た 忍 術), chronicle of soldiers where one finds mentions of the use of ninjutsu.
- *Gun Ho nor Arawareta Ninjutsu* (軍 法 に 現 れ た 忍 術), military manuscript of strategy where one finds mentions of the use of ninjutsu.
- *Kenpō to Tanren* (剣 法 と 鍛 練), manuscript of the art of the sword, and physical and mental reinforcement in relation to ninjutsu.
- *Kabuki nor Arawareta Ninjutsu* (歌 舞 伎 に 現 れ た 忍 術), manuscript of the kabuki and other theater mentioning ninjutsu.
- *Meiji Taishō no Ninjutsu* (明 治 大 正 の 忍 術), document of the Meiji and Taishō periods mentioning ninjutsu.

7. Tobe Shinjūrō, op. cit., Chap. 153.

8. In Koyama Ryūtarō, op cit. Chap. 1.

9. *Buyō Benryaku* (武 用 弁 略) was compiled in 1684 by Kinoshita Gishun, when it gives one of the first definitions of ninjutsu: *The ninja were people who could be distributed undetected in their hometowns as well as in the other provinces. Among them, some knew secret techniques and could infiltrate an enemy castle in full safety. They were native to the provinces of Iga and Kōga, which were for a very long time a crucible for the type of warrior who excelled in this art. It is said that they*

*transmitted their knowledge from generation to generation...*, In Sasama Yoshihiko, *Buke Senjin Sakuhō Shūsei*, 武 家 戦 陣 作 法 衆、ED. Kōdansha, Tokyo, 1970, pp. 84−85.

10. In Miura Jōshin, *"Hōjō Godai-ki"*, 北 条 五 代 記, *in Sengoku Shiryō Sōshō*, 2nd series, Vol. 1, ED. Kōdansha, Tokyo, 1965−67, pp. 395−397.

11. For all the names indicating the ninja in the history of Japan, consult Appendix C.

12. In Tobe Shinjūrō, op. cit p. 309.

13. ibid

14. The final chapter of the treatise of Sun Zi is entirely devoted to the methods of espionage and named spies. *Kanchō* ( 間 諜). Sun Zi distinguishes five types of spies and points out the role of these ninja:

*Inkan* (隠 間), was a native of the area, generally a peasant or a villager, who was employed for espionnage and to locate the positions of enemy troops. As he was not regarded as one who would be involved with this type of mission, he was seldom suspected.

*Naikan* (内 間), acted inside the family to which he belonged. There were many reasons why this type of agent would betray his Master: desire for independence, revenge, desire for social advancement, and so forth. He was the perfect agent in the sense that he acted on the inside, sowing disorder and confusion. Information that he offered was of a greater use than even that of the *inkan*.

*Yūkan* (友 間), was a typical double agent, changing loyalties when it served him.

*Shikan* (死 間), was the carrier of death. When captured, he deliberately gave false information, causing confusion and disorder in the enemy's designs. Even if he were put at death, which was often the case, the distored information that he had given beforehand would have already bourne fruit.

*Shōkan* (初 間), was the traditional ninja who infiltrated the enemy camps and returned with invaluable information. For this type of mission, these men had to have great capabilities and knowledge of combat and espionage. They were necessarilly well-equipped, patient and nimble. Sun Zi puts this type of spy on a pedestal compared to the others. he was very loyal to the general, who in turn rewarded him liberally. In Sasama Yoshihiko, op cit. pp. 88.

15. Koyama Kyūtaro, op cit. p. 21, and Tobe Shinjuro, op cit. p. 236 to 251.

16. In Sugiyama Hiroshi, op. cit chap. 10, pp. 101.

17. ibid

18. The *Kurama* temple (鞍 馬 寺) was built in 770 and belonged to the current *Tendai* (天 台 宗). The god Bishamonten (毘 沙 門 天) was venerated there. This temple is not only known to be the place where Minamoto Yoshitsune (1159−1189) accepted the transmission of the various techniques of combat by *tengu* (天 狗), but is also affiliated with many other schools of *bujutsu*. Well before the birth of the three main branches* of *bujutsu*, *Tenshin Shōden Katori shintō-ryū*, *Kage-ryū*, and *Nen-ryū*, there were the *Eight Schools of the Kansai* (京 八 流) and the *Seven Schools of Kantō* (関 東 七 流), originating from the *Katori* and *Kashima* temples, named *Kashima no Tachi* (鹿 島 之 太 刀) or *Katori no Tachi* (香 取 之 太 刀).† According to the various manuscripts, such as that of *Yoshitune-ki* (義 経 記), a master, and an expert in *bujutsu* and the science of *Onmyōdō* ( 陰 陽 道),‡ named Kiichi Hōgen (鬼 一 法 眼), was the founder of the school *Kuruma-ryū* (鞍 馬 流). He transmitted his knowledge to eight monks who founded the eight offshoots of *Kurama-ryū*. However, information about Kiichi Hōgen is scarce, and far from being very reliable. According to legend, when Yoshitsune was a young man, he wished to acquire the famous treatise on the art of war: *Rikutō sanryaku* (六 韜 三 略). To learn its secrets, he charmed Kiichi Hōgen's daughter in order to steal the coveted *densho* containing all the secret techniques of combat. One of the schools that would be the last offshoot of the *Eight Schools of the Kansai* was the renowned *Yoshioka-ryū* (吉 岡 流), from which sprang the famous *Yoshioka kenpō* (吉 岡 憲 法). This school had the misfortune to be in the path of a certain Miyamoto Musashi. All the schools related to *Yoshitsune-ryū* ( 義 経 流), *Hankan-ryū* (判 管 流) *Yoshioka-ryū*, were the source of transmission for *Kurama-ryū*. The *Yoshitsune-ryū* school appears to have been the school of ninjutsu. Its transmission remained in the stronghold of the Fukui family (福 井), and a *densho*, *Taiyōshū* (待 用 集) written in 1618 by Ogasawara Sakuun Nyūdō, contains a chapter entitled *Yoshitsune Hyakushū* (義 経 百 首). This chapter describes in the form of a poem written in *kanbun*, the attitude to be adopted in many types of situations in relation to combat, which resembles the precepts that one finds in the schools of ninjutsu, in particular in the texts resulting

---

* The creation of these three branches goes back, without any doubt, to the period Muromachi (1333−1467). They are called the three branches of origins of the use of the sword, *kenjutsu no sandai genryū* (剣 術 の 三 大 源 流). The names of these three movements are as follows: *Tenshin shōden katori shintō-ryū* (天 真 正 伝 香 取 神 道 流), founded by Iizasa Chōisai Ienao (飯 篠 長 威 斎 家 直 1387−1488), *Kage-ryū* (影 流), founded by Aisu Ikōsai (愛 洲 移 香 斎 1452−1538) and *Nen-ryū* (念 流), founded by Summon Shirō Yoshimoto (相 馬 四 朗 義 元 1350−?), better known by the name *Nenami Jion* (念 阿 弥 慈 恩). Although these three branches are known for their use of the sword, the teaching of each school rests on a broad range of weapons and techniques of combat of which the central teaching remains the rational use of the body as a whole. The generic term for the teaching of these schools is *bugei jūhappan* (武 芸 十 八 般), the *18 warlike disciplines*. Thus, the founders of these three branches were all masters in the use of several weapons and could pass from the one to the other without constraining their movement.

† Of the seven schools that were born from *Kashima no Tachi*, the name of only two families, Kitsukawa (吉 川) and Matsuoka (松 岡) are mentioned. The other names do not appear in any of the various documents relating to the history of the *bujutsu* of the two temples Katori and Kashima.

‡ *Onmyōdō* (陰 陽 道: sees ying and yang), is a science of predicting the future based, among other things, on the astronomy of ancient China and the theory of the five phases, male and female (五 行 説: *gogyō setsu*).

from *Iga-ryū ninjutsu*, where the resemblances are striking. Thus, we can make the assumption that it is very probable that parallel to the teaching of combat techniques and strategy, a form of ninjutsu was also disseminated in secrecy and to the elite, and sometimes to only one person. One can even advance the idea that some of the instructors had a dual identity of ninja and monk. Remember that the ninja was to have a double identity to act as secrecy, and that in the guise of a monk it was easier to circulate in order to collect information. Also note that Kyōtō, the imperial city was not far from the provinces of Iga and Kōga, whose author of *Iran-ki* (伊 乱 記), Kikuoka Nyōgen (菊 岡 如 幻) wrote in 1679 the following sentence: "*It is told that a certain Oirota Yuya had transmited a subtle science of combat and that this was to become a specific source of knowledge in the province of Iga for generations to come.*" This same name is often quoted in the genealogy of the *Kurama-ryū*.

19. *Nen-ryū* (念 流) is one of the principal branches of *kenjutsu* of Japan. Its history is closely dependant on the Higuchi family and, of course, on a place named Maniwa, which is in the town of Takazaki in the prefecture of Gunma. This school remains active and has existed for a very long time, being founded at the start of the Muromachi period by Sōma Shirō Yoshimoto (相 馬 四 朗 義 元). Reliable historical documents concerning him are scarce. His story seems fairly typical, wanting to avenge the death of his father, he entered the *Kurama* temple (鞍 馬 寺) at a very young age. There he received the transmission that he mastered very quickly. Then he took a tour of various temple known to transmit teachings on *bujutsu*, such as the *Jufuku-JI* (寿 福 寺) of Kamakura, in order to receive there the mysteries of the art. At the age the eighteen, he entered the *Anraku* temple (安 楽 寺) and there received the total transmission. After having put an end to his search of revenge, he became a monk and took the name Jion Nen Washō (慈 音 念 和 尚). It is under the pseudonym of Nen-washō, that the school that he created will be known until our day: *Nen-ryū*. The name *Nen* (念), is not arbitrary. It is in reference to one of the ultimate lessons of the school. In fact, it refers to the ability to detect motives and intentions in the enemy's movements. This shows the high level of refinement to which the deeply disciplined movements, positions and various sword (*tachi*) techniques were out. It is very interesting to note that this attribute is found in various schools such as *Kage-ryū* (影 流), *Shinkage-ryū* (新 影 流), *Nitō-ryū* (二 刀 流), and so on. Indeed, the founders of these schools included controlled *Nen-ryū* as a common point in their practice. Jion transmitted his knowledge only to fourteen disciples. It is thought that the tradition according to which a master granted only one act of transmission of his art to only one disciple in each province, the famous "*ikkoku hitori inka sōden*" (一 国 一 人 印 可 相 伝), was continued by Jion. Continuation of this system of transmission was perpetuated within the *Shinkage-ryū* through Kamiizumi Isenokami. Of his fourteen disciples, three would make a mark on the history of the Japanese *bujutsu*: Chūjō Hyōgo no Kami, Higuchi Tarō Kanemori, and Akamatsu Sanshuza. Chūjō Hyōgo no Kami went on to create the school *Chūjō-ryū* (中 條 流), which would be perpetuated through the school *Toda-ryū* (富 田 流) established by his best disciple, Toda Seigen, and finally one can find the teaching of these two schools within the school *Ittō-ryū* (一 刀 流), founded by Itō Ittōsai. Higuchi Tarō Kanemori was designated by Jion to be his single successor, and the transmission of *Nen-ryū* was exclusively transmitted within the Higuchi family until our day. One of the fundamental characteristics of the schools was to teach the form of the art as it was created by its founder. A type of protection was created with a kind of *fukuro shinai*, allowing the practice of combat. It should be noted here that one never seeks to touch the wrists, but always the head. The teaching of the school also required that the art of the *naginata*, the *bōjutsu*, and a form of *jūjutsu* were not to be taught indiscriminately. Another fundamental characteristic of *Nen-ryū* is its assertion that it is a *goshin-jutsu* (護 身 術), that is, an art of protection and defense. The goal is not to kill or wound anyone, when a form of interdiction will answer any provocation. Here is a translation of the beginning of the *densho* entitled *Nen-ryū Heihō Shintoku* (念 流 兵 法 心 得):

> *This school (*Nen-ryū*) conforms to the order of the universe. The art of our school is practiced through multitudes of things. When a disciple manages to acquire the* shinmyōken *(心 明 剣)\* of our school, he can understand and control the things before they occur and thus follow what is intended for him. This destiny lies in each thing and action, which we must correctly achieve without any negligence.* In Nihon Budō Taikei, op. cit. Vol. 2, pp.393 and 426.

20. *At seven years, Yoshitsune, then named Ushijakumaru, entered the* Kurama *temple of Kyōto. There, he accepted the teaching of Kiichi Hōgan. This teaching comprised the strategy of* Rikutō Sanryaku *(六 韜 三 略) and the art of the* kenjutsu. *It is told that Yoshitsune taught an art of combat called* Kurama-ryū *(鞍 馬 流) and a combat strategy that included various disciplines under the name of* Yoshitsune-ryū *(義 経 流).* In Koyama Ryūtarō, op cit., p. 46 and 50.

21. In Sugiyama Hiroshi, op. cit chap. 10.

22. In Tobe Shinjūrō, op. cit p. 251 and 265.

23. In Sugiyama Hiroshi, op cit.

24. Among the many theories on the origin of the ninjtsu, that of the immigrants from China and Korea, such as those mentioning the *shomonji* and or *Kugutsu* (傀 儡), are most widespread. Why? It is very difficult to explain it in a few lines, but I tried to show how *Nō* theater (能) and the art of the ninjutsu are related to these various theories. In the same way, it is often believed that the precursors of ninjutsu originated among *Shomonji* or *Kugutsu* coming from China and Korea.

---

\* *The shinmyōken* is a state of mind, a bodily attitude that rises from the control of three fundamental principles that one finds in the very first schools of *bujutsu* to begin with *Nen-ryū*. It is about the *kako no jutsu* (過 去 の 術), the technique of the past, *genzai no jutsu* (現 在 の 術), the technique of the present, and finally *no jutsu* (未 来 の 術) the technique of the future. It is a whole practical knowledge based on life experience that makes it possible to avoid danger and to sense what is about to occur. It is about the wisdom to apply knowledge in the moment in order to be able to envisage and avoid the things to come. It results in a state in which the the behavior of the sword reflects a luminous heart.

At the beginning of the eigth century, the festivals where *sumō* was held, named *sumō no sechi* (相撲節), became annual festivals at the court of the emperor of Japan. These festivals, accompanied by religious ceremonies to the gods, took place each year during July. They were followed by spectacles and entertainment. These festivals were held in the hope that a good harvest would usher forth a time of plenty, and of course peace. For the people of Japan of this time, and even further back in the history of Japan, the recreation, blessings, and rejoicing brought by these festivals, had spiritual implications as well. Indeed, if one took great pleasure during these festivals dedicated to the gods, they would be delighted and grant good harvests and peace in all the country. Thus, the activities and recreation went beyond personal pleasure. Among the spectacles, one found the *sangaku* (散楽), a kind of theater that showcased the talents of musicians, dancers, acrobats, puppeteers, magicians, mimes, and others. This type of theater was practiced especially by *shomonji* or *kugutsu*, which were the equivalent of the troubadours, minstrels, and gypsies in Europe. With very diverse origins, coming mainly from China or Korea, they lived as nomads. Their only sources of income came from the spectacles that they give without any other acknowledged occupation. They were consigned to the lowest social hierarchy. However, at that time the Imperial court was permeated with the culture of the continent and even with its popular culture. It is, thus, advisable to stress that, other than these direct contacts, where the nobles had fun spectacles of these actors of the street, it is mainly through immigrants that Japan knew of the cultures of the mainland. Among these immigrants there were those called the *kugutsu;* here is an example of how their way of life is reported in the oldest documents:

> They live under round tents and carry out an existence of nomads. The men are very skillful in shooting with the bow and with the throwing of knives and other objects. They are, in addition, excellent riders. They handle puppets so that they appear to be living beings. They are versed in the art of producing metals, starting from sand and stones. They know the magic that transforms plants into animals. The women make themselves up, dance, and prostite themselves. They never work in plain sight, and thus escape controls and administrative taxes. They do not recognize any hierarchy and do not respect the gods of the country. They carry out a life of ease, listen to noisy music, and have their own worship.

It was quickly noticed that there were ideal areas into which the ninja of Iga or Kōga could infiltrate to pass incognito from one area to another in order to collect information. These groups of continental origin integrated themselves with the Japanese community, either by setting up wandering groups like the *shomonji* or *kugutsu*, or by settling to cultivate the land. As I wrote before, the *kugutsu* and *shomonji* were regularly invited to the court of the emperor on certain feast days to present their art, the *sangaku*. Through their wandering life, little by little they diffused their art in the public square. Over centuries, the art of the *sangaku* became refined and elegant. In the fourteenth century, a prominent actor, Kanami (1333–1384) invented a new form of *No* Theater, which is separate from the *sangaku*. At the time, this new form of theater was called the *sarugaku* (猿楽) or *dengaku* (田楽). However, the training of the actors of *No* continued to contain elements of the *sangaku*. Most of the *No* theater performed today was composed by the son of Kanami, Zeami (1363–1443), who revolutionized the art. Zeami collaborated with his father and supplemented his work. Zeami put in writing many theoretical works on *No*. Before the time of Kanami, *No* theater did not have a precise system and comprised various forms. The relationship with ninjutsu is very simple, indeed, Kanami and Zeami came from Iga province where their family was allied with a prominent ninja family, Hattori. in those days, the inhabitants of Iga went by any of several names, and one of the more common ones was that of *musoku-nin* (無足人). This term connotes a manner of movement that stresses futiveness and subtlety. This type of movement is known by various names: the term *suri-ashi* (摺足) that one finds in certain schools of *jūjutsu* like *Takeuchi-ryū* (竹内流), or the *musoku No Ho* (無足之法) that one finds in various schools of *bujutsu* like *Kage-ryū* (陰流), *Shinkage-ryū* (新影流), *Komagawa kaishin-ryū* (駒川改心流) and of many schools of ninjutsu.

*No* theater is recognized as a highly sophisticated art. The deliberate progression of mastery of this art is representative of Japanese arts. It presents, through the epic and the music, song, decorations, esthetics characteristic of the Japanese traditional culture. Works of Zeami on *No* can be read like manuscripts on the martial arts. First of all, it should be noted that the works of Zeami were *densho*, like *Fushi kaden* (風姿家伝) or the *kakyō* (花鏡), intended for only one person. It was, thus, necessary as in the various documents of transmission of *bujutsu*, that those who were going to receive these documents could understand the instruction hidden within each character. The actual experience of the practice, and the memory of the example of the master, are the internal factors that make it possible to correctly read, understand, and interpret this type of document. Thus, by studying works of Zeami thoroughly, one notices that they refer to the techniques of the body (how to move, the transfer of weight of the body, hand and foot movements, the use of the body as a whole, etc.) and the attitude of the spirit (how to generate different types of emotions and impressions in spectators). In these writings, Zeami exposes the various expressions of force, the rhythms and the distances and their transitions. In other words, he explains how to reach the highest level, making it possible, in each moment, to sense and control every aspect of the part being played. One finds the same thing in the martial arts when the practitioner faces his adversary. By replacing the theatrical framework with a combat situation, the works of Zeami become excellent texts on the martial arts. As I mentioned before, *No* comes from the *sangaku* which featured acrobatics based on movements of various bodies and of the spectacle of magic which consisted in fooling the eyes of the spectator. Thus, a great number of researchers think that the *sangagku*, the *kugutsu*, and the *shomonji* were the origin of ninjutsu. Indeed, the techniques of *genjutsu* or *yojutsu* (conjuring) magic and acrobatics, are an integral part of ninjutsu. Moreover in the imagination of the Japanese, the ninja remains a kind of superwarrior with the capacity for magic that defied natural law. However, many factors show that it would be erroneous to believe that ninjtutsu was invented by *Kugutsu* and other *shomonji*. The latter, far from being warriors, had exceptional physical capabilities, as is the case for those in any artistic field that uses the body as the principal vector. The ninja was to remain invisible and to camouflage himself to achieve his mission, so to pass for a *kugutsu* or *shomonji* was logical.

*No* was created by eliminating the vulgar aspects from the *sangaku*, while accentuating and refining the sober character of its expression. One can also see the influence of the concept of *wabi* (佗 or 詫 び) that one finds in various Japanese traditional arts like painting and poetry. In the *Shikadō* (至 花 道),* written in 1420, Zeami writes the following explanation:

> When you move the body and the feet at the same time, your movement appears brutal. On the other hand, if you move the feet delicately when you move the body violently, your movements appear powerful but not brutal. Then, when you pose the feet with power and stir up the body delicately, your movements do not appear brutal, even if the noise of the steps is heard.

> For dancing, it is important to learn how to look forward while being vigilant behind. The impression of an actor seen by the spectators is not exactly what the actor feels. It is essential to maintain a detached view of oneself. Astute spectators are sometimes captivated by the absence of expression of an actor. They arrive at that impression when they are sensitive to the movements of the spirit of the deeply dissimulated actor. This absence of expression corresponds to a state of emptiness exists between two techniques of expression.

Of course, for a follower of ninjutsu or any other school of *bujutsu*, one finds much in common with the attitude and the movements that one finds in the explanations of Zeami. However the difference is serious. Indeed, *No* remains theater, even on a high level, and ninjutsu remains a method of survival and predicting danger. However, let me state that if Zeami could reach so major a level of comprehension of the mechanisms of the body, one can be sure that he had already achieved an uncommonly controlled way of moving. The second point is that all the work of Zeami, every bit an art form as painting and other arts of this time, are all dominated by the omnipresence of the sword, that is, a tension that leads to deep introspection, because there is no certainty of continued existence. Indeed, during the period when Kanami and Zeami lived, the skillful utilization of hands and swords was not just for show.

From the seventeenth century on, manuscripts on the art of the *bujutsu* and *kenjutsu* multiply, and a great number of them borrow the technical vocabulary and sentences written by Zeami. Thus, one finds in a great number of the *densho* of *bujutsu* schools the following sentence of Zeami: "One should not forget the initial thought." Many terms, words, and expressions of the techniques of combat come from *No*, which shows that the exchanges between various arts like *No* and the various schools of ninjutsu and *bujutsu* are very important.

25. In Sugiyama Hiroshi, op. cit., chap. 10.

26. ibid

27. In Koyama Ryūtaro, op. cit., chap. 1, p. 18.

28. In Tobe Shinjūrō, op. cit., pp. 22 and 37.

29. In Sugiyama Hiroshi, op. cit.

30. In Sugiyama Hiroshi, op. cit.

31. In Sugiyama Hiroshi, op. cit., chap. 11, p. 205 and in Yamaguchi, op. cit., p. 110. (One finds the same quotation in the works of Tobe Shinjūrō and Koyama Ryūtaro). He cites the following quotation of *Ōmi Kochi shirayku* (近 江 興 地 誌 略): "That who one calls ninja comes from the provinces from Iga and Kōga. He is able to freely infiltrate enemy castles, to spy on people in their most secret conversations, and to make known the content of these conversations to their close relations."

32. ibid

33. In Sugiyama Hiroshi, op. cit., chap. 11

34. In Pierre F. Souyri, *Iga, Kōga, Oyamoto: Social Construction in the Mountainous Areas in the Southeast of Kyōto in the fifteenth and sixteenth centuries*, p. 5 and 7.

35. ibid, p. 7.

36. ibid, p. 8.

37. In Koyama Ryūtaro, op. cit., p. 58.

38. In Sugiyama Hiroshi, op. cit., chap. 12.

39. In Yamaguchi, op. cit., p. 25. (One finds the same quotation in the works of Tobe Shinjūrō, Koyama Ryūtaro, and Sugiyama Hiroshi).

40. All the facts recalling the actions of the ninja of Kōga in the account of Tokugawa Ieyasu are brought back in *Mikawa Go fūdo-ki* (三 河 後 風 土 記), in *Kaitei Mikawa Go Fūdo-ki* (改 訂 三 河 後 風 土 記), Kurita Tadachika, ED. Shinbutsu Yūraisha, Tokyo, 1977, Vol. 1, p. 244 with 248.

---

* In the writings of Zeami, the flower symbolizes the ultimate state of the theatrical expression of *No*. One of the *densho* of Zeami, *Fūshi kaden* (風 姿 家 伝), is a remarkable example. For Zeami, *No* is like a flower. Among the plants, the flowers bloom, each one in its turn, causing astonishment and the awakening of major emotions. Like the spirit, they are interesting and rare at the same time. Their aspect is beautiful, but their beauty is transitory, like the glory of the dew of the morning, a recurring image in poetry and Buddhism. The flower in the martial arts, like the bamboo, is a very major symbolic element because it shows the character of the practitioner. He must have the "character of the flower," beautiful, soft, and as flexible as the bamboo, as the *gokui* testifies to regarding ninjutsu, *Kajō Chikusei* (花 情 竹 性). Another *gokui*, *Kajō Waraku* (花 情 和 楽), can be translated in the following way: the main characteristic of each mouvment, action, intention, must lend harmony and peace, such is the "character of the flower." The flower, thus, has a significance in practice martial arts and ninjutsu in particular. One can add expressions like "the fine flower of knighthood", "the flower of knowledge", or in religion, one finds the "Lotus of the Limit."

41. ibid, p. 244.

42. In Yamaguchi H., op.cit., p. 52.

43. In Kurita, op. cit., p. 244.

44. ibid

45. In *Sengoku Shiryō Sōshō, Hōjō Godai-ki* (北 条 五 代 記) Miura Jōshin, second series, Vol. 1, ED. Kōdansha, Tokyo, 1965, p. 395 and 397.

46. ibid

47. ibid (One finds the presentation of the same manuscript in the works of the authors quoted above.)

48. ibid (One finds the presentation of the same manuscript in the works of the authors quoted above.)

49. ibid (One finds the presentation of the same manuscript in the works of the authors quoted above.)

50. *Kōyō Gunkan* (甲 陽 軍 鑑), work in twenty volumes divided into three parts. Written by Takasaka Tomonobu, a vassal of Takeda Shingen (1521−1573), which tells the history of Shingen and Takeda Katsuyori (1546−1582). This text contains the strategies of combat, the types of relations, and the political system used by the Takeda family. The work is also known under the title of *Kōshū-ryū Gungakusho* (甲 州 流 軍 学 書), Study of the Military Work of the Kōshū School. It is an invaluable work for understanding the mentality of the Sengoku period. The text was surely compiled in 1615 at the request of Tokugawa Ieyasu, who held the talents of Takeda Shingen in high regard. It is interesting to note the influence of the treatise of Sun Zi on the various names of the various groups of army, infantry, cavalry, and other elements of the armed forces of Takeda. *Fūrinkazan* (風 林 火 山). In Tobe Shinjūrō, op. cit., p. 110.

51. ibid

52. In Miura Jōshin, op. cit., second series, Vol. 1, the history mentioning *Kusa* is on pages 395−397.

53. ibid

54. ibid, p. 397−398.

55. ibid, p. 398−400. *Fukuroku-ju* (福 禄 寿), is one of the seven divinities of happiness. He is often represented with a long body, a large head, a lot of hair, and a large beard.

56. Or *Eikyo Gunki* (奥 武 永 亨 軍 記) recalls the heroic defense of the castle of Hataya by Eguchi Goenjō, honest vassal of Mogami Yoshiaki (1546−1614). This chronicle is recounted in *Sengoku Shiryō Sōshō*, op. cit., second series, Vol. 3 and 4. The history mentioning the ninja appears in Vol. 4, p. 308.

57. *Chūgoku Chiran-ki* (中 國 知 覧 記) recalls the wars between the Mōri and Amako families on the shores of the inland sea. This chronicle is recounted in *Sengoku Shiryō Sōshō*, op. cit., second series, Vol. 9, p. 17 and 47, the history mentioning the ninja appears on page 21.

58. In Yamaguchi, op. cit., p. 109.

59. Sugiyama, op. cit., Vol. 11: Sengoku daimyō, p. 107−109.

60. ibid

61. Tsukahara Bokuden Takamoto (塚 原 卜 伝 1489−1571) celebrated swordsman Miyamoto Musashi like this. He was born into a family of a Shintō priest from the sanctuary of Kashima where, according to the legend, the priests had transmitted the techniques of combat since antiquity. He studied with his father the art of the school *Katori Shintō-ryū*. In 1505, at seventeen years age, he engaged in his first duel with a sword and killed his adversary. He then engaged in nineteen duels and took part in thirty-seven battles. He was locked up in the sanctuary of Kashima for a thousand days and had an inspiration about the art of the sword. On the basis of the teaching of his father and his master, Matsumoto Bizen no Kami Masabobu (1468−1524), founder of *Kashima Shin-ryū* and Iizasa Chōisai, founder of *Katori shintō-ryū*, he founded the *Shintō-ryū* (新 当 流) school, whose ultimate technique is *Hitotsu no Tachi*, (一 之 太 刀) "the single sword." Bokuden traversed various areas during three journeys, during which he met followers of various schools and transmitted and disseminated the art of his school. Here is a passage from the *Nihon Kengō Retsuden* (日 本 剣 豪 列 伝: Writings on the Masters of the Japanese Sword), ED. Gendai Kōyō Bunko, Tokyo, 1970, p. 10:

> *In his quest to develop his strategy, Tsukahara Bokuden traveled by horse with three replacement horses, carrying three falcons for hunting. Eighty men followed him. Thus, for his quest, the lords as well as their followers treated him with respect. Bokuden was a true follower of the sword.*[*]

In Kyōto, Bokuden successively taught his art of the sword to the three shōgun of Ashikaga, Yoshiharu (1511−1550), Yoshiteru (1536−1565) and Yoshiaki (1537−1597). In terms of Katori and Kashima, the affiliation of Iizasa Chōisai, Matsumoto Bizen, and Tsukahara Bokuden Takamoto is well known. In Nihon Budō Taikei, op. cit., Vol. 3, p. 9.

62. The author, Kikuoka Nyogen, is one of the very first people to have been interested in ninjutsu and the history of Iga and *Kōga mono no*, more commonly known under the name of ninja. He left us a great number of manuscripts which remain prominent historical documents of foreground for the study of the ninjutsu as well as the historical context of the province of Iga and Kōga. (For the other works of Kikuoka, refer to Appendix E). *Iran-ki* (伊 乱 記) is a chronicle of war, *senki* (戦 記), in four booklets written in 1679. The author reports all the facts relating to the invasion of Iga by the armies of Oda Nobunaga between the 6th year (1579) and the 9th year (1982) of the Tenshō era. He also reports, certain great feats of arms of the ninja until the destruction of the province of Iga. The first booklet carries the title of *Iga Fūzoku no Koto* (伊 賀 風 俗 之 事) and

---

[*] Extract comes from the beginning of the *Kōyō Gunkan* (甲 陽 軍 鑑).

starts with the following paragraph:

> *The moment has come to tell the history and the circumstances of the inhabitants of this province (Iga), which was held between the Shōkei era (1332–1338) and the middle of the Tenshō era (1573–1592). We don't have the words to describe these men, whose prowesses in combat reflected a faultless courage, but who were reluctant to fight an enemy if another solution could be found.... From the start of the day until the end of the morning, they applied themselves to various types of work, inventing all types of intruments, and after midday to the last ray of the sun, they polished their combat techniques and other tactics, all while improving in* Sokuin-jutsu *(*測 隠 術*)....*

Of course, one notices the immense respect with which Kikuoka describes these generations of warriors to Iga through these lines. The term *sokuin-jutsu*, which can be considered *sokuon jutsu*, refers directly to the practice of ninjutsu. The character *soku* (測) can be read *hakaru*. The meaning of this character is "to probe" or "to measure." Paired with the character *Kakusu* (隠), "to hide," one obtains: *"to probe, or measure from a hiding-place; to observe while being hidden."* In ninjutsu practice, it is not just a question of using espionage techniques, but, it's also necessary to be able to measure technical level of the adversary without them discovering that they've been compromised. Here, one finds here one of the thrusts of *Kage-ryū* and other schools of *bujutsu*. The most well-known version of *Iranki* is the *Kosei Iranki*, published in 1897 in Ueno by Momochi Orinosuke, twentieth generation since Momochi Sandayū, a famous ninja of the province of Iga.

63. In *Seishū Heiran-ki*, compiled in 1639; it appears in the vol. 25, of *Kaitei Shiseki Shūran*, (改 訂 史 籍 周 覧), ED. Shin jinbutsu Yūraisha, Tokyo, 1965, pp. 585–601.

64. In Tobe Shinjūrō, op. cit., p. 52.

65. ibid and for Koyama, in Koyama Ryūtaro, op. cit., p. 86.

66. In Momochi, Iranki, op. cit., Vol. 2, p. 2

67. ibid. p. 2, Tozawa (戸 沢), Fujiwara (藤 原), Minamoto (源), Taira (平), Momochi (百 地), Hattori (服 部), Izumo (出 雲), Ōkuni (大 國), Tsustumi (堤), Arima (有 馬), Hata (畑), Mizuhara (水 原), Shima (志 摩), Togakure (戸 隠), Ise (伊 勢), Sakagami (坂 上), Narita (成 田), Oda (小 田), Mōri (??), Abe (阿 部), Ueno (上 野), Otsuka (大 塚), Ibuki (伊 吹), Kaneko (兼 子), Kotani (小 谷), Shindō (進 藤), Iida (飯 田), Kataoka (片 岡), Kanbe (神 戸), Sawada (沢 田), Kimata (木 又), Toyota (豊 田), Toda (戸 田), Suzuki (鈴 木), Kashiwabara (柏 原), Fukui (福 井), Iga (伊 賀), Kuriyama (栗 山), Ishitani (石 谷), Ōyama (大 山), Sugino (杉 野), Hanbe (伴 部).

68. Two versions of this letter are reproduced respectively in *Shinchōkō-ki* (p. 262 in Sugiyama H., Sengoku Daimyō, op. cit.) and in *Iran-ki* (Vol. 2, p. 13.).

69. In Momochi, Iran-ki, op. cit., Vol. 3, p. 7.

70. In Momochi, Iran-ki, op. cit., Vol. 7, p. 4.

71. ibid, p. 9.

72. ibid, Vol. 6, p. 1.

73. ibid, p. 7.

74. In Momochi, op. cit., Vol. 4, p. 4.

75. In Kurita Tadachika, op. cit., Vol. 2, p. 191.

76. ibid, p. 191–192.

77. There are highly reliable historical documents on the Hattori family, we noted the most important in Appendix E.

78. This quotation from the *Mikawa Monogatari* (三 河 物 語) is used again by many authors in particular those whom I presented at the beginning of this chapter. In Yamaguchi, op. cit., p. 21.

79. *Taikō-ki* (太 閣 記) is a love song based on the life of Toyotomi Hideyoshi written by Takenouchi Kakusai and illustrated by Okada Gyokuzan, published in Osaka by Kobayashi Rokubei in 1882. The history mentioning the infiltration by a ninja of the *Chigūju* fortress appears in Vol. 3, pp. 107–108.

80. In Sugiyama Hiroshi, op. cit., chap. 13.

81. in Yamaguchi, op. cit., p. 59.

This group of Kōga ninja consisted of ten people; here are their names and ages at the time of the mission:

Mochizuki Heidayū, 63 years.
Mochizuki Ataemon, 33 years.
Akutagawa Seizaemon, 60 years.
Akutagawa Shichirōhei, 25 years.
Hango hei, 53 years.
Yamanaka Jyūdayū, 24 years.
Natsumi Kakkai, 41 years.
Iwane Kanbei, 45 years.
Iwane Kaneimon, 56 years.

82. ibid

83. ibid

84. ibid

85. ibid

86. There is, however, another chronicle of which it is necessary for us to present the contents even if there is no historical

proof in connection with the facts that it presents. *Iga Fused Shucchō* (伊賀付差出帳) written in 1637, presents various groups, of which only one really consisted of ninja, *Shinobi no Shū* (忍び ノ 衆). In this group, one name seems to top all the others: Sawamura Sakurō. The Sawamura family's base of operation was in the village of Mibuno (壬生野) in the province of Iga and was known to be *Ninke* (忍家), a house where a form of ninjutsu was transmitted. The family specialized in *kayakujutsu* (火薬術), the art of the use of the explosives and gunpowder; they left a great number of *densho* that deal with their talent as bomb disposal experts and warriors. This family was noticed very early, and it was on many occasions in the service of the Tōdō family (藤堂), as a family specializing in the use of ninjutsu. Among the documents[*] that reached us from this family, is a work entitled *Sawamura-ke Yusho-sho* (澤村家由諸諸), which is most interesting. In 1852 (year 2 of the *Kaei* era), the ships of Commodore Perry arrived at Japan and forced the shōgun to open the country. The *bakufu* ordered the Tōdō family, lords of the provinces of Iga and Kōga, to send a ninja of Iga on a mission. It seems that a ninja joined a group of people accompanying the bakufu on board Perry's vessel. The role of *Onmitsu* had been restricted and their capacity had decreased very much by the end of the Edo period, one needed a type of person who had continued the practice ninjutsu and who could still pass unperceived. The Tōdō family gave the order to the most outstanding family: Sawamura. The one who completed the mission was none other than the head of the household. his name was Sawamura Jinsaburō Hōji. He embarked on the boat with the invited delegation from the bakufu, fulfilled his mission, and returned to his place. He carried with him certain stolen objects as proof of his passage: soap, a candle, matches and tobacco, two letters written in Dutch and two pairs of pants. The letters are preserved by the members of the family like a treasure. One contains the following sentences written in Dutch:

> *Englesch meid in bed. Fransch meid in keuken*
> "寝室に於ける英国の下婢料理部屋に於ける仏蘭西の下婢 (...)"
> *"English maid in bed. French maid in the kitchen."*
> *Stille toilets heeft diept grond*
> "音無川は水深し"
> *"Still waters run deep."*

For a long time, the members of the Sawamura family believed that they were words written by Commodore Perry, but that was not the case. They were only two letters that belonged to one of the sailors of a ship of Dutch origin. In addition, the Netherlands is the only country that maintained trade with Japan in spite of the closing of the country. A great amount of knowledge about medicine, techniques, customs, and habits of the Western countries were conveyed to Japan via books written in Dutch. The Dutch Studies, *rangaku* (蘭学), were very developed.

However, this chronicle[†] raises many points that still remain obscure. First of all, the document of the Sawamura family does not reveal other details, such as during which visit the ninja carried out his mission, the names and rank of the members of the delegation of the bakufu, and so forth. Moreover, Commodore Perry came to Japan twice. Thus, one can say that there were two occasions on which contact could occur, but no other indication. Let me state that to infiltrate any ship, much less Commodore Perry's, was no small matter, even if that was the speciality of the ninja. What exactly was the purpose of the mission and the nature of the orders he received from his superiors? Was it to uncover something of value, in connection with a weapon, a chart, instruments, or a special technique of naval action or navigation? All these questions remain unanswered.

With regard to the arrival of Perry in Japan, the chronicle *Nihon Ensei-ki* (日本遠征記), recalls all the historical facts and shows an exemplary objectivity. Of course, in this chronicle there is no mention of any ninja exploit. From the observations of many researchers such as Tobe Shinjūrō and Okuse Heishichirō, the stolen logbook from Perry's ship is reasonable evidence enough to believe that this exploit was the last to credited to the ninja of Kōga or Iga. However, doubt remains and that proves only one thing: in the art of ninjutsu one seeks not to leave of trace; one leaves only tracks to confound those who come later. The goal is to never be recognized or known.

87. In Tobe Shinjūrō, op. cit., p. 181.
88. In Yamaguchi, op. cit., p. 31.
89. n Koyama Ryūtarō, op. cit., p. 102–121.

## Chapter 3: The Private History of Ninjutsu

1. The school *Takeuchi-ryū* (竹内流) or *Takenouchi-ryū*, is the oldest school of *jū-jutsu* of Japan for which one has reliable documents of transmission. These make it possible to follow the affiliations of the school since its creation by Takenouchi Nakatsu Kasadayū Hisamori (1503−1596), lord of the Ichinose castle in the province of Sakushū (prefecture of Okayama), to the present day. It is by far the most important school of *jū-jutsu* in Japan because it gave rise to the different branches of *jū-jutsu*, *kenjutsu*, *buki-jutsu*, and so forth. Indeed, according to the *Keisho Kogoden* (系書古語伝), a *densho* of the school

---

[*] The Sawamura family left with a great number of *densho* among which one finds a version of *Bansenshū Kai* (万川集海) and *Shinobi no Michi Kaitei Ron* (忍道楷梯論). Another *densho*, *Ninki Jūroku-shu Mokuroku* (忍器十六種目録), which explains in detail the ninja's weapons, their use, and their manufacture.

[†] *Yusho-sho* (由諸書), a chronicle preserved by the Inamasu family, a family of ninja of Iga, corroborates the facts and stipulates that a ninja was introduced onto Perry's ship. Another chronicle *Onmitsu Yōsokin kōkō* (隠密用相勤候桱), quoted the surname Sawamura and the same exploit.

that reports the creation of the school and the history of its founder, the school was created at the beginning of the Sengoku period in 1532, and was known by the name *Takenouchi-ryū koshi no Mawari* (竹內流腰之廻) or *Hinoshita Torite Kaisan Takenouchi-ryū* (日下捕手開山竹内流). Like the majority of the schools of this period, it was created as a result of a dream or of divine inspiration, *shinden* (神伝). Here is how the *Keisho Kogoden* reports this episode:

> *During his tender childhood, Hisamori loved the art of* kenjutsu *passionately. Although he practiced unceasingly, he was always dissatisfied with his own practice and his level. On the 24th day of the 6th month of the first year of the Tenmon era (1532), he withdrew to* Haga *temple* (垪和), *which venerated the god Atago. Each day, he carried out three ritual washings, with deep devotion to the god Atago, and he devoted himself to the practice of* bujutsu *with enthusiasm. He exercised it against the trees of the sanctuary with a* bokutō *(wooden sword) measuring 2 shaku, 3 sun (72 cm.). The 6th night of the 6th day, with his body and spirit exhausted, he fell asleep with his* bokutō. *From nowhere a* yamabushi *with long white hair emerged and called to him. When Hisamori opened his eyes, he saw in front of him a man of strong and strange stature whose size bordered on 7 shaku (2 m.). At the time, Hisamori exclaimed "do not approach me!", The yamabushi told him "You show much enthusiasm in your practice, and your faith is without fault. I will show you my art." Hisamori seized his* bokutō *to attack, but the yamabushi easily countered the attack, and Hisamori found himself on the ground. Hisamori attacked repeatedly, employing various attacks, but the yamabushi, without using any weapon, disarmed and controlled all of Hisamori's attacks. It was really an unbelievable technique! Hisamori understood that he could not defeat this strange character and asked to receive his superior combat science. The yamabushi said: "This combat science consists of being able to make the enemy surrender quickly in any situation. Now, I will show you the mechanisms of this combat science." The yamabushi transmitted various techniques to him. Then he seized Hisamori's* bokutō, *broke it in two and declared: "When the weapon is too long, its advantages decrease!" The yamabushi grasped one of the broken ends of the* bokutō *and added: "With this type of weapon at your side, you begin the science* kogusoku (小具足)." *Now, a very small weapon will be used as a* kodachi *(short sword), such is the science of* kogusoku. *Hisamori accepted the major transmission of each technique, and the yamabushi also taught him the art of* musha garami (武者搦) *which consists of tying up an adversary with a leather cord that was 7 shaku 5 sun (2.5 m.) in length. This science of tying up one's adversary in combat is called* Hayanawa (迅縄).\* *While Hisamori was acquiring this transmission of an unknown knowledge, the daybreak began. And, strangely the silhoutte of the yamabushi disappeared with a flash of light and a thunder clap.... One does not know what became of him....*

> *Hisamori spent the next night waiting with enthusiasm, but strange the yamabushi did not return again. The hand-to-hand combat techniques that he had accepted from the yamabushi formed the basis of Takeuchi-ryū. He named them* Torite gokajō (捕手五ヶ条). *The techniques using a short weapon like the* kogusoku *or the* kodachi, *the* kogusoku kumiuchi (小具足組討), *were named* Koshi no Mawari (腰之廻). *Hisamori carried this art to a transcendent level of application.*

This quotation in the *Keisho Kogoden* is used the most to present the creation of the *Takenouchi-ryū* school. *The Keisho Kogoden* was written during Hisamori's life time and was then transmitted in the Takenouchi family. All the other writings relating to *jūjutsu* that would be written thereafter would all, without exception, reference the *Keisho Kogoden*. In volume 10 of *Honchō Bugei Shōden* (本朝武芸小伝) written in 1714 by Hinatsu Hyosuke, a *Tendō-ryū kenjutsu* (天道流剣術) schoolmaster, one can read a similar explanation concerning *Takenouchi-ryū*:[†]

> Takenouchi-ryū *is a multi-faceted school. It proffers a vast repertoire of combat and weapons-handling techniques on the basis of the* Koshi no Mawari *which is also called* kogusoku Kumiuchi (小具足組討: *techniques where one uses short weapons in armored combat). Its technical curriculum vitae also includes* torite (捕手: *combat techniques that consist of applying torsions, blows, and percussions to control and make the adversary surrender),* torinawa (捕縄: *use of cord to control the adversary),* hade (羽手: *a form of* jū-jutsu *known by the name* kenpōtaijutsu, *mainly a technique consisting of blows and percussions),* saide (斎手 kenjutsu), iai-jutsu (居合術), bōjutsu (棒術), sōjutsu (槍術), jōjutsu (杖術), naginata-jutsu (薙刀術), tessen-jutsu (鉄扇術), jūtte-jutsu (十手術), kusarigama-jutsu (鎖鎌術), nabebutajutsu (鍋蓋 art of using the shield), tegasa-jutsu (手傘術 art of using the sunshade), shurikenjutsu (手裏剣), kasatsu-jutsu (活殺術), kappō-jutsu (活法術). *Also note that* Takenocuhi–ryū *is the first school of* jūjutsu *that has a proper technical lexicon, and names like* Koshi no Mawari (腰之廻), Saide (斎手), Hade (羽手), *with technical characteristics that are clear to him. One finds these terms entrenched in the various branches that result from this school such as* Takenouchi une-ryū (竹内畝流), Futakami-ryū (二上流), Takagi-ryū (高木流), Rikishin-ryū (力信流), Araki-ryū (荒木流) Goose-ryū (御

---

\* *Haya-nawa* is a term like the terms *Torinawa-jutsu, Shubaku-jutsu, hojō-jutsu,* and so forth.

[†] Tere was a man of the Takenouchi family who was present at the introduction of the arts of *kogusoku* and *torite*. It is he who gave his mark of nobility to the use of the kogusoku. Today, one calls this art *Koshi no Mawari*. This man of the village of Haga in Sakushū, answering to the name of Takenouchi Nakatsu Kasadayū, was known to be a master of *kogusoku*. He named his art *Takenouchi-ryū Koshi no Mawari*. One finds the teaching of his school in several provinces. According to the family *densho*, the twenty-fourth day of the sixth month of the Tenmon era (1532), a *shugenja* came in the residence from Takenouuchi and transmitted five techniques of Hobaku (捕縛). Nobody knows what became of the *shugenja*. Takenouchi always prayed to the god Ako with enthusiasm. It is thought that the *shugenja* that appeared in front of Takenouchi was an emanation of the god Ako. It is told that Takenouchi always had a deep respect and faith in this god. His son, Hitachi Nosuke, and his grandson, Kagasuke, inherited the family transmission. This name is known and respected in all the country.

家 流), Tonteki-ryū (呑 敵 流), Takenouchi santō-ryū (竹 内 三 統 流), *and others.*

*All the secrets of the school,* densho, makimono *and weapons were always transmitted within the Takenouchi family until the ninth genration when they started to adopt in order to perpetuate the Takenouchi surname; the same process is perpetuated in the Higuchi family of the school* Maniwa nen-ryū (馬 庭 念 流). *The second teacher of Hisamori, Hisakatsu, left for a journey of initiation, applying the art during eight years throughout all Japan. He codified, in the form of kata, the various combat techniques that he used during actual combat; these kata number eight and are called* Hakkejō no koto (八 ヶ 条 之 事). *Its fame came to the ears of Toyotomi Hideyoshi (1536–1598). Hideyoshi invited him in 1592, and followed his teaching. Hisakatsu accepted the title Hitachi no Suke (常 陸 介). In 1618, he opened a dōjō in his native village (today the town of Takebe in Okayama prefecture). This dōjō still exists today and is classified as a national treasure. The documents of the family are preserved there. In 1620, Hisakatsu accompanied by his son, Hisakichi, gave a demonstration in front of the Gomizunoo emperor. The very impressed emperor decreed that be given the title of Hinohita Torite Kaisan (日 下 捕 手 開 山 竹 内 流) "Hisakatsu, the founder of the torite (*jūjutsu*) of Japan."*

As a gift, he also accepted a violet cord to tie part of the *kanmuri,* clothing worn solely by the guards dedicated to the protection of the emperor. It is with this cord that the techniques of haya-nawa from then on would be carried out. Hisakatsu died in 1663 at the age of 97 years. His son, Hisakichi, the third generation of the school, just like his father and grandfather, practiced the family *bujutsu* passionately. He reached a very high level of control and taught the art of *Takenouchi ryū* throughout all Japan. He supplemented the style by bringing in many technical inventions, kata, and improved the understanding of the essential techniques transmitted from his grandfather. He admitted that it is through Hisakichi that the name of *Takenouchi-ryū* was known through all Japan and that he supplemented the transmission received from his father. In 1663, like his father, he received the title of Hinoshita Torite Kaisan of Kanpaku Takatsukasa. Hisakatsu disseminated the knowledge of his school, and the texts report that he had approximately 300 pupils. He died in 1671 at 69 years of age. Another characteristic of *Takenouchi-ryū* is its integration in the social life of the stronghold where it was established. All the various generations of the school taught the art of *bō-jutsu* to the peasants in the surrounding area of Sakushū (today's Okayama prefecture). The Takenouchi family held a place in the hearts of the inhabitants of this area, and today a great number of anecdotes are still transmitted. Another characteristic of it is a form of belief paired with a religious practice. When one visits the area where the Takenouchi family was established, the place of the genesis of the style, one is struck by the spiritual dimension of the place. Indeed, it is a wild and difficult place to access, very appropriate for asceticism and the religious practice just as for the intense practice of *bujutsu.* The prohibition against eating certain foods on a particular date, the ritual cleansings, chanting and other religious litanies are integral parts of the practice of *Takenouchi-ryū.* There is no doubt that it is thanks to this ingrained faith that the technical capabilities of the first three generations of Takenouchi were descibed by the term *mahō no hijutsu* (魔 法 之 秘 術: incredible secret technique). One of the *Gokui no Atu* (極 意 之 歌), poems that present the essence of the art, of *Takenouchi-ryū Dōka* (竹 内 流 道 歌) illustrates well the spiritual asceticism and mental outlook that the practice of this school requires: "You must learn how to polish your heart as the surface of a mirror so that each movement and impression of your adversary is reflected there."* In *Nihon Budō Taikei,* op. cit., vol. 6, pp. 8–77, and in *Hiden Nihon Bujutsu,* op. cit, pp. 21–70.

2. It is wise to highlight certain important points in the study of the *densho* relating to the practice of ninjutsu. Historically, the appearance of the first manuscripts, *densho,* and *makimono,* comprising a passage, a chapter, or a part on ninjutsu in the manuscripts of military strategy, goes back to the Muromachi period. The passages in these manuscripts treating ninjutsu cover the following disciplines: *sakusen* (作 戦: tactics of combat and guerilla warfare), *chikujō* (築 城: construction of fortresses and castles), *chōkei* (諜 計: espionage), *dan-yaku* (弾 薬: explosives and pharmacology), *ryōshoku* (糧 食: food, rationing), *iryō* (医 療: medicine and treatment), *tenmon* (天 文: astrology), *jujutsu* (呪 術: magic), and *onmitsu* (隠 密). These disciplines formed the basis of the training for all well-read men, as well as warriors wishing to become *heigakusha,* (兵 学 者), the strategists. The majority of these treatises on ninjutsu use various names to conceptualize a facet of ninjutsu. Here are the most frequent: *yōkan gyōnin no ho* (用 間 行 人 之 法), *gokan no ho* (五 間 之 法), *shinobi* (志 能 便), *dakkō* (奪 口), *unki sakki-jutsu* (雲 気 察 気), *sokuon-jutsu* (測 隠 術), *fudamono* (牒 者), *suppa* (素 破), *grated* (乱 破), *nokizaru* (坦 猿), *mono mitsu* (三 者), *shinobi* (窃 盗), *onmitsu* (隠 密), *rōen* (狼 煙), *ongyō-jutsu* (隠 形), and *sōho-jutsu* (早 歩 術).

3. The original of *Bansen Shūkai* (万 川 集 会) was transmitted from generation to generation, in the same family. The original, by the hands of Fujibayashi Masayoshi (the names of Masatake or Yasutake also exist), ninja of an important family of Iga, as well as Momochi and Hattori, is a work very well-known to historians and researchers who consider the history of ninjutsu. The manuscript consists of twenty-two volumes on the formation and organization, techniques, and thought of forty-nine schools of ninjutsu in the provinces of Iga and Kōga. These twenty-two volumes are divided into six fields of studies, the first is *Origins and Development of Ninjutsu* (忍 術 之 起 原 と 発 達), the second is *The Spiritual Principles of the Ninja* (忍 者 之 精 神 綱 領), the third is *Treatise on the Method* (方 法 論), the fourth is *Yōnin and Innin* (陽 忍 と 陰 忍), the

---

* In the martial arts, as in the majority of the religions, the heart is very often compared to a mirror. Indeed, all impurities must be removed from the mirror to reflect the mysteries. The effect of gradual corruption of certain actions, attitudes, and so forth, on the heart resembles the slow accumulation of rust on metal. Thus, in the traditional martial arts, as in ninjutsu, asceticism is consequently compared to polishing. In one of the very many letters written by Sensei Takamatsu in Hatsumi Masaaki, one can read the following recommendation: "Each one, according to the measurement of his illumination, proportionally sees the invisible things with the polishing of the mirror of the heart. The more he polishes, the more he sees and more visible the shape of the invisible things appears to him. This effort and this asceticism are in proportion to the inspiration of the practitioner. "A man obtains only the fruit of his tribulation." In the personal collection of Hatsumi Masaaki.

fifth is *Ninjutsu and Astronomy*, atmospheric phenomena (忍 術 と 天 文 気 象), and, finally the sixth, *Ninjutsu and the Tools and Ustensils* (忍 術 と 道 具), which is divided into five sections: *Ninki* (忍 器: weapons or tools allowing one to survive), *Tōki* (登 器: weapons or tools making it possible to climb or cross a high obstacle), *Suiki* (水 器: weapons or tools allowing one to use a waterway), *Kaiki* (開 器: weapons or tools allowing one to infiltrate a house or castle), and finally *Hiki* (火 器: weapons or tools allowing one to use gunpowder and set fires). All of these mansucrits are written in *Kanbun*.

The manuscript[*] followed two affiliations, the first among the families of Iga and the other, among the families of Kōga. The most well-known copies are in the Library of the Diet in Tokyo and in the private collection of the Ōhara family of Kōga. But the version belonging to the Okimori family of Iga is the oldest and remains the most complete by far, as attested to by the signature of the author. It should be noted, however, that certain private collections have incomplete copies of the same manuscripts. Thus a kirigami[†] going back to 1789, preserved in the files of the temple of Ise, attests to transmission of a copy of the manuscript (incomplete) of the Ōhara family to the Yamanaka family. The manuscript of the latter is preserved along with the kirigami. The version that was transmitted in the province of Iga, namely the original, was transmitted through several families, each of which would make a copy, often incomplete, and add their own notes or other volumes entirely. The most well-known affiliation in Iga is as follows: Okimori, Taki, Sawamura as well as Ōsawa. The difference between the version that was transmitted in the families of Iga and that of the families of Kōga is very simple, by checking two lineages one notices that the version from Kōga does not have all the details of the original and attests to the fact that the *Bansenshūkai* was written by a native of Kōga, which is not true, because the author, Fujibayashi Yasutake was a native of Iga. Although this manuscript is very rich for the theoretical study of ninjutsu, it remains only a document that does not capture the flavor of the living practice. Ninjutsu cannot be transmitted through documents; it is first and foremost about mental and physical training stripped of any expression or written explanation.

4. In research on ninjutsu, *Shōninki* (正 忍 記) is, like *Bansenshūkai*, a primary *densho*. The original, written in 1681 by Natori Sanjūrō Masazumi (also known by the names Fujinoissui Masatake, Natori Sanjūrō Masatake and Fujibashi Masatake), is preserved at the library of the Japanese Diet. The *densho* is composed of three volumes divided into four parts (the preamble, *shokan*, *chūkan* and *gekan*). At the end of the last volume one can read the inscription: "(This *densho* was) transmitted in the third year of the Kanpō era (1743) to Watanabe Rokurō Saemon by Natori Keisaemon." Shōninki is a *densho* of the *Kishū-ryū ninjutsu* school (紀 州 流 忍 術). This school is known under the name *Shin Kusunoki-ryū* (新 楠 流). After the battle of Iga, *Tenshō Iga no Ran*, the surviving ninja fled towards other provinces. According to one of the most commonly made assumptions, notorious Momochi Tanba, one of the chiefs of Iga, escaped towards the province of Kishū in Saiga in an area where *Negoro-shū* (根 来 衆) was very active. According to this same assumption, this escape would mark the genesis of the *Kishū-ryū* school. However, when one thoroughly studies the *Shōninki* and *Bansen Shūkai* which gathers all the knowledge of *Iga-ryū* and *Kōga-ryū*, one notices that there is a great deal of difference between the method and theory of the practice of ninjutsu transmitted in Iga and Kōga and that of *Kishū-ryū*. The founder of the *Kishū-ryū* school is also the author of the *Shōninki*, Natori Sanjūrō Masazumi. His family had accepted the transmission of the *Kōshū-ryū Gunpō* school (甲 州 流 軍 法)[‡] of Hansuke Heiken, and the head of the Natori household, Masago, had changed the name to *Natori-ryū* (名 取 流), then *Shin Kusunoki-ryū* and, finally, *Kishū-ryū*. The *Shōninki* seems to be at the origin of another *densho*, entitled *Kōketsu Hichū* (口 決 秘 注: *Secret Notes on Orally Transmitted Secrets*)[§] which covers weapons and armor, as well as of the movement of troops and the use of spies. All the chapters are divided into three parts, without exception: *shu, ri, ha*,[¶] which indicates the stages of transmission and training. It seems that the first appearance of the principle, in three terms, *shu-ri-ha* or *shu-ha-ri*, recurs in almost all the schools of *bujutsu*, theater, and *sadō*,[**] from the Edo period comes from the treatise of the school known as *Shin*

---

[*] Today one finds seven copies of the manuscript of which the most important was transmitted within the Okimori family of Iga and is preserved by Okimori Nao Saburō. This manuscript contains three *densho* which is *Shinobi no Michi Kaitei Ron* (忍 道 楷 梯 論), *Wakan ninri shōgo Shū* (和 漢 忍 利 証 語 集) in three volumes, and *Shinobi Mondō* (忍 問 答) in one volume. The six other copies belong to the following families or organizations: the Library of the Japanese Diet, Ōhara family, Fujita family, Ōsawa family, Taki family, and Sawamura family.

[†] With regard to the copy of the manuscript and conditions of transmission and study, the *kirigami* recalls the following sentence: "This manuscript should in no case be mentioned, shown, or presented to a person other than a member of the family. Treason of this will bring terrible punishment from the Gods and the Buddha."

[‡] This school is known to be branch of *Takeda-ryū* (武 田 流), *Shingen-ryū* (信 玄 流), or *Kaishū-ryū* (甲 州 流), and therefore related to the science of the combat and military strategy transmitted within the Takeda family. The principal influence of *Kishū-ryū* emanates primarily from *Kōshū-ryū* whose origin is *Kusunoki-ryū gungaku* (楠 流 軍 学). During the Edo period it was at the origin of a great number of new schools, which diffused the bujutsu and the military strategy (*gungaku*). Throughout the Edo period of the *kusunoki-ryū*, of the Sengoku period was split into several branches of which *Yōōden kusunoki-ryū* (陽 翁 伝 楠 流), *Nanki-ryū* (南 木 流), *Kayō-ryū* (河 陽 流). Natori Sanjūrō Masazumi studied *Kusunoki-ryū* and received the teaching of various Zen masters. From this diverse knowledge, he created his *Shin kusunoki-ryū* (新 楠 流) school. He became an instructor of the stronghold of Kishū, and his school trained the spies of this stronghold. Many sources of information show that the spies of this stronghold formed *Oniwaban* (御 庭 番), a group set up by the eighth shōgun, Tokugawa Yoshimune (1684–1751).

[§] Private collection.

[¶] *Shu* (守) literally means "to protect, preserve, and respect", *ha* (破) can mean "to break or infringe on", and *ri* (離) "to be detached, move away, or leave." This principle evokes an idea of eternal return. It is indeed a nonlinear but repetitive training of a concentic type from which can arise not only the formation from a philosophy of the training itself, but also the intuitive creation of a philosophical ideal. It is interesting to note a major bond with the *Sanshin no Kata* transmitted to Hatsumi Masaaki by his master, Takamatsu.

[**] The master of the *sadō* (茶 道), Kawakami Fuhaku (川 上 不 白 1719–1807) wrote in the *Fuhaku Hikki* (不 白 筆 記: *Notes of Fuhaku*) the following explanation: "There is a rule in the art of warfare in three characters: *shu-ha-ri*. *Shu* means to respect, *ha* to engage, *ri* to leave. When

*kusunoki-ryū* under the name of *Natori-ryū*. The first chapter, *shu*, covers the teaching of fundamental principles. The second, *ha*, deals with application and variants. Finally, the third, *ri*, discusses the spiritual dogmas concerning the need to not rely on objects or techniques and to not fear death. In the first chapter, *shu*, one learns all the precise details of wearing armor starting from the bottom elements; the *ha* chapter covers various possible alternatives, according to the need of the moment, whereas the *ri* chapter describes other alternatives. For example, if one lacks time, it is possible not to change but to directly thread the armor over the clothing which one wears, or not to wear all the elements of the armor. And finally this chapter finishes with the assertion that one does not escape death thanks to armor. When armor is worn, it should be with the thought that one wears the clothing of death, *Kyōkata-bira* (経 帷 子). Thus, life and death rest ultimately in the hands of destiny.

5. *Ninpiden* (忍 秘 伝) is the third-most important *densho* after the two cited before. It is on the first day of the second month of third year of the Eiroku era (1560) on which Hattori Hanzō Yasunaga gave *Ninpiden* to his son, Hanzō Masanari. The first sentence of the preamble immediately states the secret nature of the text and how it must be transmitted:

> *The families of Iga and Kōga have many relatives. However, in the shadow of all these family bonds, the essence of our way hides and lies in secret laws according to which nobody can receive the transmission apart from the close relationship that binds a father to his son. This essence was born from the heart and the flesh of man.*

Upon reading of these lines, one immediately understands that the *Ninpiden* will be transmitted only in the Hattori family, to only one son, who would receive the full measure of it. Indeed, very few of the Hattori children had all of the points of transmission of this *densho* and the science that goes with. The *ninpiden* was transmitted to Hattori Mimasaka Saburō, who went on to write the four volumes in their entirety in 1656. The years passed, and Hattori Saburō's version was transmitted from generation to generation until Katō Sakuemon, who received on the first day of the first month of sixteenth year of the Kyōhō era (1736). The version currently preserved is that written by Hattori Saburō. *The ninpiden* gives many explanations of the use of the tools of the ninja (*nin-dōgu*) without overly exaggerating the use of the tools or the aptitudes of the practitioner.

6. In *Togakure-ryū densho*, private collection, Hatsumi Masaaki thirty-fourth successor of the school since the founder, Noda-shi Chiba-ken, date of writing not communicated.

7. ibid
8. ibid
9. ibid
10. ibid
11. ibid
12. ibid
13. ibid
14. ibid
15. ibid
16. ibid

17. According to all the manuscripts and researchers on the schools of traditional *bujutsu* and *jūjutsu*, *Takenouchi-ryū* is the oldest school of *jūjutsu* in Japan. However, according to *densho* of *Shoshō-ryū* (諸 賞 流), the latter would opened up by Fujiwara Kamatari (614–669), great partisan of the reform of *Taika* (大 化). According to same the *densho*, the school at that time was called *Koden-ryū* (孤 伝 流). With the death of Kamatari, the school makes a reapearance under another name, *Kanze-ryū* (観 世 流) thanks to the shōgun, Sakanoe Tamuramaro (758–811). Lastly, the seventeenth successor of *Kanze-ryū*, Mōri Uheita Kunitomo changed the name to *Shoshō-ryū*. Thus, it seems true that the history of this school, just like its decendants, is not ancient. The renaming is also registered in the training of the school. The stages of control are as follows: the first level is nakakurai (中 位), named *Shoshō-ryū*, the second level is *menkyo* (免 許) named *Kanze-ryū*, and the third level is *inka* (印 可), the *koden-ryū*, and, finally, the *inka kaiden* (印 可 皆 伝), which is the ultimate certificate of control of the style bears the name of "*Kanze-teki shin-shoshō yōgan Koden-ryū*" (観 世 的 真 諸 賞 要 眼 孤 伝 流). Among the schools of *bujutsu*, the *Shoshō-ryū* is the only one that uses the character *wa* (和) with the reading *will yawara* instead of the character *jū* (柔) for *jūjutsu*. It is interesting to note that this school is exclusively transmitted in the stronghold of Morioka under the name *Otome bujutsu* (御 留 武 術). It was said to be a school exclusive to the stronghold, of a family of warriors of high rank, who were the lords of the stronghold. This is why there are no other schools of *Shoshō-ryū* in the other provinces of Japan. Its transmission was restricted to people of the stronghold within only one family of high-ranking warriors. This school proposes a single system of practice and technique of combat with and without weapons, a method of blows and strikes for combat in armor.

Indeed, one of its most notorious characteristics is its art of the *atemi* (当 身) with a very high level of control and destructive precison. The art of *atemi* used kicks and elbow strikes never before seen in the other schools of *jūjutsu* in Japan. One

---

one teaches his disciples, it is a question of *shu*. When they have assimilated the level of shu well and progressed, of themselves, spontaneously, they engage him. It is because they have become able to do as I have just said. It is the stage of ability. However, *shu* like *ha* is insufficient. After that, there is the level of the expert who has exceeded these two levels. He joins them together and transcends them, at the same time as he respects them. But this respect (*shu*) is not of the same nature as in the beginning. How remote is it? This level constitutes in truth an essential teaching. Reflect on this well, reflect on this well." In Nishiyama Matsunosuke, Kinsei Geidō Ron (近 世 芸 道 論: *Theories on Art in Modern Times*), Tokyo, Iwanami Shoten, Nihon Shisō Taikei (日 本 思 想 大 系), Vol. 61, p.619–620.

of the most well-known anecdotes about this school is that when that one of the masters of this style fought, he could break armor with his foot or elbow, however, when this kind of combat took place in front of the lord of the stronghold, so as not to appear coarse one did not use the kicks but only the elbows to destroy armor. Thus, it was never broken outside but on the interior, a rather incredible thing considering the hardness of the armor. In-depth study of the *atemi* of this school will reveal a form of very effective strike that makes it possible to either to kill or wound an adversary. The blow was carried out without any injury to the one who delivered it. That shows that this school had a form of reinforcement and conditioning, and uncommon flexibility of the body.

Another characteristic of this system is a method of practice called *Sanjūtori* (三 重 取). This method of practice and application of the techniques is performed upright, on the ground and with weapons, and is divided into three levels: *Omote* (表), *Hogure* (解), and *Ura* (裏). The first level, *omote keiko*, gathers all the techniques of blow and strikes, control of bones, torsions, strangulations, and projections. The second level, *hogure keiko*, gathers all counter-techniques, or how to escape and to demolish techniques. Lastly, *Ura keiko*, remained the most grueling test, and even today it is carried out with great caution; only the *sōke* of the school and those with top grades have the right to participate. People who are still practicing the first two levels and any foreign visitors at the school cannot participate in this practice, as it is very taxing. The candidate must realize and apply the techniques of combat without half-measures. The practitioner must perform the techniques with an experienced partner or the *sōke* himself and the techniques had to be carried out approximately 1000 times without making any errors. This test started at the beginning of evening and finished very late in the night. At the end of this incredible practice, the candidate saw himself giving the *kazu keiko mokuroku* (数 稽 古 目 録). The mental and physical states that should be reached here are to feel the harmony that a flexible body, unbound, freely achieves as this motto of the school reveals: "When one finishes Kazukeiko, all the unused power and the tensions of the body disappear and leave the body empty. In the happy medium state between that which is visible and invisible, the true flexibility of harmony pours out."

The movements and the techniques of this school require a flexibility of the body in its totality. Techniques like being able to leap out of a sitting position and to strike while kicking at the same time, all the while wearing armor, show that art of this school depends on a very high level of use of the body and especially flexibility, which is not simply a technique but a physical and mental attitude. *Shoshō-ryū* is another school that is very close to *Muhen-ryū* (無 辺 流). Some know techniques of this school, such as *nawa-jutsu*, which were studied by many different *shoshō-ryū*. The *Muhen-ryū* also uses a broad range of weapons like *bōjutsu*, *kenjutsu*, the *naginata*, *yari-jutsu*, and others. One of the *gokui* of this school which arises from the *ichi ate* (一 当: only one strike or attack), recalls the principle of the *ichi* (一: the 1 or the unit) and of the *jū* (十: ten or the multiplicity), which we already discussed in Appendix A. "The *1 is the 10, and the 10 is the 1. One never should forget the spirit of the beginning.*"[*] The *Shoshō-ryū* school is one of the most interesting schools of *bujutsu* of Japan. The transmission is ensured by the current *sōke*, the sixty-eighth generation since the founder, Mr. Takahashi. In *Hiden Nihon Jūjutsu*, op. cit., pp. 125–174.

18. I have already presented the treatises *Its Shi No heihō* (孫 子 之 兵 法) and *Rikutō Sanryaku* (六 韜 三 略). Here are the other treatises that were essential to the training of any high-ranking warrior:

*Goshi* (呉 子): A work on military strategy written by a Chinese strategist named Gi, who lived during the Warring Kingdoms period. Its treatise comprises six chapters and, like the treaty of Sun Zi, it covers all the aspects of the preparation of a battle in order to carry it out.

*Shibahō* (司 馬 法): A work written by Shiba (Sima) a government official during the Han period. A fine politician and expert in military strategy, he left a single work the *shibahō*.

*Utsu ryōshi* (尉 繚 子): A military treatise in five volumes written by a Chinese strategist of the Warring Kingdoms period called Utsuryō.

19. In *Togakure-ryū ninpō densho*, op. cit. One of the many letters that Hatsumi Masaaki received from Master Takamatsu, contains the following explanations:

> In connection with the origins of the ninjutsu and its power, I think that there are many errors circulating. There are people who think that it is a science of combat that comes from China, other researchers form their theories only based on conjectures and theories in books. I think that all these theories are not founded on a correct transmission. Thanks to my master (Toda sensei) I had a great number of chronicles and memoirs on ninjutsu, then as part of my personal practice I carried out much research. Lastly, thanks to the teaching in ninjutsu that I received from my other master, Ishitani Matsutarō, I understood that ninjutsu did not come from China: that it is erroneous to think that ninjutsu was an independant science of survival or Chinese technology for combat; it did not come from China but could have only developed in Japan. Ikai came from China, but he had been voluntarily exiled from Japan. This man with transmitted Kosshi-jutsu, and the essence of the Kosshi-jutsu basics. It is composed of two sciences: taijutsu (体 術) and tobikiri (飛 切 り). These two combat sciences that went hand in hand with kosshi-jutsu, came from China, and one can, thus, think that there are points common with the forms of combat practiced in Shōrinji-ryū (少 林 寺 流).[†] But, the Chinese basics, even those of the techniques of combat, tōte (唐 手), do not seem to be the taijutsu. Just as for the types of combat of the

---

[*] One finds this teaching in all the traditional schools like ninjutsu. In fact, it is a question here of understanding that unit arises from the multiplicity and vice versa. This unit is in practice of only one basic element that makes it possible to understand any other technique because it is the essence of any multiplicity. It is, in some ways, one of the essential basics of the *bugei jūhappan*, *ninja hachimon* or *hakkei*, *jūppō sesshō No jutsu*, *happō biken*, *kihon happō*, and so on. Note the preponderance of the characters *ichi*, *jū* and *hachi*, which is not arbitrary.

[†] The famous temple Shaolin, Shōrin in Japanese pronunciation, was built in 496.

*schools that emanate from* Shōrinji, *there are technical points that seem to be* taijutsu. *From Japan, men and deposed warriors from the Fujiwara family, from the wars between Minamoto and Taira, as well as wars of Nanbokuchō, voluntarily exiled themselves in the provinces of Iga and Kōga and settled there. In these remote areas, they studied taijutsu and kosshi-jutsu, and in order to live in peace, they decided never to steal, use violence, and to adapt to the good of others. They practiced various techniques of combat, such as, among other things,* kenpō *(剣法),* bō-jutsu, kyū-jutsu, *and* yari-jutsu *by constantly adding innovations to it, and the fruit of this evolutionary research was the creation of the science of* Happōbiken *(八法秘剣). These exiles were sought for their aptitudes. They naturally developed the use of gun powder and pharmacology as a* ningu *(忍具)\* and, thus ninjutsu was born from the fruit of their research, inventions, the rational use of the body, and* kosshi-jutsu.... *I end the translation here. In the private collection of Mr. Hatsumi Masaaki.*

20. In *Togakure-ryū ninpō densho*, op. cit.

21. ibid

22. ibid

23. One finds this remark in the majority of the works of the authors whom we already quoted, namely, Koyama, Tobe, Yamaguchi, and so forth.

24. In *Togakure-ryū ninpō densho*, op. cit.

25. Ibid

26. ibid

27. There are two manuscripts that present the genealogy of the Hattori family in a very concise way. The first manuscript was a work that was carried out by a *daimyō* and his *hatamoto* for the *bakufu*. It carries the title of *Kansei Chōshū Shokafu* (寛政重修諸家譜), and is also called *Kanseifu* (寛政譜). It is a manuscript written about the beginning of the Edo period. The second manuscript, *Imabari Shūi* (今治拾遺), was written by the son of Hattori Hanzō Masanari, Hattori Masahiko, who became a member of the stronghold of Imabari. In *Imabari Shūi* one finds a part entitled "Hattori Haya Mimasanobu Kafu" (服部速水正宣家譜), also known by the title "Hayami Kafu" (速水家譜). This document gives direct relationships since the first generation of Hattori, Hattori Hanzō Yasunaga. The information that it presents on the family remains the most reliable by far from the historical point of view.

28. The origin of the name Hattori came from Hastened-ori (機織り) and many common points show that there is a profound bond with the former Hata family (秦), which was originated on the continent. This family came from the continent under the reign of the Ōjin emperor in the fifth century. However, it there no historical document that shows the bonds between the Hata and Hastened-ori families.

29. One finds information relating to the Momochi family in several documents and chronicles on the history of the ninja of Iga, in addition to the documents preserved by the descendants of the Momochi family, one finds *Igakuni Daison Momochike Yusho-sho* (伊賀国喰代村百地家由緒書), which, in a single volume, recalls the entire history of the family in addition to the exploits of Momochi Tanba no Kami. The author is unknown as is the date of writing. Broad reference is found to the Momochi family and Momochi Tanba no Kami in the works written by Kikuoka Nyōgen. *Iran-ki* (伊乱記) in four volumes, *Isui Onko* (伊水温古) in five volumes written in 1706, and *Isui Onkō* (伊水温故) in four volumes written in 1687.

30. There are two documents that have the same title but different authors. The oldest document titled *Zokku Hisei dan* (賊禁秘誠談), a single volume written by Tōbu Zankō that dates from 1668. The author reports it as the history of Sandayū and Ishikawa Goemon. The second document, composed of four volumes, was written in 1788 by Nagai Yoshie.

31. In *Togakure-ryū ninpō densho*, op. cit.

31. ibid

## Chapter 4: The Essence of Ninjutsu

1. The whole title of the article is: "Shinden Shura Roppō Meiji. Taishō. Shōwa No san dai nor ikiru kukishinden happō biken nijyū shichi dai Takamatsu Toshitsugu" (神伝修羅六方明治大正昭和の三代に生きる九鬼神伝八法秘剣二十七代高松寿嗣)

This article was written by Takamatsu at 78 years age in 1965 for issue 38 of the monthly review magazine *Budō Shunjū* (武道春秋) published in Nara. The article that we received is a photocopy of the original where on the first page there are a photocopy in black and white showing Takamatsu Toshitsugu in front of his house in the town of Kashiwara in the prefecture of Nara. In this article, Takamatsu was interviewed by Mr. Koizumi for *"Tokyo Spotsu."* It is a short article where Takamatsu primarily speaks about his initiatory course in ninjutsu. It is one of a series of twelve articles that starts with issue 22, and ends with issue 33, published in 1963 by *Tokyo Spotsu*, a publisher in the town of Yokohama. Issue 33 is rather symbolic, when it is announced that Hatsumi Masaaki received the *menkyo kaiden* that makes of him the thirty-fourth *sōke* of *Togakure-ryū ninjutsu* and thus the successor of Takamatsu Toshitsugu, the first day of thirty-third year of the Shōwa era. Moreover, Takamatsu Toshitsugu was the thirty-third *sōke* of the *Togakure-ryū* school. The last article, in issue 33, has as the title "Ishin Den Shin no Shitei" (以心伝心の師弟: "Transmission from Heart to Heart between the Master and the Disciple"), shows

---

\* The *nin gu* (忍具) is often translated as weapons or tools of the ninja, but this translation does not really capture the depth of the sense evoked by the character nin (忍). They are tools and weapons invented to be able to survive and endure in any situation. In fact, it is necessary that the weapon be capable of being used as tool and the tool as a weapon.

that Hatsumi Masaaki is the future successor of Takamatsu Toshitsugu. A very interesting anecdote in connection with these articles deserves to be presented. The journalist, Mr. Koizumi, did not believe the remarks of Master Takamatsu. Takamatsu made an appointment to meet him at his place. In his garden, in front of a tree, Takamatsu made an astonishing demonstration of his knowledge. He took up an attitude of combat and the expression of his face became more intense, and he struck the tree with his fingers. His fingers were inserted in the bark of the tree to a depth of 2 cm! It seems that after this astonishing demonstration, the whole attitude of Koizumi changed. I was told this story by the journalist himself who I was able to meet thanks to a very generous friend who I thank in passing.

2. In the Japanese language, one finds two different characters that can be used to write the word *kata*. This word has two meanings. The first character, (形), means *"form"* with the etymological sense of: *"to trace with the brush an exact image."* The second character, (型), means *"mold"* with the etymological sense of: *"original form made out of earth."* A kata can, in many ways, be regarded as a form being used as a mold. The term brings to mind the concept of an empty container.

This character has also represented, for a very long time, the concepts of "trace", "ideal form", "law", and "practice." the word *kata* thus evokes at the same time the image of an ideal form to reproduce and its rigidity, but one is unaware of precisely the time from which it was used to indicate the fixing and the transmission of knowledge as a basis for codifying gestural technique. This historical aspect is not the least important. The *kata*, thus, fits into a long Japanese tradition and cannot be understood without certain historical references. Fundamental stages of the history of Japan make it possible to explain some aspects of the concept of *kata* and clarify facts or many behaviors. In the martial arts, a *kata* is a codified sequence of pre-determined techniques, considered to be a complete series. More precisely, within the framework of the traditional schools specialized in the handling various weapons where the practitioner confronts two people, the word *kata* indicates the total sequence formed by the codified exchange of pre-determined techniques between two adversaries. It should, however, be noted that, although the word *kata* is currently the most widely-used generic term, I did not find it in the *densho* and another treatises of the Edo period of earlier times. Thus in the *Shinkage-ryū Heihō Mokuroku* (新影流兵法目録) of Kamiizumi Isenokami Nobutsuna, the word *kata* indicates the *daitō*, or large sword. The narrower term that one finds in the *densho* and treatises and that is always used for the *kata* of the schools of *bujutsu* in particular *kenjutsu*, *sōjutsu*, and the like, is *tachi-awase* (太刀合わせ). The *kata* is still present today in many fields, even if the Japanese themselves are not always aware of it. Other cultural elements were grafted onto the *kata* forming with it, over the length of the centuries, a structure on which are based many characteristics of Japan.

3. *Meiji Mōroku Otoko* (明治毛六男) is sole autobiography written by Master Takamatsu. It contains all the details of the life of Master Takamatsu. It was given to Hatsumi Masaaki with all the other documents and material concerning the art of the ninjutsu and various *bujutsu*. There is only one copy of this autobiography, and no one beside the alumni of Hatsumi Masaaki has ever read it.

3. In Martin Lings, *What is Sufism?*, George Al & Unwin Ltd, London, 1975, and in Annemarie Schimmel's *Mystical Dimensions of Islam*, ED. University of North Carolina, 1975.

4. In the private collection of Mr. Hatsumi Masaaki.

5. In Dr. Ahmed hamid Bhrahimi, *Acupuncture*, Algiers Ed.Mussart-Press, 1996.

7. In Annemarie Schimmel, op. cit., this maxim probably comes from the Gospels.

8. In private collection, op. cit.

9. ibid

10. In Annemarie Schimmel, op. cit.

11. In Martin Lings, op. cit., this esoteric teaching is found in a great number of religions.

12. In Takamatsu Toshitsugu, *Ninjutsu Hiketsu-bun*, date of drafting unknown.

13. In private collection, op. cit.

14. In Louis Massignon, *The Passion of Hallaj, Mystical Martyr of Islam*, vol. 2, Paris, 1922, new ED.

15. In Annemarie Schimmel, op. cit.

## Chapter 5: Autobiography of a Ninja Master

1. In Takamatsu Toshitsugu, *Shinden Shūra Roppō, Budō Shunjū Zashi*, 1965, *nanajū hachi seisō*, p. 48.

2. ibid Nakimuso.

3. In Takamatsu Toshitsugu, *Shinden Shūra Roppō, Budō Shunjū Zashi*, 1965, pp. 48–49: *Toda dōjō nyūmon*.

4. *Shinden Fudō-ryū daken-taijutsu* or *taijutsu* (神伝不動流) is a school that was founded in the middle of the twelfth century by Genpachirō Tameyoshi of Iga, starting from the techniques of *Koppō-taijutsu* (technique based on the human framework) taught by Izumo Kanja Yoshiteru. The school was noted for its form of *iai-nuki*, *sōjutsu* and *taijutsu*. The characteristic of this school of combat is not to adopt a warlike attitude or stance. I should state that many things and characteristics of this school are not currently taught. Takamatsu was the twenty-second successor of this school. In Watatani Kiyoshi, *Bugei ryūha Daijiten* (武芸流派大事典), Akita Shoten, Tokyo, 1979, pp. 414–415.

5. In *Shinden Shūra Roppō, Budō Shunjū Zashi*, op. cit., Naimuso Haigyō, p. 49.

6. ibid Kotengu, p. 49.

7. The character *tō* (唐) of *tōte* (唐手), means that in the beginning the *koppō jutsu* was subject to a Chinese influence in its primitive form. We can even say that it is in its Chinese primitive form that it was introduced in Japan and that it developed

with it, just as Okinawa *Tōte-jutsu* (唐手術) is the technique of combat from the island of Okinawa whose origin is Chinese. However, in this case, it is very easy to see the resemblance at the level of the types of combat between the different styles from the island of Okinawa and the branches of *Shaolin* of the north and the techniques of combat that were transmitted in the south of China. Thus, it is necessary to see in this term only one reference to a remote influence or origin and not a direct or indirect relationship with one of the branches of karate developed in Okinawa or Japan. *Kotō-ryū koppō-jutsu* (虎倒流骨法術) was founded in the middle of the sixteenth century by Toda Sakyō Ishinsai, starting from *Gyokkō-ryū kosshi-jutsu* (骨指術: techniques based on the striking of the bodies and vital organs) of a monk named Gyokkan. *Koppō-jutsu* is a science born in China, where it was called *Gohō* (強法). In addition to using a significant number of short and long weapons, this school has a teaching on the science of the vital points. Takamatsu was the fifteenth successor of this school. In *Bugei ryūha Daijiten*, op. cit., p. 296.

8. In *Shinden Shūra Roppō, Budō Shunjū Zashi*, op. cit, *Rokujū Tai Ichi*, p. 49.

9. ibid, *Musashi-ryū to no Shitō*.

10. The origin of *Takagi Yōshin-ryū Jū-taijutsu* (高木揚心流柔体術) goes, according to the *Bugei ryū Daijiten*, back to the sixteenth century when it was founded by Takagi Setsuemon Shigetoshi, starting from the school *Takenouchi-ryū* (竹内流). This school was transmitted jointly with another school, *Kukishinden-ryū Happōbiken* (九鬼神伝流八法秘剣), through generations until Takamatsu, who was the sixteenth successor. In addition to teaching a great number of weapons (*bō-jutsu, yari-jutsu, naginata, shuriken-jutsu,* etc.), it specializes in *jū-taijutsu* (柔体術), techniques of combat with the bare hands. At the time of fusion between the *Takagi-ryū* and the *Kukishin-ryū*, the techniques of the two schools underwent a deep change, and little by little, they became the support of the technical concepts of ninjutsu. Moreover, Sensei Takamatsu received as sources two transmissions of *Takagi yōshin-ryū*, one by Sensei Mizutani and the other by Sensei Ishitani, who was also a sōke of *Kukishin-ryū ninjutsu*. This explains why the movements, techniques, *densho*, makimono, and so forth that Hatsumi Masaaki inherited from Master Takamatsu are different from the other sources, which claim these two schools and that followed the official line of descent. In *Bugei ryūha Daijiten*, op. cit., pp. 524–525.

11. In *Shinden Shūra Roppō, Budō Shunjū Zashi*, op. cit, *Kukihappō Hiken no Jutsu*, p. 52.

*Kukishinden-ryū Happōbiken* (九鬼神伝流八法秘剣) was founded during period of Northern and Southern Courts (1336–1392) by Yakushimaru Kurando Takamasa, a guard of the Godaigo emperor. This school remained then with a notorious family of pirates of Ise, the Kuki, known for their unorthodox methods and techniques. It is thought that one of these pirates was the famous Aisu Ikōsai, founder of *Kage-ryū* (陰流), who was known to have roamed the seas. The technical teaching of this school includes a great number of disciplines (*bō-jutsu, ken-jutsu* of various lengths, *shuriken-jutsu, jutte-jutsu,* kusari-*gamma-jutsu,* etc.) whose joint basis resides in *Daken taijutsu*, the type of close combat in armor, which arises from *Koppō-jutsu*. School of pirates; this school also specialized in combat on the sea. Takamatsu was the twenty-seventh successor of this school. In *Bugei ryū Daijiten*, op. cit., pp. 240–241.

12. Takamatsu divides into two sciences the *happō biken*, which are linked. Here it is how he describes these two combat sciences:

> "What one calls *happō* is an entire science of the combat that includes the following disciplines: 1. *taijutsu* (体術), *hichō-jutsu* (飛鳥術), *nawajutsu* (縄術). 2. *koppō-jutsu* (骨法術), *jū-taijutsu* (柔体術). 3. *Sōjutsu* (槍術), *naginata-jutsu* (薙刀術). 4. *bōjutsu, jōjutsu, hanbō-jutsu*. 5. *tenpan stroke jutsu* (磐投術), *ken stroke* (剣投), *shuriken-jutsu*. 6. *ka-jutsu* (火術), *sui-jutsu* (水術). 7. *Chikujō gunryaku heihō* (築城軍略兵法). 8. *Onshin-jutsu* (隠身術)."

> "The art of the *hiken* consists in knowing how to handle any type of sabre among which *ken* (剣), the *kotachi* (小太刀) and the last science, are the *jutte-jutsu* (十手術). Thus to protect his body, his flesh, and to demolish the enemy with the *jutte* or the *tessen*, such is the major principle of the art of the sabre. This science bears also the name of *Jūppō sesshō no jutsu* (十法折衝之術)." In private collection op. cit.

13. In *Shinden Shūra Roppō, Budō Shunjū Zashi*, op. cit., *Shōbei Seikatsu Ikka Nen*, p. 50.

14. *Shōrin-Ryū* (少林流) is the current Chinese main approach to the techniques of combat. The name of the school refers to the *Shaolin* Temple in the province of Henan, known in China under the name Shaolin Quan or Chuan. According to the legend, this school was founded by Daruma or Bodhidarma. In China, one distinguishes two branches, that of the North (*Changquan*) and that of the South (*Nanquan*). The styles of the North are famous for their attacks at long distances, the striking down speed of their sequences, the strength and the amplitude of the movements, the stressing of the rate/rhythm, the frequency of the jumps, and rotations. The large variety of the techniques of foot and leg movement makes the reputation of the schools of North. South of the Chang Jiang river, the styles are characterized by the use of the strong power of the upper limbs, through movements of low amplitude that are very varied in the shapes of hands. The postures are low and the legs are used like catapults to launch the movements of the upper limbs. The execution of the movements is punctuated by cries (*shenfa*) which accompany discharges of explosive power (*fajing* or *fali*). One distinguishes six areas of influence in the Chinese martial arts:

- *EIB Shaolin ji* (Shaolin of the North)
- *Chen gia gou* (Chen style of tai ji quan)
- *Cangzhou* (Muslim boxing)
- *Wudang shan* (Taoist boxing)

- *Nan Sholin* (Shaolin of the South)
- *Siming shan* (boxing of the school interns)

In Matsuda Ryuichi, *Zusetsu Chūgoku Bujutsu Shi* (図 説 中 國 武 術 史), *Shin jinbutsu will ōrai sha*, Tokyo, 1976, pp. 21–49.

15. *Nihon Kokumin Seinen Butokutai* (日 本 国 民 青 年 武 德 会) was an institute that exempted a technique of combat. It followed upon the centers of martial education set up by the various warlike families during the Edo period, *Kobusho* (講 武 所). These centers became branches of *Dainippon Butokukai* (大 日 本 武 德 会: *the Association of the Warlike Virtues of Great Japan*). Founded in 1895 after the victory over China, it developed the *bujutsu taisō ho* (武 術 体 操 法: *methods of gymnastics by the techniques of combat*), which praised the merits of the techniques of combat, effective not only as a physical but also a moral education. Their practice formed "warlike," that is, patriotic, spirit. From 1905, at the time of the victory over Russia, it created a center of training for teachers in techniques of combat, *bujutsu kyōin yōseijō* (武 術 教 員 養 成 所). The seat of *Butokukai* was inside the enclosure of the sanctuary of Heian, set up to commemorate the 1,100th birthday of the establishment of the capital in Kyōto. Its acknowledged goal was to encourage the practice of the techniques of combat and to develop the warlike virtues. It included sections that taught various disciplines of the *bujutsu* like kendō, jūdō, aikidō, *bōjutsu, yarijutsu, naginatajutsu,* and so forth. Its method of attribution for the title of Masters of *Budō* comprised three degrees in ascending order: *Renshi* (錬 士), *Kyōshi* (教 士), and *Hanshi* (範 士). The examination was organized by the Association of Masters in techniques of combat, highest ranked of the *Butokukai*. It was affiliated with the network of the police organization, and became, about 1907, an organization of national scale, with local sections throughout the country whose directors were the prefects of the departments. It would be dissolved after the Second World War, and ceased issuing diplomas. At the present time, there is a federation called Kokusai Kobudō Renmei (I.M.A.F: International Martial Arts Federation) which deals with distinguishing the title as well as the most important ranks. In *Nihonshi Kohyaka Budō*, 日 本 史 小 百 科 (*Small Encyclopedia of the History of the Japanese Martial Arts*), p. 190, Tōkyōdō Edition, Tokyo, 1994.

16. Any follower of combat was to leave for an initiatory journey in order to improve his art. Generally done to confront the reality of combat, the practice of the "voyage of perfection," known by the name of *musha-shugyō* (武 者 修 行), appears in the fourteenth century with the first schools of combat and swordsmanship, and became standard practice among warriors. Some travelled with the objective to find a lord, others to look further into their art, others still with this double objective. For the feudal lords, to accommodate men in *musha-shugyō* made it possible to collect information on the other areas. And for the potential vassals, the knowledge which they accumulated during these initiatory voyages formed useful luggage. During this voyage, a warrior traveled by foot and, if he met a follower of the martial arts worthy of being faced, he asked him to fight. If this follower were a master of a *dōjō*, it was often necessary to fight initially against his disciples. In any case, this type of meeting resulted in serious wounds, or even death, if one lost. Even if the engagements were won, one could not remain always unscathed. Many followers of the martial arts perished during this journey of improvement and deepening knowledge. Towards the end of the Edo period, the use of armor spread and accidents decreased considerably, but during the previous period, a meeting between followers often caused the death of one of the protagonists. *The musha-shugyō* was, therefore, a voyage where one invested his life to go further in the selected way. Retirement to the mountains for type of practice was not rare either, and it is not surprising that this old habit of the *musha-shugyō* continued among followers into the Meiji and Taishō eras. Ibid, chap. 48, p. 123.

17. In *Shinden Shūra Roppō, Budō Shunjū Zashi*, op. cit, p. 52, lig. 9.

18. Before the creation of the University of Kenkoku (建 国), *Daidō Gakuin* (大 道 学 院) was created in Manchuria, occupied in 1932, especially to groom Japanese students for high administration. As in the University of Kenkoku, one took courses of history and Manchu and Chinese culture. This university was the first center where the *aiki-budō* was taught. The University of Kenkoku was established in Manchuria in 1938, by the General Matsudaira, a pupil of Ueshiba. After a memorable presentation of Ueshiba in front of the first president of the University of Kenkoku, Sakura Seichi, and a chairman of the University of Tokyo, Sensei Kakei, the teaching of the *aiki-budō* (old name of the aikidō) was accepted at the University of Kenkoku. The central *dōjō* named *Kobukan* (皇 武 館: the current world center of aikidō known by the name of *Aikikai hombu dōjō* in Shinjuku, Tokyo) was to send a teacher to oversee the associated courses. And on a recommendation of Ueshiba, Tomiki Kenji (1900–1979) was sent to Kenkoku to teach the techniques of combat with *aiki-budō*. However, he seems to have widened his activities beyond the *aiki-budō* and gave courses to the military police force. Tomiki Kenji (1900–1979) born in Kakunodate, prefecture of Akita. He graduated with a degree in economy from the University of Waseda. He had achieved a high grade in *jūdō* (eighth dan) which he began studying at ten years of age. He met Ueshiba in 1926. March 1936, he indicated by Kanō and Ueshiba to go to teach at the University of Kenkoku and Daidō Gakuin in Manchuria. He also gave courses to the military police force. Imprisoned in Manchuria at the end of the Second World War, he remained a prisoner in the Soviet Union for three years before being repatriated to Japan. In 1949, at the University of Waseda where he taught jūdō, He created the first aikidō center that bears the name of his style, Tomiki Aikidō. In Ueshiba Kisshōmaru, *Aikidō Kaiso Ueshiba Morihei Den* (合 気 道 開 祖 植 芝 盛 平 伝), ED. Kōdansha, Tokyo, 1977, pp. 177–258.

19. In Ian Nish, *A Spy in Manchuria: Ishimitsu Makiyo, Proceedings of the British Association for Japanese Studies*, 1986, p. 1.

20. In Onoda Hirō, *Tatta Hitori no 30 Nen Sensō* (た っ た 一 人 の 30 年 戦 争), Tokyo, 2004, editon of Onoda Hirō, *No Surrender—My Thirty-Year War*, translated by Charles S. Terry, ED. Firebird Books, U.K, 1975, p. 32.

21. ibid, p. 33.

22. ibid, p. 34.

23. In an interview Onoda Hirō explains why the techniques of combat taught at the Nakano school came from jūdō, karate, aikidō, and a form of use of the sword *Shoshu Guntō-jutsu* (諸 手 軍 刀 術). According to Onoda, Ueshiba Morihei, the founder of aikidō, came to teach a class there. In *Hiden Budō Bujutsu* (秘 伝 武 道 武 術), ED. Bab Japan, number 7, July 2004, pp. 32–36.

24. In Onoda Hirō, op. cit., p. 34.

25. ibid, p. 35.

26. Fujita Seiko remains very well-known as the fourteenth *sōke* of *Kōga-ryū ninjutsu*; however, many facts remain obscure about him. First of all, the school of Fujita was not, as he affirmed, original *Kōga-ryū* but another branch resulting from original *Kōga-ryū*. Its school bore the name of *Kōga-ryū Wadaha* (甲 賀 流 和 田 派), and he inherited it from his maternal grandfather. The speciality of this school remained espionage and information gathering. There no proof of the existence of techniques of combat. However, although the official history presented Fujita in its works as a ninja, there are other testimonies of very serious people who I met and who affirmed to me the opposite, especially because one of these people knew Fujita personally. In these first works where he was shown in the costume of a ninja and carrying out incredible physical feats worthy of faquir and a yogi,* he was presented like a *shugenja* and not in the form of a ninja. Indeed, it seems that he was an excellent artist who copied the *densho* and other *makimono* and he carried out a great deal of research on ninjutsu, including a great piece on *Bansen-shūkai* of which he had one of the seven representatives. However, a true ninja, in the real sense of the term is not seen and does not pose for posterity in the black garb of combat. There are many paradoxes that surround this man; his knowledge of *jōjutsu*, *jūjutsu* and of the *shuriken*, as well as his collection of *densho* and his talent as a counterfeiter, and the way he came into contact with many masters of *Kenyūkai*. Although it is said that he did not take pupils, he made an exception for Iwada Bansai. He was introduced to Bansai by Kenwa Mabuni, the founder of *Shitō-ryū* (糸 東 流), a member of the *Kenyukai* and close friend of Fujita, Ueno Takashi, and the like. He succeeded Fujita as the head of *Namba satō-ryū*, and became the fourth *sōke* of this school. Today, it is the son of Iwada, Genzō, who is the fifth *sōke* of this school. The complete name of the school is *Nanbam Satō-ryū kempō* (南 蛮 殺 到 流 拳 法). This school was founded during the Meiji era by Hashimoto Ippusai, with the stated goal to eliminate all the foreigners living in Japan! The school of combat specialized in the blows and strikes that do not share any technical or historical bond with ninjutsu. It was attended by a great number of nationalists. Fujita was the successor of Ippusai. More significant information on Fujita is that he was an instructor at the military academy of Toyama during the war. He would have taught espionage there. In that context, his name mingled with a murky story of experiments† conducted on human guinea-pigs in connection with research on the effectiveness of attacking the vital points. But he was not judged for war crimes during the trials‡ after the Japanese defeat. It is necessary to emphasize his particular relation to another man, Donn F. Dreager who played a decisive part in the lifting of the prohibition of the practice of martial arts imposed by SCAP. The entire bibliography used by Dreager for his works, in particular *Asian Fighting Arts* (ED. kōdansha, Tokyo, 1969) was given to him by Fujita Seiko. In connection with the Japanese sources of the book, Dreager wrote in *Asian Fighting Arts*: "The best sources were the unpublished writings of Fujita Seiko, which cover the breadth of martial Japanese arts."§ Many photographs and witnesses still living today prove that Dreager often came to visit Hatsumi Masaaki in his residence in the town of Noda. Dreager was an insatiable researcher and no source was ever left unchecked; his various works are proof of this. Regarding the collection of weapons and manuscripts belonging to Fujita, it was all bequeathed to the museum and the library of Iga Ueno in the Mie prefecture.

---

\* I found, in the files of the *asahi shinbun*, the following testimony of a person who had met Fujita for an interview. Here is the content:

*Seiko Fujita, is a 65-year-old Tokyoite who styles himself the "fourteenth master Koga school of ninjutsu". Trained by his grandfather in the arts of the ninja, Fujita claims to be able to "concentrate his senses" to see eight times better and hear fourteen times better. To condition himself to pain, Fujita stuck hundreds of needles in his flesh and learned to tolerate poison, He says, "I ate sulphuric acid, rat poison, wall lizards...Fujita, who claims that he is the last of the ninja and that the secret off the craft "will die with me" deplores the current marketing of ninja in Japan.*

† In 1935, a brilliant scientist, professor Ishii Shiro, proposed to make the army Japanese invulnerable and to support the victory by the bacteriological weapon. Named general, he built research units, of which largest was Unit 731, located at the center of Manchuriua, in Pingfan. On 12 ha, in an ultramodern complex (the first of the kind in the world) an army of 3000 scientists carried out experiments, on prisoners of war, Chinese and Russian, concerning typhus, the bubonic plague, tetanus, tuberculosis (which devastated civil Japanese), dysentery, cholera, refrigeration (to -50°C), etc. Experiments on a large scale was also made on a population of fogs with toxic spray. Unit 731 provided 8 tons of bacilli each month. For the experiments, the human guinea-pigs were designated by the name *maruta*, literally "wood end." In 1942, when the United States entered the war (Pearl Harbor), thousands of prisoners were used as *maruta* at Mukden, a unit close to Pingfan. At the end of the year 1943, with defeat being projected, the number of researchers reached 10,000 (of which masters of martial arts were requisitioned to try out the vital points and the *kuatsu*: not to reanimate a person). Each researcher had a white chart and ten *maruta* at their disposal. One, thus, can estimate the number of prisoners thus sacrificed. Japan officially recognizes only 3000 of them. In 1945, to erase the evidence, the buildings of the research units were completely destroyed, obliterating at the same time the prisoners who were there and who could have testified against the atrocities. During the prosecution of the war criminals of 1946, the activities of the units of experiments were never evoked. Professor Ishii Shiro was not worried and was even invited in the United States, in 1950, for a series of conferences on the reaction of the body to the various infections."

‡ I should note that after the surrender of Germany, imunity was granted to certain scientists responsible for the V1 and V2 flying bombs, such as Werner von Braun, (who died in Virginia in 1977) to whom one owes the space flights, in particular the Jupiter and Saturn rockets. Teams of American scientists came to Japan to study the conclusive reports/ratios of the units of research: "Many of these experiments could not be carried out in our laboratories because of our great scruples about the human experimentation". In *Fires of History*, Gallimard, 1989, Vol. 6, the *war crimes: the lawsuit of Nuremberg*, pp.80–150.

§ in Dreager & Smith, *Asian Fighting Arts*, ED. Kōdansha, Tokyo, 1969, p. 193: Select Bibliography.

27. The term *jōnin* (上 忍) rendered with this character can be misunderstood. When one uses the term *jōnin* with the following characters, it refers to the distinction between the three type of ninja during the Sengoku period, namely, *jōnin* (上 人), *chūnin* (中 人), and *genin* (下 人). However, in the *densho* and *makimono* of ninjutsu written before or at the beginning of the Edo period, the term *jōnin* rendered with the following character: (上 忍), means that the person has reached the ultimate state of endurance, perseverance and patience. *Bansen-shūkai* described it in the following way: "*They make no noise, they do not have a particular odor and do not even make mention of their names and prowesses. Their merits are similar to the existence of the sky and the earth, they are experienced by all, but remain unsoundable.*"

28. My humble research on the jumble of old traditional schools and disciplines of Japan and China led me to write many articles, of which one very long one had as a subject the school *Asayama ichiden-ryū*. At the time of my long course of studies in Japan, I was lucky to be able to meet many traditional schoolmasters. It is on such an occasion that I became acquainted with Master Sakai Eiji, teacher of Master Sakai Uichirō who was the direct disciple of Okura, the thirteenth *sōke* of the school *Asayama ichiden-ryū*. Master Sakai Eiji showed me the original of the Chi no Maki written by the hand of Okura to the attention of his father, Sakai Uichirō. I was able to admire the penmanship of *sōke* Okura and check the authenticity of the *makimono*. During a discussion that wrapped up late in one night, I had the occasion to see and undergo a private hearing, to receive from the hands of Master Sakai, in front of all the alumni (3 in all), a book carried out in the invaluable form of a *densho* containing extremely rare photographs of Master Sakai Uichirō demonstrating all the techniques of the school. The *densho* that I was offered was signed with two seals, that of the late father and that of the son, Sakai Eiji. Consequently it was easy for me to see the difference between the many people who claim this school. Master Sakai Eiji does not wish to open his school to a greater number of pupils and does not seek publicity. He practices the art of this school as a family transmission which he accepted from his father. He has only two disciples, and sometimes the alumni who had practiced with him under the directions of his father come to join the practice. The course proceeds in the residence of the Master, the blows are carried out thoroughly but the whole is carried out with admirable control. Master Sakai Eiji is an open person, extremely pleasant, very attentive, and faithful to the practice and the experience which he accumulated under the direction of his amazing father who continued to transmit knowledge until a very advanced age. I hold much gratitude for Master Sakai, and the *shihan* Ota and Miyamoto for their kindness and all the documents that they gave me for my research on this school.

## Chapter 6: The Secret Text of Ninjutsu

1. The original text was written by Takamatsu Toshitsugu (1886–1972) thirty-third successor of *Togakure-ryū ninpō* and head teacher of eight other schools of ninjutsu. The original is in the possession of Hatsumi Masaaki, his single successor, and there is not another copy. The part presented is only the beginning of the manuscript.

2. Master Uehara died in 2004 at 100 years of age. At the time of the writing of this book he was still alive and although he was weakened by cancer, he continued to practice with enthusiasm. His manner of moving and his vitality make of him an example for many practitioners.

3. In the *Book of the Tricks*, op. cit., "Antara, teacher of Chaddâd, mystical poet and man who lived before the birth of Islam, between the end of the sixth century and the beginning of the seventh century" (cf Arab Poetry, Seghers, p. 50–52.).

4. In James Jones, *The Thin Red Line (the Red Line)*, ED. Contempory Books, Inc, U.S.A, republication of 1998, pp. 80–125.

5. Miyamoto Musashi (1584–1646) is a legendary Master of the sword. During his youth, between thirteen and twenty-nine years of age, he fought more than sixty times, sometimes against several adversaries, and always won. Musashi spent most of his life traveling in order to improve his art, meeting many followers of the sword. He taught only a few years, in two periods, when he wa around forty years of age, then again at the end of his life, when he was accommodated at the court of great feudal lords. He also practiced other arts, reaching a very high level of skill in penmanship, painting, poetry, sculpture and the tea ceremony. In spite of his fame, his teaching remained very personal and his school did not continue after his death. He believed that his experience was applicable to combat in a number of ways and would have liked to have employed his theories and his capabilities as chief of war. But the time in which he lived was that of the end of the wars, and of the establishment of peace and the bureaucracy. Musashi thus did not have the occasion to develop his capacities as a man of war and to reach the corresponding social status. This is why, in spite of the development that he brought to the art of the sword, his teachings did not give rise to a lasting school, like that of Yagyū.

However, after his death, swordsmen often read his works. He died at sixty-two years of age. He wrote several works and the last, written at the age of sixty years, is regarded as the most concise formulation of his thought. This work, *Gorin No sho* (五 輪 書: *The Book of Five Rings*), is composed of five divisions. The first, the ring of the ground (地 巻), indicates the general system of his school, then the ring of water (水 巻) specifically described his techniques; the ring of the wind (風 巻) contained criticism of other schools; and the ring of the sky (空 巻 or open space), is very short, and brings his conclusion: "...From this moment, I was at the very end of this way. And this enabled me to be a master in all the fields of arts." in Ezaki Shunpei, *Nihon Kengō Retsuden* (日 本 剣 豪 列 伝), ED. Gendai Kōyō bunko, Tokyo, 1970.

6. Yagyū Munenori (1571–1646), teacher of Yagyū Muneyoshi Sekishusai (1529–1606) and the sword master Tokugawa Ieyasu. Munenori became the master of the sword of the family of the shōgun and because of this acquired important political power. His political and cultural influence on the third shōgun, Iemitsu (shōgun of 1623 to 1651), was significant. His knowledge was then transmitted to his descendants, putting them at the same rank as feudal lords. He exerted great influence on the

*bushi* of the later period that practiced the sword in his school. In his advancement of the way of the sword, he was strongly influenced by the Zen Buddhism, and his relationship with Master Takuan (1573–1645) show through clearly in his work. It was mainly as a spiritual technique that Zen interested Munenori. It was he who first explicitly affirmed that the sword and Zen are, in a certain manner, the same thing. He affirmed that belief after having reached a very high level of swordsmanship. At that time, the idea that the sword and Zen are the same thing began to spread, and while being popularized, this idea was distilled. What was left is the concept that *Ken* (the sword) = Zen. Munenori himself practiced No theater, as it was related to his practice of the sword. In addition to *Shinkage-ryū Mokuroku* (新影流兵法目録), there is a family document written by his father, Muneyoshi. Munenori wrote *Heihō Kaden Sho* (兵法家伝書: *Family Transmission of the Strategy*),* which presents his designs for the way of the sword which he applies, like Musashi, to many fields. In Siba Ryōtarō, *Nihon kenkyaku den*, Vol. 2, (History of the Followers of the Japanese sword), ED. Asahi Shinbun sha, Tokyo, 1985, pp. 70–90.

---

\* Here an extract of the Heihō Kadensho which shows us the high level that Munenori had reached:

*In the beginning, as one knows nothing, one does not doubt anything. After having entered study, various things occupy the spirit; one is obstructed by it, and all becomes difficult. Then, as soon as one does not wonder any more about what one learns, the idea of rules does not have any more impact. Thus, one does not stick to them anymore to exert the techniques of the various ways, which come from themselves and are then in true harmony with the rules. While thus acting, one naturally harmonizes some with the rules. It is necessary to follow the way of the combat, by understanding this well. To involve oneself by learning the beginning weapons techniques, and all the rules, postures of the body, manners of perceiving... is to deploy intelligence. When one has gained control, these many rules disappear from the intellectual conscienceness. Without conscience reflection, one reaches the heart of the things. After having assimilated many rules, the merits of the approach being accumulated, the movements are in the legs, the arms, the body, they are no more in the spirit. One moves away from the rules, but one conforms to them. In all circumstances the techniques become spontaneous. Alone, thought does not stick to anything, and thus, not even the demons can disturb it. It is to reach this stage that one learns. When the rules were assimilated, they disappear.*

In Yagyū Munenori, *Heihō Kadensho*, Tokyo, Iwanami shōten, 1983, p. 29–30.

# Bibliography

## 1- Texts of Reference

- Takamatsu Toshitsugu, *Ninjutsu Hiketsu Bun*, 忍術秘訣文, (*Secret Text of Ninjutsu*) date of drafting unknown, private collection.
- Takamatsu Toshitsugu, *Togakure-ryū Ninpō no Makimono*, 戸隠流忍法巻物, (*Scroll of Togakure-ryū Ninpō*), private collection.
- Takamatsu Toshitsugu, *Shinden Shura Roppō Meiji. Taishō. Shōwa no san dai ni ikiru kukishinden happō biken nijyū shichi dai Takamatsu Toshitsugu* (神伝修羅六方明治大正昭和の三代に生きる九鬼神伝八法秘剣二十七代高松寿嗣), *Budō Shunjū*, 1965, Nara.
- *Takamatsu Toshitsugu no Tegami*, 高松寿嗣の手紙, (letter of Takamatsu Toshitsugu), private collection (written between 1958 and 1972).

## 2-Works in Japanese on Ninjutsu and the Ninja

- Koyama Ryūtarō, *Shinsetsu Nihon Ninja Retsuden*, Ed. Arechi, Tōkyō 1964.
- Yamaguchi Masayuki, *Ninja no seikatsu*, Ed.Ozan kyakan, Tōkyō 1962.
- Tobe Shinjūrō, *Ninja to Tōzoku Nihon-shi Kage no Jinbutsu-shi*, Ed. Nihon shoseki, Tōkyō, 1978.
- Tobe Shinjūrō, *Ninja to Ninjutsu*, Ed. Mainichi, Tōkyō, 1996.
- Tobe Shinjūrō, *Ninja no hekireki sho*, Ed. Asashi shinbun-sha, Tōkyō, 1987.
- Tobe Shinjūrō, *Hattori Hanzō*, in five volumes, Ed. Mainichi shinbun-sha, Tōkyō, 1993.
- Hassai Tomeya, *Ninjutsu Ronkō*, Ed. Nihon sheru shuppan, Tōkyō, 1980.
- Okuse Heishichirō, *Ninjutsu: Sono Rekishi to Ninja*, Ed. Jinbutsu yuraisha, Tōkyō, 1953.
- Okuse Heishichirō, *Ninpō Sono Hiden to Jitsurei*, Ed. Jinbutsu yuraisha, Tōkyō, 1964.
- Tamura Eitarō, *Kōshō: Ninja Monogatari*, Ed. Yusan Kyaku, Tōkyō, 1968.
- Fukuyama Matsuo, *Kōga-ryū Ninjutsu*, Ed. Jinrui Kagaku kenkyūjo, Tōkyō, 1953.
- Nawa Yūmio, *Anata Ni Mo Ninja Ni Nare*, Ed. Shōbunkan, Tōkyō, 1966.
- Nawa Yūmio, *Ninjutsu no Kenkyū*, Ed. Shōbunkan, Tōkyō, 1968.
- Fujita Seiko, *Ninjutsu Hiroku*, Ed. Chyoda Shoin, Tōkyō, 1936.
- Fujita Seiko, *Doron Ron*, Ed. Nihon Shūhōsha, Tōkyō, 1958.
- Amano Hitoshi, *Ninja no Rabirensu*, Ed. Sodosha, Tōkyō, 2001.
- Hatsumi Masaaki, *Hiden Ninja*, Ed. Keibunsha, Tōkyō, 1991.
- Higuchi Kiyoyuki & Hatsumi Masaaki, *Sengoku Ninpō Zukan*, Ed. Shin jinbutsu Yuraisha, Tōkyō, 1978.

## 3-Works in English on Ninjutsu and the Ninja

- Draeger & Smith, *Understanding Asian Fighting Arts*, Ed. Kōdansha International, translation and republication, Tōkyō, 1985.
- Turnbull Stephen, *The True Story of Japan's Secret Warrior Cult*, Ed. Firebird Book, U.K, 1991.
- Adams Andrew, *Ninja: The Invisible Assassin*, Ed. Ohara Publications, Inc., U.S.A, 1970.

## 4-General Works on the Martial Arts

- Yagyū Muneyoshi Sekishūsai, *Shinkage Ryū Heihō Mokuroku Koto, Index of the Techniques and the Strategy of the Shinkage School*, 1601, the original is preserved at Hōzanji in Nara.
- Yagyū Munenori, *Heihō Kaden-Sho, Treaty on the Family's Transmission of the Strategy*, Tōkyō, 1636, the original belongs to the private collection of Yagyū Nobuharu. One finds, however, a very beautiful copy preserved at the library of Tenri University.
- Kotōda Yahei Toshisada Ittōsai, *Ittōsai Sensei Kenpō Sho, Treatise on the Laws Governing the Handling of the Sword of the Master*, 1653. (This text is presented in a collection of old works that include part of the *densho* presented in *Budō hōkan*, Precious *Texts of Budō*, compiled and assembled by the *Dai nippon butokukai*, before the second world war, published for the first time in 1970 by Kōdansha).
- Hinatsu Shigetaka, *Honchō Bugei Shōden, Short Histories of the Martial Arts of Japan*, Japan, 1715.
- Tetsuya Sokushirō, *Nihon Chūkō Bujutsu Keifu Ryaku, Lineages of the Schools of Bujutsu of Japan*, Japan, 1791.
- Minamoto Tokushū, *Gekiken Sōdan, Treaty on the Art of Handling the Sword*, Japan, 1848. Minamoto Tokushū was a master of *kenjutsu* and traveled for more than ten years, visiting the various schools of swords and martial arts. This work describes the documents that he collected.
- Under the direction of Imamura Yoshio, *Nihon Budō Taikei*, ten volumes, Ed. Dōbōi, Tōkyō, 1982.
- Several authors, *Nihonshi Kohyaka budō*, Tōkyōdō Edition, Tōkyō, 1994.
- Ezaki Shunpei, *Nihon Kengō Retsuden*, Ed. Gendai Kōyō bunko, Tōkyō, 1970.
- Shiba Ryōtarō, *Nihon Kenkyaku Den*, Vol.2, Ed. Asahi shinbunsha, Tōkyō, 1982.
- Gima Shinkin and Fujiwara Ryozō, *Kindai Karatedō no Rekishi wo Kataru*, Ed. BB, Tōkyō 1980.
- Watanabe Ichirō, *Shiryō Meiji Budō-shi*, Ed. Ed. Shin Jinbutsu Yūraisha, Tōkyō, 1970.
- Otaki Tadao, *Kanō jigorō: Watashi no Shōrai to Jūdō*, Ed. Shin Jinbutsu Yūraisha, Tōkyō, 1950.
- Katō Jinpei, *Kanō Jigorō*, collection *Shin Taiikugaku Kōza* (新体育学講座), Ed. Shōyō Shoin, Tōkyō, 1964.
- Matsuda Ryūchi, *Hiden Nihon Jūjutsu*, Ed. Sōjinsha, Tōkyō, 1978.
- Matsuda Ryuichi, *Zusetsu Chūgoku Bujutsu Shi*, Ed. Shin jinbutsu ōrai sha, Tōkyō, 1976.
- Kasao Kyōji, *Chūgoku Kenpō-den*, Ed. Fukuodō, Tōkyō, 1972.
- Watatani Kiyoshi & Yamada Chushi, *Bugei Ryūha Daijiten*, Ed. Tōkyō Copy shuppanbu, Tōkyō, 1969.
- Ueshiba Kisshōmaru, *Aikidō Kaiso Ueshiba Morihei Den*, Ed. Kōdansha, Tōkyō, 1977.

- Kisshomaru Ueshiba, *Ueshiba Morihei Tanjyō Hyakunen Kaiso Aikidō*, Ed. Kōdansha, Tōkyō, 1977.
- Sasama Yoshihiko, *Nihon budō Jiten*, Ed. Kashiwa Shobo, Tōkyō, 1982.
- Katō Hiroshi & Nishimura Ryō, *Budō Kotoba Gogenjiten*, Ed. Tōkyōdō, Tōkyō, 1995.
- Several authors, *Budō Bunka no Tankyū*, Ed. Fumaido, Tōkyō, 2003.
- Morita Sakae, *Ittō-ryū Heihō Shikō*, Ed. NGS, Osaka, 1980.
- Sasamori Junzō, *Ittō-ryū Gokui*, ED Reirakudō, Tōkyō, 1986.
- Toyama Mitsuru, *Bakumatsu Sanshū-den*, Ed. Shimazu shoten, Tōkyō, 1997.
- Kaku Kōzō, *Miyamoto Musashi Jiten*, Ed. Tōkyōdō shuppan, Tōkyō, 2001.
- Kaku Kōzō, *Bujutsuka Budōka Reisuden*, Ed. Shimazu shobo, Tōkyō, 1998.
- Kōno Yoshinori, *Ken no Seishin-shi*, Ed. Shinyōsha, Tōkyō, 1991.
- Katō Kenji, *Budō no Kenkyū*, Ed. Shimazu Shobō, Tōkyō, 1990.

## 5- General Works on History

- Sugiyama Hiroshi, *Nihon no Rekishi*, Vol.11, 5th edition, Shōgakukan, Tōkyō, 1980,
- Miura Joshin, *Hōjō Godai-ki*, in *Sengoku Shiryō Sōshō*, 2nd series, Vol.1, Tōkyō, 1967.
- Hisaki Fujiki, *Sengoku Shakai shi ron*, Ed. Tōkyō daigaku shuppankai, Tōkyō, 1974.
- Several authors, *Sengoku 13 Nin no Mei Gunshi*, Ed. Shin jinbutsu yūraishi, Tōkyō, 1999.
- Several authors, *Nihon-shi Jinbutsu Sōran*, Ed.Shin jinbutsu Yūraisha, Tōkyō, 1983.
- Several authors, *Nihon Rekishi Denki Sōran*, Shin jinbutsu yūraisha, Tōkyō, 1980.
- Several authors, *Zuroku Nihon-shi Sōran*, Shin jinbutsu yūraisha, Tōkyō, 1985.
- Several authors, *Nihon Shūkyō Sōran*, Shin jinbutsu yūraisha, Tōkyō, 1986.
- Several authors, *Meishō no Kage Musha*, Shin jinbutsu Yūraisha, Tōkyō, 1962.

- Chisatsu Hikotoshi, *Sen Nin no Kenkyū*, Ed. Tairiku shobō, Tōkyō, 1976.
- Kurita Tadachika, *Kasei Mikawa Go Fudo-ki*, Ed. Shinbutsu yuraisha, Tōkyō, 1977.
- Watanabe Ichirō, Nishiyama Matsunosuke, *Kindai Geidō Ron*, collection *Nihon Shisō Taikei*, Vol. 61, Ed. Iwanami shoten, Tōkyō, 1970.
- Francine Hérail, *Histoire du Japan*, Ed. Horvath, Paris, 1988.
- Several authors, *Les Brûlures de l'histoire*, Vol. 6, Ed. Gallimard, Paris, 1995
- Michel Life, *Le Japon et le Monde au 20ᵉ Siècle*, Ed. Masson, Paris, 1995.

## 6-Studies

- Pierre F. Souyri, *Iga, Kōga, Oyamoto: Social Construction in the Mountainous Areas Southeast of Kyoto in the 15th and 16th Centuries*, I.N.A.L.C.O, 1998.
- Ian Nish, *A Spy in Manchuria: Ishimitsu Makiyo*, Proceedings off the British Studies, U.K, 1985.
- Louis Al, *The Nakano School*, Proceedings of the British Studies, U.K, 1985.

## 7-Works on War and Strategy

- Rene R. Khawan, the *Le Livre des Ruses : la stratégie politique des Arabes*, (integral translation on original manuscripts), Ed. Phébus, Paris 1976.
- Sun Zi, *The Art of War*, translation of Samuel B. Griffith, Ed. Contemporary Books Inc., U.S.A, 1980.
- Moriya Hiroshi, *Rikutō San Ryaku no Heihō*, Ed. Purejidento-sha, Tōkyō, 1994.
- Kessler Ronald, *Moscow Station*, Ed. Contemporary Books Inc., U.S.A, 1984.

## 8-Novels

- Onoda Hirō, *No Surrender- My Thirty Year War*, translated by Charles S. Terry, Firebird Book, U.K, 1975.
- Onoda Hirō, *Tatta Hitori no 30 Nen Sensō*, Ed. Bab Japan, Tōkyō, 2004

## 9-Works on Spirituality and Medicine

- Annemarie Schimmel, *Mystical Dimensions of Islam*, Ed. University off North Carolina Near, 1975.
- Martin Lings, *What Is Sufism?*, Ed. George Al &Unwin Ltd., 1971.
- Dr. Hamed-hmid Bhrahimi, *Acupuncture*, Ed. Mussart-press, Algiers, 1996.
- Several authors, *Mikkyō no Hon*, Ed. Gakken, Tōkyō, 1992.
- Several authors, *Fūsui no Hon*, Ed. Gakken, Tōkyō, 1991.
  Several authors, *Tendai Mikkyō no Hon*, Gakken, Tōkyō, 1990.
- Several authors, *Shingon Mikkyō no Hon*, Ed.Gakken, Tōkyō, 1989.
- Several authors, *Jukyō no Hon*, Ed.Gakken, Tokyo, 1991.
- Several authors, *Shugendō no Hon*, Ed.Gakken, Tōkyō, 1992.
- Several authors, *Onmyōdō no Hon*, Ed.Gakken, Tōkyō, 1992.
- Several authors, *Dōkyō no Hon*, Ed.Gakken, Tōkyō, 1992.
- Several authors, *Koshintō no Hon*, Ed.Gakken, Tōkyō, 1992.
- Izitsu Toshihikō, *Isulamu Shisō-shi*, Ed. Chūkō bunko, Tōkyō, 1990.

## 10-Reviews

- *Hiden, Budō Bujutsu*, monthly magazine published by BAB Japan, Tōkyō, issues throughout the years 1995 to 2000.
- *Budō, Nihon Budokan*, monthly magazine published by Nihon Budōkan Shuppan, Tōkyō, throughout the years 1998 to 2001.

## 11-Dictionaries

- *Kokugo Jiten*, Ed. Shōgakukan, Tōkyō, 1982.
- *Kojien*, Ed. Iwanami, Tōkyō, 1967.
- *Shinjigen*, Ed. Kakugawa shoten, Tōkyō, 1997.
- *Kokugo*, Ed.Sanshōdo, Tōkyō, 2001
- *Kanjikai*, Ed. Sanshōdō, Tōkyō, 2000.
- *Nihonshi jiten*, Ed. Kōdansha, Tōkyō, 1980
- *Kanji no gogen*, Ed. Kakodawa, Tōkyō, 1985.
- *Koji to Kotowaza no Jiten*, Ed. Haga shoten, Tōkyō, 1975.

# Acknowledgments

To Him we give thanks for every moment, be it in the secrecy of night, or in broad daylight. Thanks to my parents, my family, and my sensei in the practice of ninjutsu. I particularly want to thank Mr. Christopher Davy, as well as all members of Yume Dōjō (Tony, Ethan, Steve, Brian, Ilan, David), and Mr. Ray A. Letter, without whom this version would never have seen the light of day.

Many photographs and scrolls were reproduced in this publication. From the bottom of my heart I wish to thank the following people, museums, universities, companies and private organizations for their valuable assistance and for their collaboration:

Bab Japan shuppan sha
Shin jinbutsu yuraisha
NHK Publications
QUEST Company
National Diet Library
National Library of Australia
British Library
Société Française des Etudes Japonaises
British Association for Japanese Studies
Japan Society
Musée des Armées de Paris
Gaikokugo University Library
Tsukuba University Library
Saitama University Library
Tenri University Library
Tokyō University Library
Kodōkan jūdō
Nihon budō gakkai
Nihon Budōkan
Musée de Ueno
Ueno Library
Shiga Library
Musée de Tokyō

Maître Hatsumi Masaaki, Ishizuka Tetsuji, Tobe Shinjūrō, Koyoma Ryūtarō, Nawa Yumio, Yamaguchi Masayuki, Ohara Tami, Okuse Heishichirō, Nakajima Atsumi (soke de l'école Hoki ryū jūjutsu), Nobuyuki Hirakami (menkoykaiden de plusieurs Koryū et chercheur), Sakai Eiji (Okura-den Asayama ichiden ryū dai- shihan), Ota Nobuaki (Asayama Ichiden ryū Researcher chief), Higashi Kenichi (gaikoku go university), Tōdō Yoshiaki (Tsukuba University), Kazuma Kōji (Kōgakuin University), Yoshio Mifuji (Nippon budōkan), Yoshino Yoshinobu (Nippon budōkan),Masatoshi Taya (Nippon budōkan), Yoshikane Hirayama (Nipon budōkan), Naoki Murata (Kōdōkan Jūdō Museum), Kōno Yoshinori, Kuroda Tetsuzan (Shinbukan), Kogure Yuji, Stephen Turnbull, Pierre F.Souyri (Inalco), Francois Macé (Inalco), Jean Noel Robert (Sorbone Ecole Pratique des Hautes Etudes), François Lachaud (EFO).